Who Else

writes like ... ■■■

A readers' guide to fiction authors

Fourth Edition

Edited by
Roy and Jeanne Huse

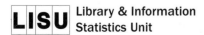

LISU Library & Information
Statistics Unit

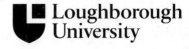

**Loughborough
University**

HUSE, Roy and Jeanne, Editors

Who else writes like ...? A readers' guide to fiction authors

First published 1993, 4th edition 2002

ISBN 1 901786 57 9

Cover design by
Mary Ashworth & Sharon Fletcher, LISU
and Esther Bexon, Media Services, Loughborough University

Inside pages designed and typeset in Lucida Sans and Verdana by
Mary Ashworth & Sharon Fletcher, LISU

Printed by
Polar Print Group Ltd, Venturi House, 9-17 Tuxford Road,
Hamilton Industrial Park, Leicester LE4 9TZ

Published and distributed by
Library and Information Statistics Unit (LISU)
Loughborough University, Loughborough, LE11 3TU
Tel: +44 (0)1509 223071 Fax: +44 (0)1509 223072
E-mail: lisu@lboro.ac.uk
Web: www.lboro.ac.uk/departments/dis/lisu/lisuhp.html

Contents

Acknowledgements

This fourth edition of the Readers' Guide could not have been produced without the support of many librarians and their authorities. A considerable amount of time and, above all, professional expertise has been willingly given to help the editors produce what is essentially a librarians' guide for library users. As with the last edition help was given in two stages and we are most grateful to all of the following:

Stage One

Angus Council	*John MacRitchie*
Blaenau Gwent County Borough Council	*Mary Jones*
East Dunbartonshire	*Doreen Fergusson*
Sutton Libraries	*Anita Myatt*
Thurrock Council	*Bob Wilde*

Stages One and Two

Dumfries and Galloway	*Terri Coy*
East Riding of Yorkshire Libraries	*Margaret Sumner with Ian Sumner*
Halton Borough Council	*Trudy Burr*
Herefordshire Libraries	*Carolyn Huckfield*
Middlesbrough Libraries	*Alyson Perry*
Reading Borough Council	*Elizabeth Lea*
Southampton City Libraries	*Ian Lawrence*
Trafford MBC	*Mark Ramsden*
West Dumbarton	*Ian Baillie*
West Sussex County Library	*David Kendall*

We would also like to thank the Registrar of Public Lending Right, Dr Jim Parker, for supplying statistics which, as in previous editions, have formed the basis for the core list of authors. We have had considerable assistance from Michael Marston and David Gates of Macaulay Library Services while the staff of our local libraries at Bognor Regis and Willowhale have been unfailingly helpful. Our thanks also to Eric Pascal for his technological support.

As always we have had consistent support from our publisher Dr Eric Davies, Director of LISU and from the LISU Advisory Committee, but our special thanks must go to Mary Ashworth and Sharon Fletcher of LISU, who have continued to take such a personal interest in *Who else writes like...?* and who have done so much to maintain the highest possible standard in the design and production of this Guide.

Roy and Jeanne Huse
Aldwick

August 2002

ii

Introduction

Who else writes like ...? seeks to help anyone who enjoys reading fiction to expand the number of writers that they read. It is designed to address the dilemma one faces when, having exhausted the output from a particular author, one ponders – "What shall I read next?" The book lists over 1,800 authors, and with each name suggests others who write in a similar way. The number of alternative authors listed for each entry is between three and twelve. Alternative ways of finding suitable reading are through the index of genres, or the list of prize winners at the back of the book. There is also an index to characters in fiction as well as a list of further reading, which includes some useful websites and other fiction guides. The entry for each author offers copious detail to help make a choice.

The basis for the initial selection of authors continues to be the most popular according to the Public Lending Right lists, with additions suggested by a number of professional librarians from England, Scotland and Wales. In the main, authors are only included when they have three books to their name and when their novels are easily obtainable from bookshops and libraries. Inclusion is therefore determined by a mixture of objective and subjective criteria. Inevitably some cherished favourites may be omitted as a result, and for this we are sorry.

This is the fourth edition of what has now become an established tool for readers and those advising readers in their quest to derive the utmost pleasure from fiction. This edition is bigger and better than ever. We conducted a readership survey to help shape it. The main features of the earlier editions have been retained, but there are also one or two refinements and additions.

Each time we have brought out *Who else writes like ...?* it has grown in size. This edition continues the trend with a net gain of around a fifth in the number of authors listed. Within this figure, 394 new authors have been added and there have been 188 deletions of writers whom our advisors felt were no longer widely read. We have expanded the **How to use this guide** section to accommodate the additional features that are in the entries. Brief details of prizes are now included in author entries as well as more comprehensively in an index. The Internet has impinged on a number of fiction writers and many now have their own websites through which more can be learned about their lives and work. In this edition we have included website addresses when we have discovered them - these are live at the time of going to print but we realise that in the course of time some may change.

Any reference work worthy of the name must continue to evolve in line with changing circumstances and demands. We welcome comments from users of this edition regarding how we can make the next one even better.

How to use this Guide

The main list of authors is in alphabetical order. Each name is followed by a list of suggested alternatives. So pick out an author whose books you like, and see which other writers are recommended underneath. For instance, if you like **J M Coetzee**, *Who else writes like ...?* suggests that you might also like **Murray Bail,** or **James Bradley,** and so on.

Additional information is given with many of the author entries:

- author's dates of birth and death, where known
- nationality (or place of birth) of authors who are not English, where known (see abbreviations used on page vi)
- the genre and/or subgenre, or type of novel (eg **Crime: PI** or **Glitz & glamour**)
- name of main character(s), preceded by ⚲ (eg **Cooper MacLeish**)
- environment and/or occupation (eg **Chicago** or **'Kingsmarkham'** - quotation marks ('xxx') indicate a fictional environment - and **taxi driver**)
- pseudonym(s): **also writes as** or **is**
- author's own website (eg www.martell-reaves.com) or websites with more details about an author and their books (eg www.twbooks.co.uk)
- prizes won with dates (see abbreviations used on page vi)

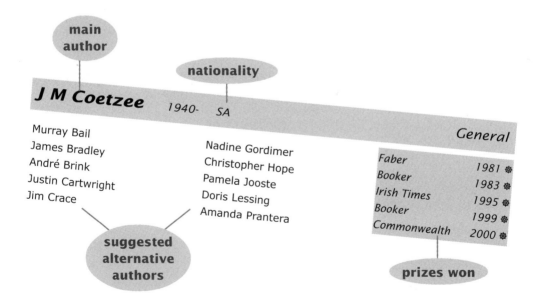

main author

nationality

J M Coetzee *1940- SA*

Murray Bail
James Bradley
André Brink
Justin Cartwright
Jim Crace

Nadine Gordimer
Christopher Hope
Pamela Jooste
Doris Lessing
Amanda Prantera

General

Faber   1981 ❀
Booker   1983 ❀
Irish Times   1995 ❀
Booker   1999 ❀
Commonwealth   2000 ❀

suggested alternative authors

prizes won

An increasing number of established authors are writing in alternative genres. These are shown in the main sequence as well as in the genre listings at the end of the book. Where an author writes under the same name but under two different genres, we have given two entries: for example, **Lynda La Plante** *(General)* and **Lynda La Plante** *(Crime: Police work)*.

Authors who usually write in one category may occasionally produce a book in a quite different genre - so if genre is important to you, check the jacket details of a book before you read it.

If you want to start by consulting a list of authors who write in a particular category, go to **Authors listed by genre** beginning on page 312. Some of the genres are further sub-divided - for instance, *Crime* is divided into Humour, Private investigator (PI), and so on. *Romance* and *Western* writers do not appear in the main sequence but are retained, under their respective headings, in the genre listings. Authors classified as *General* have not been listed.

Another possible starting point is to look at the lists of prize-winning books in **Literary prizes and awards**, which begin on page 348.

Who else writes like ...? apart, there is an increasing number of guides to novelists and their works. Some of these are listed in **Further reading** on page 374.

An index of **Characters**, **Series** and **Families**, listed alphabetically by surname, begins on page 331.

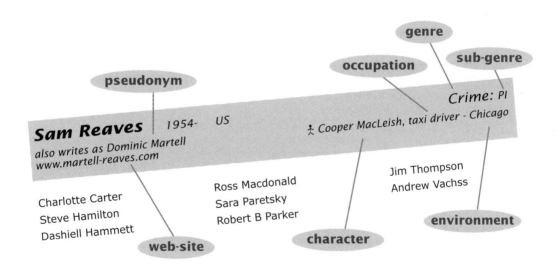

Abbreviations

The nationality or place of birth (where known) of those authors who are not English is indicated in the main list by an abbreviation or, in a few places, by the name of the country in full. The following is a full list of these countries.

Aus	Australia	Ire	Ireland	SA	South Africa
Belg	Belgium	Isr	Israel	Sco	Scotland
Braz	Brazil	It	Italy	Sing	Singapore
Can	Canada	Ja	Japan	Spain	Spain
Carib	Caribbean	Lebanon	Lebanon	Sri Lan	Sri Lanka
Chi	Chile	Mex	Mexico	Swe	Sweden
Colombia	Colombia	Neth	Netherlands	Tai	Taiwan
Cz	Czechoslovakia	NZ	New Zealand	US	United States of
Den	Denmark	Nigeria	Nigeria		America
Fr	France	Peru	Peru	Wales	Wales
Ger	Germany	Pol	Poland	Zan	Zanzibar
Guy	Guyana	Port	Portugal	Zim	Zimbabwe
Ind	India	Rus	Russia		

Literary prizes and awards

The following are the abbreviations used in the main body of the guide for winners of prizes. These are listed in full with their descriptions in the list of Literary prizes and awards (pages 348-373).

Authors	Authors' Club First Novel Award
Black	James Tait Black Memorial Prizes
Booker	Booker Prize for Fiction
H Bowling	Harry Bowling Prize
BSFA	British Science Fiction Association Awards
Arthur C Clarke	Arthur C Clarke Award
Commonwealth	Commonwealth Writers Prize
CWA	Crime Writers' Association
Encore	Encore Award
Faber	Geoffrey Faber Memorial Prize
Guardian	Guardian Fiction Prize / First Book Award
Hawthornden	Hawthornden Prize
Higham	David Higham Prize for Fiction
Holtby	Winifred Holtby Memorial Prize
IMPAC	International IMPAC Dublin Literary Award
Independent	'Independent' Foreign Fiction Award
Irish Times	Irish Times International Fiction Prize
Mail	Mail on Sunday / John Llewellyn Rhys Prize
S Maugham	Somerset Maugham Awards
McKitterick	McKitterick Prize
Orange	The Orange Prize
Parker	Parker Romantic Novel of the Year
Pulitzer	Pulitzer Prize for Fiction
Sagittarius	Sagittarius Prize
W H Smith	W H Smith - Book Awards
Sunday Times	Sunday Times Young Writer of the Year Award
TGR	Thumping Good Read Book Award
Tom-Gallon	Tom-Gallon Trust
Betty Trask	Betty Trask Awards
Whitbread	Whitbread Book of the Year and Literary Awards
Wingate	Jewish Quarterly / Wingate Literary Prize for Fiction

The Readers' Guide
An Alphabetical List

A

Peter Ackroyd *1949-*   *General*

John Banville
Julian Barnes
William Bedford
Anthony Burgess
John Fowles

Maggie Gee
Robert Nye
Iain Sinclair
Jill Paton Walsh

S Maugham	1984	❀
Guardian	1985	❀
Whitbread	1985	❀

Paul Adam *1958-*   *Adventure/Thriller*

David Armstrong
Paul Carson
Robin Cook

Tess Gerritsen
Roy Lewis
Ken McClure

Leah Ruth Robinson
Stella Shepherd

Douglas Adams *1952-2001*   *Science Fiction: Humour*
www.douglasadams.com

Neil Gaiman
Rob Grant

Tom Holt
Terry Pratchett

Robert Rankin
Bob Shaw

James Adams *1951-*   *Adventure/Thriller*

Ted Allbeury
James Buchan
Stephen Coonts
Clive Egleton

James Follett
Frederick Forsyth
Alan Furst

John Lawton
Terence Strong
Robert Wilson

Jane Adams *1960-*   *Crime: Police work - Br*
⚕ *DI Mike Croft - Psychological* ▪ *DS Ray Flowers - Norfolk*

Lisa Appignanesi
Hilary Bonner
Deborah Crombie

Frances Fyfield
P D James
Danuta Reah

Alison Taylor
Aline Templeton
Margaret Yorke

Don't forget lists of: *Genres* * *Characters* * *Literary prizes* * *Further reading* ☞

Jessica Adams   *Aus*   *Chick Lit*

Geraldine Bedell   Anna Davis   Alexandra Potter
Susie Boyt   Chris Manby   Fiona Walker

Richard Adams   *1920-*   *General*

Jonathan Carroll   Joyce Stranger
William Horwood   Henry Williamson

Elizabeth Adler   *Saga*

Lisa Appignanesi   Barbara Taylor Bradford   Elizabeth Villars
Charlotte Bingham   Anita Burgh   Penny Vincenzi
Rose Boucheron   Sidney Sheldon

Joan Aiken   *1924-*   *General*

Jane Austen   Elizabeth Harris   Iris Murdoch
Charles Dickens   Susan Hill   Emma Tennant

Catherine Aird   *1930-*   *Crime: Police work - Br*
is Kinn Hamilton McIntosh   ☆ *DI Sloan & DS Crosby - 'Calleshire'*

Vivien Armstrong   W J Burley   Ann Cleeves
Brian Battison   Joanna Cannan   Gladys Mitchell
M C Beaton   Agatha Christie   John Penn
Pauline Bell

Rosemary Aitken   *Saga*
also writes as Rosemary Rowe

Gloria Cook   Elizabeth Ann Hill   Susan Sallis
Anne Goring   Malcolm Ross   Barbara Whitnell
Winston Graham

Don't forget lists of: *Genres * Characters * Literary prizes * Further reading* ☞

Brian W Aldiss 1925- Science Fiction

www.brianwaldiss.com

Isaac Asimov	Brian Herbert	BSFA	1982 ❀
J G Ballard	Frank Herbert	BSFA	1985 ❀
Greg Bear	Vernor Vinge		
Arthur C Clarke	Kurt Vonnegut		
Joe Haldeman	John Wyndham		
Robert A Heinlein			

Bruce Alexander 1932- US Crime: Historical

is Bruce Cook 🏃 Sir John Fielding, Bow Street magistrate
www.angelfire.com/ct/TORTUGA/fielding.html C18th London

Stephanie Barron	Deryn Lake	Hannah March
Gwendoline Butler	Janet Laurence	Fidelis Morgan
Keith Heller	Margaret Lawrence	

Kate Alexander Saga

is Tilly Armstrong

Charlotte Bingham	Elizabeth Elgin	Patricia Wendorf
Betty Burton	Juliette Mead	Sarah Woodhouse
Elizabeth Darrell	Mary Jane Staples	

Vanessa Alexander Historical

also writes as Anna Apostolou, Michael Clynes, Paul Doherty, P C Doherty & Paul Harding

Evelyn Anthony	Elizabeth Darrell
Helen Cannam	Norah Lofts

Ted Allbeury 1917- Adventure/Thriller

James Adams	Len Deighton	Brian Freemantle
Eric Ambler	Clive Egleton	Palma Harcourt
Evelyn Anthony	Colin Forbes	John Lawton
Victor Davis		

Charlotte Vale Allen 1941- Can Saga

www.charlottevaleallen.com

Janet Dailey	Lavyrle Spencer	Nicola Thorne
Claire Lorrimer	Danielle Steel	Elizabeth Walker
Audrey Reimann		

Isabel Allende   1942-   Chi   General
www.isabelallende.com

Gail Anderson-Dargatz	Louise Erdrich	Ángeles Mastretta
Margaret Atwood	Laura Esquivel	Lisa St Aubin de Terán
Mário de Carvalho	Gabriel Garcia Márquez	Mario Vargas Llosa

Jay Allerton   Sco   Saga
also writes as Frances Paige

Josephine Cox	Evelyn Hood	Eileen Ramsay
Elizabeth Darrell	Nora Kay	Harriet Smart
Doris Davidson	Alexandra Raife	Dee Williams

Margery Allingham   1904-66   Crime: PI
                                                    ⚐ Albert Campion

Joanna Cannan	Michael Innes	Dorothy L Sayers
Agatha Christie	Ngaio Marsh	Josephine Tey
Edmund Crispin	Emma Page	Patricia Wentworth
Elizabeth Ferrars		

Catherine Alliott   Chick Lit

Alexandra Campbell	Wendy Holden	Sue Margolis
Lucy Ellman	Christina Jones	Carole Matthews
Maeve Haran	Kathy Lette	Melissa Nathan
Sarah Harvey	Jill Mansell	Fiona Walker

Lisa Alther   1944-   US   General

Beryl Bainbridge	Susan Isaacs	Marge Piercy
Ethan Canin	Toni Morrison	Tom Robbins
Zoë Fairbairns	Ann Oakley	

Eric Ambler   1909-98   Adventure/Thriller

Ted Allbeury	Robert Harris	CWA	1972 ✹
John Buchan	Joseph Kanon		
Peter Driscoll	John Le Carré		
Ian Fleming	Robert Littell		
John Gardner	J K Mayo		
Palma Harcourt			

Stephen Amidon   *1959-   US*   *General*

Ethan Canin   Ben Elton   Tom Wolfe
Don DeLillo   Garrison Keillor

Kingsley Amis   *1922-95*   *General*

Terence Blacker   Stanley Middleton   *Booker   1986* ✱
Malcolm Bradbury   David Nobbs
Joseph Connolly   Keith Waterhouse
Michael Frayn   A N Wilson
David Lodge

Martin Amis   *1949-*   *General*
http://martinamis.albion.edu/

Paul Auster   Tim Lott   Brian Moore
Iain Banks   Ian McEwan   Vladimir Nabokov
Julian Barnes   Thomas McGuane   Will Self
Justin Cartwright

Poul Anderson   *1926-2001   US Science Fiction: Space opera*
www.lafterhall.com/poulanderson.html

Isaac Asimov   David Brin   Jack McDevitt
Stephen Baxter   Alan Dean Foster   Roger Zelazny
Ray Bradbury   Joe Haldeman

Gail Anderson-Dargatz   *Can*   *General*

Isabel Allende   Barbara Kingsolver   Lisa St Aubin de Terán
Margaret Atwood   Alice Munro   Anne Tyler

Colin Andrews   *1946-   US*   *Adventure/Thriller*
also writes as F Paul Wilson

Jonathan Aycliffe   Ken McClure   Richard Preston
Robin Cook   Michael Palmer   Morris West
Michael Crichton

Don't forget lists of: *Genres* ∗ *Characters* ∗ *Literary prizes* ∗ *Further reading* ☞

Lyn Andrews 1943- Saga
previously wrote as Lynn M Andrews
Liverpool Irish

Anne Baker	Katie Flynn	Maureen Lee
Donna Baker	June Francis	Elizabeth Murphy
Jane Brindle	Ruth Hamilton	Margaret Thornton
Josephine Cox	Joan Jonker	

Phil Andrews Crime: PI
₣ Steve Strong - Soccer

Marc Blake	Raymond Chandler	Chris Niles
John Burns	Frank Lean	

Virginia Andrews 1936-86 US General
also writes as V C Andrews (with Andrew Neiderman)
www.fantasticfiction.co.uk/authors/Virginia_Andrews.htm

Jane Brindle	Judith Kelman	Daoma Winston
Diane Guest	Nora Roberts	Anne Worboys
Gwen Hunter		

Evelyn Anthony 1928- Adventure/Thriller: Spy
₣ Davina Graham

Ted Allbeury	Clare Francis	Palma Harcourt
David Brierley	Alan Furst	Lindsay Townsend
Colin Forbes		

Evelyn Anthony 1928- Historical

Vanessa Alexander	Victoria Holt	Diana Norman
Cynthia Harrod-Eagles	Genevieve Lyons	Jean Plaidy

Mark Anthony 1966- US Fantasy: Epic
www.thelastrune.com

Chaz Brenchley	Stephen Donaldson	Robert Jordan
Steven Brust	Terry Goodkind	Guy Gavriel Kay
Jonathan Carroll		

Don't forget lists of: *Genres * Characters * Literary prizes * Further reading* ☞

Piers Anthony 1934- US

www.hipiers.com

Fantasy: Humour
Xanth Series

Steven Brust
L Sprague de Camp

Alan Dean Foster
Craig Shaw Gardner

Terry Pratchett

Lisa Appignanesi 1946- Pol

General

Elizabeth Adler
Sally Beauman
Helen Dunmore

Jill Gascoine
Lesley Glaister
Josephine Hart

Judith Krantz
Ann Oakley

Lisa Appignanesi 1946- Pol

Adventure/Thriller:
Psychological

Jane Adams
Clare Francis

Nicci French
Robert Goddard

Barbara Vine

Diana Appleyard

Aga Saga

Judy Astley
Geraldine Bedell
Charlotte Bingham
Cindy Blake

Anna Cheska
Victoria Clayton
Nina Dufort

Sarah Grazebrook
Mary Sheepshanks
Joanna Trollope

Geoffrey Archer 1944-

Adventure/Thriller
⚑ Sam Packer

Stephen Coonts
Graham Hurley
Philip Kerr
Stephen Leather

Mike Lunnon-Wood
Chris Ryan
Julian Jay Savarin

Tim Sebastian
Craig Thomas

Jeffrey Archer 1940-

General

Harry Bingham
Michael Dobbs
Arthur Hailey
Colin Harrison

Philip Hensher
David Mason
Peter Rawlinson
Lawrence Sanders

Michael Shea
Sidney Sheldon
John Trenhaile

Don't forget lists of: *Genres * Characters * Literary prizes * Further reading* ☞

A

Tom Arden   1961-   Aus

Fantasy: Epic
Orokon Series

David Eddings
Terry Goodkind
Kate Jacoby

Robert Jordan
Nick Nielsen
K J Parker

Freda Warrington
David Zindell

William Ardin

Crime
🏃 *Charles Ramsay - Antiques & art*

Jonathan Gash
Philip Hook

John Malcolm
Iain Pears

Derek Wilson

Aileen Armitage   1930-

Saga
🏃 *Eva Bower - Yorkshire ▪ Hawksmoor Series - Yorkshire*

Jessica Blair
Helen Cannam
Joan Eadith

Audrey Reimann
Ann Victoria Roberts
Kay Stephens

Margaret Sunley
Elizabeth Walker

Campbell Armstrong   1944-   Sco   Adventure/Thriller

Harold Coyle
Colin Forbes
Glenn Meade

David Morrell
Julian Jay Savarin

Tim Sebastian
John Trenhaile

David Armstrong   1946-

Crime: Police work - Br
🏃 *DI Frank Kavanagh ▪ DC Jane Salt - Birmingham*

Paul Adam
Jeffrey Ashford
John Harvey

Donna Leon
Roy Lewis
Barry Maitland

Janet Neel
Frank Palmer
Stewart Pawson

Vivien Armstrong

Crime: Police work - Br
🏃 *DI Ian Preston - Great Yarmouth*

Catherine Aird
Stephen Booth
Ken Bruen
Joanna Cannan

Mary Clayton
Brian Cooper
Raymond Flynn
Malcolm Forsythe

Alan Hunter
P D James
Susan Kelly
Ann Quinton

Catherine Arnold US Crime: Legal/financial
♣ Karen Perry-Mondori, Attorney - Florida

A

Rankin Davis	Linda Fairstein	Steve Martini
Alan M Dershowitz	Philip Friedman	Lisa Scottoline
Dexter Dias		

Jake Arnott 1961- Crime

Adam Baron	Jeff Gulvin	Jerry Raine
Nicholas Blincoe	Toby Litt	Mark Timlin
Jeremy Cameron	Marc Pye	

Jane Asher 1946- General

Jane Gordon	Elizabeth Jane Howard	Deborah Moggach
Julia Hamilton	Shena Mackay	

Jeffrey Ashford 1926- Crime: Police work - Br
is Roderic Jeffries

David Armstrong	Kate Ellis	Bill Knox
Hilary Bonner	J M Gregson	Roy Lewis
Martin Edwards	Bill James	Ian Rankin

Sherry Ashworth 1953- Humour

Anne Atkins	Helen Fielding	Kate O'Riordan
Victoria Colby	Kathy Lette	Arabella Weir

Isaac Asimov 1920-92 US Science Fiction: Space and time
www.asimovonline.com

Brian W Aldiss	John Brunner	Robert A Heinlein
Poul Anderson	Arthur C Clarke	Larry Niven
Gregory Benford	Philip K Dick	Clifford D Simak
Ben Bova		

Don't forget lists of: *Genres * Characters * Literary prizes * Further reading* ☞

9

Robert Asprin   1946-   US
Fantasy: Epic
also writes as Robert Lynn Asprin   *Myth Adventures Series ▪ Phule's Saga*

L Sprague de Camp   Terry Goodkind   Terry Pratchett
Alan Dean Foster   Andrew Harman   Martin Scott
Craig Shaw Gardner   Tom Holt

Judy Astley
Aga Saga

Diana Appleyard   Anne Doughty   Sophia Watson
Raffaella Barker   Nina Dufort   Madeleine Wickham
Anna Barrie   Charlotte Moore   Marcia Willett
Victoria Clayton   Jill Roe

Ace Atkins   US
Crime
⚐ Nick Travers, Blues historian - New Orleans

James Lee Burke   Ron Ellis   James Sallis
Charlotte Carter   Michael McGarrity   Mary Wings
Thomas H Cook   Walter Mosley   Stuart Woods
Stephen Donaldson

Anne Atkins
Aga Saga

Sherry Ashworth   Charlotte Moore   Diana Saville
Marika Cobbold   Ann Purser   Rebecca Shaw
Hazel Hucker   Pam Rhodes   Madeleine Wickham
Maggie Makepeace

Kate Atkinson   1951-
General
www.geocities.com/kateatkinson14/index.htm

Beryl Bainbridge   Janice Galloway   *Whitbread   1995* ❀
Kate Bingham   Shena Mackay
Angela Carter   Mary Morrissy
Maureen Duffy   Carol Shields
Laura Esquivel   Rebecca Wells
Margaret Forster

*Don't forget lists of: Genres * Characters * Literary prizes * Further reading ☞*

A A Attanasio   1951-   US   Science Fiction: Space opera
www.fantasticfiction.co.uk/authors/A_A_Attanasio.htm

Marion Zimmer Bradley	Ursula K Le Guin	Robert Silverberg
Arthur C Clarke	Julian May	Roger Zelazny
Colin Greenland		

Margaret Atwood   1939-   Can   General
www.owtoad.com/

Isabel Allende	Nadine Gordimer	Arthur C Clarke 1987 ❀
Gail Anderson-Dargatz	Ruth Prawer Jhabvala	Booker 2000 ❀
Andrea Barrett	Annie Proulx	
Dennis Bock	David Adams Richards	
Clare Chambers	Jane Rogers	
Anita Desai	Carol Shields	

Jean M Auel   1936-   US   Historical

Louise Cooper	Pauline Gedge	Edward Rutherfurd
Stephen Donaldson	Christian Jacq	Linda Lay Shuler
Diana Gabaldon		

Jane Austen   1775-1817   General
www.pemberley.com/janeinfo/janeinfo.html

Joan Aiken	Alison Lurie	Barbara Trapido
Penelope Fitzgerald	Barbara Pym	Edith Wharton
Georgette Heyer	Emma Tennant	

Paul Auster   1947-   US   General
www.paulauster.co.uk

Martin Amis	Don DeLillo	David Mamet
Nicola Barker	E L Doctorow	Thomas Pynchon
Julian Barnes	Franz Kafka	Adam Thorpe
Terence Blacker		

Don't forget lists of: *Genres* * *Characters* * *Literary prizes* * *Further reading* ☞

A B

Jonathan Aycliffe   1949-   Horror
also writes as Daniel Easterman

Colin Andrews	Robert Girardi	Richard Matheson
Richard Bachman	Graham Joyce	Kim Newman
Clive Barker	Stephen Laws	Anne Rice
Campbell Black		

Steve Aylett   Science Fiction: Near future

J G Ballard	William Gibson	Neal Stephenson
John Barnes	Gwyneth Jones	Bruce Sterling
Alexander Besher	Ken MacLeod	Tad Williams
Eric Brown	Jeff Noon	

Marian Babson   1929-   US   Crime: Humour
is Ruth Stenstreem   ⚲ *Trixie Dolan & Evangeline Sinclair, Actresses* ⎱ *London*
            Douglas Perkins & Gerry Tate, PR Consultants ⎰

Lilian Jackson Braun	Valerie Kershaw	Simon Shaw
Simon Brett	Nancy Livingston	Charles Spencer
Anthea Fraser	Charlotte MacLeod	Susan Sussman with
Alison Joseph	Lindsay Maracotta	Sarajane Avidon

Richard Bachman   1947-   US   Horror
also writes as Stephen King

Jonathan Aycliffe	Peter James	Mark Morris
Muriel Gray	Stephen King	Dan Simmons
James Herbert	Dean R Koontz	Peter Straub

Anita Rau Badami   1967-   Can   General
www.emory.edu/ENGLISH/Bahri/Badami.html

Jung Chang	Chitra Banerjee Divakaruni	Amy Tan
Anita Desai	Rohinton Mistry	

David Baddiel   Lad Lit

Mark Barrowcliffe	Mike Gayle	Sean Thomas
Ben Elton	Nick Hornby	Matt Thorne
Stephen Fry	Tony Parsons	Nigel Williams

Desmond Bagley *1923-83* *Adventure/Thriller*

Jon Cleary
Clive Cussler
James Follett
Ken Follett

John Gardner
Jack Higgins
Hammond Innes
Geoffrey Jenkins

Duncan Kyle
Alistair MacLean
William Smethurst

Louise Bagshawe *1972-* *Chick Lit*

Pat Booth
Celia Brayfield
Lucy Ellman

Elizabeth Gage
Olivia Goldsmith
Christina Jones

Susan Lewis
Robyn Sisman
Fiona Walker

Murray Bail *1941- Aus* *General*

James Bradley
Peter Carey

Angela Carter
J M Coetzee

Robert Drewe
Michael Ondaatje

Hilary Bailey *1936-* *General*

Nina Bawden
Charlotte Bingham
Maureen Duffy

Alice Thomas Ellis
Jane Gardam
Angela Lambert

Hilary Mantel
Kate Pullinger
Emma Tennant

Beryl Bainbridge *1934-* *General*

Lisa Alther
Kate Atkinson
Pat Barker
Alice Thomas Ellis
Penelope Fitzgerald
Linda Grant

Sara Maitland
Mary Morrissy
Bernice Rubens
Teresa Waugh
Fay Weldon

Guardian	*1974* ✺
Whitbread	*1977* ✺
Whitbread	*1996* ✺
Black	*1998* ✺

Anne Baker *Saga*
Liverpool

Lyn Andrews
Donna Baker
Doreen Edwards
Katie Flynn

Helen Forrester
June Francis
Audrey Howard
Joan Jonker

Maureen Lee
Margaret Mayhew
Elizabeth Murphy

Don't forget lists of: *Genres * Characters * Literary prizes * Further reading* ☞

Donna Baker 1939-   Saga
also writes as Lilian Harry   Weavers Series ▪ Glassmakers Series - Kidderminster

Lyn Andrews	Marie Joseph	Susan Sallis
Anne Baker	Annie Murray	Sally Spencer
Jean Chapman	Audrey Reimann	Sue Sully
Meg Hutchinson		

B

John Baker 1942-   Crime: PI
www.johnbakeronline.co.uk   ☆ Sam Turner - York

Adam Baron	Reginald Hill	Martyn Waites
Eileen Dewhurst	Frank Lean	Barbara Whitehead
Martin Edwards	Cath Staincliffe	

Keith Baker 1945- Ire   Adventure/Thriller

Conor Cregan	Jack Higgins
Len Deighton	Patricia Highsmith

David Baldacci 1960- US   Adventure/Thriller
www.david-baldacci.com

Po Bronson	Paul Kilduff	TGR	1997 ❀
Nelson DeMille	Brad Meltzer		
Paul Erdman	David Morrell		
Joseph Finder	Michael Ridpath		
Craig Holden	Sheldon Siegel		

J G Ballard 1930-   Science Fiction: Technical
www.jgballard.com

Brian W Aldiss	Frank Herbert	BSFA	1979 ❀
Steve Aylett	James Lovegrove	Black	1984 ❀
Ray Bradbury	John Sladek	Guardian	1984 ❀
Philip K Dick	Kurt Vonnegut		
Thomas M Disch	Ian Watson		
Joe Haldeman	Jack Womack		

Don't forget lists of: *Genres * Characters * Literary prizes * Further reading* ☞

Iain Banks   1954-   Sco   *General*
also writes as Iain M Banks

Martin Amis	Jeremy Dronfield	Ian McEwan
Martyn Bedford	Neil Ferguson	Duncan McLean
Peter Benson	Gordon Legge	Alan Warner
Douglas Coupland	Carl MacDougall	

B

Iain M Banks   1954-   Sco   *Science Fiction: Space opera*
also writes as Iain Banks

John Barnes	Peter F Hamilton	
Greg Bear	Ken MacLeod	
David Brin	Adam Roberts	
John Brunner	Ian Watson	
Lois McMaster Bujold	David Zindell	
Orson Scott Card		

BSFA	1994 ✿
BSFA	1996 ✿

Lynne Reid Banks   1929-   *General*
www.lynnereidbanks.com

Margaret Drabble	Olivia Manning	Amos Oz
Nadine Gordimer	Edna O'Brien	Muriel Spark

Jo Bannister   1951-   *Crime: Police work - Br*
⚲ DI Liz Graham & DS Cal Donovan - 'Castlemere' ▪ *DCI Frank Shapiro*
▪ Brodie Farrell, PI - English South Coast

Simon Brett	Liz Evans	Priscilla Masters
Deborah Crombie	Jill McGown	Peter Turnbull
Marjorie Eccles	Barry Maitland	

John Banville   1945-   Ire   *General*

Peter Ackroyd	John McGahern	
Dermot Bolger	Vladimir Nabokov	
Peter Carey	William Trevor	
James Hamilton-Paterson	Barry Unsworth	

Guardian	1981 ✿

James Barclay   1965-

Fantasy: Epic
Chronicles of the Raven Series

Stephen Donaldson	Greg Keyes	George R R Martin
Steven Erikson	Juliet E McKenna	Caiseal Mor
David Gemmell	John Marco	Freda Warrington
Kate Jacoby		

Tessa Barclay   1928-   Sco

Saga

is Jean Bowden

⚐ *Craigallan, Corvill & Tramont Families*

Emma Blair	Margaret Graham	Frances Paige
Betty Burton	Isobel Neill	Nicola Thorne
Brenda Clarke	Pamela Oldfield	T R Wilson

Clive Barker   1952-

Horror

www.clivebarker.com

Jonathan Aycliffe	John Douglas	Richard Laymon
Jonathan Carroll	Dennis Etchison	Bentley Little
Simon Clark	Christopher Fowler	Dan Simmons

Nicola Barker   1966-

General

Paul Auster	Candia McWilliam	Higham	1993 ✹
Julian Barnes	Marcia Muller	Mail	1996 ✹
Saul Bellow	Will Self	IMPAC	2000 ✹
Jenny Diski			

Pat Barker   1943-

General

Beryl Bainbridge	Mary Morrissy	Guardian	1993 ✹
Louis de Bernières	Tim Parks	Booker	1995 ✹
Sebastian Faulks	Erich Maria Remarque		
Linda Grant	Bernhard Schlink		
Sebastien Japrisot	Charles Todd		
Shena Mackay			

Don't forget lists of: *Genres* * *Characters* * *Literary prizes* * *Further reading* ☞

Raffaella Barker   1964-   General

Judy Astley	Victoria Clayton	India Knight
Alexandra Campbell	Louise Doughty	Polly Samson
Anna Cheska	Kate Fenton	Isabel Wolff

Robert Barnard   1936-   Crime: Police work - Br
Det Supt Oddie & DC Charlie Peace - Yorkshire ■ Supt Perry Trehowan - London

Pauline Bell	John Harvey	Peter Robinson
Colin Dexter	Reginald Hill	Simon Shaw
Jonathan Gash	Stewart Pawson	Peter Turnbull
Patricia Hall	Nicholas Rhea	

John Barnes   1957-   US   Science Fiction: Near future

Steve Aylett	Ben Bova	Robert A Heinlein
Iain M Banks	Eric Brown	Neal Stephenson
Stephen Baxter	Pat Cadigan	Bruce Sterling
Gregory Benford		

Julian Barnes   1946-   General
also writes as Dan Kavanagh
www.julianbarnes.com

Peter Ackroyd	Bruce Chatwin	
Martin Amis	Adam Lively	*S Maugham 1981* ❀
Paul Auster	Tim Parks	*Faber 1985* ❀
Nicola Barker	Graham Swift	
Peter Benson	A N Wilson	

Linda Barnes   1949-   US   Crime: PI
www.lindabarnes.com   *Carlotta Carlyle - Boston, Mass.*

Liza Cody	Susan Moody	Sandra Scoppettone
Janet Evanovich	Marcia Muller	Mary Wings
Lauren Henderson	Sara Paretsky	

17

Zoë Barnes
Chick Lit

Maria Barrett
Cindy Blake
Susie Boyt
Rebecca Campbell

Cathy Kelly
Serena Mackesy
Jill Mansell
Sue Margolis

Carole Matthews
Freya North
Tyne O'Connell
Lesley Pearse

Adam Baron
Crime: PI
↟ Billy Rucker - London

Jake Arnott
John Baker
Jeffery Deaver

Stephen Donaldson
Frank Lean
Dennis Lehane

James Patterson
Martyn Waites

Nevada Barr   *1952-   US*
Crime
www.nevadabarr.com
↟ Anna Pigeon, US Park Ranger

Sue Grafton
Tony Hillerman

Sharyn McCrumb
Michael McGarrity

Margaret Maron
John Straley

Andrea Barrett   *1954-   US*
General

Margaret Atwood
Judy Budnitz
Patricia Gaffney

Barbara Kingsolver
Matthew Kneale
Alice Munro

Annie Proulx
Anita Shreve
Amy Tan

Maria Barrett
Glitz & Glamour

Zoë Barnes
Celia Brayfield
Laramie Dunaway

Roberta Latow
Susan Lewis

Una-Mary Parker
Lynne Pemberton

Anna Barrie   *1946-*
Aga Saga

Judy Astley
Hazel Hucker

Nora Naish
Ann Purser

Kathleen Rowntree
Henrietta Soames

Don't forget lists of: *Genres * Characters * Literary prizes * Further reading* ☞

Stephanie Barron   1963-   US   *Crime:* Historical
also writes as Francine Matthews   ⚲ *Jane Austen, Novelist - Georgian England*

Bruce Alexander
Gwendoline Butler
Keith Heller

Deryn Lake
Janet Laurence
Hannah March

Fidelis Morgan
Roberta Rogow
Kate Ross

Mark Barrowcliffe   *Lad Lit*

David Baddiel
Matthew Beaumont
Matthew Branton
Nick Earls

Mike Gayle
Alex George
Nick Hornby

Tim Lott
Tony Parsons
William Sutcliffe

Colin Bateman   1962-   Ire   *Humour*
⚲ *Dan Starkey, Journalist*

Marc Blake
Jeremy Cameron
Tim Dorsey
Roddy Doyle
Bill Fitzhugh
Maggie Gibson

Peter Guttridge
Douglas Lindsay
Toby Litt
Ardal O'Hanlon
Mike Ripley
John B Spencer

Betty Trask   1994 ❀

H E Bates   1905-74   *General*

Melvyn Bragg
R F Delderfield

Andrew Greig
Annie Leith

H E Bates   1905-74   *Humour*

E F Benson
Tom Holt

Garrison Keillor
David Nobbs

Peter Tinniswood
Keith Waterhouse

Brian Battison   1939   *Crime:* Police work - Br
⚲ *DCI Jim Ashworth & DS Holly Bedford - 'Bridgetown'*

Catherine Aird
John Creasey
Elizabeth George

John Harvey
Quintin Jardine
Priscilla Masters

Dorothy Simpson
June Thomson
Margaret Yorke

19

Nina Bawden   1925-   General

Hilary Bailey   Penelope Lively   Elizabeth Pewsey
Margaret Drabble   Alison Lurie   Kate Pullinger
Caro Fraser   Bel Mooney   Muriel Spark
Jane Gardam

B

Stephen Baxter   1957-   Science Fiction: Technical

Poul Anderson   Ian McDonald   BSFA   1995 ✹
John Barnes   China Miéville
Ben Bova   Alastair Reynolds
Arthur C Clarke   Vernor Vinge
Wil McCarthy   Ian Watson
Jack McDevitt   H G Wells

Peter S Beagle   1939-   US   Fantasy: Myth

Storm Constantine   Sara Douglass   Robert Holdstock
John Crowley   Neil Gaiman   Tanith Lee
Charles de Lint   Robin Hobb

Greg Bear   1951-   US   Science Fiction: Technical
www.gregbear.com

Brian W Aldiss   C J Cherryh   John Meaney
Iain M Banks   Arthur C Clarke   Kim Stanley Robinson
Gregory Benford   Wil McCarthy   Mary Doria Russell
David Brin

M C Beaton   1936-   Sco   Crime: Police work - Br
also writes as Marion Chesney   ☂ PC Hamish Macbeth - Scotland
                                   Agatha Raisin, Retired advertising executive

Catherine Aird   Margaret Duffy   Bill Knox
Pauline Bell   Gerald Hammond   Nancy Livingston
Clare Curzon   Joyce Holms   Ann Quinton

Sally Beauman   1944-   *Glitz & Glamour*
also writes as Vanessa James

Lisa Appignanesi   Jill Gascoine   Hilary Norman
Laramie Dunaway   Judi James   Una-Mary Parker
Julie Ellis   Susan Lewis   Lynne Pemberton
Elizabeth Gage   Judith Michael   Caroline Upcher

B

Matthew Beaumont   *Lad Lit*

Mark Barrowcliffe   Mike Gayle   Tim Lott
Nick Earls   Alex George

Geraldine Bedell   *Chick Lit*

Jessica Adams   Anna Maxted   Sue Welfare
Diana Appleyard   Stephanie Theobald   Isabel Wolff
Sarah Harris

Martyn Bedford   1959-   *Crime*

Iain Banks   Ben Richards   Tony Strong
Colin Dexter   Nicholas Royle   Barbara Vine

William Bedford   *Historical*

Peter Ackroyd   Jan Needle   Barry Unsworth
Jim Crace   Rose Tremain

Lauren Belfer   1957-   US   *General*

Joan Brady   Thomas Eidson   Annie Proulx
Caleb Carr   Stewart O'Nan

Pauline Bell   1938-   *Crime: Police work - Br*
⚗ DI Benny Mitchell ▪ CI Browne & DC Jennie Taylor - 'Cloughton', Yorkshire

Catherine Aird   Brian Cooper   Stewart Pawson
Robert Barnard   Eileen Dewhurst   Peter Robinson
M C Beaton   Marjorie Eccles   Peter Turnbull
Mary Clayton   Patricia Hall   Barbara Whitehead

21

Guy Bellamy   *Humour*

Michael Carson   Colin Douglas   Robert Llewellyn
Mavis Cheek   Michael Frayn   Ann Oakley
Jonathan Coe   Patrick Gale   Peter Tinniswood
Joseph Connolly   Annie Leith

B

Saul Bellow   *1915-   US*   *General*

Nicola Barker   Frederic Raphael   Pulitzer   1976 ✿
Don DeLillo   Philip Roth
Joseph Heller   Isaac Bashevis Singer
Amos Oz   William Styron
Thomas Pynchon   John Updike

Gregory Benford   *1941-   US*   *Science Fiction: Technical*
also writes as Sterling Blake
www.authorcafe.com/benford/index.html

Isaac Asimov   Peter F Hamilton   BSFA   1980 ✿
John Barnes   Paul J McAuley
Greg Bear   Wil McCarthy
Ben Bova   Brian Stableford
C J Cherryh   Ian Watson
Arthur C Clarke

Anne Bennett   *Saga*

Julia Bryant   Patricia Grey   Kay Stephens
Jean Chapman   Mary Minton
Brenda Clarke

Francis Bennett   *Adventure/Thriller*

David Brierley   Joseph Kanon   John Le Carré
Alan Furst   John Lawton   Robert Wilson

E F Benson   *1867-1940*   *Humour*

H E Bates   Annie Leith   P G Wodehouse
Tom Holt   Evelyn Waugh

Peter Benson   1956-   General

Iain Banks	Adam Lively	Authors	1987 ❀	Encore	1990 ❀
Julian Barnes	Graham Swift	Guardian	1987 ❀	S Maugham	1991 ❀
Robert Edric	Colm Toibin				

B

Alex Benzie   1961-   Sco   General

Margaret Forster   Gabriel Garcia Márquez   Carl MacDougall
Janice Galloway   Alasdair Gray   Allan Massie

Suzanne Berne   US   Adventure/Thriller: Psychological

Kate Grenville   Anita Shreve   Orange   1999 ❀
Harper Lee   Anne Tyler
Annie Proulx   Minette Walters

Alexander Besher   US   Science Fiction: Near future
                                                    Rim Series

Steve Aylett   Jon Courtenay Grimwood   Michael Marshall Smith
Eric Brown   Gwyneth Jones   Neal Stephenson
Pat Cadigan   Jeff Noon   Bruce Sterling
Greg Egan   Rachel Pollack   Tad Williams

Rachel Billington   1942-   General

Anne Fine   Maureen Freely   Penelope Lively
Penelope Fitzgerald   Elizabeth Jane Howard   Alison Lurie

Anne Billson   1954-   Horror

Chaz Brenchley   Nancy Collins   S P Somtow
Poppy Z Brite   Kim Newman   Steven Spruill
Simon Clark   Anne Rice

Maeve Binchy   1940-   Ire   Saga
www.randomhouse.com/features/binchy   Ireland

Elaine Crowley	Lynne Pemberton	*W H Smith* 2000 ✻
Anne Doughty	D M Purcell	
Rose Doyle	Liz Ryan	
Mary A Larkin	Mary Ryan	
Genevieve Lyons	Alice Taylor	
Imogen Parker	Kate Thompson	

B

Tim Binding   1947-   Adventure/Thriller

Michael Dibdin   Sebastian Faulks
Robert Edric   Tim Pears

Charlotte Bingham   1942-   General

Elizabeth Adler	Lucinda Edmonds	*Parker* 1995 ✻
Kate Alexander	Maeve Haran	
Diana Appleyard	Sarah Harrison	
Hilary Bailey	Erin Pizzey	
Elizabeth Buchan	Sally Spencer	

Harry Bingham   1967-   Adventure/Thriller: Legal/financial

Jeffrey Archer   John T Lescroart   Christopher Reich
Jonathan Davies   John McLaren   Michael Ridpath
Paul Kilduff   Steve Martini

Kate Bingham   General

Kate Atkinson   Sue Gee   Carol Shields
Margaret Forster   Bel Mooney

Carol Birch   1951-   General

Helen Dunmore	Deborah Moggach	*Higham* 1988 ✻
Lesley Glaister	Carole Morin	*Faber* 1991 ✻
Catherine Merriman		

Campbell Black   *Horror*

Jonathan Aycliffe   Stephen Gallagher   Phil Rickman
Ramsey Campbell   Steve Harris   Bernard Taylor
Joe Donnelly   James Herbert

B

Julia Blackburn   *1948-*   *General*

Bruce Chatwin   Esther Freud
Louis de Bernières   Anne Michaels

Terence Blacker   *Humour*

Kingsley Amis   John Lanchester   Geoff Nicholson
Paul Auster   John McCabe   Nigel Williams
Jonathan Coe

Emma Blair   *1942-   Sco*   *Saga*
✦ Drummond Family - Scotland

Tessa Barclay   Isobel Neill   Alison Skelton
Christine Marion Fraser   Eileen Ramsay   Harriet Smart
Nora Kay   Agnes Short   Jessica Stirling
Elisabeth McNeill

Jessica Blair   *1923-*   *Saga*
is William J Spence

Aileen Armitage   Margaret Graham   Margaret Thornton
Helen Cannam   Eileen Ramsay   Eileen Townsend
Joan Eadith   Audrey Reimann   Elizabeth Walker
Iris Gower

Cindy Blake   *General*

Diana Appleyard   Susie Boyt   Mary Sheepshanks
Zoë Barnes   Anna Cheska

Marc Blake · Crime: Humour

Phil Andrews
Colin Bateman
Nicholas Blincoe
Matthew Branton

John Burns
Janet Evanovich
Peter Guttridge

Carl Hiaasen
Chris Niles
Grant Stewart

Alice Blanchard · US · Adventure/Thriller

John Gilstrap
Stuart Harrison

Donald Harstad
Paullina Simons

Scott Smith
Boston Teran

Peter Blauner · 1959- · US · Adventure/Thriller

Lee Child
John Gilstrap

Douglas Kennedy
Dennis Lehane

Stuart Woods

Faith Bleasdale · Humour

Sarah Grazebrook
Wendy Holden

Chris Manby
Mary Selby

Sue Welfare
Isabel Wolff

Nicholas Blincoe · Crime
www.twbooks.co.uk/authors/nicholasblincoe.html/ · Manchester

Jake Arnott
Marc Blake
Christopher Brookmyre
Jeremy Cameron
Philip Caveney

Paul Johnston
Nick Oldham
Kevin Sampson
Mark Timlin

CWA   1998 ❁

Lawrence Block · 1938- · US · Crime
also writes as Paul Kavanagh

🏃 Bernie Rhodenbarr, Burglar ⎫
Matthew Scudder, Retired policeman ⎬ New York
John Keller, Hit man ⎭

Robert Crais
Loren D Estleman
Elmore Leonard
John D MacDonald

Ross Macdonald
Reggie Nadelson
Robert B Parker

George P Pelecanos
Robert K Tanenbaum
Donald E Westlake

Valerie Blumenthal   1950-   General

Margaret Drabble	Sian James	Libby Purves
Sue Gee	Bel Mooney	

Philip Boast   1952-   Saga

♖ Ben London - London

Harry Cole	Beryl Kingston	Victor Pemberton
Patricia Grey	Peter Ling	Elizabeth Waite
Lena Kennedy		

Dennis Bock   Can   General

Margaret Atwood	Anne Michaels	Carol Shields
Peter Matthiessen	Michael Ondaatje	

Dirk Bogarde   1921-99   General

Elizabeth Bowen	Francis King	Frederic Raphael
Rumer Godden	Barbara Neil	Tony Warren
Christopher Hudson		

Dermot Bolger   1959-   Ire   General

John Banville	Colum McCann	Joseph O'Connor
Roddy Doyle	Bernard MacLaverty	Colm Toibin
Patrick McCabe	Brian Moore	Niall Williams

Janie Bolitho   1950-   Crime: Police work - Br

♖ DCI Ian Roper ▪ Rose Trevelyan, Painter - Cornwall

W J Burley	J M Gregson	Alexander McCall Smith
Mary Clayton	Janet Harward	Sally Spencer
Kate Ellis	Peter Robinson	Alison Taylor
Ann Granger	Betty Rowlands	

Don't forget lists of: *Genres* * *Characters* * *Literary prizes* * *Further reading* ☞

Larry Bond   1951-   US   *Adventure/Thriller*

Dale Brown	Clive Cussler	Stephen Leather
Stephen Coonts	Richard Herman	James Thayer

Hilary Bonner   1949-   *Crime:* Police work - Br
DCI Rose Piper - West Country

Jane Adams	John Farrow	Alison Taylor
Jeffrey Ashford	Robert Goddard	Andrew Taylor
Stephen Booth	Alan Scholefield	

Martin Booth   1944-   *Adventure/Thriller*

James Clavell	Peter May	William Rivière
Bryce Courtenay	Marc Olden	

Pat Booth   1942-   *Glitz & Glamour*

Louise Bagshawe	Olivia Goldsmith	Roberta Latow
Sandra Brown	Judith Krantz	Johanna Lindsey
Jackie Collins	Lynda La Plante	Penny Vincenzi
Lucinda Edmonds		

Stephen Booth   1957-   *Crime:* Police work - Br
www.stephen-booth.com
DC Ben Cooper & DS Diane Fry

Vivien Armstrong	Barry Maitland	Alison Taylor
Hilary Bonner	Priscilla Masters	Aline Templeton
Jill McGown	Danuta Reah	

Alice Borchardt   US   *Fantasy:* Myth

Poppy Z Brite	Megan Lindholm	S P Somtow
Mark Chadbourn	Holly Lisle	Judith Tarr
Storm Constantine	Juliet Marillier	Freda Warrington
Katharine Kerr		

Rose Boucheron   *Saga*

Elizabeth Adler	Sarah Harrison	Beryl Kingston
Josephine Cox	Elizabeth Jane Howard	

Anthony Bourdain   1956-   US   Crime: Humour

Tim Dorsey
Bill Fitzhugh
Kinky Friedman

Vicki Hendricks
Carl Hiaasen
Joe R Lansdale

Dennis Lehane
Laurence Shames
Sheldon Siegel

Ben Bova   1932-   US   Science Fiction: Space and time
www.benbova.net

Isaac Asimov
John Barnes
Stephen Baxter
Gregory Benford

John Brunner
Thomas M Disch
Greg Egan

Larry Niven
Kim Stanley Robinson
John Sladek

Elizabeth Bowen   1899-1973   Ire   General

Dirk Bogarde
Anita Brookner
Graham Greene
Jennifer Johnston

Penelope Lively
Candia McWilliam
Olivia Manning

Iris Murdoch
V S Pritchett
William Trevor

David Bowker   Horror
♀ C S Vernon Lavelle

John Farris
Christopher Fowler

Steve Harris
Jenny Jones

Phil Rickman
Bernard Taylor

Harry Bowling   1931-99   Saga
Tanner Trilogy - London

Patricia Burns
Harry Cole
Josephine Cox
Emma Dally

Anna King
Elizabeth Lord
Margaret Pemberton

Victor Pemberton
Mary Jane Staples
Elizabeth Waite

William Boyd   1952-   General

Justin Cartwright
Giles Foden
Philip Hensher
Christopher Hope
Alan Isler

Matthew Kneale
David Lodge
Paul Micou
Tim Parks
Adam Thorpe

Whitbread	*1981* ❁
Mail	*1982* ❁
S Maugham	*1982* ❁
Black	*1990* ❁

Clare Boylan   1948-   Ire   Saga

Michael Collins	Wendy Perriam	Patricia Scanlan
Kathleen Conlon	Mary Ryan	Alice Taylor
Edna O'Brien	Diana Saville	Sue Townsend

Elizabeth Boyle   Historical

Catherine Coulter	Judith McNaught
Teresa Crane	Amanda Quick

Susie Boyt   1969-   Chick Lit

Jessica Adams	Jenn Crowell	Susan Oudot
Zoë Barnes	Lucy Ellman	Lesley Pearse
Cindy Blake	Josie Lloyd & Emlyn Rees	Lynne Truss
Jenny Colgan	Freya North	Fiona Walker

Malcolm Bradbury   1932-2000   General

Kingsley Amis	Thomas Keneally	Nicholas Shakespeare
Melvyn Bragg	David Lodge	Keith Waterhouse
Michael Frayn	John Mortimer	A N Wilson
Howard Jacobson		

Ray Bradbury   1920-   US   Science Fiction: Space and time
www.spaceagecity.com/bradbury/bio.htm

Poul Anderson	Aldous Huxley	Kim Stanley Robinson
J G Ballard	H P Lovecraft	Clifford D Simak
Dennis Etchison	Ken MacLeod	Roger Zelazny
Robert A Heinlein	George Orwell	

Tom Bradby   Adventure/Thriller

Daniel Easterman	Stephen Leather	Tim Sebastian
Clive Egleton	Robert Ludlum	Gerald Seymour
Gavin Esler	A J Quinnell	

*Don't forget lists of: Genres * Characters * Literary prizes * Further reading* ☞

Barbara Taylor Bradford 1933- Saga
www.barbarataylorbradford.com

⚲ Emma Harte

Elizabeth Adler
Frankie McGowan
Una-Mary Parker

Danielle Steel
Rosie Thomas
Nicola Thorne

Penny Vincenzi
Elizabeth Walker

James Bradley Aus General

Murray Bail
Peter Carey

J M Coetzee
Michael Ondaatje

Marion Zimmer Bradley 1930-99 US Fantasy: Epic
www.mzbfm.com

Avalon • Darkover Series

A A Attanasio
Barbara Hambly
Robert Holdstock
Helen Hollick

Tanith Lee
Holly Lisle
Juliet Marillier
Julian May

Caiseal Mor
Melanie Rawn
Jan Siegel
Sheri S Tepper

Rita Bradshaw Saga
N E England

Catherine Cookson
Ruth Hamilton

Una Horne
Meg Hutchinson

Freda Lightfoot
Annie Murray

Joan Brady 1939- US General

Lauren Belfer
Fred D'Aguiar
Pete Dexter
Ellen Gilchrist
A L Kennedy

Alison Lurie
Mary McGarry Morris
Annie Proulx
Carol Shields
Jane Smiley

Whitbread 1993 ❀

John Brady 1955- Ire Crime: Police work - foreign
⚲ Insp Matt Minogue - Dublin

Bartholomew Gill
Hugo Hamilton
P D James
Jim Lusby

Rory McCormac
Eugene McEldowney
Pauline McLynn

John Penn
Mike Ripley
Georges Simenon

Melvyn Bragg   *1939-*   *General*

H E Bates
Malcolm Bradbury
A S Byatt
Margaret Drabble
Thomas Hardy

Roy Hattersley
Catherine Merriman
Stanley Middleton
Andrew O'Hagan

W H Smith   2000 ❀

B

Sally Brampton   *1955-*   *General*

Suzanne Goodwin
Maeve Haran

Diana Stainforth
Rosie Thomas

Matthew Branton   *1971-*   *Crime*

Mark Barrowcliffe
Marc Blake

Bret Easton Ellis
Alex Garland

William Sutcliffe

Lilian Jackson Braun   *1916-   US*   *Crime: Humour*
👤 *Jim Qwilleran, Journalist - US 'Moose County'* ▪ *Yum Yum & Koto - Siamese cats*

Marian Babson
Rita Mae Brown
Paula Gosling
Emma Lathen

Nancy Livingston
Charlotte MacLeod
Margaret Maron

Susan Sussman with
  Sarajane Avidon
Kathy Hogan Trocheck

Celia Brayfield   *1945-*   *Glitz & Glamour*

Louise Bagshawe
Maria Barrett
Jackie Collins
Shirley Conran

Jilly Cooper
Barbara Delinsky
Lucinda Edmonds
Elizabeth Gage

Judith Michael
Hilary Norman
Victoria Routledge

Chaz Brenchley   *1959-*   *Horror*
www.chazbrenchley.co.uk

Mark Anthony
Anne Billson
Simon Clark
Nancy Collins

John Douglas
Sara Douglass
Stephen Gallagher

Andrew Klavan
David Martin
K J Parker

Simon Brett 1945- Crime: Humour
Charles Parris, Actor ▪ Mrs Pargeter, Widow - Sussex
Carole Seddon & Jude, PIs - 'Fethering', Sussex

Marian Babson   Tim Heald   Simon Shaw
Jo Bannister   Veronica Heley   Charles Spencer
Michael Dibdin   Joyce Holms   Stella Whitelaw
Jonathan Gash   Nancy Livingston

B

Gene Brewer Fantasy: Contemporary

Bill Fitzhugh   Nick Nielsen   Adam Roberts
John Meaney   Jeff Noon   Michael Marshall Smith

Caroline Bridgwood 1960- Aga Saga

Marika Cobbold   Sybil Marshall
Patricia Fawcett   Kathleen Rowntree

David Brierley 1936- Adventure/Thriller

Evelyn Anthony   Dick Francis   Richard Pitman
Francis Bennett   John Francome   Martin Cruz Smith
Len Deighton   David Ignatius   Gordon Stevens

David Brin 1950- US Science Fiction: Space opera
www.kithrup.com/brin

Poul Anderson   C J Cherryh   Larry Niven
Iain M Banks   Alan Dean Foster   Dan Simmons
Greg Bear   Brian Herbert   Robert Charles Wilson
Lois McMaster Bujold   Frank Herbert   David Zindell

Jane Brindle 1938- General
also writes as Josephine Cox

Lyn Andrews   Iris Gower   Barbara Michaels
Virginia Andrews   Susan Hill   Sarah Waters
Lesley Glaister

Don't forget lists of: *Genres* * *Characters* * *Literary prizes* * *Further reading* ☞

Louise Brindley
Saga
Tanquillan Series

Rosemary Enright	Sara Hylton	Titia Sutherland
Diane Guest	Susan Sallis	Margaret Thornton

B

André Brink *1935- SA*
General

J M Coetzee	Nadine Gordimer
Jim Crace	Christopher Hope

Poppy Z Brite *1964- US*
Horror

Anne Billson	Tom Holland	Anne Rice
Alice Borchardt	Brian Lumley	S P Somtow
Nancy Collins	Kim Newman	

Po Bronson *1964- US*
Crime: Legal/financial

David Baldacci	Stephen Frey	Michael Ridpath
Linda Davies	Paul Kilduff	Sheldon Siegel
Paul Erdman	Brad Meltzer	

Amanda Brookfield *1960-*
Aga Saga

Erica James	Elizabeth Pewsey	Peta Tayler
Karen Nelson	Jill Roe	Sophia Watson
Elizabeth Palmer	Titia Sutherland	Madeleine Wickham

Christopher Brookmyre *1968- Sco*
Crime
www.brookmyre.co.uk
⚐ Jack Parlabane, Journalist - Scotland

Nicholas Blincoe	Jack Harvey	Douglas Lindsay
Jeremy Cameron	James Hawes	David Peace
Philip Caveney	Carl Hiaasen	Kevin Sampson
Bill Fitzhugh		

Anita Brookner   1928-   General

Elizabeth Bowen	Sue Gee	Booker 1984 ⊛
A S Byatt	Penelope Lively	
Isabel Colegate	Barbara Pym	
Helen Dunmore	Bernice Rubens	
Penelope Fitzgerald	Salley Vickers	

B

Terry Brooks   1944-   US   Fantasy: Epic
www.terrybrooks.net

Kate Elliott	Mike Jefferies	J R R Tolkien
Raymond E Feist	John Marco	Margaret Weis
Maggie Furey	Elizabeth Moon	Tad Williams
David Gemmell	Mickey Zucker Reichert	Philip G Williamson

Dale Brown   1956-   US   Adventure/Thriller
www.megafortress.com   ⚐ Patrick McLanahan - Aviation

Larry Bond	Richard Herman	Julian Jay Savarin
Tom Clancy	Graham Hurley	Douglas Terman
Stephen Coonts	Patrick Robinson	Craig Thomas
Bart Davis		

Eric Brown   1960-   Science Fiction: Near future
www.ericbrown.co.uk

Steve Aylett	William Gibson	Adam Roberts
John Barnes	K W Jeter	Neal Stephenson
Alexander Besher	Paul Johnston	Bruce Sterling
Pat Cadigan	James Lovegrove	Tad Williams

Lizbie Brown   Crime
                          ⚐ Elizabeth Blair, Quilt shop owner - Bath

Mary Clayton	Hazel Holt	Rebecca Tope
Ann Granger	Betty Rowlands	

Rita Mae Brown   1944-   US   Crime: Humour
www.ritamaebrown.com   ⚐ Mary Haristean & Mrs Murphy (a cat) - Crozet, Virginia

Lilian Jackson Braun	Susan Isaacs
Sparkle Hayter	Donald E Westlake

Sandra Brown   1948-   US   Glitz & Glamour
also writes as Laura Jordan, Rachel Ryan & Erin St Claire
www.sandrabrown.net

Pat Booth	Judi James	Harold Robbins
Elizabeth Gage	Jayne Ann Krentz	Penny Vincenzi
Olivia Goldsmith	Roberta Latow	

Ken Bruen   Ire   Crime: Police work - Br
⚡ DCI Roberts & DS Brant - London

Vivien Armstrong	Russell James	Peter Turnbull
Paul Charles	David Ralph Martin	Martyn Waites
Patricia Hall	David Peace	R D Wingfield
Bill James	June Thomson	

John Brunner   1934-95   US   Science Fiction: Near future

Isaac Asimov	Jack Vance	BSFA	1969 ❀
Iain M Banks	Ian Watson	BSFA	1970 ❀
Ben Bova	Jack Womack		
Thomas M Disch	John Wyndham		
Bob Shaw			

Steven Brust   1955-   US   Fantasy: Epic
www.dreamcafe.com   Vlad Taltos Series

Mark Anthony	Fritz Leiber	Janny Wurts
Piers Anthony	Margaret Weis	Roger Zelazny
Elizabeth Haydon		

Julia Bryant   Saga
⚡ Forrest Family - Portsmouth

Anne Bennett	June Francis
Elizabeth Elgin	Anna Jacobs

Elizabeth Buchan   1948-   Aga Saga

Charlotte Bingham	Juliette Mead	Parker	1994 ❀
Kate Fenton	Kate Sharam		
Eileen Goudge	Fay Weldon		
Angela Huth	Sarah Woodhouse		

James Buchan 1954- Adventure/Thriller

James Adams	Alan Judd	Guardian 1984 ❀
Victor Davis	John Le Carré	Guardian 1995 ❀
Gavin Esler	Gerald Seymour	Whitbread 1995 ❀

B

John Buchan 1875-1940 Sco Adventure/Thriller

Eric Ambler	Lionel Davidson	Robert Goddard
Jon Cleary	Peter Driscoll	Duncan Kyle
Joseph Conrad	Ian Fleming	

Edna Buchanan 1939- US Crime

🏃 Britt Montero, Journalist - Miami

Jan Burke	Sparkle Hayter	Sara Paretsky
Sue Grafton	Laura Lippman	Laurence Shames
James Hall	Geoffrey Norman	Les Standiford

Fiona Buckley 1937- Crime: Historical
is Valerie Anand

🏃 Ursula Blanchard - C16th England

P F Chisholm	Paul Harding	Fidelis Morgan
Michael Clynes	Edward Marston	Peter Tonkin
Judith Cook		

Judy Budnitz 1973- US General

Andrea Barrett	Marianne Fredriksson	Lorrie Moore
Angela Carter	Alice Hoffman	Joyce Carol Oates

Lois McMaster Bujold 1949- Science Fiction: Space opera
www.dendarii.com

🏃 Miles Vorkosigan

Iain M Banks	Orson Scott Card	Peter F Hamilton
David Brin	C J Cherryh	Anne McCaffrey
Octavia E Butler	Colin Greenland	Elizabeth Moon

Don't forget lists of: Genres * Characters * Literary prizes * Further reading ☞

Chris Bunch 1943- US   Fantasy: Epic
                                             Sten Series

C J Cherryh	Maggie Furey	John Marco
Allan Cole	Mike Jefferies	Harry Turtledove
David A Drake	Robert Jordan	Janny Wurts
David Eddings		

John Burdett   Adventure/Thriller: Legal/financial

Tom Clancy	Robert Ludlum
John Le Carré	Gerald Seymour

Anthony Burgess 1917-93   General

Peter Ackroyd	Vladimir Nabokov	Salman Rushdie
Gabriel Garcia Márquez	George Orwell	Angus Wilson
William Golding		

Anita Burgh 1937-   General
also writes as Annie Leith
www.anitaburgh.com

Elizabeth Adler	Winston Graham	Sue Sully
Teresa Crane	Erin Pizzey	

James Lee Burke 1936- US   Crime: Police work - US
www.webfic.dk/jlb/jlb.asp   � *Dave Robicheaux - Louisiana*
                                       Billy-Bob Holland, Attorney - Texas

Ace Atkins	Tony Hillerman	*CWA* *1998* ❀
Michael Connelly	Martin Limon	
John Connolly	George P Pelecanos	
James Crumley	James Sallis	
John Farrow	John Sandford	
James Hall	Les Standiford	

Don't forget lists of: *Genres * Characters * Literary prizes * Further reading* ☞

Jan Burke   1953-   US   Crime
www.janburke.com   ☶ Irene Kelly, Journalist - California

Edna Buchanan   Laurie R King   Margaret Maron
John Burns   Martha Lawrence   Chris Niles
Sue Grafton   Laura Lippman   Kathy Hogan Trocheck
Faye Kellerman   Claire McNab

B

W J Burley   1914-   Crime: Police work - Br
                                             ☶ Supt Wycliffe - Cornwall

Catherine Aird   Kate Ellis   Alan Scholefield
Janie Bolitho   Janet Harward   June Thomson
Mary Clayton   Roger Ormerod   M J Trow
Ann Cleeves   John Penn

Mark Burnell   1964-   Crime: Modern
                                   ☶ Stephanie Patrick - Northumberland

Robin Cook   Jefferson Parker   Tim Wilson
Patricia Hall   Chris Petit

John Burns   1946-   Crime: Humour
                                   ☶ Max Chard, Journalist - London

Phil Andrews   Peter Guttridge   Chris Niles
Marc Blake   Valerie Kershaw   Mike Ripley
Jan Burke   Claire McNab
Denise Danks

Patricia Burns   Saga
                                                   London

Harry Bowling   Lena Kennedy   Jeanne Whitmee
Harry Cole   Beryl Kingston   Dee Williams
Elizabeth Daish   Peter Ling   Sally Worboyes
Patricia Grey   Elizabeth Lord

Guy Burt
Adventure/Thriller: Psychological

Michel Faber
John Fowles

Stephen King
Duncan McLean

Alan Warner

B

Betty Burton
Saga

♣ Lu Wilmott - London ▪ Nugent Family - Hampshire

Kate Alexander
Tessa Barclay
Elizabeth Daish
Elizabeth Darrell

Harriet Hudson
Freda Lightfoot
Pamela Oldfield

Sally Stewart
Alison Stuart

Gwendoline Butler   1922-
also writes as Jennie Melville

Crime: Police work - Br

♣ Com John Coffin - London
Major Mearns & Sgt Denny - C18th England

Bruce Alexander
Stephanie Barron
Ann Cleeves
Cynthia Harrod-Eagles
Keith Heller
Alan Hunter

Alanna Knight
Deryn Lake
Margaret Lawrence
Hannah March
Fidelis Morgan
Iain Pears

CWA	*1973* ❀
Parker	*1981* ❀

Octavia E Butler   1947-   US   Science Fiction: Space and time

Lois McMaster Bujold
Gwyneth Jones

Ursula K Le Guin
Ken MacLeod

Sheri S Tepper
Connie Willis

A S Byatt   1936-
www.asbyatt.com

General

Melvyn Bragg
Anita Brookner
Angela Carter
Margaret Drabble
Angela Huth

Penelope Lively
Candia McWilliam
Barbara Neil
Angus Wilson

Booker	*1990* ❀
Irish Times	*1990* ❀

*Don't forget lists of: Genres * Characters * Literary prizes * Further reading* ☞

Colette Caddle   Ire   Chick Lit

Martina Devlin   Marian Keyes   Patricia Scanlan
Cathy Kelly   Kate O'Riordan   Kate Thompson

Pat Cadigan   1953-   US   Science Fiction: Near future
users.wmin.ac.uk/~fowlerc/patcadigan.html

John Barnes   James Lovegrove   *Arthur C Clarke   1992* ❀
Alexander Besher   Ian McDonald   *Arthur C Clarke   1995* ❀ **C**
Eric Brown   Jeff Noon
Greg Egan   Rachel Pollack
Jon Courtenay Grimwood Jack Womack
K W Jeter

Brian Callison   1934-   Sco   Sea: Modern

Alan Evans   James Pattinson   Charles Whiting
Alexander Fullerton   Douglas Reeman   Richard Woodman
Geoffrey Jenkins   Antony Trew

Claire Calman   Chick Lit

Jenny Colgan   Christina Jones   Kate Saunders
Maeve Haran   Tyne O'Connell   Isabel Wolff
Wendy Holden

Jeremy Cameron   Crime: Modern
                                      ⚥ Nicky Burkett - London

Jake Arnott   Christopher Brookmyre Paul Johnston
Colin Bateman   Martina Cole   Mark Timlin
Nicholas Blincoe   James Hawes

Alexandra Campbell   Glitz & Glamour

Catherine Alliott   Jilly Cooper   Madge Swindells
Raffaella Barker   Olivia Goldsmith   Caroline Upcher

Bethany Campbell   US   Adventure/Thriller

Philip Caveney   Joy Fielding   Judith Kelman
Mary Higgins Clark   Iris Johansen   Gloria Murphy
Kit Craig

Ramsey Campbell   1946-   Horror
www.herebedragons.co.uk/campbell

C Campbell Black   Steve Harris   Michael Slade
Jonathan Carroll   Stephen Laws   Whitley Strieber
Joe Donnelly   H P Lovecraft   T M Wright
Christopher Fowler

Rebecca Campbell   Chick Lit

Zoë Barnes   Jenny Colgan   Josie Lloyd & Emlyn Rees
Anna Cheska   Lisa Jewell

Albert Camus   1913-60   Fr   General

William Golding   Jack Kerouac
Franz Kafka   Ivan Klima

Ethan Canin   1960-   US   General

Lisa Alther   Jonathan Franzen   Sue Miller
Stephen Amidon   Henry James   Mary McGarry Morris
E L Doctorow   Garrison Keillor   John Updike
F Scott Fitzgerald

Helen Cannam   Saga

Vanessa Alexander   Elizabeth Elgin   Kay Stephens
Aileen Armitage   Sheelagh Kelly   Eileen Townsend
Jessica Blair   Elvi Rhodes   Elizabeth Walker
Joan Eadith

Don't forget lists of: *Genres* * *Characters* * *Literary prizes* * *Further reading* ☞

Joanna Cannan　　1898-1961　　　　Crime: Police work - Br
↟ Insp Guy Northeast - 'Loamshire'

Catherine Aird
Margery Allingham
Vivien Armstrong
B M Gill

Caroline Graham
Patricia Hall
Susan Kelly
Ngaio Marsh

Gladys Mitchell
David Roberts
Dorothy L Sayers

Stephen J Cannell　　1941-　US　　Adventure/Thriller
www.cannell.com

C

John Lawton
Robert Littell

David Mason
Martin Cruz Smith

Truman Capote　　1924-84　US　　　　　　General

Raymond Carver
Ernest Hemingway
Carson McCullers

Armistead Maupin
J D Salinger

Gore Vidal
Tom Wolfe

Lorenzo Carcaterra　　1954-　US　　Adventure/Thriller

Richard Condon
George V Higgins

Mario Puzo
Sidney Sheldon

Orson Scott Card　　1951-　US　Science Fiction: Space opera
www.hatrack.com

Iain M Banks
Lois McMaster Bujold
C J Cherryh
Alan Dean Foster

Colin Greenland
Joe Haldeman
Brian Herbert
China Miéville

Mary Doria Russell
Dan Simmons
Connie Willis
David Zindell

Helen Carey　　　　　　　　　　　　　Saga
Lavender Road Series - London

Harry Cole
Pamela Evans
Lilian Harry
Anna King

Beryl Kingston
Margaret Mayhew
Sally Spencer

Mary Jane Staples
Elizabeth Waite
Dee Williams

Peter Carey   1943-   Aus   General

Murray Bail	Thomas Keneally	
John Banville	David Malouf	
James Bradley	Charles Palliser	
Robert Drewe	Patrick White	
Rodney Hall	Tim Winton	
Tim Jeal		

Booker	1988 ❀
Commonwealth	1998 ❀
Booker	2001 ❀
Commonwealth	2001 ❀

C Caleb Carr   1955-   US   Crime: Historical
late C19th New York

Lauren Belfer	Sharyn McCrumb	Iain Pears
E L Doctorow	Stewart O'Nan	Anne Perry
Umberto Eco	Charles Palliser	Tom Wolfe
Laurie R King		

Irene Carr   1920s-   Saga
NE England

Joan Eadith	Anna Jacobs	Denise Robertson
Valerie Georgeson	Sheila Jansen	Wendy Robertson
Elizabeth Gill	Brenda McBryde	Janet MacLeod Trotter
Una Horne		

John Dickson Carr   1906-77   US   Crime
also wrote as Carter Dickson   ⚗ Dr Gideon Fell - Medical

Paul Carson	Michael Innes	Gladys Mitchell
John Creasey	Stuart M Kaminsky	Dorothy L Sayers
Edmund Crispin	Ngaio Marsh	Rex Stout
Erle Stanley Gardner		

Philippa Carr   1906-93   Historical
also wrote as Victoria Holt & Jean Plaidy

Joy Chambers	Valerie Georgeson	Pamela Hill
Emma Drummond	Cynthia Harrod-Eagles	Dinah Lampitt
Barbara Erskine	Caroline Harvey	Diana Norman
Diana Gabaldon		

Don't forget lists of: *Genres * Characters * Literary prizes * Further reading* ☞

Gerry Carroll   *d 1996*   US   *Sea: Modern*

Bart Davis
P T Deutermann
Duncan Harding
Hammond Innes

A E Langsford
Sam Llewellyn
Alistair MacLean

Douglas Reeman
Patrick Robinson
Peter Tonkin

Jonathan Carroll   *1949-*   US   *Horror*
www.jonathancarroll.com

Clive Barker
Ramsey Campbell
James Cobb

Christopher Fowler
Robert Jordan

Graham Joyce
Peter Straub

C

Jonathan Carroll   *1949-*   US   *Fantasy: Dark*
www.jonathancarroll.com

Richard Adams
Mark Anthony
John Crowley
Stephen Donaldson

Robert Jordan
Michael Moorcock
Sheri S Tepper

Tad Williams
Janny Wurts
Jonathan Wylie

Michael Carson   *1946-*   *General*

Guy Bellamy
Jonathan Coe
Patrick Gale

Alan Hollinghurst
Adam Mars-Jones
Armistead Maupin

Tony Warren
Edmund White

Paul Carson   *1949-*   Ire   *Crime: Medical*

Paul Adam
John Dickson Carr
Robin Cook

Patricia D Cornwell
Tess Gerritsen
Ken McClure

Michael Palmer
Leah Ruth Robinson

Angela Carter   *1940-92*   *General*

Kate Atkinson
Murray Bail
Judy Budnitz
A S Byatt
Alice Thomas Ellis
Ben Okri

Michèle Roberts
Iain Sinclair
Marina Warner
Fay Weldon
Jeanette Winterson

Black   *1984* ✿

Charlotte Carter   US   Crime
♪ Nanette Hayes, Saxophonist - New York

Ace Atkins   Sara Paretsky   Alexander McCall Smith
Kinky Friedman   Sam Reaves   Les Standiford
John Harvey   James Sallis   Valerie Wilson Wesley

Nicholas Carter   Historical

Bernard Cornwell   Allan Mallinson   Nigel Tranter
Garry Douglas   Edith Pargeter

Justin Cartwright   1945-   SA   General

Martin Amis   Christopher Hope   *Whitbread   1998* ❀
William Boyd   John Updike
J M Coetzee   Evelyn Waugh
Graham Greene   Rebecca Wells

Raymond Carver   1939-88   US   General

Truman Capote   Philip Hensher   Alice Munro
Richard Ford   David Mamet   Joyce Carol Oates
Ernest Hemingway

Peter Cave   War: Modern

Shaun Clarke   Andy McNab   Chris Ryan
Murray Davies   John Nichol

Philip Caveney   1951-   Wales   Crime: Modern

Nicholas Blincoe   Jeff Gulvin   Kevin Sampson
Christopher Brookmyre   David Martin   Tim Willocks
Bethany Campbell   Jerry Raine

Mark Chadbourn   1960-   Fantasy: Contemporary
www.markchadbourn.com   *Age of Misrule Series*

Alice Borchardt   David Eddings   Katharine Kerr
Charles de Lint   Terry Goodkind   Jan Siegel
Stephen Donaldson   Guy Gavriel Kay   David Zindell

C

Elizabeth Chadwick
also writes as Nancy Herndon

Historical

Dorothy Dunnett
Barbara Erskine
Georgette Heyer

Rosalind Laker
Norah Lofts

Sharon Penman
Kate Ross

Clare Chambers   *1966-*

General

C

Margaret Atwood
Katie Fforde

Elizabeth Pewsey
Mary Wesley

Joy Chambers   *Aus*
www.joychambers.com

Historical

Philippa Carr
Elizabeth Darrell

Emma Drummond
Wilbur Smith

Raymond Chandler   *1888-1959*   *US*

Crime: PI

www.geocities.com/Athens/Parthenon/3224

⚐ Philip Marlowe
John Delmas } Los Angeles

Phil Andrews
James Hadley Chase
Robert Crais
Stuart M Kaminsky

John D MacDonald
Ross Macdonald
Reggie Nadelson
Kem Nunn

George P Pelecanos
Donald Rawley
James Sallis

Jung Chang

General

Anita Rau Badami
Arthur Golden

Catherine Lim
Timothy Mo

Amy Tan
Reay Tannahill

Jean Chapman

Saga

Donna Baker
Anne Bennett
June Francis
Elizabeth Gill

Una Horne
Rosalind Laker
Maureen Lee

Annie Murray
Denise Robertson
Wendy Robertson

Kate Charles *1950- US* *Crime*

www.twbooks.co.uk/authors/katecharles.html

☥ David Middleton-Brown & Lucy Kingsley, Solicitor

D M Greenwood
Paul Harding
Alison Joseph
Dorothy L Sayers
Derek Wilson

Paul Charles *Crime: Police work - Br*

☥ DI Christy Kennedy - London

C

Ken Bruen
Brian Cooper
Judith Cutler
Colin Dexter
B M Gill
Patricia Hall
Russell James
Susan Kelly
David Ralph Martin
Maureen O'Brien
Martyn Waites

James Hadley Chase *1906-85 US* *Crime*

was Rene Brabazon Raymond
also wrote as James L Docherty, Ambrose Grant & Raymond Marshall

Raymond Chandler
Dashiell Hammett
Stuart M Kaminsky
John D MacDonald
Ross Macdonald
Robert B Parker
Rex Stout

Bruce Chatwin *1940-89* *General*

Julian Barnes
Julia Blackburn
David Cook
John Fowles
Patrick McCabe
Robert Nye
Barry Unsworth

Black	*1982* ❁
Whitbread	*1982* ❁

Amit Chaudhuri *1962- Ind* *General*

John Masters
Gita Mehta
Rohinton Mistry
R K Narayan
Arundhati Roy
Salman Rushdie
Vikram Seth
Zadie Smith

Betty Trask	*1991* ❁
Encore	*1994* ❁

Mavis Cheek *Humour*

Guy Bellamy
Isla Dewar
Catherine Feeny
Jane Gordon
Jane Green
Sue Limb
Shena Mackay
Helen Muir
Kate Pullinger
Ben Richards
Lynne Truss
Arabella Weir

C J Cherryh 1942- US Science Fiction: Space opera
www.cherryh.com

Greg Bear
Gregory Benford
David Brin

Lois McMaster Bujold
Orson Scott Card
Alan Dean Foster

Colin Greenland
Peter F Hamilton
Vernor Vinge

C J Cherryh 1942- US Fantasy: Myth
www.cherryh.com

Chris Bunch
Allan Cole
Kate Elliott
Barbara Hambly

Stephen R Lawhead
Ursula K Le Guin
Megan Lindholm

George R R Martin
L E Modesitt Jr
Sheri S Tepper

C

Anna Cheska General

Diana Appleyard
Raffaella Barker

Cindy Blake
Rebecca Campbell

Jean Saunders

Marion Chesney 1936- Sco Historical
also writes as M C Beaton

Catherine Coulter
Jude Deveraux

Georgette Heyer
Amanda Quick

Tracy Chevalier 1962- US Historical
www.tchevalier.com

Stevie Davies
Maggie Gee
Philippa Gregory
Anne Haverty

Pamela Hill
Katharine McMahon
Deborah Moggach
Maureen Peters

Jane Stevenson
Rose Tremain
Sarah Waters

Lee Child 1954- Adventure/Thriller
www.leechild.com ⚘ Jack Reacher, ex military policeman - Florida

Peter Blauner
Kit Craig
Conor Cregan
Jeffery Deaver
William Diehl
John Gilstrap

James Hall
Graham Hurley
Greg Iles
Donald James
Martin Limon
Peter May

TGR 1999 ❀

P F Chisholm 1958-   Crime: Historical
also writes as Patricia Finney   ⚐ *Sir Robert Carey - C16th London*

Fiona Buckley	Edward Marston	Kate Sedley
Michael Clynes	Fidelis Morgan	Peter Tonkin
Judith Cook		

Windsor Chorlton 1948-   Adventure/Thriller

C

Nicholas Coleridge	John Gordon Davis
Michael Crichton	Ken McClure

Agatha Christie 1890-1976   Crime: PI
also wrote as Mary Westmacott   ⚐ *Miss Marple*
www.agathachristie.com   Hercule Poirot

Catherine Aird	Kay Mitchell	Julian Symons
Margery Allingham	John Penn	June Thomson
Ngaio Marsh	David Roberts	Patricia Wentworth
Gladys Mitchell	Dorothy L Sayers	

Tom Clancy 1947- US   Adventure/Thriller
                                           ⚐ *Jack Ryan* ▪ *Net Force Explorers*

Dale Brown	Eric L Harry	John Nichol
John Burdett	Stephen Hunter	Henry Porter
James Cobb	David Mason	Douglas Terman
P T Deutermann	John R Maxim	James Thayer

Alys Clare   Crime: Historical
www.alysclare.com ⚐ *Abbess Helewise & Josse D'Aquin - C12th Kent 'Hawkenlye Abbey'*

Paul Doherty	Viviane Moore	Candace Robb
Paul Harding	Ian Morson	Kate Sedley
Michael Jecks	Ellis Peters	Peter Tremayne
Bernard Knight		

Lucy Clare   Aga Saga

Patricia Fawcett	Hazel Hucker	Jill Roe
Kate Fenton	Erica James	Mary Sheepshanks
Katie Fforde		

Candida Clark
General

Josephine Hart
Ann Oakley

Libby Purves
Rosie Thomas

Carol Higgins Clark   1956-   US
Crime: PI
🏃 Regan Reilly - Missouri

Liza Cody
Sue Grafton
Laura Lippman

Margaret Maron
Marcia Muller

Sara Paretsky
Nancy Taylor Rosenberg

Mary Higgins Clark   1929-   US
Adventure/Thriller: Psychological

www.maryhigginsclark.com

Bethany Campbell
Kit Craig
Joy Fielding

Frances Galleymore
Richard Greensted
Jonathan Kellerman

Gloria Murphy
Hilary Norman
Melanie Tem

Simon Clark   1958-
Horror

Clive Barker
Anne Billson
Chaz Brenchley

John Douglas
Dennis Etchison
Muriel Gray

Shaun Hutson
Bentley Little
Mark Morris

Arthur C Clarke   1917-
Science Fiction: Technical

Brian W Aldiss
Isaac Asimov
A A Attanasio
Stephen Baxter
Greg Bear
Gregory Benford

Robert A Heinlein
Jack McDevitt
Robert Silverberg
Dan Simmons
Vernor Vinge

BSFA   1973 ✿

Brenda Clarke   1926-
Saga
Midlands & West Country

also writes as Kate Sedley

Tessa Barclay
Anne Bennett
Suzanne Goodwin

Margaret Graham
Mary Minton
Connie Monk

Eileen Stafford
Caroline Stickland
Elizabeth Warne

Shaun Clarke
War: Modern

Peter Cave
Andy McNab
John Nichol
Chris Ryan

James Clavell
1924-94   US
Adventure/Thriller

Martin Booth
Alexander Cordell
Colin Falconer
Giles Foden

Humphrey Hawksley
Amin Maalouf
David Malouf
John Masters

Christopher Nicole
Laura Joh Rowland
Alan Savage
Peter Tonkin

Mary Clayton
1932-
Crime: PI

also writes as Mary Lide and Mary Lomer
🏃 Ex-Insp John Reynolds - Cornwall

Vivien Armstrong
Pauline Bell
Janie Bolitho
Lizbie Brown

W J Burley
Ann Cleeves
Brian Cooper
Ann Granger

Hazel Holt
Marianne MacDonald
Betty Rowlands
Rebecca Tope

Victoria Clayton
Aga Saga

Diana Appleyard
Judy Astley
Raffaella Barker
Anne Doughty

Nina Dufort
Katie Fforde
Elizabeth Jane Howard
Karen Nelson

Imogen Parker
Rosamunde Pilcher
Mary Wesley

Jon Cleary
1917-   Aus
Adventure/Thriller

Desmond Bagley
John Buchan
June Drummond
Colin Forbes

John Harris
Hammond Innes
Geoffrey Jenkins
Duncan Kyle

Derek Lambert
John Lawton
Gavin Lyall
Nevil Shute

Jon Cleary
1917-   Aus
Crime: Police work - foreign

🏃 Insp Scobie Malone - Sydney

Claire McNab
Frank Palmer

Ridley Pearson
Eric Wright

Ann Cleeves   1954-

www.twbooks.co.uk/authors/anncleeves.html

Crime: *Police work - Br*
DI Stephen Ramsay - Northumberland
DI Vera Stanhope
George & Molly Palmer-Jones, PI's, Ornithologists

Catherine Aird	Judith Cutler	Barry Maitland
W J Burley	Patricia Hall	Andrew Taylor
Gwendoline Butler	Alan Hunter	David Williams
Mary Clayton		

Douglas Clegg   *Horror* **C**

Joe Donnelly	Robert McCammon	Peter Straub
Muriel Gray	Steven Spruill	

Francesca Clementis   1958-   *Chick Lit*

Helen Fielding	Sophie Kinsella	Carole Matthews
Wendy Holden	Jill Mansell	Melissa Nathan

Carol Clewlow   1947-   *General*

J Robert Lennon	Anita Shreve	Daoma Winston
Wendy Perriam	Fay Weldon	Jeanette Winterson
Michèle Roberts		

Ajay Close   *Sco*   *General*

Isla Dewar	Frederic Lindsay	Carole Morin
Janice Galloway	Denise Mina	Manda Scott

Michael Clynes   **Crime:** *Historical*

also writes as Vanessa Alexander, Anna Apostolom,
P C Doherty, Paul Doherty & Paul Harding   *Sir Roger Shallot - C16th England*

Fiona Buckley	Bernard Knight	Fidelis Morgan
P F Chisholm	Edward Marston	Peter Tonkin
Judith Cook		

Don't forget lists of: *Genres* * *Characters* * *Literary prizes* * *Further reading* ☞

53

James Cobb US   Sea: *Modern*

↟ Com Amanda Lee Garrett - Destroyer USS Cunningham

Jonathan Carroll	Duncan Harding	James Pattinson
Tom Clancy	Eric L Harry	Douglas Reeman
Bart Davis	Richard Herman	Patrick Robinson
P T Deutermann	A E Langsford	

C

Marika Cobbold *Swe*   *Aga Saga*

Anne Atkins	Nora Naish	Peta Tayler
Caroline Bridgwood	Ann Purser	Willow Tickell
Fanny Frewen	Jill Roe	Marcia Willett
Karen Hayes		

Harlan Coben *1962-* US   Crime: *PI*

www.harlancoben.com   *↟ Myron Bolitar, Sports agent- New York*

Michael Connelly	Stuart Harrison	Kathy Reichs
Robert Crais	Jonathan Kellerman	Doug J Swanson
Loren D Estleman	Robert B Parker	Gillian White
Linda Fairstein		

Tim Cockey US   *Crime*

www.timcockey.com   *↟ Hitchcock Sewell, Mortician - Baltimore*

Tim Dorsey	Lauren Henderson	Laura Lippman
Janet Evanovich	Elmore Leonard	Rebecca Tope

Liza Cody *1944-*   *Crime*

↟ Anna Lee, PI - London ▪ Eva Wylie, Wrestler

Linda Barnes	Christine Green	CWA	1980 ✷
Carol Higgins Clark	Lauren Henderson	CWA	1992 ✷
Stella Duffy	Laura Lippman		
Sarah Dunant	Susan Moody		
Alma Fritchley	Marcia Muller		

Don't forget lists of: *Genres* * *Characters* * *Literary prizes* * *Further reading* ☞

Jonathan Coe   1961-   *Humour*

Guy Bellamy   John Lanchester   Mail   1994 ❀
Terence Blacker   Magnus Mills
Michael Carson   Geoff Nicholson
Joseph Connolly   Tim Pears
Neil Ferguson   Nigel Williams
John Irving

Paulo Coelho   1949-   *Braz*   *General* **C**

Mário de Carvalho   Umberto Eco   Gabriel Garcia Márquez

J M Coetzee   1940-   *SA*   *General*

Murray Bail   Nadine Gordimer   Faber   1981 ❀
James Bradley   Christopher Hope   Booker   1983 ❀
André Brink   Pamela Jooste   Irish Times   1995 ❀
Justin Cartwright   Doris Lessing   Booker   1999 ❀
Jim Crace   Amanda Prantera   Commonwealth   2000 ❀

Anthea Cohen   1913-   *Crime*
is Doris Simpson   ☂ *Agnes Carmichael, Nurse*

B M Gill   Christine Green   Andrew Puckett
Lesley Grant-Adamson   Patricia Highsmith   Simon Shaw

Victoria Colby   *Chick Lit*

Sherry Ashworth   Sarah Harvey   Victoria Routledge
Jenny Colgan   Freya North   Fiona Walker

Allan Cole   1943-   *US*   *Fantasy:* Epic
www.acole.com

Chris Bunch   Maggie Furey   Harry Turtledove
C J Cherryh   Melanie Rawn   Janny Wurts

Harry Cole

London

Philip Boast
Harry Bowling
Patricia Burns
Helen Carey

Pamela Evans
Patricia Grey
Anna King
Mary Jane Staples

Elizabeth Waite
Dee Williams
Sally Worboyes

C Martina Cole

Crime: Modern
🏃 *DI Kate Burrows - East End, London*

Jeremy Cameron
Colin Falconer

Lynda La Plante
Peter May

Hilary Norman
Stuart Woods

Isabel Colegate   *1931-*

General

Anita Brookner
Margaret Drabble
Penelope Fitzgerald

Penelope Lively
Anthony Powell

Barbara Pym
Muriel Spark

Nicholas Coleridge   *1957-*

Adventure/Thriller

Windsor Chorlton
Lionel Davidson

John Gordon Davis
Ken Follett

Alan Furst

Jenny Colgan   *1972-   Sco*

Chick Lit

Susie Boyt
Claire Calman
Rebecca Campbell
Victoria Colby

Amy Jenkins
L McCrossan
Jill Mansell
Melissa Nathan

Tyne O'Connell
Alexandra Potter
Stephanie Theobald
Kate Thompson

Catrin Collier   *1948-   Wales*

Saga
Heart of Gold Series - Pontypridd, Wales

Alexander Cordell
Elizabeth Daish
Sara Fraser

Iris Gower
Hilda McKenzie
Catrin Morgan

Cynthia S Roberts
Sarah Shears
Grace Thompson

Jackie Collins   1941-   Glitz & Glamour

Pat Booth   Judith Krantz   Harold Robbins
Celia Brayfield   Roberta Latow   June Flaum Singer
Joan Collins   Judith Michael   Madge Swindells
Shirley Conran   Fern Michaels

Joan Collins   1933-   Glitz & Glamour

Jackie Collins   Judi James
Elizabeth Gage   Harold Robbins

Michael Collins   1964-   Ire   General

Clare Boylan   Alice Hoffman
Louise Erdrich   Tim O'Brien

Nancy Collins   1959-   US   Horror

Anne Billson   Christopher Fowler   Anne Rice
Chaz Brenchley   Laurell K Hamilton   Dan Simmons
Poppy Z Brite   Tom Holland   S P Somtow

Richard Condon   1915-96   US   Adventure/Thriller

Lorenzo Carcaterra   Arthur Hailey   Thomas Pynchon
Michael Crichton   Mario Puzo   Sidney Sheldon

Kathleen Conlon   1943-   Saga

Clare Boylan   Elizabeth Jane Howard
Frank Delaney   Alice Taylor

C

Don't forget lists of: *Genres * Characters * Literary prizes * Further reading* ☞

Michael Connelly   1956-   US   Crime: Police work - US

www.michaelconnelly.com/

⚐ Harry Bosch ⎰ Los Angeles
Terry McCaleb, retired FBI Agent ⎱

James Lee Burke
Harlan Coben
Thomas H Cook
John Farrow

W E B Griffin
Graham Hurley
J A Jance
Martin Limon

Reggie Nadelson
John Sandford
Boston Teran

C

Tom Connery   1944-   Sea: Historical

is David Donachie

⚐ George Markham, Lieut of Marines - C18th

David Donachie
Alexander Kent
A E Langsford
Allan Mallinson

Jan Needle
Patrick O'Brian
Dan Parkinson

Dudley Pope
Victor Suthren
Richard Woodman

John Connolly   1968-   Ire   Crime: Psychological

www.johnconnolly.co.uk

⚐ Charlie 'Bird' Parker, ex New York policeman - New England

James Lee Burke
Thomas H Cook
Jeffery Deaver

Stephen Dobyns
Joy Fielding
Mo Hayder

Jonathan Kellerman
Dennis Lehane
Jefferson Parker

Joseph Connolly   1950-   Humour

Kingsley Amis
Guy Bellamy
Jonathan Coe

Colin Douglas
Geoff Nicholson

Tom Sharpe
Evelyn Waugh

Alexandra Connor   Saga

www.alexandra-connor.co.uk   Lancashire

Catherine Cookson
Ruth Hamilton
Anna Jacobs

Joan Jonker
Freda Lightfoot
Annie Murray

Kay Stephens
Margaret Thornton

Joseph Conrad   1857-1924   General

John Buchan
Louis de Bernières
Ford Madox Ford
Abdulrazak Gurnah

James Hamilton-Paterson
Ernest Hemingway
Henry James
W Somerset Maugham

V S Naipaul
Paul Theroux
Virginia Woolf

Shirley Conran *1932-*   *Glitz & Glamour*

Celia Brayfield
Jackie Collins
Jilly Cooper
Lucinda Edmonds

Olivia Goldsmith
Roberta Latow
Susan Lewis

Frankie McGowan
Erin Pizzey
Penny Vincenzi

Pat Conroy *1945- US*   *General*

Pete Dexter
Nicholas Evans
Winston Graham

Harper Lee
Larry McMurtry
Anne Rivers Siddons

Paullina Simons
William Styron
Paul Theroux

C

K C Constantine *1934- US*   *Crime: Police work - US*
www.badattitudes.com   ⚘ Chief Mario Balzac - 'Rockburg', Pennsylvania

Paula Gosling
Donald Harstad

Ed McBain
Robert B Parker

Rex Stout
Hillary Waugh

Storm Constantine *1956-*   *Fantasy*
www.grebo-heights.wox.org/bast/home.htm   *Chronicles of Magravadias*

Peter S Beagle
Alice Borchardt
Mary Gentle

Juliet Marillier
Anne Rice

Judith Tarr
Freda Warrington

David Cook *1940-*   *General*

Bruce Chatwin
Janet Frame
Francis King
Ian McEwan

Bernard MacLaverty
Brian Moore
Paul Sayer

Hawthornden 1978 ❀

Gloria Cook   *Historical*

Rosemary Aitken
Anne Goring
Iris Gower
Winston Graham

Elizabeth Ann Hill
Malcolm Macdonald
Cynthia S Roberts

Malcolm Ross
Susan Sallis
E V Thompson

Judith Cook   1933-   Crime: Historical
Dr Simon Forman & John Bradedge - C16th England

Fiona Buckley   Edward Marston   Kate Sedley
P F Chisholm   Fidelis Morgan   Peter Tonkin
Michael Clynes

Robin Cook   1940-   US   Adventure/Thriller: Medical

Paul Adam   Michael Crichton   Michael Palmer
Colin Andrews   Tess Gerritsen   Richard Preston
Mark Burnell   Patrick Lynch   Leah Ruth Robinson
Paul Carson   Ken McClure   Michael Stewart

Thomas H Cook   1947-   US   Crime: Modern

Ace Atkins   John Connolly   David Lindsey
Michael Connelly   Thomas Harris   John Sandford

Catherine Cookson   1906-98   Saga
also wrote as Catherine Marchant   *Mary Ann Shaughnessy* | NE England
                                          Tilly Trotter ▪ Bill Bailey |

Rita Bradshaw   Audrey Howard   Wendy Robertson
Alexandra Connor   Sheila Jansen   Grace Thompson
Elizabeth Gill   Marie Joseph   Janet MacLeod Trotter
Una Horne   Denise Robertson   Valerie Wood

Stephen Coonts   1946-   US   Adventure/Thriller
www.stephencoonts.com/

James Adams   Bart Davis   Julian Jay Savarin
Geoffrey Archer   Richard Herman   Murray Smith
Larry Bond   John R Maxim   Douglas Terman
Dale Brown   Matthew Reilly

Don't forget lists of: *Genres * Characters * Literary prizes * Further reading* ☞

Brian Cooper   1919-   Crime: Police work - Br
CI Mark Tench & DCI John Lubbock - Norfolk

Vivien Armstrong
Pauline Bell
Paul Charles
Mary Clayton

Colin Dexter
Raymond Flynn
Malcolm Forsythe
B M Gill

Alan Hunter
P D James
Ann Quinton

Jilly Cooper   1937-   Glitz & Glamour

C

Celia Brayfield
Alexandra Campbell
Shirley Conran

Judith Gould
Christina Jones
Judith Krantz

Jill Mansell
Lesley Pearse
Caroline Upcher

Louise Cooper   1952-   Fantasy: Epic

Jean M Auel
Barbara Hambly
Robert Jordan

L E Modesitt Jr
Michael Moorcock

Melanie Rawn
Janny Wurts

Natasha Cooper   1951-   Crime
is Daphne Wright   *Willow King, Civil Servant* London
also writes as Clare Layton   *Trish Maguire, Barrister*
www.twbooks.co.uk/authors/ncooper.html/

Frances Fyfield
Susan Kelly
Sarah Lacey

Marianne MacDonald
Jennie Melville
Janet Neel

Betty Rowlands
Veronica Stallwood
Leslie Thomas

Victoria Corby   Chick Lit

Helen Fielding
India Knight

Melissa Nathan
Adele Parks

Daisy Waugh

Alexander Cordell   1914-97   General

James Clavell
Catrin Collier
A J Cronin

R F Delderfield
Winston Graham

Malcolm Macdonald
E V Thompson

61

Bernard Cornwell 1944- War

www.bernardcornwellbooks.com — Richard Sharpe ▪ Nathaniel Starbuck

Nicholas Carter
Garry Douglas
Alan Evans
Richard Howard
Alexander Kent
Sam Llewellyn
Allan Mallinson
Steven Pressfield
Edward Rutherfurd
Simon Scarrow

C

Patricia D Cornwell 1956- US Crime

www.patriciacornwell.com — Kay Scarpetta, Pathologist; Judy Hammer, State Police — Virginia

Paul Carson
Joseph Glass
Lynn S Hightower
Tami Hoag
Rochelle Krich
Sarah Lovett
John R Maxim
Peter May
Margaret Murphy
Gemma O'Connor
Kathy Reichs
Robert W Walker

CWA	1990
CWA	1993

Catherine Coulter US Historical

Elizabeth Boyle
Marion Chesney
Teresa Crane
Victoria Holt
Genevieve Lyons
Judith McNaught
Amanda Quick
Nora Roberts

Douglas Coupland 1961- Can General

Iain Banks
Bret Easton Ellis
Alex Garland
John McCabe
Ben Richards
Rupert Thomson

Bryce Courtenay 1933- SA Adventure/Thriller

Martin Booth
Eric Lustbader
Patrick Lynch
Amin Maalouf
Jo-Anne Richards
Wilbur Smith

Josephine Cox 1938- Saga

also writes as Jane Brindle

Jay Allerton
Lyn Andrews
Rose Boucheron
Harry Bowling
Katie Flynn
Sara Fraser
Suzanne Goodwin
Meg Hutchinson
Marie Joseph
Joan O'Neill
Wendy Robertson

Harold Coyle   *1952-   US*   *Adventure/Thriller*

Campbell Armstrong	Jack Higgins	Matthew Reilly
Clive Cussler	Leo Kessler	James Thayer
Bart Davis	Stephen Leather	Craig Thomas
W E B Griffin		

Jim Crace   *1946-*   *General*

William Bedford	Jim Harrison	Guardian	1986 ✹
André Brink	Peter Matthiessen	Higham	1986 ✹
J M Coetzee	Lawrence Norfolk	Whitbread	1986 ✹
E L Doctorow	Rupert Thomson	Holtby	1994 ✹
David Guterson	Barry Unsworth	Whitbread	1997 ✹

C

Amanda Craig   *1959-*   *General*
www.amandacraig.com

Janice Galloway	Laurie Graham	Amanda Prantera
Jane Gardam	A L Kennedy	Barbara Trapido

Kit Craig   *US*   *Adventure/Thriller*
also writes as Kit Reed

Bethany Campbell	Clare Francis	Iris Johansen
Lee Child	Graham Hurley	Judith Kelman
Mary Higgins Clark	Donald James	Gloria Murphy
Joy Fielding		

Robert Crais   *1953-   US*   *Crime: PI*
www.robertcrais.com   *⚡ Elvis Cole - Los Angeles*

Lawrence Block	Reggie Nadelson	Peter Tasker
Raymond Chandler	Kem Nunn	Don Winslow
Harlan Coben	John Straley	Steve Womack
Joe R Lansdale	Doug J Swanson	

Teresa Crane   *Historical*

Elizabeth Boyle	Sara Hylton	Belva Plain
Anita Burgh	Genevieve Lyons	Judith Saxton
Catherine Coulter	Elisabeth McNeill	Eileen Townsend
Elizabeth Falconer		

John Creasey   1908-73   Crime
also wrote as Gordon Ashe & J J Marric   ⚑ The Toff ▪ The Baron ▪ DI West

Brian Battison	John Harvey	Georges Simenon
John Dickson Carr	Ed McBain	Julian Symons

Conor Cregan   1962-   Ire   Adventure/Thriller

Keith Baker	Greg Iles	David Mason
Lee Child	Donald James	Chris Ryan
Alan Furst	Robert Ludlum	

Candida Crewe   1964-   General

Catherine Feeny	Alice Hoffman	Deborah Moggach
Kate Grenville	Hilary Mantel	Anne Tyler

Michael Crichton   1942-   US   General
www.crichton-official.com

Colin Andrews	Robin Cook	Philip Kerr
Windsor Chorlton	Tess Gerritsen	Ken McClure
Richard Condon	William Gibson	Richard Preston

Edmund Crispin   1921-78   Crime
was Robert Bruce Montgomery   ⚑ Prof Gervase Fen, Academic

Margery Allingham	Georgette Heyer	Charlotte MacLeod
John Dickson Carr	Michael Innes	Gladys Mitchell

Deborah Crombie   US   Crime: Police work - Br
www.deborahcrombie.com   ⚑ Supt Duncan Kincaid & Sgt Gemma James - London

Jane Adams	Paula Gosling	Priscilla Masters
Jo Bannister	Martha Grimes	Aline Templeton
Margaret Duffy	Cynthia Harrod-Eagles	R D Wingfield
Elizabeth George		

Don't forget lists of: *Genres* ∗ *Characters* ∗ *Literary prizes* ∗ *Further reading* ☞

A J Cronin   1896-1981   Sco   *General*

Alexander Cordell   John Galsworthy   J B Priestley
R F Delderfield   Winston Graham

Amanda Cross   1926-   US   *Crime*
⚐ Kate Fansler, Academic - New York

Sarah Dunant   Nora Kelly   Emma Lathen
Elizabeth George   Laurie R King   Joan Smith
P D James

Jenn Crowell   1980-   US   *Glitz & Glamour*

Susie Boyt   Carole Morin   Sheila O'Flanagan
Lucy Ellman   Freya North

Elaine Crowley   Ire   *Saga*
⚐ O'Hara Family - Ireland

Maeve Binchy   Genevieve Lyons   D M Purcell
Frank Delaney   M R O'Donnell   Liz Ryan
Rose Doyle   Joan O'Neill   Mary Ryan
Mary A Larkin

John Crowley   1942-   US   *Fantasy: Contemporary*

Peter S Beagle   Sara Douglass   Stephen King
Jonathan Carroll   Neil Gaiman   Michael Marshall Smith
Charles de Lint   Barry Hughart   Gene Wolfe

James Crumley   1939-   US   *Crime: PI*
www.geocities.com/Athens/6384/crumley.html   *⚐ C W Sughrue - Texas*
                                                    Milo Milodragovitch - Montana

James Lee Burke   Ross Macdonald   Boston Teran
James Ellroy   Kem Nunn   Jim Thompson
Robert Ferrigno   George P Pelecanos   Andrew Vachss

Claudine Cullimore *Ire*   *Chick Lit*

Martina Devlin   Marian Keyes   Sheila O'Flanagan
Cathy Kelly   L McCrossan

Clare Curzon *1922-*   *Crime: Police work - Br*
is Rhona Petrie   *⚐ Supt Mike Yeadings &*
also writes as Marie Buchanan   *Sgt Angus Mott - Thames Valley*

M C Beaton   Caroline Graham   Dorothy Simpson
Elizabeth Gill   Ann Quinton   Barbara Whitehead

Clive Cussler *1931- US*   *Adventure/Thriller*
                                                      ⚐ Dirk Pitt

Desmond Bagley   Hammond Innes   Justin Scott
Larry Bond   James Pattinson   William Smethurst
Harold Coyle   Matthew Reilly   James Thayer
Alan Evans   Julian Jay Savarin   Craig Thomas

Judith Cutler *1946-*   *Crime*
⚐ Sophie Rivers, Lecturer • DS Kate Power, Police work - Birmingham

Paul Charles   Sarah Lacey   Michelle Spring
Ann Cleeves   Priscilla Masters   Scarlett Thomas
Martin Edwards   Nick Oldham   Rebecca Tope
Janet Harward   Manda Scott   Stella Whitelaw

Fred D'Aguiar *1960-*   *General*

Joan Brady   Pauline Melville   *Higham   1994 ❀*
David Dabydeen   Caryl Phillips   *Whitbread   1994 ❀*
Rumer Godden   Barry Unsworth
William Golding

David Dabydeen *1956-*   *General*

Fred D'Aguiar   V S Naipaul   Caryl Phillips
Sheri Holman   Ben Okri

Janet Dailey 1944- US

Charlotte Vale Allen	Judith Saxton	Elizabeth Villars
Jayne Ann Krentz	Anne Rivers Siddons	Daoma Winston
Belva Plain	Lavyrle Spencer	Barbara Wood
Nora Roberts	Diana Stainforth	

Elizabeth Daish

Saga
⚐ Emma - London ▪ Coppins Bridge Series - Isle of Wight

Patricia Burns	Elizabeth Darrell	Joan Jonker
Betty Burton	Lilian Harry	Sally Worboyes
Catrin Collier	Harriet Hudson	

D

Emma Dally 1954-

Saga

Harry Bowling	Ruth Hamilton	Margaret Pemberton
Pamela Evans	Gilda O'Neill	

Denise Danks US

Crime
⚐ Georgina Powers, Computer journalist - London

John Burns	Carol O'Connell	Valerie Kershaw
Val McDermid	Gillian Slovo	

Elizabeth Darrell
also writes as Emma Drummond

Saga
⚐ Sheridan Family

Kate Alexander	Betty Burton	June Drummond
Vanessa Alexander	Joy Chambers	Angela Huth
Jay Allerton	Elizabeth Daish	Juliette Mead

Ellen Datlow 1949- US

Fantasy: Myth

Charles de Lint	Ursula K Le Guin	Freda Warrington
Neil Gaiman	Tanith Lee	Jonathan Wylie
Robert Holdstock	Julian May	

Doris Davidson   *Sco*   *Saga*
Scotland

Jay Allerton   Elisabeth McNeill   Agnes Short
Margaret Thomson Davis   Frances Paige   Jessica Stirling
Nora Kay   Eileen Ramsay   Anne Vivis
Gwen Kirkwood

Lionel Davidson   *1922-*   *Adventure/Thriller*

John Buchan   Alan Furst

Nicholas Coleridge   Glenn Meade | CWA | 1978 ❀ |
Len Deighton   Anthony Price | CWA | 2001 ❀ |
Ken Follett   Tim Sebastian
Bryan Forbes

Jonathan Davies   *1944-*   *Crime: Legal/financial*
                                    🕅 *Jeremy Scott, Barrister*

Harry Bingham   Dexter Dias   John Grisham
Rankin Davis   Frances Fyfield   Michael Ridpath

Linda Davies   *1963- US*   *Adventure/Thriller: Legal/financial*
www.ex.ac.uk/~RDavies/arian/linda.html

Po Bronson   Frances Galleymore   Carol O'Connell
Paul Erdman   John Grisham   Michael Ridpath
Stephen Frey   Jill McGown   Sheldon Siegel

Murray Davies   *Adventure/Thriller*

Peter Cave   John Nichol
Andy McNab   Chris Ryan

Stevie Davies   *1946- Wales*   *Historical*
also writes as Stephanie Davies
www.steviedavies.com

Tracy Chevalier   Salley Vickers
Katharine McMahon   Sarah Waters

*Don't forget lists of: Genres * Characters * Literary prizes * Further reading* ☞

Anna Davis · 1971- · General

Jessica Adams
Sarah Harrison
Serena Mackesy
William Sutcliffe

Bart Davis · 1950- · US · Adventure/Thriller

Dale Brown
Gerry Carroll
James Cobb
Stephen Coonts
Harold Coyle
P T Deutermann
Duncan Harding
A E Langsford
Patrick Robinson

John Gordon Davis · SA · Adventure/Thriller

D

Windsor Chorlton
Nicholas Coleridge
Nelson DeMille
June Drummond
Daniel Easterman
Ken Follett
Alan Furst
Wilbur Smith

Lindsey Davis · 1949- · Crime: Historical

www.lindseydavis.co.uk

⚐ Marcus Didius Falco - Ancient Rome

Allan Massie
Rosemary Rowe
Laura Joh Rowland
Steven Saylor
Simon Scarrow
Marilyn Todd
Peter Tremayne
David Wishart

Authors	1989 ✿
CWA	1999 ✿

Margaret Thomson Davis · 1926- · Sco · Saga

⚐ Andrina McPherson ▪ Monkton Family ▪ Breadmakers Series - Scotland

Doris Davidson
Christine Marion Fraser
Meg Henderson
Evelyn Hood
Marie Joseph
Isobel Neill
Frances Paige
Alexandra Raife
Alison Skelton
Jessica Stirling

Rankin Davis · Crime: Legal/financial

is Keith Rankin & Tony Davis

Catherine Arnold
Jonathan Davies
Dexter Dias
John Grisham
Michael Ridpath
Sheldon Siegel

Victor Davis — Adventure/Thriller

Ted Allbeury
James Buchan

Ian Fleming
Colin Forbes

Frederick Forsyth
Daniel Silva

Jill Dawson — General

Catherine Feeny
Deborah Moggach

Elizabeth Pewsey
Kate Pullinger

Mary Selby

Louis de Bernières 1954- — General

Pat Barker
Julia Blackburn
Joseph Conrad
Tibor Fischer
James Hamilton-Paterson

Christopher Hudson
Sebastien Japrisot
Lisa St Aubin de Terán
Nicholas Shakespeare
Mario Vargas Llosa

CWA   1995 ✳

L Sprague de Camp 1907-2000 US — Fantasy: Humour
www.lspraguedecamp.com

Piers Anthony
Robert Asprin
Alan Dean Foster

Tom Holt
Greg Keyes
Fritz Leiber

Robert Rankin
Jack Vance

Mário de Carvalho 1944- Port — General

Isabel Allende
Paulo Coelho

Umberto Eco
Gabriel Garcia Márquez

Ángeles Mastretta

Charles de Lint 1951- Can — Fantasy: Contemporary
www.charlesdelint.com

Peter S Beagle
Mark Chadbourn
John Crowley
Ellen Datlow

Sara Douglass
Neil Gaiman
Robert Holdstock

Guy Gavriel Kay
Juliet Marillier
Caiseal Mor

D

Don't forget lists of: *Genres * Characters * Literary prizes * Further reading* ☞

Jeffery Deaver   *1950-   US*   *Crime*
www.jefferydeaver.com   🏃 *Lincoln Rhyme, Forensic scientist*
Rune, Film maker - New York ▪ John Pellam, Film location scout

Adam Baron	James Patterson	*TGR 2001* ✹
Lee Child	Ridley Pearson	
John Connolly	Kathy Reichs	
Mo Hayder	Paullina Simons	
Rochelle Krich	Rex Stout	
Lindsay Maracotta	Stuart Woods	

Len Deighton   *1929-*   *Adventure/Thriller*
🏃 *Bernard Samson*

D

Ted Allbeury	Clive Egleton	Gavin Lyall
Keith Baker	Bryan Forbes	Anthony Price
David Brierley	Donald James	Nigel West
Lionel Davidson	John Lawton	Barnaby Williams

Frank Delaney   *1942-   Ire*   *Saga*
🏃 *Kane Family*

Kathleen Conlon	Mary A Larkin	D M Purcell
Elaine Crowley	M R O'Donnell	Liz Ryan
Rose Doyle	Joan O'Neill	Mary Ryan

R F Delderfield   *1912-72*   *Saga*
🏃 *Craddock Family ▪ Swann Family*

H E Bates	John Galsworthy	Malcolm Macdonald
Alexander Cordell	Jenny Glanfield	J B Priestley
A J Cronin	Winston Graham	E V Thompson

Don DeLillo   *1936-   US*   *General*

Stephen Amidon	David Mamet	*Irish Times 1989* ✹
Paul Auster	Haruki Murakami	
Saul Bellow	Thomas Pynchon	
Jonathan Franzen	William Styron	
Norman Mailer	John Updike	

Barbara Delinsky   1945-   US   *Glitz & Glamour*
also writes as Billy Douglass & Bonnie Drake
www.barbaradelinsky.com

Celia Brayfield	Jayne Ann Krentz	Belva Plain
Laramie Dunaway	Judith McNaught	Lavyrle Spencer
Penny Jordan	Una-Mary Parker	Danielle Steel

Nelson DeMille   1943-   US   *Adventure/Thriller*
www.nelsondemille.net/   ⚑ *Det John Corey & Kate Mayfield*

David Baldacci	Daniel Easterman	Wilbur Smith
John Gordon Davis	Ken Follett	John Trenhaile
Peter Driscoll		

D

Alan M Dershowitz   1938-   US   *Crime: Legal/financial*

Catherine Arnold	John Grisham	Nancy Taylor Rosenberg
Linda Fairstein	Steve Martini	Scott Turow
Philip Friedman		

Anita Desai   1937-   Ind   *General*

Margaret Atwood	Lee Langley	R K Narayan
Anita Rau Badami	Gita Mehta	Salman Rushdie
Chitra Banerjee Divakaruni	Rohinton Mistry	Amy Tan
Ruth Prawer Jhabvala		

Agnes Desarthe   Fr   *General*

Penelope Fitzgerald	Muriel Spark
Alison Lurie	Anne Tyler

P T Deutermann   US   *Sea: Modern*

Gerry Carroll	James Cobb	W E B Griffin
Tom Clancy	Bart Davis	Patrick Robinson

*Don't forget lists of: Genres * Characters * Literary prizes * Further reading* ☞

Jude Deveraux   1947-   US   Glitz & Glamour

Marion Chesney   Johanna Lindsey   Nora Roberts
Olivia Goldsmith   Fern Michaels   Danielle Steel
Judith Krantz   Belva Plain

Martina Devlin   Ire   Chick Lit
www.martinadevlin.com

Colette Caddle   Claire Naylor   Adele Parks
Claudine Cullimore   Sheila O'Flanagan   Patricia Scanlan
Sarah Harris   Kate O'Riordan   Kate Thompson
Anna Maxted

D

Isla Dewar   Sco   General

Mavis Cheek   Janice Galloway   Anna Maxted
Ajay Close   L McCrossan   Agnes Owens
Roddy Doyle   Carole Matthews   Lynne Truss

Eileen Dewhurst   1929-   Crime
                                      ⚐ Phyllida Moon, Doctor

John Baker   Caroline Graham   Alan Hunter
Pauline Bell   Ann Granger   Ann Quinton

Colin Dexter   1930-   Crime: Police work - Br
                                         ⚐ DI Morse - Oxford

Robert Barnard   M R D Meek   CWA   1979 ❀
Martyn Bedford   Roger Ormerod   CWA   1981 ❀
Paul Charles   Peter Robinson   CWA   1989 ❀
Brian Cooper   Stella Shepherd   CWA   1992 ❀
Susan Kelly   Sally Spencer
Henning Mankell   Veronica Stallwood

Pete Dexter   1943-   US   General

Joan Brady   David Guterson   Thomas McGuane
Pat Conroy   Jim Harrison   Peter Matthiessen
Richard Ford   William Kennedy   Larry Watson

Dexter Dias
Crime: Legal/financial
London

Catherine Arnold
Jonathan Davies
Rankin Davis

Philip Friedman
Douglas Kennedy

Richard North Patterson
Scott Turow

Michael Dibdin 1947-
Crime: Police work - foreign
⚐ Aurelio Zen - Italy

Tim Binding
Simon Brett
Stephen Dobyns
Nicolas Freeling
J Robert Janes

Donna Leon
Manuel Vázquez Montalbán
Magdalen Nabb
Barbara Nadel
Daniel Pennac

CWA   1988 ✿
CWA   1990 ✿

D

Philip K Dick 1928-82 US
Science Fiction: Space and time

Isaac Asimov
J G Ballard
Thomas M Disch
Robert A Heinlein
K W Jeter

Michael Moorcock
Jeff Noon
Tim Powers
John Sladek
Kurt Vonnegut

BSFA   1978 ✿

Charles Dickens 1812-70
General

Joan Aiken
W Somerset Maugham

Rohinton Mistry
Iain Sinclair

Anthony Trollope
Tom Wolfe

Margaret Dickinson 1942-
Saga
also writes as Everatt Jackson
⚐ Kate Hilton - Lincolnshire

Judith Glover
Elizabeth Jeffrey
Mary Mackie
Sybil Marshall

Catrin Morgan
Lynda Page
Mary E Pearce

Pamela Pope
Judy Turner
T R Wilson

William Diehl 1924- US
Crime: Legal/financial
⚐ Martin Vail

Lee Child
Ed McBain
Phillip M Margolin

David Morrell
Richard North Patterson

Scott Turow
Joseph Wambaugh

Des Dillon *Sco* *General*

James Kelman
Gordon Legge
Duncan McLean
Alan Spence
Irvine Welsh

Thomas M Disch *1940- US* *Science Fiction: Technical*

J G Ballard
Ben Bova
John Brunner
Philip K Dick
Jeff Noon
John Sladek
Kurt Vonnegut

Jenny Diski *1947-* *General*

Nicola Barker
Maggie Gee
Lesley Glaister
Frances Hegarty
Joyce Carol Oates

Chitra Banerjee Divakaruni *Ind* *General*

Anita Rau Badami
Anita Desai
V S Naipaul
Meera Syal

Michael Dobbs *1948-* *General*

Tom Goodfellow, MP ▪ Francis Urquhart Trilogy, MP

Jeffrey Archer
Philip Hensher
Peter Rawlinson
Michael Shea

Stephen Dobyns *1941- US* *Crime: PI*

Charlie Bradshaw - Saratoga Springs, New York State

John Connolly
Michael Dibdin
Nicci French
Steve Hamilton
Thomas Harris
Dennis Lehane
Sara Paretsky
Jefferson Parker

E L Doctorow *1931- US* *General*

Paul Auster
Ethan Canin
Caleb Carr
Jim Crace
F Scott Fitzgerald
Craig Holden
Thomas Keneally
William Kennedy
John Updike

Paul Doherty   1946-   Crime: *Historical*

also writes as Vanessa Alexander,   ☨ *Sir Hugh Corbett & Brother Athelstan - C13th England*
Anna Apostolou, Michael Clynes,   *Miriam Bartimeus - C3rd BC Greece*
P C Doherty & Paul Harding   *Amerotke - Ancient Egypt*

Alys Clare	Bernard Knight	Ian Morson
Susanna Gregory	Edward Marston	Ellis Peters
Michael Jecks	Viviane Moore	Candace Robb

David Donachie   1944-   Sco   Sea: *Historical*

also writes as Tom Connery   ☨ *Harry Ludlow, Privateer*

Tom Connery	Jan Needle	Dan Parkinson
C S Forester	James L Nelson	Dudley Pope
Alexander Kent	Patrick O'Brian	Richard Woodman
A E Langsford		

Anabel Donald   1944-   Crime

☨ *Alex Tanner, TV Researcher*

Sarah Dunant	Sarah Lacey	Veronica Stallwood
Anne Fine	Joan Smith	Leslie Thomas
Susan Isaacs		

Stephen Donaldson   1947-   US   Fantasy: *Epic*

also writes as Stephen R Donaldson   *Thomas Covenant Chronicles*

Mark Anthony	Mark Chadbourn	Anne McCaffrey
Jean M Auel	Steven Erikson	John Marco
James Barclay	Raymond E Feist	Julian May
Jonathan Carroll	Paul Kearney	Philip Pullman

Stephen Donaldson   1947-   US   Crime: *PI*

also writes as Stephen R Donaldson & Reed Stephens   ☨ *Ginny Fistoulari &*
Mick 'Brew' Axbrewder

Ace Atkins	James Ellroy	Mary Wings
Adam Baron	Walter Mosley	

Don't forget lists of: *Genres* * *Characters* * *Literary prizes* * *Further reading* ☞

Joe Donnelly   *1950-   Sco*   *Horror*

Campbell Black   Peter James   Stephen Laws
Ramsey Campbell   Graham Joyce   Mark Morris
Douglas Clegg   Andrew Klavan   Kim Newman
Steve Harris

Emma Donoghue   *1969-   Ire*   *General*

Joanne Harris   Michele Roberts   Jeanette Winterson
Anne Haverty   Alice Walker

Tim Dorsey   *1961-   US*   *Crime: Humour*
www.timdorsey.com   🏃 *Serge Storms - Florida*

Colin Bateman   Kinky Friedman   Laurence Shames
Anthony Bourdain   Vicki Hendricks   Grant Stewart
Tim Cockey   Douglas Lindsay   Donald E Westlake
Bill Fitzhugh

Anne Doughty   *Ire*   *General*

Judy Astley   Victoria Clayton   Joanna Trollope
Maeve Binchy   Kate Fenton

Louise Doughty   *General*

Raffaella Barker   Lesley Glaister   Margaret Yorke
Janet Evanovich   Jenny Maxwell

Colin Douglas   *1945-   Sco*   *Humour*

Guy Bellamy   Tom Holt   David Nobbs
Joseph Connolly   David Lodge   Nigel Williams

Garry Douglas   *1941-*   *War: Historical*
also writes as Garry Kilworth   🏃 *Sgt Jack Crossman - Crimean War*

Nicholas Carter   Richard Howard
Bernard Cornwell   Allan Mallinson

John Douglas   1955-   Horror

Clive Barker	Thomas Harris	Richard Laymon
Chaz Brenchley	Shaun Hutson	David Morrell
Simon Clark	Dean R Koontz	Michael Slade

Sara Douglass   Aus   Fantasy: Epic
www.saradouglass.com

Peter S Beagle	Julia Gray	Megan Lindholm
Chaz Brenchley	Kate Jacoby	Judith Tarr
John Crowley	Gwyneth Jones	Janny Wurts
Charles de Lint		

D

Arthur Conan Doyle   1859-1930   Crime
⚘ Sherlock Holmes & Dr John Watson

Laurie R King	Anne Perry	June Thomson
Alanna Knight	Roberta Rogow	M J Trow
Peter Lovesey	Norman Russell	

Roddy Doyle   1958-   Ire   Humour

Colin Bateman	Magnus Mills	*Booker* 1993 ⚘
Dermot Bolger	David Nobbs	
Isla Dewar	Joseph O'Connor	
Stephen Fry	Ardal O'Hanlon	
Patrick McCabe	Irvine Welsh	

Rose Doyle   Ire   General

Maeve Binchy	Frank Delaney	Joan O'Neill
Elaine Crowley	Mary A Larkin	D M Purcell

Margaret Drabble   1939-   General

Lynne Reid Banks	A S Byatt	Bel Mooney
Nina Bawden	Isabel Colegate	Bernice Rubens
Valerie Blumenthal	Sara Maitland	Madeleine St John
Melvyn Bragg		

Don't forget lists of: *Genres * Characters * Literary prizes * Further reading* ☞

David A Drake　1945-　US　　　Fantasy: Epic
www.david-drake.com

Chris Bunch　　　　George R R Martin　　Margaret Weis
Terry Goodkind　　L E Modesitt Jr　　　Tad Williams
Robert Jordan　　　R A Salvatore

Robert Drewe　1943-　Aus　　　　General

Murray Bail　　　　Rodney Hall　　　　David Malouf
Peter Carey　　　　Thomas Keneally　　Patrick White

Peter Driscoll　1942-　　　Adventure/Thriller

Eric Ambler　　　　June Drummond　　　J K Mayo
John Buchan　　　　Iris Johansen　　　Wilbur Smith
Nelson DeMille

Jeremy Dronfield　1965-　Wales　　Adventure/Thriller: Psychological
http://vzone.virgin.net/jeremy.dronfield

Iain Banks　　　　Laurie R King　　　Barbara Vine
Nicci French　　　Ian McEwan

Emma Drummond　　　　　　Historical
also writes as Elizabeth Darrell

Philippa Carr　　　Cynthia Harrod-Eagles　Patricia Shaw
Joy Chambers　　　Victoria Holt

June Drummond　1923-　SA　　Adventure/Thriller

Jon Cleary　　　　Peter Driscoll　　　Alan Scholefield
John Gordon Davis　Derek Lambert　　　Wilbur Smith

June Drummond　1923-　SA　　　Historical

Elizabeth Darrell　　Jane Aiken Hodge
Winston Graham　　　Barbara Michaels

Daphne Du Maurier   1907-89   General
www.westwind.co.uk/westwind/cornwall/daphne/maurier.html

Susan Hill	Susanna Kearsley	Mary Stewart
Joanna Hines	Charlotte Lamb	Sue Sully
Susan Howatch	Anya Seton	

Brendan Dubois   US   Adventure/Thriller
www.brendandubois.com
                                                    ⚡ Lewis Cole

Robert Harris	Robert Ludlum
Derek Lambert	Lawrence Sanders

D Andre Dubus   US   General

Richard Ford	J Robert Lennon	Anne Tyler
Jane Hamilton	Anita Shreve	

Margaret Duffy   1942-   Sco   Crime: Police work - Br
                                          ⚡ Insp James Carrick - Bath

M C Beaton	Caroline Graham	Bill Knox
Deborah Crombie	Ann Granger	Priscilla Masters

Maureen Duffy   1933-   General

Kate Atkinson	Zoe Fairbairns	Marge Piercy
Hilary Bailey	Margaret Forster	Amanda Prantera

Stella Duffy   1963-   Crime: PI
                                          ⚡ Saz Martin - London

Liza Cody	Val McDermid	Manda Scott
Alma Fritchley	Claire McNab	Mary Wings
Ellen Hart	Marcia Muller	

Nina Dufort   Aga Saga

Diana Appleyard	Elizabeth Falconer	Katie Fforde
Judy Astley	Kate Fenton	Maggie Makepeace
Victoria Clayton		

Sarah Dunant 1950-

Crime: PI

🏃 Hannah Wolfe - London

Liza Cody
Amanda Cross
Anabel Donald
Nicci French
Lesley Grant-Adamson

Nora Kelly
Manda Scott
Gillian Slovo
Joan Smith

CWA	1993 ✿

Laramie Dunaway 1952- US

Glitz & Glamour

Maria Barrett
Sally Beauman
Barbara Delinsky

Lucinda Edmonds
Julie Ellis
Elizabeth Gage

Olivia Goldsmith
Judith Krantz

D

Inga Dunbar Sco

Saga

Barbara Erskine
Diana Gabaldon
Evelyn Hood

Alison McLeay
Frances Paige
Alison Skelton

Kay Stephens
Reay Tannahill
Valerie Wood

Helen Dunmore 1952-

General

Lisa Appignanesi
Carol Birch
Anita Brookner
Suzannah Dunn
Alice Thomas Ellis
Catherine Merriman

Bel Mooney
Carole Morin
Barbara Neil
Madeleine St John
Gillian White

McKitterick	1994 ✿
Orange	1996 ✿

Suzannah Dunn 1963-

General

Helen Dunmore
Esther Freud

Sian James
Lorrie Moore

Anne Tyler

Catherine Dunne

General

Catherine Fox
Jane Hamilton

Joan O'Neill
Joanna Trollope

Anne Tyler

Don't forget lists of: *Genres* * *Characters* * *Literary prizes* * *Further reading* ☞

Dominick Dunne   1925-   US   *General*

F Scott Fitzgerald	Jay McInerney	TGR	1994 ❀
Richard Ford	Marge Piercy		
Arthur Hailey	Tom Wolfe		

Dorothy Dunnett   1923-2001   Sco   *Historical*
also wrote as Dorothy Halliday   ☥ Francis Crawford of Lymond - C15th England

Elizabeth Chadwick	Jean Plaidy	Jane Stevenson
Diana Gabaldon	Mary Renault	Reay Tannahill
Geraldine McCaughrean	Edward Rutherfurd	Nigel Tranter
Sharon Penman		

D
E

Lawrence Durrell   1912-90   *General*

| John Fowles | Olivia Manning |
| Robert Graves | Thomas Pynchon |

Joan Eadith   *Saga*
Manchester

Aileen Armitage	Irene Carr	Elvi Rhodes
Jessica Blair	Una Horne	Eileen Townsend
Helen Cannam	Anna Jacobs	Elizabeth Walker

Nick Earls   1963-   Aus   *Lad Lit*
www.nickearls.com

| Mark Barrowcliffe | Matthew Beaumont | Mike Gayle |

Daniel Easterman   1949-   *Adventure/Thriller*
also writes as Jonathan Aycliffe

Tom Bradby	James Follett	John R Maxim
John Gordon Davis	Patrick Lynch	Murray Smith
Nelson DeMille	Amin Maalouf	John Trenhaile

Don't forget lists of: *Genres * Characters * Literary prizes * Further reading* ☞

Marjorie Eccles   1927-   Crime: Police work - Br
also writes as Judith Bordill & Jennifer Hyde   ♟ DI Abigail Moon & Supt Gil Mayo - Midlands
                                                        DI Tom Richmond - Yorkshire

Jo Bannister   Patricia Hall   Ann Quinton
Pauline Bell   Janet Harward   Betty Rowlands
Elizabeth George   Priscilla Masters

Umberto Eco   1932-   It   General
www.themodernword.com/eco/

Caleb Carr   Jostein Gaarder   Iain Pears
Paulo Coelho   William Golding   Patrick Süskind
Mário de Carvalho   Ross King   Jill Paton Walsh
John Fowles   Lawrence Norfolk

David Eddings   1931-   US   Fantasy: Epic
                ♟ The Belgariad ▪ The Mallorean ▪ The Ellenium ▪ The Tamuli   **E**

Tom Arden   Terry Goodkind   Mickey Zucker Reichert
Chris Bunch   Elizabeth Haydon   Robert Silverberg
Mark Chadbourn   Robert Jordan   J R R Tolkien
Kate Elliott   Paul Kearney   Tad Williams

Lucinda Edmonds   1966-   Glitz & Glamour

Charlotte Bingham   Shirley Conran   Judith Michael
Pat Booth   Laramie Dunaway   Fiona Walker
Celia Brayfield

Robert Edric   1956-   Historical

Peter Benson   Geraldine McCaughrean   Black   1985 ✹
Tim Binding   Chris Paling
Giles Foden   Tim Pears
Janice Graham   Jane Thynne
Adam Lively

Doreen Edwards   Wales   Saga

Anne Baker   Sheelagh Kelly   Ann Victoria Roberts
Audrey Howard   Audrey Reimann

Martin Edwards   1955-   Crime
♁ Harry Devlin, Solicitor - Liverpool

Jeffrey Ashford	Ron Ellis	M R D Meek
John Baker	Bill James	Gillian Slovo
Judith Cutler		

Ruth Dudley Edwards   1944-   Ire   Crime: Humour
www.ruthdudleyedwards.co.uk   *♁ Robert Amiss & Baroness Troutbeck*

B M Gill	Rory McCormac	Janet Neel
Bartholomew Gill	Fidelis Morgan	Tom Sharpe
Tim Heald		

Greg Egan   1961-   Aus   Science Fiction: Near future
www.netspace.net.au/~gregegan/

E

Alexander Besher	Jon Courtenay Grimwood	John Meaney
Ben Bova	Ian McDonald	Neal Stephenson
Pat Cadigan	Ken MacLeod	David Wingrove
William Gibson		

Clive Egleton   1927-   Adventure/Thriller
♁ Peter Ashton

James Adams	Bryan Forbes	Anthony Price
Ted Allbeury	Colin Forbes	Kenneth Royce
Tom Bradby	Frederick Forsyth	Murray Smith
Len Deighton	Palma Harcourt	

Thomas Eidson   US   General

Lauren Belfer	Stewart O'Nan	*TGR* 1995 ✿
Barbara Esstman	Annie Proulx	
Nicholas Evans	Jane Smiley	
Charles Frazier	Jane Urquhart	
Cormac McCarthy	Larry Watson	

Kerstin Ekman   1933-   Swe   Crime: Psychological

Peter Hoeg	Amy Tan	Minette Walters
Henning Mankell	Barbara Vine	

Elizabeth Elgin
Saga
⚐ *Sutton Family - Yorkshire*

Kate Alexander
Julia Bryant
Helen Cannam

Anna Jacobs
Margaret Mayhew
Wendy Robertson

Susan Sallis
Kay Stephens
Margaret Sunley

Kate Elliott 1958- US
Fantasy: Epic
also writes as Alis A Rasmussen
www.sff.net/people/Kate.elliott/index.htp
Jaran Series

Terry Brooks
C J Cherryh
David Eddings
Raymond E Feist

Maggie Furey
Terry Goodkind
J V Jones
Paul Kearney

Holly Lisle
Elizabeth Moon
Melanie Rawn

Alice Thomas Ellis 1932-
General

E

Hilary Bailey
Beryl Bainbridge
Angela Carter
Helen Dunmore

Sarah Grazebrook
Penelope Lively
Sara Maitland
Edna O'Brien

Barbara Pym
Bernice Rubens
Barbara Trapido

Bret Easton Ellis 1964- US
General

Matthew Branton
Douglas Coupland
Jay McInerney

Haruki Murakami
Tim Parks
Will Self

Matt Thorne
Tom Wolfe

Julie Ellis 1933- US
Glitz & Glamour

Sally Beauman
Laramie Dunaway
Judith Krantz

Lynda La Plante
Carole Matthews
Fern Michaels

Una-Mary Parker
June Flaum Singer

Kate Ellis 1953-
Crime: Police work - Br
www.kateellis.co.uk
⚐ *DS Wesley Peterson - West Country*

Jeffrey Ashford
Janie Bolitho
W J Burley

Janet Harward
P D James
Roy Lewis

Barry Maitland
Jessica Mann

Ron Ellis   1941-   Crime

Johnny Ace, Disc jockey - Liverpool

Ace Atkins	Valerie Kershaw	Robert T Price
Martin Edwards	Chris Niles	Cath Staincliffe

Lucy Ellman   1956-   US   General

Catherine Alliott	Joanne Harris
Louise Bagshawe	Pauline Melville
Susie Boyt	Ann Oakley
Jenn Crowell	Lynne Truss
Anne Fine	Harriet Waugh

Guardian   1988 ❀

James Ellroy   1948-   US   Crime: Modern

www.twbooks.co.uk/authors/jellroy.html   Los Angeles

E

James Crumley	Stuart M Kaminsky	Peter Tasker
Stephen Donaldson	David Peace	Boston Teran
Loren D Estleman	Mario Puzo	Jim Thompson
George V Higgins	John B Spencer	Joseph Wambaugh

Ben Elton   1959-   Lad Lit

Stephen Amidon	Robert Llewellyn
David Baddiel	John McCabe
Stephen Fry	Tony Parsons
James Hawes	Keith Waterhouse
Charles Higson	

CWA   1996 ❀

Sally Emerson   General

Janice Galloway	Agnes Owens
Candia McWilliam	Jane Rogers

Rosemary Enright   Saga

Louise Brindley	Sue Sully
Lilian Harry	Margaret Thornton

Don't forget lists of: *Genres * Characters * Literary prizes * Further reading* ☞

Paul Erdman   *1932-   US*   *Crime: Legal/financial*

David Baldacci   Joseph Finder   John McLaren
Po Bronson   Stephen Frey   Michael Ridpath
Linda Davies

Louise Erdrich   *1954-   US*   *General*

Isabel Allende   Alison Lurie   Jane Smiley
Michael Collins   Lorrie Moore   Larry Watson
William Faulkner   Stewart O'Nan   Rebecca Wells
Barbara Kingsolver   Annie Proulx

Steven Erikson   *Can*   *Fantasy: Epic*
Malazan Series

James Barclay   David Gemmell   John Marco
Stephen Donaldson   Greg Keyes   George R R Martin
Raymond E Feist   Juliet E McKenna

E

Barbara Erskine   *1944-*   *Historical*

Philippa Carr   Domini Highsmith   Alison McLeay
Elizabeth Chadwick   Helen Hollick   Magda Sweetland
Inga Dunbar   Dinah Lampitt   Reay Tannahill
Elizabeth Harris

Gavin Esler   *1953-   Sco*   *Adventure/Thriller*

Tom Bradby   Stephen Leather   Gerald Seymour
James Buchan   Kenneth Royce   Terence Strong
Humphrey Hawksley   Tim Sebastian

Laura Esquivel   *1950-   Mex*   *General*

Isabel Allende   Gabriel Garcia Márquez   Jeanette Winterson
Kate Atkinson   Ángeles Mastretta

Barbara Esstman   *US*   *General*

Thomas Eidson   Larry McMurtry   Jane Urquhart
Jim Harrison   Ann Patchett

Loren D Estleman   1952-   US   Crime: PI
www.lorenestleman.com/   ♟ Amos Walker - Detroit ▪ Peter MacKlin, Hitman

Lawrence Block	Dashiell Hammett	Reggie Nadelson
Harlan Coben	Joseph Hansen	Robert K Tanenbaum
James Ellroy	Jon A Jackson	Steve Womack
Steve Hamilton		

Dennis Etchison   1943-   US   Horror

Clive Barker	Simon Clark	Peter Straub
Ray Bradbury	Richard Matheson	

Janet Evanovich   1943-   US   Crime
also writes as Steffie Hall
www.evanovich.com   ♟ Stephanie Plum, Bail bondswoman - Newark, New Jersey

E

Linda Barnes	Valerie Kershaw	CWA	1995 ✿
Marc Blake	Pauline McLynn	CWA	1997 ✿
Tim Cockey	Lindsay Maracotta		
Louise Doughty	Scarlett Thomas		
Liz Evans	Kathy Hogan Trocheck		
Alma Fritchley	Valerie Wilson Wesley		

Alan Evans   1930-   Sea: Modern

Brian Callison	Clive Cussler	Max Hennessy
Bernard Cornwell	Duncan Harding	Peter Tonkin

Christopher Evans   1951-   Wales   Science Fiction:
                                                                Space and time

Colin Greenland	Ken MacLeod	BSFA	1993 ✿
Paul J McAuley	Brian Stableford		

Liz Evans   Crime: PI
                              ♟ Grace Smith - 'Seatoun', South Coast, England

Jo Bannister	Irene Lin-Chandler	Scarlett Thomas
Janet Evanovich	Pauline McLynn	Rebecca Tope
Sparkle Hayter	Susan Sussman with	Stella Whitelaw
Joyce Holms	Sarajane Avidon	

Nicholas Evans   1950-   *General*
www.randomhouse.com/features/nickevans

Pat Conroy	Jim Harrison	Nicholas Sparks
Thomas Eidson	Stuart Harrison	Joyce Stranger
Charles Frazier	William Horwood	Marly Swick
David Guterson	Larry McMurtry	Robert James Waller

Pamela Evans   *Saga*
London

Helen Carey	Elizabeth Lord	Alison Stuart
Harry Cole	Victor Pemberton	Elizabeth Waite
Emma Dally	Sally Spencer	Jeanne Whitmee
Elizabeth Hawksley	Mary Jane Staples	Dee Williams

Penelope Evans   1959-   Wales   *Crime:* Psychological   **E**
F

Faye Kellerman	Jenny Maxwell	Barbara Vine
Elizabeth McGregor	Ruth Rendell	Minette Walters

Michel Faber   1960-   Neth   *General*
www.thebookreport.com/authors/au-faber-michel.asp

Guy Burt	A L Kennedy	Magnus Mills
Alasdair Gray	Ian McEwan	Rupert Thomson
Franz Kafka	Duncan McLean	Alan Warner
James Kelman	W Somerset Maugham	

Zoe Fairbairns   1948-   *General*

Lisa Alther	Kate Hatfield	Kate Saunders
Maureen Duffy	Susan Howatch	Titia Sutherland
Philippa Gregory	Sara Maitland	

Linda Fairstein   1947-   US   *Crime:* Legal/financial
www.lindafairstein.com/   *Alexandra Cooper, Assistant DA - New York*

Catherine Arnold	Lisa Gardner	Nancy Taylor Rosenberg
Harlan Coben	John T Lescroart	Lisa Scottoline
Alan M Dershowitz	Steve Martini	Robert K Tanenbaum
Elaine Feinstein	Kathy Reichs	

Colin Falconer 1953- Adventure/Thriller

James Clavell   Eric Lustbader
Martina Cole   Christopher Nicole

Elizabeth Falconer Aga Saga

Teresa Crane   Amanda Prantera   Joanna Trollope
Nina Dufort   Alexandra Raife   Mary Wesley
Elizabeth Pewsey

David Farland 1957- US Fantasy: Epic
www.runelords.com

Kate Jacoby   Robert Jordan   Jane Welch
J V Jones   Juliet E McKenna   Philip G Williamson

John Farris 1936- Horror
also writes as Steve Brackeen
www.fantasticfiction.co.uk/authors/John_Farris.htm

David Bowker   H P Lovecraft   Anne Rice
Stephen Gallagher   Robert McCammon   Peter Straub
Stephen King   Graham Masterton   Whitley Strieber
Richard Laymon

John Farrow 1947- Can Crime: Police work - foreign
is Trevor Ferguson   ☀ DS Emile Cinq-Mars - Montreal

Hilary Bonner   Michael Connelly   Kathy Reichs
James Lee Burke   Donald James

Howard Fast 1914-92 US General
also wrote as E V Cunningham

Winston Graham   James A Michener   Nigel Tranter
Robert Graves   Mary Renault   Leon Uris
Georgette Heyer

F

Don't forget lists of: Genres * Characters * Literary prizes * Further reading ☞

William Faulkner   1897-1962   US   General
http://www.mcsr.olemiss.edu/~egjbp/faulkner/faulkner.html

Louise Erdrich
Connie May Fowler
Ellen Gilchrist
James Joyce

Cormac McCarthy
Carson McCullers
Toni Morrison

Joyce Carol Oates
Amos Oz
William Styron

Sebastian Faulks   1953-   General

Pat Barker
Tim Binding
Giles Foden
Andrew Greig

Sebastien Japrisot
Juliette Mead
Chris Paling
Piers Paul Read

Erich Maria Remarque
Jane Thynne
Paul Watkins

Patricia Fawcett   Aga Saga

Caroline Bridgwood
Lucy Clare

Jill Roe
Rebecca Shaw

Peta Tayler

Catherine Feeny   1957-   General **F**

Mavis Cheek
Candida Crewe
Jill Dawson

Anne Fine
Kathy Lette
Deborah Moggach

Elizabeth Pewsey
Salley Vickers

Elaine Feinstein   1930-   General
www.elainefeinstein.com

Linda Fairstein
Margaret Forster

Lisa Gardner
Susan Hill

Michele Roberts

Raymond E Feist   1945-   US   *Fantasy:* Epic
www.fantasticfiction.co.uk/authors/Raymond_E_Feist.htm   *Riftwar Saga*

Terry Brooks
Stephen Donaldson
Kate Elliott
Steven Erikson

Maggie Furey
Barbara Hambly
Brian Herbert
Mike Jefferies

Paul Kearney
John Marco
Mickey Zucker Reichert
Janny Wurts

Kate Fenton 1954-   Aga Saga

Raffaella Barker   Nina Dufort   Kate Sharam
Elizabeth Buchan   Sue Limb   Mary Sheepshanks
Lucy Clare   Maggie Makepeace   Joanna Trollope
Anne Doughty   Melissa Nathan   Madeleine Wickham

Neil Ferguson 1947-   General

Iain Banks   Geoff Nicholson   Graham Swift
Jonathan Coe   Tim Pears

Elizabeth Ferrars 1907-95   Crime
was Morna Doris Brown   ⚲ Andrew Basnett • Felix Freer

Margery Allingham   Ngaio Marsh   June Thomson
Anthea Fraser   Maureen O'Brien   Patricia Wentworth
Alison Joseph   Roger Ormerod   Barbara Whitehead
Emma Lathen   John Penn   Margaret Yorke

F Robert Ferrigno 1948- US   Crime
www.robertferrigno.com

James Crumley   David Lindsey   Carol O'Connell
James Hall   Michael McGarrity   Boston Teran
Tony Hillerman

Katie Fforde 1952-   Aga Saga

Clare Chambers   Julia Hamilton   Ann Swinfen
Lucy Clare   Maggie Makepeace   Alan Titchmarsh
Victoria Clayton   Elizabeth Palmer   Mary Wesley
Nina Dufort   Henrietta Soames

Helen Fielding 1958-   Chick Lit

Sherry Ashworth   Amy Jenkins   Stephanie Theobald
Francesca Clementis   Serena Mackesy   Lynne Truss
Victoria Corby   Alexandra Potter   Daisy Waugh
Jane Green   Yvonne Roberts   Arabella Weir

Joy Fielding 1945- Can   Crime: Psychological
www.joyfielding.com

Bethany Campbell   Thomas Harris   Gloria Murphy
Mary Higgins Clark   Faye Kellerman   Margaret Murphy
John Connolly   Judith Kelman   Melanie Tem
Kit Craig

Kate Fielding   Aga Saga
also writes as Jenny Oldfield   Ravensdale Series - Yorkshire

Fanny Frewen   Erica James   Elizabeth Pewsey
Hazel Hucker   Jan Karon   Rebecca Shaw

Joseph Finder 1958- US   Adventure/Thriller

David Baldacci   Tony Hillerman
Paul Erdman   Robert Ludlum

Anne Fine 1947-   General
www.annefine.co.uk

F

Rachel Billington   Catherine Feeny   Joan Lingard
Anabel Donald   Maureen Freely   Will Self
Lucy Ellman   Lesley Glaister   Harriet Waugh

Tibor Fischer 1959-   General

Louis de Bernières   John Irving   Ivan Klima
Joseph Heller   Franz Kafka   Ian McEwan

F Scott Fitzgerald 1896-1940 US   General
www.sc.edu/fitzgerald

Ethan Canin   Ford Madox Ford   Carson McCullers
E L Doctorow   E M Forster   John Steinbeck
Dominick Dunne   Ernest Hemingway

Don't forget lists of: *Genres * Characters * Literary prizes * Further reading* ☞

Penelope Fitzgerald   1916-2000   General

Jane Austen	Penelope Lively	
Beryl Bainbridge	Geraldine McCaughrean	
Rachel Billington	Emma Tennant	
Anita Brookner	Salley Vickers	
Isabel Colegate	Edith Wharton	
Agnes Desarthe		

Booker   1979 ✷

Bill Fitzhugh   US   Crime: Humour
www.billfitzhugh.com

Colin Bateman	Christopher Brookmyre	Joe R Lansdale
Anthony Bourdain	Tim Dorsey	Laurence Shames
Gene Brewer	Carl Hiaasen	

Ian Fleming   1908-64   Adventure/Thriller

Eric Ambler	Brian Freemantle	Alistair MacLean
John Buchan	John Gardner	J K Mayo
Victor Davis	Gavin Lyall	Daniel Silva
James Follett		

F

Katie Flynn   1936-   Saga
also writes as Judith Saxton & Judy Turner   ⚘ Lilac Larkin - Liverpool

Lyn Andrews	Ruth Hamilton	Marie Joseph
Anne Baker	Audrey Howard	Maureen Lee
Josephine Cox	Anna Jacobs	Elizabeth Murphy
Helen Forrester	Joan Jonker	

Raymond Flynn   1940-   Crime: Police work - Br
                                    ⚘ DCI Robert Graham - 'Eddathorpe', East Anglia

Vivien Armstrong	Reginald Hill	Frank Palmer
Brian Cooper	Alan Hunter	Stewart Pawson
Malcolm Forsythe	Nick Oldham	Leslie Thomas

Don't forget lists of: Genres * Characters * Literary prizes * Further reading ☞

Giles Foden 1967-   General

William Boyd	Tim Jeal	Whitbread 1998 ❋
James Clavell	Pamela Jooste	Holtby 1998 ❋
Robert Edric	Paul Theroux	S Maugham 1999 ❋
Sebastian Faulks		

James Follett 1939-   Adventure/Thriller

James Adams	John Harris	Justin Scott
Desmond Bagley	John Lawton	Craig Thomas
Daniel Easterman	Alistair MacLean	Glover Wright
Ian Fleming	Matthew Reilly	

Ken Follett 1949-   Adventure/Thriller
www.ken-follett.com

Desmond Bagley	Nelson DeMille	John Lawton
Nicholas Coleridge	Clare Francis	Michael Shea
Lionel Davidson	Palma Harcourt	William Smethurst
John Gordon Davis	Humphrey Hawksley	Gordon Thomas

Bryan Forbes 1926-   Adventure/Thriller

Lionel Davidson	Humphrey Hawksley	Tim Sebastian
Len Deighton	John Le Carré	Gerald Seymour
Clive Egleton		

Colin Forbes 1923-   Adventure/Thriller

Ted Allbeury	Victor Davis	Palma Harcourt
Evelyn Anthony	Clive Egleton	Geoffrey Jenkins
Campbell Armstrong	Frederick Forsyth	John Trenhaile
Jon Cleary		

Ford Madox Ford 1873-1939   General

Joseph Conrad	E M Forster
F Scott Fitzgerald	Henry James

F

Richard Ford   1944-   US   General

Raymond Carver	Garrison Keillor	
Pete Dexter	Thomas McGuane	
Andre Dubus	Tim O'Brien	
Dominick Dunne	John Steinbeck	
David Guterson	William Styron	
Jim Harrison		

Pulitzer   1996 ✣

C S Forester   1899-1966   Sea: Historical
⚐ Horatio Hornblower - C18th/19th England

David Donachie	Jan Needle	Dan Parkinson
Alexander Kent	James L Nelson	Dudley Pope
A E Langsford	Patrick O'Brian	Showell Styles
Jonathan Lunn	Marcus Palliser	Victor Suthren

Helen Forrester   1919-   Saga
www.helenforrester.com/   Liverpool

F

Anne Baker	Audrey Howard	Maureen Lee
Katie Flynn	Joan Jonker	Mary Mackie
June Francis	Marie Joseph	Elizabeth Murphy

E M Forster   1879-1970   General

F Scott Fitzgerald	Francis King	H G Wells
Ford Madox Ford	Anthony Powell	Edith Wharton
Henry James	Paul Scott	Virginia Woolf
Ruth Prawer Jhabvala		

Margaret Forster   1938-   General

Kate Atkinson	Elaine Feinstein	Anna Quindlen
Alex Benzie	Sue Gee	Kate Sharam
Kate Bingham	Linda Grant	Elizabeth Tettmar
Maureen Duffy	Mary Morrissy	Rebecca Wells

Don't forget lists of: Genres * Characters * Literary prizes * Further reading ☞

Frederick Forsyth　1938-　　　　　　　　Adventure/Thriller

James Adams
Victor Davis
Clive Egleton
Colin Forbes

Derek Lambert
Stephen Leather
Mike Lunnon-Wood
Andy McNab

David Mason
Glenn Meade
Daniel Silva
James Thayer

Malcolm Forsythe　1921-　　　　Crime: Police work - Br
is Malcolm Hutton　　　　　　　　　⚷ DCI Millson & DS Scobie - Norfolk

Vivien Armstrong
Brian Cooper

Raymond Flynn
Alan Hunter

Ann Quinton
Ruth Rendell

Alan Dean Foster　1946-　US　Science Fiction: Space opera
www.alandeanfoster.com　　　　　　　　　　　　Spellsinger Series

Poul Anderson
Piers Anthony
Robert Asprin
David Brin

Orson Scott Card
C J Cherryh
L Sprague de Camp

Simon R Green
Colin Greenland
Elizabeth Haydon

F

Christopher Fowler　1953-　　　　　　　　　Horror
www.christopherfowler.co.uk

Clive Barker
David Bowker
Ramsey Campbell
Jonathan Carroll

Nancy Collins
Robert Girardi
Jenny Jones
Graham Joyce

Graham Masterton
Kim Newman
Michael Marshall Smith

Connie May Fowler　1958-　US　　　　　　　General

William Faulkner
Ellen Gilchrist

J Robert Lennon
Carson McCullers

Joyce Carol Oates
Anita Shreve

John Fowles　1926-　　　　　　　　　　　General
www.fowlesbooks.com

Peter Ackroyd
Guy Burt
Bruce Chatwin
Lawrence Durrell

Umberto Eco
Maggie Gee
William Golding
Alasdair Gray

Thomas Hardy
Robert Nye
Graham Swift
Rupert Thomson

Catherine Fox 1961-   General

Catherine Dunne   Elizabeth Jane Howard   Sara Maitland
Eileen Goudge   Susan Howatch   Barbara Trapido
Julia Hamilton

Janet Frame 1924- NZ   General

David Cook   Paul Sayer   Commonwealth 1989 ❀
Elizabeth Jolley   Fay Weldon
Doris Lessing

Ronald Frame 1953- Sco   General

Robert Goddard   Bernard MacLaverty   Paul Micou
Kazuo Ishiguro   Allan Massie   William Trevor

Clare Francis 1946-   Adventure/Thriller

Evelyn Anthony   Frances Galleymore   Duncan Kyle
Lisa Appignanesi   Paula Gosling   Gloria Murphy
Kit Craig   Geoffrey Jenkins   Hilary Norman
Ken Follett

F

Dick Francis 1920-   Crime
Horse racing

David Brierley   Gavin Lyall   CWA   1979 ❀
John Francome   Richard Pitman

June Francis   Saga
Liverpool

Lyn Andrews   Helen Forrester   Maureen Lee
Anne Baker   Ruth Hamilton   Gilda O'Neill
Julia Bryant   Joan Jonker   Sally Spencer
Jean Chapman   Lena Kennedy   Margaret Thornton

John Francome 1952- Crime
Horse racing

David Brierley
Dick Francis

Gavin Lyall
Richard Pitman

Jonathan Franzen 1959- US General
www.jonathanfranzen.com

Ethan Canin
Don DeLillo

Richard Powers
Annie Proulx

John Updike

Anthea Fraser 1930- Crime: Police work - Br
� DCI David Webb & DS Ken Jackson - 'Broadshire', Home Counties, England

Marian Babson
Elizabeth Ferrars

Ann Granger
June Thomson

Caro Fraser Sco General

Nina Bawden
Elizabeth Ironside

John Mortimer
Mary Ryan

Joanna Trollope

F

Christine Marion Fraser 1945- Sco Saga
Rhanna Series ▪ Kings Series ▪ Noble Series - Scotland

Emma Blair
Margaret Thomson Davis
Nora Kay
Gwen Kirkwood

Walter Macken
Isobel Neill
Pamela Oldfield
Frances Paige

Jessica Stirling
Anne Vivis
Kirsty White
Mary Withall

George MacDonald Fraser 1925- Humour

Joseph Heller
Tom Holt

Tom Sharpe
Leslie Thomas

Peter Tinniswood

Don't forget lists of: *Genres * Characters * Literary prizes * Further reading* ☞

Sara Fraser 1937-   Saga
also writes as Roy Clews   🏃 *Tildy Crawford - Midlands*

Joyce Bell	Meg Hutchinson	Harriet Smart
Catrin Collier	Annie Murray	Alison Stuart
Josephine Cox	Lynda Page	Janet Tanner
Patricia Grey		

Michael Frayn 1933-   Humour

Kingsley Amis	Malcolm Bradbury	Francis King
Guy Bellamy	Howard Jacobson	David Lodge

Charles Frazier 1950-   US   General

Thomas Eidson	Thomas Keneally	Stewart O'Nan
Nicholas Evans	Cormac McCarthy	Larry Watson
David Guterson	Larry McMurtry	

Marianne Fredriksson 1927-   Swe   General

F

Judy Budnitz	Peter Hoeg
Sue Gee	Katharine McMahon

Nicolas Freeling 1927-   Crime: *Police work - foreign*
🏃 *Henri Castang - France • Insp Van Der Valk - Netherlands*

Michael Dibdin	Donna Leon	Daniel Pennac
Juliet Hebden	Henning Mankell	Georges Simenon
Mark Hebden	Barbara Nadel	Janwillem van de Wetering
J Robert Janes		

Maureen Freely 1952-   General

Rachel Billington	Esther Freud	Michele Roberts
Anne Fine	Joan Lingard	Meera Syal

Don't forget lists of: *Genres* ∗ *Characters* ∗ *Literary prizes* ∗ *Further reading* ☞

Brian Freemantle   1936-   Adventure/Thriller
also writes as John Maxwell   ⚘ *Charlie Muffin - MI6*

Ted Allbeury   John Gardner   Anthony Price
Ian Fleming   John Le Carré

Nicci French   1958-   Adventure/Thriller: Psychological
is Nicci Gerrard   ⚘ *Dr Samantha Laschen*

Lisa Appignanesi   Joseph Glass   Elizabeth McGregor
Stephen Dobyns   Richard Greensted   J Wallis Martin
Jeremy Dronfield   Frances Hegarty   Gemma O'Connor
Sarah Dunant   Alice Hoffman

Esther Freud   1963-   General

Julia Blackburn   Alex Garland   Polly Samson
Suzannah Dunn   Ian McEwan   Meera Syal
Maureen Freely   Shena Mackay   Emma Tennant
Jane Gardam   Terry McMillan   Harriet Waugh

Fanny Frewen   1924-   Aga Saga

Marika Cobbold   Nora Naish   Rebecca Shaw
Kate Fielding   Elizabeth Pewsey   Titia Sutherland
Erica James   Kathleen Rowntree   Mary Wesley

Stephen Frey   US   Crime: Legal/financial

Po Bronson   John Grisham   Brad Meltzer
Linda Davies   John McLaren   Michael Ridpath
Paul Erdman   Phillip M Margolin

Kinky Friedman   1944-   US   Crime
www.kinkyfriedman.com/   ⚘ *Kinky Friedman, Country & Western singer - New York*

Anthony Bourdain   Sparkle Hayter   Robert B Parker
Charlotte Carter   Susan Isaacs   Laurence Shames
Tim Dorsey   Elmore Leonard   Doug J Swanson
James Hawes

F

Philip Friedman   1944-   US   Crime: Legal/financial

Catherine Arnold	John Grisham	Richard North Patterson
Alan M Dershowitz	Steve Martini	Nancy Taylor Rosenberg
Dexter Dias		

Alma Fritchley   1954-   Crime: Humour
⚐ *Letty Campbell, Chicken farmer - Yorkshire*

Liza Cody	Lauren Henderson	Manda Scott
Stella Duffy	Val McDermid	Michelle Spring
Janet Evanovich	Marianne MacDonald	Cath Staincliffe
Ellen Hart		

Stephen Fry   1957-   Humour

David Baddiel	Howard Jacobson	Mark Wallington
Roddy Doyle	Tim Lott	Nigel Williams
Ben Elton	Geoff Nicholson	P G Wodehouse
Charles Higson	David Nobbs	

F

Alexander Fullerton   1924-   Adventure/Thriller

Brian Callison	Hammond Innes	James Pattinson
Duncan Harding	Philip McCutchan	Richard Woodman
Max Hennessy		

Maggie Furey   1955-   Fantasy: Epic

Terry Brooks	Raymond E Feist	J V Jones
Chris Bunch	Terry Goodkind	Paul Kearney
Allan Cole	Julia Gray	George R R Martin
Kate Elliott	Mike Jefferies	Roger Taylor

Alan Furst   1941-   US   Adventure/Thriller

James Adams	Conor Cregan	Alan Judd
Evelyn Anthony	Lionel Davidson	Robert Littell
Francis Bennett	John Gordon Davis	Gordon Stevens
Nicholas Coleridge	David Ignatius	Robert Wilson

Frances Fyfield 1948- Crime
also writes as Frances Hegarty

♣ Helen West & DS Geoffrey Bailey
London Crown Prosecution Service

Jane Adams	Sarah Lovett	CWA	1990 ❀
Natasha Cooper	M R D Meek	CWA	1991 ❀
Jonathan Davies	Margaret Murphy		
Elizabeth George	Maureen O'Brien		
B M Gill	Robert K Tanenbaum		
Joanna Hines	Laura Wilson		

Jostein Gaarder 1952- Nor General

Umberto Eco   Peter Hoeg
Gabriel Garcia Márquez   Iris Murdoch

Diana Gabaldon 1950- US Historical
www.cco.caltech.edu/~gatti/gabaldon/gabaldon.html

Jean M Auel   Dorothy Dunnett   Magda Sweetland
Philippa Carr   Judith Lennox   Reay Tannahill
Inga Dunbar   Alison McLeay   Patricia Wendorf

Patricia Gaffney US General
www.sff.net/people/PGaffney/

Andrea Barrett   Libby Purves   Joanna Trollope
Barbara Kingsolver   Anita Shreve   Anne Tyler
Sue Miller

Elizabeth Gage 1943- US Glitz & Glamour
also writes as Lavyrle Spencer

Louise Bagshawe   Joan Collins   Judith Gould
Sally Beauman   Laramie Dunaway   Freya North
Celia Brayfield   Olivia Goldsmith   June Flaum Singer
Sandra Brown

Neil Gaiman 1960- Fantasy: Contemporary
www.neilgaiman.com

Douglas Adams   Ellen Datlow   Philip Pullman
Peter S Beagle   Charles de Lint   Martin Scott
John Crowley   Tim Powers

F
G

103

Patrick Gale *1962-*   *General*

Guy Bellamy   Alan Hollinghurst   Paul Micou
Michael Carson   Armistead Maupin   Edmund White

Stephen Gallagher *1954-*   *Horror*
www.stephengallagher.com

Campbell Black   Steve Harris   Graham Masterton
Chaz Brenchley   James Herbert   Mark Morris
John Farris   Peter James   T M Wright
Muriel Gray   Dean R Koontz

Frances Galleymore *1946-*   *US*   *Adventure/Thriller*

Mary Higgins Clark   Philip Hook   Carol O'Connell
Linda Davies   Graham Hurley   Barbara Vine
Clare Francis   Gloria Murphy

Janice Galloway *1956-*   *General*

Kate Atkinson   Isla Dewar   Agnes Owens
Alex Benzie   Sally Emerson   Alan Spence
Ajay Close   A L Kennedy   Mary Wesley
Amanda Craig   Andrew O'Hagan

G

John Galsworthy *1867-1933*   *General*

A J Cronin   D H Lawrence   Christina Stead
R F Delderfield   J B Priestley   Anthony Trollope

Gabriel Garcia Márquez *1928-*   *Colombia*   *General*

Isabel Allende   Mário de Carvalho   Ángeles Mastretta
Alex Benzie   Laura Esquivel   Ben Okri
Anthony Burgess   Jostein Gaarder   Mario Vargas Llosa
Paulo Coelho   David Grossman   Niall Williams

Don't forget lists of: *Genres * Characters * Literary prizes * Further reading* ☞

Jane Gardam   1928-   General

Hilary Bailey	Joan Lingard	*Higham* 1975 ❀
Nina Bawden	Kate Pullinger	*Whitbread* 1991 ❀
Amanda Craig	Jane Rogers	
Esther Freud	Salley Vickers	
Susan Hill	Jill Paton Walsh	
Jennifer Johnston	Teresa Waugh	

Craig Shaw Gardner   1949-   US   Fantasy: Humour

Piers Anthony	Andrew Harman	Terry Pratchett
Robert Asprin	Tom Holt	

Erle Stanley Gardner   1889-1970   US   Crime:
also wrote as A A Fair, Charles M Green,   Legal/financial
Carleton Kendrake & Charles J Kenney
www.erlestanleygardner.com   ⚲ Perry Mason, Lawyer

John Dickson Carr	John D MacDonald	Rex Stout
Dashiell Hammett	Lisa Scottoline	Charles Willeford

John Gardner   1926-   Adventure/Thriller
                                              ⚲ Big Herbie Kruger

G

Eric Ambler	Brian Freemantle	Gavin Lyall
Desmond Bagley	Palma Harcourt	J K Mayo
Ian Fleming	Jack Higgins	Julian Rathbone

Lisa Gardner   US   Adventure/Thriller
www.lisagardner.com

Linda Fairstein	Tami Hoag
Elaine Feinstein	Iris Johansen

Alex Garland   1970-   General
www.thaistudents.com/thebeach/alexgarland.html

Matthew Branton	Jack Kerouac	*Betty Trask* 1997 ❀
Douglas Coupland	Tim Lott	
Esther Freud	Timothy Mo	
William Golding	William Sutcliffe	
James Hamilton-Paterson	Paul Theroux	

Jill Gascoine 1937-   General

Lisa Appignanesi   Josephine Hart   Ann Oakley
Sally Beauman   Alice Hoffman   Rosie Thomas

Jonathan Gash 1933-   Crime
is John Grant & also writes as Jonathan Grant   ⚐ *Lovejoy, Antique dealer - London*
Dr Clare Burtonall & Bonn, Doctor & gigolo

William Ardin   Alison Joseph   CWA   1977 ❀
Robert Barnard   Valerie Kershaw
Simon Brett   John Malcolm
Gerald Hammond   Iain Pears
Tim Heald   Charles Spencer
Philip Hook   David Williams

Mike Gayle   Lad Lit
www.hha.com.au/author_mikeg.htm

David Baddiel   Nick Earls   Tony Parsons
Mark Barrowcliffe   Alex George   Kevin Sampson
Matthew Beaumont

Pauline Gedge 1945- NZ   Historical

G Jean M Auel   Simon Scarrow
Christian Jacq   Wilbur Smith

Maggie Gee 1948-   General

Peter Ackroyd   Jenny Diski   Graham Swift
Tracy Chevalier   John Fowles   Rose Tremain

Sue Gee 1947-   General

Kate Bingham   Charlotte Lamb   Parker   1997 ❀
Valerie Blumenthal   Joan Lingard
Anita Brookner   Deborah Moggach
Margaret Forster   Bel Mooney
Marianne Fredriksson   Iris Murdoch
Ivan Klima   Jane Thynne

David Gemmell *1948-*

Fantasy: Epic
Drenai Series

James Barclay	J V Jones	Adam Nichols
Terry Brooks	Paul Kearney	Michael Scott Rohan
Steven Erikson	Valery Leith	Jane Welch
Simon R Green		

Mary Gentle *1956-*

Fantasy: Epic

Storm Constantine	Michael Moorcock	*BSFA* 2000 ✿
Colin Greenland	Tim Powers	
Gwyneth Jones	Philip Pullman	
Ursula K Le Guin	Sheri S Tepper	
China Miéville		

Alex George *1970-*

Lad Lit

Mark Barrowcliffe	Mike Gayle	Tony Parsons
Matthew Beaumont	Nick Hornby	

Elizabeth George *1949-   US*

Crime: Police work - Br
⚲ DCI Thomas Lynley & DS Barbara Havers - London

Brian Battison	Frances Fyfield	Sarah Lovett
Deborah Crombie	Martha Grimes	Barry Maitland
Amanda Cross	P D James	Maureen O'Brien
Marjorie Eccles	Alison Joseph	

Margaret George *1943-   US*

Historical

Christian Jacq	Edith Pargeter	Wilbur Smith
Colleen McCullough	Jean Plaidy	Gore Vidal
Rosalind Miles		

Valerie Georgeson

Historical

Irene Carr	Una Horne	Pamela Oldfield
Philippa Carr	Sheila Jansen	Janet MacLeod Trotter
Elizabeth Gill	Brenda McBryde	

G

Tess Gerritsen   1953-   US   Crime: Medical
www.tessgerritsen.com/

Paul Adam	Michael Crichton	Ken McClure
Paul Carson	Mo Hayder	Michael Palmer
Robin Cook	Tami Hoag	Leah Ruth Robinson

Maggie Gibson   Ire   Humour

Colin Bateman	L McCrossan
Sparkle Hayter	Pauline McLynn

William Gibson   1948-   US   Science Fiction: Near future

Steve Aylett	Rachel Pollack	Vernor Vinge
Eric Brown	Alastair Reynolds	Kurt Vonnegut
Michael Crichton	Lucius Shepard	Connie Willis
Greg Egan	Michael Marshall Smith	David Wingrove

Ellen Gilchrist   1935-   US   General

Joan Brady	Jane Hamilton	Lorrie Moore
William Faulkner	Barbara Kingsolver	Mona Simpson
Connie May Fowler	Sue Miller	Jane Smiley

G

B M Gill   1921-   Crime: Police work - Br
is Barbara Trimble & also writes as Margaret Blake   ⚇ DCI Maybridge

Joanna Cannan	Ruth Dudley Edwards		
Paul Charles	Frances Fyfield	CWA	1984 ✹
Anthea Cohen	P D James		
Brian Cooper	Julian Symons		

Bartholomew Gill   1943-   US   Crime: Police work - foreign
also writes as Mark McGarrity   ⚇ Insp Peter McGarr, Irish Garda

John Brady	Jim Lusby	Eugene McEldowney
Ruth Dudley Edwards	Rory McCormac	Ian Rankin
Hugo Hamilton		

Elizabeth Gill   1950-   Saga
also writes as Elizabeth Hankin

Irene Carr	Valerie Georgeson	Freda Lightfoot
Jean Chapman	Una Horne	Elvi Rhodes
Catherine Cookson	Sheila Jansen	Janet MacLeod Trotter
Clare Curzon		

John Gilstrap   1957-   US   Adventure/Thriller
www.johngilstrap.com

Alice Blanchard	Rochelle Krich	Scott Smith
Peter Blauner	Jefferson Parker	Stuart Woods
Lee Child	Paullina Simons	

Robert Girardi   US   Horror

Jonathan Aycliffe	Richard Matheson
Christopher Fowler	Nicholas Royle

Lesley Glaister   1956-   General

Lisa Appignanesi	Joanna Hines	
Carol Birch	Catherine Merriman	*S Maugham 1991* ✱
Jenny Diski	Julie Myerson	
Louise Doughty	Marina Warner	
Anne Fine	Gillian White	

G

Jenny Glanfield   General

R F Delderfield	Malcolm Macdonald
Winston Graham	Rosamunde Pilcher

Joseph Glass   Crime
🕯 *Dr Susan Shader, Criminal psychiatrist - Chicago*

Patricia D Cornwell	Val McDermid
Nicci French	Kathy Reichs

Don't forget lists of: *Genres * Characters * Literary prizes * Further reading* ☞

Judith Glover   1943-   Saga

Margaret Dickinson   Annie Murray   Judith Saxton
Alison McLeay   Pamela Oldfield   Sally Spencer
Anne Melville   Rosamunde Pilcher

Robert Goddard   1954-   Adventure/Thriller

Lisa Appignanesi   Susanna Kearsley   TGR   1992 ✿
Hilary Bonner   J Robert Lennon
John Buchan   Gemma O'Connor
Ronald Frame   Charles Palliser
Gregory Hall   Tony Strong
Elizabeth Ironside   Charles Todd

Rumer Godden   1907-98   General

Dirk Bogarde   Ruth Prawer Jhabvala   John Masters
Fred D'Aguiar   Elizabeth Jolley   R K Narayan
Elspeth Huxley   Olivia Manning   Vikram Seth

Arthur Golden   1957-   US   General

Jung Chang   Catherine Lim   Amy Tan
Kazuo Ishiguro   Timothy Mo

G

William Golding   1911-93   General

Anthony Burgess   Graham Greene   Booker   1980 ✿
Albert Camus   Thomas Hardy
Fred D'Aguiar   Ernest Hemingway
Umberto Eco   Anthony Trollope
John Fowles   Patrick White
Alex Garland   Marianne Wiggins

Olivia Goldsmith   1954-   US   Glitz & Glamour

Louise Bagshawe   Shirley Conran   Anne Rivers Siddons
Pat Booth   Jude Deveraux   Robyn Sisman
Sandra Brown   Laramie Dunaway   Elizabeth Villars
Alexandra Campbell   Elizabeth Gage   Penny Vincenzi

Terry Goodkind   1948-   US

www.terrygoodkind.com/

Fantasy: Epic

Richard Cypher • Sword of Truth Series

Mark Anthony	David A Drake	Mike Jefferies
Tom Arden	David Eddings	Robert Jordan
Robert Asprin	Kate Elliott	Mickey Zucker Reichert
Mark Chadbourn	Maggie Furey	Jane Welch

Suzanne Goodwin   1916-

also writes as Suzanne Ebel

Saga

Sally Brampton	Josephine Cox	Elvi Rhodes
Brenda Clarke	Margaret Graham	Diana Stainforth

Nadine Gordimer   1923-   SA

General

Margaret Atwood	Pamela Jooste	Booker 1974 ❀
Lynne Reid Banks	Doris Lessing	
André Brink	Paul Scott	
J M Coetzee	Patrick White	
Christopher Hope		

Jane Gordon

General

Jane Asher	Laurie Graham
Mavis Cheek	Robyn Sisman

G

Anne Goring

Historical

Rosemary Aitken	Elizabeth Ann Hill	Susan Sallis
Gloria Cook	Malcolm Ross	E V Thompson

Paula Gosling   1939-   US

also writes as Ainslie Skinner

Crime: Police work - US

Lt Jack Stryker - 'Blackwater Bay', Michigan
Prof Kate Trevorne - Mid West, US

Lilian Jackson Braun	Laurie R King	CWA	1978 ❀
K C Constantine	Jill McGown	CWA	1985 ❀
Deborah Crombie	Jennie Melville		
Clare Francis	Anne Perry		
Martha Grimes	Hillary Waugh		

Eileen Goudge 1950- US General
www.eileengoudge.com

Elizabeth Buchan	Elizabeth Jane Howard
Catherine Fox	Joan Lingard

Judith Gould 1952- US Glitz & Glamour
is Nicholas Bienes & also writes as W R Gallaher

Jilly Cooper	Jayne Ann Krentz	Judith Michael
Elizabeth Gage	Susan Lewis	Caroline Upcher
Judith Krantz	Judith McNaught	

Iris Gower 1939- Wales Saga
Cordwainer Series - South Wales ▪ Sweet Rosie Series ▪ Firebird Series

Jessica Blair	Una Horne	Sally Spencer
Jane Brindle	Catrin Morgan	Grace Thompson
Catrin Collier	Joan O'Neill	Barbara Whitnell
Gloria Cook	Cynthia S Roberts	Barbara Wood

Sue Grafton 1940- US Crime: PI
www.suegrafton.com/ ⚐ Kinsey Millhone - 'Santa Teresa', California

Nevada Barr	Joseph Hansen	Sandra Scoppettone
Edna Buchanan	Martha Lawrence	Alexander McCall Smith
Jan Burke	Laura Lippman	Susan Sussman with
Carol Higgins Clark	Carol O'Connell	Sarajane Avidon

G

Caroline Graham 1931- Crime: Police work - Br
⚐ DCI Tom Barnaby & Sgt Troy - 'Midsomer Worthy'

Joanna Cannan	Veronica Heley	Stella Shepherd
Clare Curzon	Kay Mitchell	Dorothy Simpson
Eileen Dewhurst	Ann Quinton	Sally Spencer
Margaret Duffy	Nicholas Rhea	

Janice Graham General

Robert Edric	Barbara Kingsolver
Alice Hoffman	Robert James Waller

Laurie Graham   1947-   General

Amanda Craig   Elinor Lipman   Yvonne Roberts
Jane Gordon   Helen Muir   Sue Townsend
Sue Limb   Ben Richards   Arabella Weir

Margaret Graham   1945-   Saga

Tessa Barclay   Brenda Clarke   Pamela Pope
Jessica Blair   Suzanne Goodwin   Denise Robertson

Winston Graham   1909-   General

Pat Conroy   Howard Fast   Malcolm Macdonald
A J Cronin   Jenny Glanfield   Claire Rayner
R F Delderfield   Joanna Hines   Jean Stubbs

Winston Graham   1909-   Historical

Rosemary Aitken   June Drummond   Cynthia S Roberts
Anita Burgh   Elizabeth Hawksley   Malcolm Ross
Gloria Cook   Joanna Hines   Nigel Tranter
Alexander Cordell   Jane Aiken Hodge   Kate Tremayne

Ann Granger   1939-   Crime: Police work - Br **G**
also writes as Ann Hulme   ⚡ *Fran Varady, PI - London*
                        Div Supt Alan Markby & Meredith Mitchell - Cotswolds, England

Janie Bolitho   Margaret Duffy   Betty Rowlands
Lizbie Brown   Anthea Fraser   Stella Shepherd
Mary Clayton   J M Gregson   Sally Spencer
Eileen Dewhurst   Hazel Holt   Rebecca Tope

Jonathan Grant   1933-   Historical
is John Grant & also writes as Jonathan Gash

Philippa Gregory   Pamela Pope   Judy Turner
Mary Mackie   Malcolm Ross   T R Wilson
Connie Monk

Don't forget lists of: *Genres * Characters * Literary prizes * Further reading* ☞

Linda Grant 1951- General

Beryl Bainbridge	Mary Morrissy	Higham 1996 ❀
Pat Barker	Anna Quindlen	Orange 2000 ❀
Margaret Forster	Teresa Waugh	

Rob Grant Science Fiction: Humour

Douglas Adams Terry Pratchett Bob Shaw
Harry Harrison Robert Rankin

Lesley Grant-Adamson 1942- Crime

Anthea Cohen P D James Gemma O'Connor
Sarah Dunant Val McDermid Joan Smith
Patricia Highsmith

Robert Graves 1895-1985 General

Lawrence Durrell Valerio Massimo Manfredi Erich Maria Remarque
Howard Fast Olivia Manning Mary Renault
Ross Leckie Allan Massie Gore Vidal
Colleen McCullough Steven Pressfield

G Alasdair Gray 1934- Sco General

Alex Benzie	A L Kennedy	Guardian 1992 ❀
Michel Faber	Agnes Owens	Whitbread 1992 ❀
John Fowles	Iain Sinclair	
James Kelman		

Julia Gray Fantasy: Epic

Sara Douglass Kate Jacoby Adam Nichols
Maggie Furey Guy Gavriel Kay Jane Welch

Muriel Gray 1959- Sco Horror

Richard Bachman Douglas Clegg Bentley Little
Simon Clark Stephen Gallagher Mark Morris

Richard Grayson 1922-
is Richard Grindal

Crime: Historical
🏃 Insp Jean-Paul Gauthier - Belle Epoque, Paris

Laurie R King
Alanna Knight

Deryn Lake
Gillian Linscott

Amy Myers
Anne Perry

Sarah Grazebrook

General

Diana Appleyard
Faith Bleasdale

Alice Thomas Ellis
M J Trow

Sue Welfare

Christine Green 1944-
www.christine-green.com

Crime: Police work - Br
🏃 Kate Kinsella, Nurse
DCI Connor O'Neill & DS Fran Wilson, Police - 'Fowchester'
DI Thomas Rydell & Sgt Denise Caldecote - 'Marston'

Liza Cody
Anthea Cohen

Val McDermid
Andrew Puckett

Claire Rayner

Jane Green

Chick Lit

Mavis Cheek
Helen Fielding
Lisa Jewell

Marian Keyes
Sue Limb

Linda Taylor
Lynne Truss

G

Simon R Green 1955-

Fantasy: Epic

Alan Dean Foster
David Gemmell
Holly Lisle

L E Modesitt Jr
Adam Nichols
Terry Pratchett

Martin Scott
Jane Welch

Graham Greene 1904-91

General

Elizabeth Bowen
Justin Cartwright
William Golding
Pauline Melville

Brian Moore
V S Naipaul
George Orwell
Anthony Powell

Piers Paul Read
Paul Scott
Nicholas Shakespeare
Morris West

Colin Greenland 1954- Science Fiction: Space opera

A A Attanasio
Lois McMaster Bujold
Orson Scott Card
C J Cherryh
Christopher Evans

Alan Dean Foster
Mary Gentle
Peter F Hamilton
Harry Harrison
Brian Stableford

BSFA 1990 ✿
Arthur C Clarke 1991 ✿

Richard Greensted Adventure/Thriller

Mary Higgins Clark
Nicci French

James Kelman
Michael Stewart

Andrew Taylor
Gillian White

D M Greenwood Crime
⚐ Deacon Theodora Braithwaite - Church

Kate Charles
Hazel Holt

John Sherwood
Staynes & Storey

Barbara Whitehead

Philippa Gregory 1954- Historical

Tracy Chevalier
Zoe Fairbairns
Jonathan Grant
Caroline Harvey
Tim Jeal
Alison McLeay

Robin Maxwell
Julian Rathbone
Edward Rutherfurd
Kate Saunders
Reay Tannahill
Sarah Waters

Parker 2002 ✿

G

Susanna Gregory 1958- Crime: Historical
⚐ Matthew Bartholomew - C14th England

Paul Doherty
Michael Jecks
Bernard Knight

Edward Marston
Viviane Moore
Ian Morson

Ellis Peters
Candace Robb
Kate Sedley

J M Gregson Crime: Police work - Br
also writes as Jim Gregson
⚐ DI Percy Peach - East Lancashire
Det Lambert & Det Hook

Jeffrey Ashford
Janie Bolitho
Ann Granger

Alan Hunter
Kay Mitchell
Ann Quinton

Nicholas Rhea
Sally Spencer

Andrew Greig   1951-   Sco   General

H E Bates   Carl MacDougall   Alan Spence
Sebastian Faulks   Andrew O'Hagan   Jane Thynne

Kate Grenville   1950-   Aus   General
www.users.bigpond.com/kgrenville/

Suzanne Berne   Barbara Kingsolver | Orange | 2001 ❀ |
Candida Crewe   Jane Smiley

Patricia Grey   Saga
                                                                    London

Anne Bennett   Harry Cole   Elizabeth Lord
Philip Boast   Sara Fraser   Elizabeth Waite
Patricia Burns   Anna King   Jeanne Whitmee

W E B Griffin   1929-   US   War: Modern
is William E Butterworth III & also writes as Alex Baldwin
www.nmark.com/webgriffin/   Series: Corps • Badge of Honour • Brotherhood of War

Harold Coyle   Graham Hurley   Derek Robinson
P T Deutermann   Robert Jackson   Terence Strong
John Harris   Matthew Reilly

G

W E B Griffin   1929-   US   Crime: Police work - US
is William E Butterworth III & also writes as Alex Baldwin   Philadelphia
www.nmark.com/webgriffin/

Michael Connelly   Ed McBain   Ridley Pearson
Donald Harstad   Margaret Maron   Joseph Wambaugh

Martha Grimes   1931-   US   Crime: Police work - Br
www.marthagrimes.com/   ⚡ DCI Richard Jury - London

Deborah Crombie   Janet Harward   Maureen O'Brien
Elizabeth George   Gillian Linscott   Dorothy L Sayers
Paula Gosling   Kay Mitchell   Charles Todd

Don't forget lists of: *Genres * Characters * Literary prizes * Further reading* ☞

Jon Courtenay Grimwood
www.j-cg.co.uk
Science Fiction: Near future

Alexander Besher	John Meaney	Bruce Sterling
Pat Cadigan	Jeff Noon	Tad Williams
Greg Egan	Rachel Pollack	David Wingrove
Ian McDonald	Neal Stephenson	

John Grisham   1955-   US
www.jgrisham.com
Crime: Legal/financial

Jonathan Davies	Stephen Frey	John McLaren
Linda Davies	Philip Friedman	Christopher Reich
Rankin Davis	Craig Holden	Lisa Scottoline
Alan M Dershowitz	John T Lescroart	Sheldon Siegel

David Grossman   1954-   Isr
General

Gabriel Garcia Márquez	Amos Oz	Isaac Bashevis Singer
Primo Levi	Salman Rushdie	

Diane Guest   US
Horror

G

Virginia Andrews	Jenny Jones	Stephen King
Louise Brindley	Judith Kelman	Barbara Michaels
James Herbert		

Sandra Gulland
Historical

Ross King	Norah Lofts	Jean Plaidy
Rosalind Laker	Robin Maxwell	

Jeff Gulvin   1962-
Crime: Police work - Br
⚹ DCI Aden Vanner - London

Jake Arnott	Quintin Jardine	R D Wingfield
Philip Caveney	Jerry Raine	

Don't forget lists of: *Genres * Characters * Literary prizes * Further reading* ☞

Abdulrazak Gurnah   1948-   Zan   General

Joseph Conrad   Rohinton Mistry   Paul Theroux
Ruth Prawer Jhabvala V S Naipaul

David Guterson   1956-   US   General

Jim Crace   Charles Frazier   Harper Lee
Pete Dexter   Peter Hoeg   Cormac McCarthy
Nicholas Evans   Stuart M Kaminsky   Jacquelyn Mitchard
Richard Ford   Michael Kimball   Jane Urquhart

Peter Guttridge   1951-   Crime: Humour
www.peterguttridge.com   ⚐ Nick Madrid, Journalist

Colin Bateman   Carl Hiaasen   Laurence Shames
Marc Blake   Claire McNab   Charles Spencer
John Burns   Chris Niles

Arthur Hailey   1920-   Can   Adventure/Thriller

Jeffrey Archer   Harold Robbins   Wilbur Smith
Richard Condon   Sidney Sheldon   Morris West
Dominick Dunne

G
H

Joe Haldeman   1943-   US   Science Fiction: Space opera

Brian W Aldiss   Orson Scott Card   Lucius Shepard
Poul Anderson   Harry Harrison   Robert Silverberg
J G Ballard   Robert A Heinlein   Dan Simmons

Gregory Hall   1948-   Crime: Psychological

Robert Goddard   Mark Hebden   Andrew Taylor
Juliet Hebden   Elizabeth Ironside

James Hall   1947-   US   Crime: PI
www.jameswhall.com/   ⚐ Thorn - Florida

Edna Buchanan   Robert Ferrigno   Laurence Shames
James Lee Burke   John D MacDonald   Les Standiford
Lee Child   Geoffrey Norman

Patricia Hall 1940-
is Maureen O'Connor

Crime: Police work - Br
♁ DCI Michael Thackeray & Laura Ackroyd, Journalist - 'Bradfield', Yorkshire

Robert Barnard
Pauline Bell
Ken Bruen
Mark Burnell

Joanna Cannan
Paul Charles
Ann Cleeves

Marjorie Eccles
Stewart Pawson
Barbara Whitehead

Rodney Hall 1935- Aus
General

Peter Carey
Robert Drewe

Thomas Keneally
David Malouf

Patrick White
Tim Winton

Barbara Hambly 1951- US
Fantasy
www.barbarahambly.com/

Marion Zimmer Bradley
C J Cherryh
Louise Cooper
Raymond E Feist

Mercedes Lackey
Anne McCaffrey
Julian May
Elizabeth Moon

Tim Powers
Melanie Rawn
Sheri S Tepper

Hugo Hamilton 1953- Ire
Crime: Police work - foreign
♁ Pat Coyne

John Brady
Bartholomew Gill

Jim Lusby
Rory McCormac

Eugene McEldowney

H Jane Hamilton 1957- US
General

Andre Dubus
Catherine Dunne
Ellen Gilchrist
Barbara Kingsolver

Shena Mackay
Sue Miller
Alice Munro
Ann Patchett

Anita Shreve
Mona Simpson
Jane Smiley

Julia Hamilton 1956-
Aga saga

Jane Asher
Katie Fforde

Catherine Fox
Hazel Hucker

Catherine Merriman

Don't forget lists of: *Genres * Characters * Literary prizes * Further reading*☞

Laurell K Hamilton   US   Horror
www.laurellkhamilton.org   ⚘ Anita Blake, Necromancer & crime investigator

Nancy Collins   Kim Newman   Judith Tarr
Jeanne Kalogridis   Anne Rice   Melanie Tem
Holly Lisle   Steven Spruill

Peter F Hamilton   1960-   Science Fiction: Space opera
www.peterhamilton.com   Greg Mandell Series ▪ Night Dawn Trilogy

Iain M Banks   C J Cherryh   Larry Niven
Gregory Benford   Colin Greenland   Alastair Reynolds
Lois McMaster Bujold   Robert A Heinlein   Dan Simmons

Ruth Hamilton   Saga
www.ruthhamilton.co.uk   Liverpool & Lancashire

Lyn Andrews   Katie Flynn   Maureen Lee
Rita Bradshaw   June Francis   Freda Lightfoot
Alexandra Connor   Meg Henderson   Elizabeth Murphy
Emma Dally   Audrey Howard   Margaret Thornton

Steve Hamilton   1961-   US   Crime: PI
www.authorstevehamilton.com   ⚘ Alex McKnight - 'Paradise', Michigan

Stephen Dobyns   Michael McGarrity   Les Standiford
Loren D Estleman   Walter Mosley   John Straley
Elmore Leonard   Sam Reaves   Robert K Tanenbaum

James Hamilton-Paterson   1941-   General

John Banville   Timothy Mo
Joseph Conrad   William Rivière   Whitbread   1989 ❂
Louis de Bernières   Nicholas Shakespeare
Alex Garland

Dashiell Hammett   1894-1961   US   Crime: PI
                ⚘ Sam Spade - San Francisco ▪ The Continental Op - San Francisco

James Hadley Chase   Stuart M Kaminsky   Sam Reaves
Loren D Estleman   Ross Macdonald   Andrew Vachss
Erle Stanley Gardner   Walter Mosley

H

Gerald Hammond   1926-   Crime

also writes as Arthur Douglas   ⚐ *Keith Calder, Gunsmith* ⎱ *Scottish Borders*
                                              John Cunningham, Kennel owner ⎰

M C Beaton   Joyce Holms   John Sherwood
Jonathan Gash   Bill Knox   Margaret Yorke
Tim Heald

Joseph Hansen   1923-   US   Crime: PI

                                  ⚐ *Dave Brandstetter, Insurance investigator - California*

Loren D Estleman   Ross Macdonald   Sara Paretsky
Sue Grafton   Marcia Muller   Don Winslow

Maeve Haran   1950-   General

Catherine Alliott   Claire Calman   Kathleen Rowntree
Charlotte Bingham   Sarah Harrison   Diana Stainforth
Sally Brampton   Ann Oakley

Palma Harcourt   Adventure/Thriller

also writes as John Penn

Ted Allbeury   Clive Egleton   John Gardner
Eric Ambler   Ken Follett   Julian Rathbone
Evelyn Anthony   Colin Forbes

H

Duncan Harding   1926-   Sea: Modern

also writes as Leo Kessler & Charles Whiting

Gerry Carroll   Bart Davis   Alexander Fullerton
James Cobb   Alan Evans   Peter Tonkin

Paul Harding   Crime: Historical

is Paul Doherty & also writes as Anna Apostolou,   ⚐ *Sir John Cranston &*
Michael Clynes & P C Doherty   *Brother Athelstan - C14th London*

Fiona Buckley   Bernard Knight   Ellis Peters
Kate Charles   Viviane Moore   Candace Robb
Alys Clare   Ian Morson   Peter Tremayne
Michael Jecks

Thomas Hardy   1840-1928   General

Melvyn Bragg   William Golding   Adam Thorpe
John Fowles   D H Lawrence   Edith Wharton

Andrew Harman   1964-   Fantasy: Humour

Robert Asprin   Tom Holt   Robert Rankin
Craig Shaw Gardner   Terry Pratchett   Martin Scott

Elizabeth Harris   General

Joan Aiken   Dinah Lampitt
Barbara Erskine   Barbara Michaels

Joanne Harris   1974-   General

Emma Donoghue   Hilary Mantel   Barbara Trapido
Lucy Ellman   Michele Roberts   Salley Vickers
Alice Hoffman   Polly Samson   Barbara Wood

John Harris   1916-91   Adventure/Thriller
also wrote as Mark Hebden & Max Hennessy

Jon Cleary   Jack Higgins   Julian Rathbone
James Follett   A E Langsford

John Harris   1916-91   War: Modern **H**
also wrote as Mark Hebden & Max Hennessy

W E B Griffin   Leo Kessler   Derek Robinson
Max Hennessy   Nicholas Monsarrat   Charles Whiting
Robert Jackson

Robert Harris   1957-   Adventure/Thriller

Eric Ambler   Robert Littell   *TGR*   1993 ✸
Brendan Dubois   Glenn Meade
David Ignatius   Henry Porter
Greg Iles   Michael Shea
Donald James   Martin Cruz Smith
Joseph Kanon   Barnaby Williams

Sarah Harris   1967-   Chick Lit

Geraldine Bedell   Chris Manby   Claire Naylor
Martina Devlin   Jill Mansell   Adele Parks
Sarah Harvey

Steve Harris   1954-   Horror

Campbell Black   Joe Donnelly   Peter James
David Bowker   Stephen Gallagher   Phil Rickman
Ramsey Campbell   James Herbert   John Saul

Thomas Harris   1940-   US   Adventure/Thriller: Modern
www.randomhouse.com/features/thomasharris/hannibal.html

⚗ Dr Hannibal Lecter, Serial Killer

Thomas H Cook   Andrew Klavan   John Sandford
Stephen Dobyns   David Lindsey   Steven Spruill
John Douglas   Phillip M Margolin   Boston Teran
Joy Fielding   Chris Petit   Tim Willocks

Colin Harrison   1960-   US   Adventure/Thriller
www.bookreporter.com/authors/au-harrison-colin.asp

Jeffrey Archer   Phillip M Margolin   Scott Turow
Paul Kilduff   Lawrence Sanders   Tom Wolfe
Michael Kimball

H   Harry Harrison   1925-   US   Science Fiction: Humour
www.harryharrison.com

Rob Grant   Robert A Heinlein   Robert Rankin
Colin Greenland   Tom Holt   Martin Scott
Joe Haldeman   Larry Niven   Bob Shaw

Jim Harrison   1937-   US   General

Jim Crace   Richard Ford   David Mamet
Pete Dexter   Cormac McCarthy   Peter Matthiessen
Barbara Esstman   Thomas McGuane   Larry Watson
Nicholas Evans   Larry McMurtry

Ray Harrison   1928-   Crime: Historical
† Sgt Bragg & PC Morton - C19th London

Alanna Knight   Amy Myers   Norman Russell
Deryn Lake   Anne Perry   Julian Symons
Gillian Linscott   Roberta Rogow   M J Trow
Peter Lovesey   Kate Ross

Sarah Harrison   1946-   General

Charlotte Bingham   Susan Howatch   Jill Roe
Rose Boucheron   Susan Isaacs   Diana Saville
Anna Davis   Andrea Newman   Grace Wynne-Jones
Maeve Haran   Wendy Perriam

Stuart Harrison   Adventure/Thriller

Alice Blanchard   Tami Hoag   Grant Stewart
Harlan Coben   Cormac McCarthy   Stuart Woods
Nicholas Evans

Cynthia Harrod-Eagles   1948-   Historical
www.twbooks.co.uk/authors/cheagles.html   *Morland Dynasty*

Evelyn Anthony   Victoria Holt   *Parker   1993* ✿
Pamela Belle   Rosalind Laker
Philippa Carr   Reay Tannahill
Emma Drummond   E V Thompson
Pamela Hill   Patricia Wendorf

H

Cynthia Harrod-Eagles   1948-   Crime: Police work - Br
www.twbooks.co.uk/authors/cheagles.html   *† DI Bill Slider - London*

Gwendoline Butler   Barry Maitland
Deborah Crombie   Alan Scholefield

Eric L Harry   1958-   US   War: Modern
www.eharry.com

Tom Clancy   Max Hennessy
James Cobb   Johnny 'Two Combs' Howard

Lilian Harry   1939-   *Saga*
also writes as Donna Baker   Portsmouth

Helen Carey   Margaret Mayhew   Victor Pemberton
Elizabeth Daish   Mary Minton   Elizabeth Warne
Rosemary Enright

Donald Harstad   US   Crime: Police work - US
                          ⋏ *Dep Sheriff Carl Houseman - Nation County, Iowa*

Alice Blanchard   J A Jance   Scott Smith
K C Constantine   Ed McBain   Boston Teran
W E B Griffin   Michael McGarrity   Hillary Waugh
Tony Hillerman   Ridley Pearson   Eric Wright

Ellen Hart   1949-   US   *Crime*
www.ellenhart.com   ⋏ *Jane Lawless, Restaurateur - Minneapolis*

Stella Duffy   Claire McNab   Manda Scott
Alma Fritchley   Margaret Maron   Mary Wings
Val McDermid   Carol O'Connell

Josephine Hart   1942-   Ire   *General*

Lisa Appignanesi   Andrea Newman   Ann Oakley
Candida Clark   Hilary Norman   Rosie Thomas
Jill Gascoine

H Caroline Harvey   1943-   *Historical*
is Joanna Trollope

Philippa Carr   Victoria Holt
Philippa Gregory   Judith Lennox

Jack Harvey   1960-   Sco   *Adventure/Thriller*
also writes as Ian Rankin

Christopher Brookmyre   Frank Lean   Terence Strong
Graham Hurley   David Martin   Douglas Terman

John Harvey   *1938-*

www.mellotone.co.uk/

Crime: Police work - Br

🏃 *DI Charlie Resnick - Nottingham*

David Armstrong	Graham Hurley	*Higham* 1979 ✿
Robert Barnard	Jim Lusby	
Brian Battison	William McIlvanney	
Charlotte Carter	Chris Paling	
John Creasey	Nicholas Royle	
Reginald Hill	Sally Spencer	

Sarah Harvey

Chick Lit

Catherine Alliott	Sarah Harris	Cathy Kelly
Victoria Colby	Christina Jones	Victoria Routledge

Janet Harward

Crime: Police work - Br

🏃 *DI Josephine Blake - Devon & Birmingham*

Janie Bolitho	Marjorie Eccles	H R F Keating
W J Burley	Kate Ellis	Ngaio Marsh
Judith Cutler	Martha Grimes	Gladys Mitchell

Kate Hatfield

also writes as Daphne Wright

General

Zoe Fairbairns	Andrea Newman	Mary Wesley
Angela Lambert	Kate Saunders	

Roy Hattersley   *1932-*

General **H**

Melvyn Bragg	John Mortimer	Tony Warren
Meg Hutchinson	Annie Murray	

Anne Haverty   *Ire*

Historical

Tracy Chevalier	Sheri Holman
Emma Donoghue	Sarah Waters

Don't forget lists of: *Genres * Characters * Literary prizes * Further reading* ☞

James Hawes   1960-   Wales   Humour

Christopher Brookmyre   Carl Hiaasen   Tom Sharpe
Jeremy Cameron   Charles Higson   Grant Stewart
Ben Elton   John McCabe   Louisa Young
Kinky Friedman   Patrick McCabe

Elizabeth Hawksley   Historical

Pamela Evans   Georgette Heyer
Winston Graham   Jane Aiken Hodge

Humphrey Hawksley   Adventure/Thriller
www.hhawksley.co.uk

James Clavell   Ken Follett   Alan Judd
Gavin Esler   Bryan Forbes   Tim Sebastian

Mo Hayder   Crime: Psychological
                                                  ⚐ DI Jack Caffery - London

John Connolly   Tess Gerritsen   Michael Palmer
Jeffery Deaver   Jonathan Kellerman   James Patterson

Elizabeth Haydon   US   Fantasy: Epic
www.elizabethhaydon.com   Rhapsody Trilogy

Steven Brust   Alan Dean Foster   Juliet E McKenna
David Eddings   Anne McCaffrey

Karen Hayes   General
also writes as Karen Nelson

Marika Cobbold   Rebecca Shaw   Willow Tickell
Karen Nelson   Mary Sheepshanks   Joanna Trollope
Jill Roe   Peta Tayler

H

Don't forget lists of: *Genres * Characters * Literary prizes * Further reading* ☞

Sparkle Hayter 1958- Can

Crime: Humour

http://server108.hypermart.net/sparklevhayter/index.html

≛ Robin Hudson, TV journalist - New York

Rita Mae Brown
Edna Buchanan
Liz Evans
Kinky Friedman
Maggie Gibson

Lauren Henderson
Susan Isaacs
Pauline McLynn
Lindsay Maracotta

Susan Sussman with
  Sarajane Avidon
Scarlett Thomas
Valerie Wilson Wesley

Tim Heald 1944-

Crime: Humour

also writes as David Lancaster

≛ Simon Bognor, Board of Trade Inspector

Simon Brett
Ruth Dudley Edwards

Jonathan Gash
Gerald Hammond

Juliet Hebden

Crime: Police work - foreign

≛ Insp Evariste Pel - Burgundy, France

Nicolas Freeling
Gregory Hall
Mark Hebden
J Robert Janes

Roderic Jeffries
H R F Keating
Donna Leon

Magdalen Nabb
Georges Simenon
Janwillem van de Wetering

Mark Hebden 1916-91

Crime: Police work - foreign

was John Harris & also wrote as Max Hennessy

≛ Insp Evariste Pel - Burgundy, France

Nicolas Freeling
Gregory Hall
Juliet Hebden
J Robert Janes

Roderic Jeffries
H R F Keating
Donna Leon

Magdalen Nabb
Georges Simenon
Janwillem Van De Wetering

H

Frances Hegarty 1948-

Crime: Psychological

also writes as Frances Fyfield

Jenny Diski
Nicci French

Jonathan Kellerman
Judith Kelman

Gloria Murphy
Barbara Vine

Robert A Heinlein 1907-88 US Science Fiction: Space & Time
www.nitrosyncretic.com/rah

Brian W Aldiss
Isaac Asimov
John Barnes
Ray Bradbury

Arthur C Clarke
Philip K Dick
Joe Haldeman
Peter F Hamilton

Harry Harrison
Jules Verne
John Wyndham

Veronica Heley 1933- Crime
⚥ Ellie Quick

Simon Brett
Caroline Graham

Marianne MacDonald
Annette Roome

Betty Rowlands
Alexander McCall Smith

Joseph Heller 1923-99 US General

Saul Bellow
Tibor Fischer
George MacDonald Fraser
John Irving

Norman Mailer
Tim O'Brien
Thomas Pynchon
Tom Robbins

Derek Robinson
Philip Roth
Leslie Thomas

Keith Heller 1949- Crime: Historical
⚥ George Man - C18th England

Bruce Alexander
Stephanie Barron
Gwendoline Butler

Deryn Lake
Janet Laurence

Margaret Lawrence
Hannah March

H Ernest Hemingway 1898-1961 US General
www.hemingway.org

Truman Capote
Raymond Carver
Joseph Conrad
F Scott Fitzgerald

William Golding
Norman Mailer
Nevil Shute
John Steinbeck

William Styron
Paul Theroux
Paul Watkins

Lauren Henderson 1966- Crime: PI
⚥ Sam Jones, Sculptress - London

Linda Barnes
Tim Cockey
Liza Cody
Alma Fritchley

Sparkle Hayter
Irene Lin-Chandler
Pauline McLynn
Susan Moody

Mike Phillips
Gillian Slovo
Scarlett Thomas
Stella Whitelaw

Meg Henderson *Saga*

Margaret Thomson Davis
Ruth Hamilton

Evelyn Hood
Meg Hutchinson

Gilda O'Neill
Frances Paige

Vicki Hendricks   *1951-*   US *Crime*
www.vickihendricks.com *Miami*

Anthony Bourdain
Tim Dorsey

Carl Hiaasen
Kem Nunn

Max Hennessy   *1916-91* *War: Modern*
was John Harris & also wrote as Mark Hebden

Alan Evans
Alexander Fullerton
John Harris

Eric L Harry
Johnny 'Two Combs' Howard
Philip McCutchan

Derek Robinson
John Winton

Philip Hensher *General*

Jeffrey Archer
William Boyd
Raymond Carver
Michael Dobbs

Adam Mars-Jones
Peter Rawlinson
Tom Sharpe

S Maugham   1997 ❀

Brian Herbert   *1947-*   US   *Science Fiction: Space opera*

Brian W Aldiss
David Brin
Orson Scott Card

Raymond E Feist
Frank Herbert

Kristine Kathryn Rusch
Jack Vance

H

Frank Herbert   *1920-86*   US   *Science Fiction: Space opera*

Brian W Aldiss
J G Ballard
David Brin

Brian Herbert
Ursula K Le Guin
Larry Niven

Adam Roberts
Sheri S Tepper
Jack Vance

James Herbert *1943-* *Horror*

Richard Bachman
Campbell Black
Stephen Gallagher
Diane Guest
Steve Harris
Peter James
Jenny Jones
Stephen Laws
Bentley Little
Phil Rickman
Steven Spruill
Bernard Taylor

Richard Herman *1939-* *US* *Adventure/Thriller*

Larry Bond
Dale Brown
James Cobb
Stephen Coonts
Graham Hurley
John Nichol
Justin Scott
Douglas Terman
James Thayer

Georgette Heyer *1903-74* *Crime*

Supt Hannasyde & DI Hemingway

Edmund Crispin
Gladys Mitchell
David Roberts
Dorothy L Sayers
Patricia Wentworth

Georgette Heyer *1903-74* *Historical*

Jane Austen
Elizabeth Chadwick
Marion Chesney
Howard Fast
Elizabeth Hawksley
Jane Aiken Hodge
Rosalind Laker
Norah Lofts
Diana Norman
Amanda Quick
Kate Ross

H

Carl Hiaasen *1953-* *US* *Crime: Humour*

www.carlhiaasen.com/

Florida

Marc Blake
Anthony Bourdain
Christopher Brookmyre
Bill Fitzhugh
Peter Guttridge
James Hawes
Vicki Hendricks
Douglas Lindsay
John B Spencer
Doug J Swanson
Donald E Westlake
Don Winslow

CWA *1992*

George V Higgins *1939-99* *US* *Crime*

New England

Lorenzo Carcaterra
James Ellroy
Elmore Leonard
Mario Puzo
John B Spencer
Jim Thompson
Charles Willeford

Jack Higgins *1929-*
is Harry Patterson

Adventure/Thriller

♔ *Sean Dillon*

Desmond Bagley	John Harris	James Thayer
Keith Baker	Duncan Kyle	Craig Thomas
Harold Coyle	Stephen Leather	Glover Wright
John Gardner		

Domini Highsmith *1942-*
also writes as Domini Wiles

Historical

Barbara Erskine	Dinah Lampitt	Anya Seton
Jane Aiken Hodge	Claire Lorrimer	

Patricia Highsmith *1921-95* US

Crime: *Psychological*

♔ *Tom Ripley - London*

Keith Baker	Douglas Kennedy	Josephine Tey
Anthea Cohen	Simon Shaw	Stuart Woods
Lesley Grant-Adamson	Julian Symons	

Lynn S Hightower *1956-* US

Crime: *Police work - US*

♔ *Det Sonora Blair - Cincinnati*

Patricia D Cornwell	Sarah Lovett	Sandra Scoppettone
Tami Hoag	Kathy Reichs	Robert W Walker
Rochelle Krich		

Charles Higson *1958-*

Humour H

Ben Elton	James Hawes
Stephen Fry	John McCabe

Elizabeth Ann Hill

Saga

Rosemary Aitken	Connie Monk	Eileen Stafford
Gloria Cook	Malcolm Ross	E V Thompson
Anne Goring	Susan Sallis	Elizabeth Warne
Elizabeth Jeffrey		

Pamela Hill   1920-   Sco   *Historical*
also writes as Sharon Fiske

Philippa Carr	Rosalind Laker	Edith Pargeter
Tracy Chevalier	Norah Lofts	Maureen Peters
Cynthia Harrod-Eagles		

Reginald Hill   1936-   *Crime:* Police work - Br
also writes as Patrick Ruell & Charles Underhill
www.randomhouse.com/features/reghill/

⚐ DS Pascoe & DI Dalziel - Yorkshire
Joe Sixsmith, PI - Luton

John Baker	Bill Knox		
Robert Barnard	Frank Lean	CWA	1990 ❀
Raymond Flynn	Emma Page		
John Harvey	Frank Palmer		
Graham Hurley	Aline Templeton		
Bill James	Hillary Waugh		

Susan Hill   1942-   *General*

Joan Aiken	Penelope Lively		
Jane Brindle	Charles Palliser	Mail	1972 ❀
Daphne Du Maurier	Ann Patchett	Whitbread	1972 ❀
Elaine Feinstein	Kate Pullinger		
Jane Gardam	William Trevor		
Jennifer Johnston	Teresa Waugh		

Tony Hillerman   1925-   US   *Crime:* Police work - US
⚐ Jim Chee & Joe Leaphorn - Navajo Reservation, Arizona

Nevada Barr	Donald Harstad	Michael McGarrity
James Lee Burke	J A Jance	Alexander McCall Smith
Robert Ferrigno	Ed McBain	John Straley
Joseph Finder	Sharyn McCrumb	Christopher West

Joanna Hines   1949-   *Adventure/Thriller:* Psychological

Frances Fyfield	Minette Walters
Lesley Glaister	Gillian White

Joanna Hines   1949-   *Historical*

Daphne Du Maurier	Winston Graham	Susanna Kearsley

Tami Hoag   1959-   US   Crime: Psychological

Patricia D Cornwell   Lynn S Hightower   Rochelle Krich
Lisa Gardner   Gwen Hunter   James Patterson
Tess Gerritsen   Stephen Hunter   Nancy Taylor Rosenberg
Stuart Harrison   Iris Johansen   Scott Smith

Robin Hobb   1952-   US   Fantasy: Epic
is Megan Lindholm
www.robinhobbonline.com

Peter S Beagle   Caiseal Mor   Jane Welch
Guy Gavriel Kay   Jennifer Roberson   Tad Williams
Katherine Kurtz   Kristine Kathryn Rusch Philip G Williamson
Juliet Marillier   Jan Siegel

Jane Aiken Hodge   1917-   Historical

June Drummond   Georgette Heyer   Barbara Michaels
Winston Graham   Domini Highsmith   Jean Plaidy
Elizabeth Hawksley   Victoria Holt

Peter Hoeg   1957-   Den   General

Kerstin Ekman   Henning Mankell   CWA   1994 ✿
Marianne Fredriksson   Haruki Murakami
Jostein Gaarder   Annie Proulx
David Guterson   Jane Smiley
Stuart M Kaminsky   Jane Urquhart

H

Alice Hoffman   1952-   US   General
www.alicehoffman.com

Judy Budnitz   Jill Gascoine   Carson McCullers
Michael Collins   Janice Graham   Jacquelyn Mitchard
Candida Crewe   Joanne Harris   Mona Simpson
Nicci French   Janette Turner Hospital Nicholas Sparks

Don't forget lists of: *Genres * Characters * Literary prizes * Further reading* ☞

Craig Holden US — Crime: Legal/financial

www.craigholden.com

David Baldacci
E L Doctorow

John Grisham
Lisa Scottoline

Scott Turow

Wendy Holden — Chick Lit

Catherine Alliott
Faith Bleasdale
Claire Calman
Francesca Clementis

Amy Jenkins
Lisa Jewell
L McCrossan
Melissa Nathan

Yvonne Roberts
Daisy Waugh
Sue Welfare
Isabel Wolff

Robert Holdstock 1948- — Fantasy: Literary

also writes as Robert Black, Chris Carlsen & Robert Faulcon
www.mythago.tuatha.org/main.html

Peter S Beagle
Marion Zimmer Bradley
Ellen Datlow
Charles de Lint
Graham Joyce

Guy Gavriel Kay
Tim Powers
Jan Siegel
Judith Tarr
Gene Wolfe

BSFA	1984 ❀
BSFA	1988 ❀

Tom Holland 1947- — Horror

Poppy Z Brite
Nancy Collins
Brian Lumley

Kim Newman
Anne Rice

Iain Sinclair
S P Somtow

H

Helen Hollick — Historical
Arthurian Trilogy

Marion Zimmer Bradley
Barbara Erskine

Stephen R Lawhead
Rosalind Miles

Sharon Penman
Mary Stewart

Alan Hollinghurst 1954- — General

Michael Carson
Patrick Gale
Francis King

Adam Mars-Jones
Armistead Maupin
Edmund White

S Maugham	1989 ❀
Black	1994 ❀

Sheri Holman   US   Historical

David Dabydeen   Ross King   Sarah Waters
Anne Haverty   Rose Tremain

Joyce Holms   Sco   Crime: PI
Fizz Fitzgerald & Tam Buchanan, Legal student & lawyer - Edinburgh

M C Beaton   Quintin Jardine   Betty Rowlands
Simon Brett   Bill Knox   Scarlett Thomas
Liz Evans   Janet Laurence   Rebecca Tope
Gerald Hammond   M R D Meek   Stella Whitelaw

Hazel Holt   1928-   Crime: PI
Sheila Malory - 'Taviscombe'

Lizbie Brown   Marianne MacDonald   Dorothy Simpson
Mary Clayton   Betty Rowlands   Staynes & Storey
Ann Granger   John Sherwood   Rebecca Tope
D M Greenwood

Tom Holt   1961-   Humour

H E Bates   Garrison Keillor   Peter Tinniswood
E F Benson   David Nobbs   Sue Townsend
Colin Douglas   Tom Sharpe   P G Wodehouse

Tom Holt   1961-   Fantasy: Humour

H

Douglas Adams   Craig Shaw Gardner   Terry Pratchett
Robert Asprin   Andrew Harman   Robert Rankin
L Sprague de Camp   Harry Harrison   Martin Scott
George MacDonald Fraser Nick Nielsen   Bob Shaw

Victoria Holt   1906-93   Historical
also wrote as Philippa Carr & Jean Plaidy

Evelyn Anthony   Caroline Harvey   Norah Lofts
Catherine Coulter   Jane Aiken Hodge   Claire Lorrimer
Emma Drummond   Harriet Hudson   Anya Seton
Cynthia Harrod-Eagles   Sara Hylton   Daoma Winston

Evelyn Hood   *1936-*   *Sco*   *Saga*
Scotland

Jay Allerton	Gwen Kirkwood	Alison Skelton
Margaret Thomson Davis	Freda Lightfoot	Linda Sole
Inga Dunbar	Isobel Neill	Mary Withall
Meg Henderson	Malcolm Ross	Valerie Wood

Philip Hook   *Adventure/Thriller*
Art world

William Ardin	Jonathan Gash	John Malcolm
Frances Galleymore	Graham Hurley	Iain Pears

Christopher Hope   *1944-*   *SA*   *General*

William Boyd	Nadine Gordimer	*Higham*	*1981* ❀
André Brink	Pamela Jooste	*Whitbread*	*1984* ❀
Justin Cartwright	Amos Oz		
J M Coetzee			

Nick Hornby   *1957-*   *Lad Lit*
www.penguin.co.uk/static/packages/uk/articles/hornby

David Baddiel	Ardal O'Hanlon	*W H Smith* *2001* ❀
Mark Barrowcliffe	Ben Richards	
Alex George	Kevin Sampson	
Gordon Legge	Polly Samson	
Tim Lott	William Sutcliffe	
John McCabe	Sean Thomas	

H

Una Horne   *Saga*
NE England

Rita Bradshaw	Joan Eadith	Sheila Jansen
Irene Carr	Valerie Georgeson	Brenda McBryde
Jean Chapman	Elizabeth Gill	Wendy Robertson
Catherine Cookson	Iris Gower	Janet MacLeod Trotter

William Horwood   *1944-*   *Fantasy: Epic*

Richard Adams	Joyce Stranger
Nicholas Evans	Henry Williamson

Janette Turner Hospital   1942-   Aus   General

Alice Hoffman
Elizabeth Jolley
Thomas Keneally

David Malouf
Toni Morrison

Michele Roberts
Salman Rushdie

Audrey Howard   1929-   Saga
Liverpool & Lancashire

Anne Baker
Catherine Cookson
Doreen Edwards
Katie Flynn
Helen Forrester
Ruth Hamilton

Anna Jacobs
Marie Joseph
Audrey Reimann
Arabella Seymour
Sue Sully
Valerie Wood

Parker   1988 ✹

Elizabeth Jane Howard   1923-   General

Jane Asher
Rachel Billington
Rose Boucheron
Victoria Clayton

Kathleen Conlon
Catherine Fox
Eileen Goudge
Angela Lambert

Charlotte Moore
Anna Quindlen
Ann Swinfen
Elizabeth Tettmar

Johnny 'Two Combs' Howard   1960-   War: Modern

Eric L Harry
Max Hennessy

David Mason
John Nichol

Chris Ryan

Richard Howard   War: Historical   H
⚔ Sgt Alain Lausard - C18th French Dragoon ▪ Bonaparte Series

Bernard Cornwell
Garry Douglas

Philip McCutchan
Allan Mallinson

Patrick O'Brian

Susan Howatch   1940-   Saga
Church of England Series

Daphne Du Maurier
Zoe Fairbairns
Catherine Fox
Sarah Harrison

Susanna Kearsley
M R O'Donnell
Jean Stubbs

Sue Sully
Kate Tremayne
Anthony Trollope

Hazel Hucker   1937-   *Aga Saga*

Anne Atkins	Julia Hamilton	Rebecca Shaw
Anna Barrie	Erica James	Mary Sheepshanks
Lucy Clare	Julia Lisle	Madeleine Wickham
Kate Fielding		

Christopher Hudson   1946-   *General*

Dirk Bogarde	M M Kaye	W Somerset Maugham
Louis de Bernières	Francis King	

Harriet Hudson   *Saga*
also writes as Amy Myers

Betty Burton	Margaret Pemberton	Patricia Wendorf
Elizabeth Daish	Caroline Stickland	Audrey Willsher
Victoria Holt	Alison Stuart	Sally Worboyes
Sara Hylton		

Barry Hughart   1934-   US   *Fantasy: Myth*

John Crowley	Terry Pratchett	Gene Wolfe
Tanith Lee	David Wingrove	

Sean Hughes   1965-   Ire   *Humour*

James Kelman	Ardal O'Hanlon	Irvine Welsh
Patrick McCabe	Will Self	

H

Alan Hunter   1922-   *Crime: Police work - Br*
                                                          ⚐ Supt George Gently - Norfolk

Vivien Armstrong	Eileen Dewhurst	J M Gregson
Gwendoline Butler	Raymond Flynn	Nicholas Rhea
Ann Cleeves	Malcolm Forsythe	David Williams
Brian Cooper		

Don't forget lists of: *Genres * Characters * Literary prizes * Further reading* ☞

Gwen Hunter 1956- US Adventure/Thriller

also writes as Gary Hunter
www.gwenhunter.com

Virginia Andrews | Stephen Hunter | Paullina Simons
Tami Hoag | Peter Rawlinson |

Stephen Hunter 1946- US Adventure/Thriller

Tom Clancy | John R Maxim | John Sandford
Tami Hoag | Geoffrey Norman | Paullina Simons
Gwen Hunter | Chris Ryan |

Graham Hurley 1946- Crime: Police work - Br

www.grahamhurley.co.uk

⚐ *DI Joe Faraday - Portsmouth*

Michael Connelly | Quintin Jardine | Michelle Spring
John Harvey | Peter Robinson | M J Trow
Reginald Hill | Betty Rowlands |

Graham Hurley 1946- Adventure/Thriller

www.grahamhurley.co.uk

Geoffrey Archer | Frances Galleymore | Philip Hook
Dale Brown | W E B Griffin | Chris Ryan
Lee Child | Jack Harvey | Gordon Thomas
Kit Craig | Richard Herman |

Meg Hutchinson Saga

also writes as Margaret Astbury Birmingham

H

Donna Baker | Roy Hattersley | Lynda Page
Rita Bradshaw | Meg Henderson | Jessica Stirling
Josephine Cox | Annie Murray | Audrey Willsher
Sara Fraser | |

Angela Huth 1938- General

Elizabeth Buchan | Angela Lambert | Deborah Moggach
A S Byatt | Shena Mackay | Elizabeth Tettmar
Elizabeth Darrell | Margaret Mayhew |

Shaun Hutson   1958-   Horror

Simon Clark	Graham Masterton	John Saul
John Douglas	Mark Morris	Guy N Smith
Richard Laymon	Christopher Pike	Whitley Strieber
Bentley Little	Phil Rickman	

Aldous Huxley   1894-1963   General

Ray Bradbury	George Orwell
D H Lawrence	Anthony Powell

Elspeth Huxley   1907-97   General

Rumer Godden	Lee Langley	Toni Morrison
M M Kaye	Doris Lessing	

Sara Hylton   Saga

Louise Brindley	Harriet Hudson	Margaret Pemberton
Teresa Crane	Marie Joseph	Judith Saxton
Victoria Holt	Claire Lorrimer	Elizabeth Walker

David Ignatius   1950-   US   Adventure/Thriller
www.davidignatius.com

David Brierley	Robert Harris	Martin Cruz Smith
Alan Furst	Philip Kerr	Gordon Stevens

Greg Iles   US   Adventure/Thriller
www.gregiles.com/

Lee Child	Donald James	Robert Ludlum
Conor Cregan	Alan Judd	Glenn Meade
Robert Harris		

Hammond Innes   1913-98   Adventure/Thriller

Desmond Bagley	Alexander Fullerton	James Pattinson
Gerry Carroll	Duncan Kyle	Douglas Reeman
Jon Cleary	Alistair MacLean	Nevil Shute
Clive Cussler	Nicholas Monsarrat	Peter Tonkin

H
I

Michael Innes 1906-94

Crime: Police work - Br
⚘ DI John Appleby - London

Margery Allingham
John Dickson Carr
Edmund Crispin

Gladys Mitchell
Dorothy L Sayers

Josephine Tey
Patricia Wentworth

Elizabeth Ironside   Crime

Caro Fraser
Robert Goddard

Gregory Hall
Andrew Taylor

CWA   1984 ⚘

John Irving 1942- US   General

Jonathan Coe
Tibor Fischer
Joseph Heller
Terry McMillan

Larry McMurtry
Rick Moody
Tim O'Brien

Thomas Pynchon
Tom Robbins
John Updike

Susan Isaacs 1943- US   General
www.susanisaacs.com

Lisa Alther
Rita Mae Brown
Anabel Donald
Kinky Friedman

Sarah Harrison
Sparkle Hayter
Pauline McLynn
Lindsay Maracotta

Anna Quindlen
Susan Sussman with
  Sarajane Avidon

Kazuo Ishiguro 1954- Ja   General

Ronald Frame
Arthur Golden
Franz Kafka
Timothy Mo
Haruki Murakami

Vladimir Nabokov
Michael Ondaatje
Graham Swift
Adam Thorpe
Mario Vargas Llosa

Holtby   1982 ⚘
Whitbread   1986 ⚘
Booker   1989 ⚘

I

Alan Isler 1934- US   General

William Boyd
Howard Jacobson
Amos Oz

Philip Roth
Bernhard Schlink

Tom Sharpe
Isaac Bashevis Singer

Jon A Jackson　1938-　US　　Crime: Police work - US
www.jonajackson.com　　　　　　　　⚲ Sgt 'Fang' Mulheisen - Detroit

Loren D Estleman　　　Dennis Lehane　　　Ridley Pearson
Joe R Lansdale　　　　Ed McBain　　　　　Charles Willeford

Robert Jackson　1941-　　　　　　　War: Modern

W E B Griffin　　　　Derek Robinson　　　Charles Whiting
John Harris　　　　　Julian Jay Savarin

Anna Jacobs　　　　　　　　　　　　Saga
also writes as Sherry-Anne Jacobs & Shannah Jay　⚲ Annie Gibson - Lancashire
www.annajacobs.com

Julia Bryant　　　　Elizabeth Elgin　　　Penny Jordan
Irene Carr　　　　　Katie Flynn　　　　　Marie Joseph
Alexandra Connor　Audrey Howard　　　Maureen Lee
Joan Eadith　　　　Joan Jonker　　　　　Mary Minton

Jonnie Jacobs　US　　　　　　　　　Crime
⚲ Kali O'Brien, Attorney - San Francisco ▪ Kate Austen, Single mother - California

J A Jance　　　　　　John T Lescroart　　Lisa Scottoline
Jonathan Kellerman　Marcia Muller　　　Sheldon Siegel

Howard Jacobson　1942-　　　　　General

Malcolm Bradbury　Amos Oz　　　　　　Wingate　　1999 ✲
Michael Frayn　　　Frederic Raphael
Stephen Fry　　　　Philip Roth
Alan Isler　　　　　Tom Sharpe
David Lodge

Kate Jacoby　Aus　　　　　　　Fantasy: Epic
www.katejacoby.com　　　　　　　　　　Elita Series

Tom Arden　　　　Julia Gray　　　　　K J Parker
James Barclay　　Robert Jordan　　　Freda Warrington
Sara Douglass　　Juliet E McKenna　Jane Welch
David Farland

J

Christian Jacq   1947-   Fr   Historical

Jean M Auel   Ross Leckie   Linda Lay Shuler
Pauline Gedge   Colleen McCullough   Wilbur Smith
Margaret George   Valerio Massimo Manfredi

Bill James   1929-   Wales   Crime: Police work - Br
is James Tucker   🏃 *Ch Supt Colin Harpur & ACC Desmond Iles - Wales*
also writes as David Craig & Judith James   *Simon Abelard, Intelligence Officer*

Jeffrey Ashford   Eugene McEldowney   Jerry Raine
Ken Bruen   David Ralph Martin   Mark Timlin
Martin Edwards   David Peace   David Williams
Reginald Hill   Robert T Price

Donald James   1931-   Adventure/Thriller
                                                 🏃 *Inspector Vadim - Moscow*

Lee Child   John Farrow   Glenn Meade
Kit Craig   Robert Harris   Reggie Nadelson
Conor Cregan   Greg Iles   Martin Cruz Smith
Len Deighton   Joseph Kanon

Erica James   1960-   General

Amanda Brookfield   Hazel Hucker   Ann Purser
Lucy Clare   Jan Karon   Mary Selby
Kate Fielding   Julia Lisle   Rebecca Shaw
Fanny Frewen   Melissa Nathan

Henry James   1843-1916   US   General

Ethan Canin   Ford Madox Ford   Edith Wharton
Joseph Conrad   E M Forster   Patrick White

Judi James   Glitz & Glamour

J

Sally Beauman   Susan Lewis   Una-Mary Parker
Sandra Brown   Judith Michael   June Flaum Singer
Joan Collins

Don't forget lists of: *Genres * Characters * Literary prizes * Further reading* ☞

P D James   1920-   Crime: Police work - Br
🏃 Supt Adam Dalgleish ▪ Cordelia Gray, PI - London

Jane Adams	Elizabeth George	CWA	1971 ✻
Vivien Armstrong	B M Gill	CWA	1975 ✻
John Brady	Lesley Grant-Adamson	CWA	1986 ✻
Brian Cooper	Morag Joss		
Amanda Cross	M R D Meek		
Kate Ellis	Julian Symons		

Peter James   1948-   Horror
www.peterjames.com

Richard Bachman	Steve Harris	Bernard Taylor
Joe Donnelly	James Herbert	Tim Wilson
Stephen Gallagher	Stephen King	

Russell James   1942-   Crime
www.russelljames.co.uk

Ken Bruen	Jonathan Kellerman	Jim Thompson
Paul Charles	Julian Rathbone	Charles Willeford

Sian James   Wales   General

Valerie Blumenthal	Bel Mooney	Joanna Trollope
Suzannah Dunn	Libby Purves	

J A Jance   1944-   US   Crime: Police work - US
🏃 Det J P Beaumont - Seattle
Sheriff Joanna Brady - Bisbee, Arizona
www.jajance.com

Michael Connelly	Ed McBain	Claire McNab
Donald Harstad	John D MacDonald	Robert B Parker
Tony Hillerman	Michael McGarrity	Ridley Pearson
Jonnie Jacobs		

J

Don't forget lists of: *Genres* * *Characters* * *Literary prizes* * *Further reading* ☞

J Robert Janes
1935-   Can   *Crime: Police work - foreign*
ⵣ *Jean-Louis St-Cyr & Hermann Kohler - Occupied France*

Michael Dibdin	Juliet Hebden	Philip Kerr
Nicolas Freeling	Mark Hebden	Georges Simenon

Sheila Jansen
Saga
Newcastle, NE England

Irene Carr	Una Horne	Denise Robertson
Catherine Cookson	Brenda McBryde	Wendy Robertson
Valerie Georgeson	Lynda Page	Janet MacLeod Trotter
Elizabeth Gill		

Sebastien Japrisot
1931-   Fr   *General*
is Jean Baptiste Rossi

Pat Barker	Sebastian Faulks
Louis de Bernières	Paul Theroux

Quintin Jardine
1945-   Sco   *Crime: Police work - Br*
also writes as Matthew Reid   ⵣ *Oz Blackstone & Primavera Phillips, PIs - Glasgow*
www.twbooks.co.uk/authors/quintinjardine.html   *DCI Bob Skinner - Edinburgh*

Brian Battison	Paul Johnston	William McIlvanney
Jeff Gulvin	Bill Knox	Denise Mina
Joyce Holms	Frederic Lindsay	Nicholas Royle
Graham Hurley	Jim Lusby	Peter Turnbull

Tim Jeal
1945-   *Historical*

Peter Carey	Philippa Gregory
Giles Foden	Ross King

Michael Jecks
1960-   *Crime: Historical*
www.michaeljecks.co.uk   ⵣ *Sir Baldwin Furnshill & Simon Puttock, Bailiff - C14th Devon*

J

Alys Clare	Bernard Knight	Ellis Peters
Paul Doherty	Edward Marston	Kate Sedley
Susanna Gregory	Viviane Moore	Peter Tonkin
Paul Harding	Ian Morson	Peter Tremayne

Mike Jefferies   1943-   Fantasy: Epic

Terry Brooks   Maggie Furey   Harry Turtledove
Chris Bunch   Terry Goodkind   Janny Wurts
Raymond E Feist   J V Jones

Elizabeth Jeffrey   Historical

Margaret Dickinson   Beryl Kingston   Mary Mackie
Elizabeth Ann Hill   Peter Ling   Sarah Shears
Lena Kennedy

Roderic Jeffries   1926-   Crime: Police work - foreign
also writes as Peter Alding, Jeffrey Ashford & Roderic Graeme   ⚐ *DI Alvarez - Mallorca, Spain*

Juliet Hebden   Magdalen Nabb   Julian Symons
Mark Hebden   Michael Pearce   Christopher West
Manuel Vázquez Montalbán

Amy Jenkins   Chick Lit

Jenny Colgan   Wendy Holden   Isabel Wolff
Helen Fielding   Stephanie Theobald

Geoffrey Jenkins   1920-   Ire   Adventure/Thriller

Desmond Bagley   Clare Francis   Nevil Shute
Brian Callison   Alistair MacLean   Wilbur Smith
Jon Cleary   Douglas Reeman   Charles Whiting
Colin Forbes

K W Jeter   1950-   US   Science Fiction: Technical
www.europa.com/~jeter

Eric Brown   Philip K Dick   Ian McDonald
Pat Cadigan   Gwyneth Jones

J

Lisa Jewell
www.lisa-jewell.co.uk

Chick Lit

Rebecca Campbell
Jane Green
Wendy Holden
Josie Lloyd & Emlyn Rees

L McCrossan
Anna Maxted
Claire Naylor
Freya North

Adele Parks
Victoria Routledge
Daisy Waugh

Ruth Prawer Jhabvala   1927-   US

General

Margaret Atwood
Anita Desai
E M Forster
Rumer Godden
Abdulrazak Gurnah

Lee Langley
John Masters
V S Naipaul
Paul Scott

Booker	*1975* ❀

Iris Johansen   US

Crime

www.randomhouse.com/features/johansen/   ⚐ *Eve Duncan, Forensic sculptor*
Sarah Patrick & Monty, Search & rescue worker & dog

Bethany Campbell
Kit Craig
Peter Driscoll

Lisa Gardner
Tami Hoag

Judith Kelman
Gloria Murphy

Jennifer Johnston   1930-   Ire

General

Elizabeth Bowen
Jane Gardam
Susan Hill
Joan Lingard
Shena Mackay

Iris Murdoch
Edna O'Brien
Colm Toibin
William Trevor
Niall Williams

Authors	*1973* ❀
Whitbread	*1979* ❀

Paul Johnston   1957-   Sco

Crime: PI

⚐ *Quintilian Dalrymple - C21st Edinburgh*

Nicholas Blincoe
Eric Brown
Jeremy Cameron
Quintin Jardine

Douglas Lindsay
Paul J McAuley
Ian Rankin

CWA	*1997* ❀

J

149

Elizabeth Jolley   1923-   Aus   General

Janet Frame   David Malouf   V S Naipaul
Rumer Godden   Hilary Mantel   Barbara Pym
Janette Turner Hospital   Alice Munro

Christina Jones   1948-   Chick Lit

Catherine Alliott   Jilly Cooper   Jill Mansell
Louise Bagshawe   Sarah Harvey   Fiona Walker
Claire Calman   Kathy Lette

Gwyneth Jones   1952-   Science Fiction: Near future
also writes as Ann Halam
www.boldaslove.co.uk

Steve Aylett   Ian McDonald   Arthur C Clarke 2002 ✺
Alexander Besher   Mary Doria Russell
Octavia E Butler   Neal Stephenson
Sara Douglass   Sheri S Tepper
Mary Gentle   Ian Watson
K W Jeter   David Wingrove

J V Jones   1963-   Fantasy: Epic
www.jvj.com

Kate Elliott   Mike Jefferies   Jennifer Roberson
David Farland   Katherine Kurtz   Kristine Kathryn Rusch
Maggie Furey   Valery Leith   Freda Warrington
David Gemmell   Megan Lindholm   Philip G Williamson

Jenny Jones   1954-   Horror
                                                        Flight Over Fire Series

David Bowker   Diane Guest   Stephen King
Christopher Fowler   James Herbert   Melanie Tem

J

Joan Jonker
Saga
Liverpool

Lyn Andrews
Anne Baker
Alexandra Connor
Elizabeth Daish

Katie Flynn
Helen Forrester
June Francis
Anna Jacobs

Penny Jordan
Maureen Lee
Freda Lightfoot
Margaret Mayhew

Pamela Jooste   SA
General

J M Coetzee
Giles Foden

Nadine Gordimer
Christopher Hope

Doris Lessing
Jo-Anne Richards

Penny Jordan   1946-
Saga

Barbara Delinsky
Anna Jacobs
Joan Jonker

Jayne Ann Krentz
Judith McNaught

Mary Minton
Una-Mary Parker

Robert Jordan   1948-   US
Fantasy: Epic
is James Oliver Rigney Jr & also writes as Chang Lung,
Regan O'Neal, Jackson O'Reilly & Regan O'Reilly
Wheel of Time Series

Mark Anthony
Tom Arden
Chris Bunch
Jonathan Carroll

Louise Cooper
David A Drake
David Eddings
David Farland

Terry Goodkind
Kate Jacoby
John Marco
J R R Tolkien

Alison Joseph   1958-
Crime: PI
⚗ *Sister Agnes Bourdillon, Nun*

Marian Babson
Kate Charles
Elizabeth Ferrars
Jonathan Gash

Elizabeth George
Morag Joss
Valerie Kershaw

Sarah Lacey
Marianne MacDonald
Stella Shepherd

J

Don't forget lists of: *Genres * Characters * Literary prizes * Further reading* ☞

Marie Joseph

Saga
Lancashire

Donna Baker
Catherine Cookson
Josephine Cox
Margaret Thomson Davis
Katie Flynn
Helen Forrester

Audrey Howard
Sara Hylton
Anna Jacobs
Lena Kennedy
Mary Minton
M R O'Donnell

Parker	*1987* ❀

Morag Joss

Crime
🏃 *Sara Selkirk, Cellist - Bath*

P D James
Alison Joseph
Marianne MacDonald

Gemma O'Connor
Ruth Rendell
Roberta Rogow

Annette Roome
Norman Russell

Graham Joyce   1954-

Horror

www.grahamjoyce.net

Jonathan Aycliffe
Jonathan Carroll
Joe Donnelly

Christopher Fowler
Robert Holdstock
David Martin

Mark Morris
Phil Rickman
Michael Stewart

James Joyce   1882-1941   Ire

General

William Faulkner
Franz Kafka

D H Lawrence
John McGahern

Vladimir Nabokov
Virginia Woolf

Alan Judd   1946-

Adventure/Thriller
🏃 *Charles Thoroughgood*

James Buchan
Alan Furst
Humphrey Hawksley
Greg Iles

John Le Carré
Andy McNab
Daniel Silva

Guardian	*1991* ❀
Holtby	*1992* ❀

J

*Don't forget lists of: Genres * Characters * Literary prizes * Further reading* ☞

Franz Kafka *1883-1924 Cz*   *General*

Paul Auster	Tibor Fischer	Ivan Klima
Albert Camus	Kazuo Ishiguro	George Orwell
Michel Faber	James Joyce	Patrick Süskind

Jeanne Kalogridis *1954- US*   *Horror*
http://jeannekalogridis.com   ☆ *Family Dracul, Vampire*

Laurell K Hamilton	Anne Rice	Steven Spruill

Stuart M Kaminsky *1934- US*   *Crime: PI*
www.stuartkaminsky.com   ☆ *Toby Peters - Hollywood, Los Angeles*
Portiry Petrovich Rostnikov, Police - Moscow

John Dickson Carr	James Ellroy	Peter Hoeg
Raymond Chandler	David Guterson	Philip Kerr
James Hadley Chase	Dashiell Hammett	

Joseph Kanon *1946- US*   *Adventure/Thriller*
www.josephkanon.com

Eric Ambler	Donald James	Peter Matthiessen
Francis Bennett	John Lawton	Charles Whiting
Robert Harris	John Le Carré	

Jan Karon *1937- US*   *General*
www.mitfordbooks.com   *Mitford Series - USA*

Kate Fielding	Garrison Keillor	Miss Read
Erica James	Ann Purser	Rebecca Shaw

Guy Gavriel Kay *1954- Can*   *Fantasy: Epic*
www.brightweavings.com

Mark Anthony	Robin Hobb	Stephen R Lawhead
Mark Chadbourn	Robert Holdstock	Michael Scott Rohan
Charles de Lint	Katharine Kerr	J R R Tolkien
Julia Gray	Greg Keyes	Jane Welch

K

Don't forget lists of: *Genres * Characters * Literary prizes * Further reading* ☞

Nora Kay
Saga
Scotland

Jay Allerton
Emma Blair
Doris Davidson
Christine Marion Fraser

Isobel Neill
Frances Paige
Eileen Ramsay
Harriet Smart

Jessica Stirling
Anne Vivis
Mary Withall

M M Kaye   1908-
General

Christopher Hudson
Elspeth Huxley
Lee Langley

John Masters
Gita Mehta

Paul Scott
Mary Stewart

Paul Kearney   1967-   Ire
Fantasy: Epic
www.paulkearneyonline.com

Stephen Donaldson
David Eddings
Kate Elliott
Raymond E Feist

Maggie Furey
David Gemmell
Stephen R Lawhead
Valery Leith

Roger Taylor
Harry Turtledove
Freda Warrington
Jonathan Wylie

Susanna Kearsley   1966-   Can
General

Daphne Du Maurier
Robert Goddard

Joanna Hines
Susan Howatch

Mary Stewart

H R F Keating   1926-
Crime: Police work - foreign
also writes as Evelyn Hervey
🏃 *Ins Ghote - Bombay*
DCI Harriet Martens - 'Greater Birchester'

Janet Harward
Juliet Hebden
Mark Hebden
Lynda La Plante
Priscilla Masters
Magdalen Nabb

Michael Pearce
Daniel Pennac
Georges Simenon
Janwillem van de Wetering
Christopher West

CWA   1980 ✿

Garrison Keillor   1942-   US
Humour
http://phc.mpr.org/cast/garrison_keillor.shtml

K

Stephen Amidon
H E Bates
Ethan Canin

Richard Ford
Tom Holt

Jan Karon
William Kennedy

Faye Kellerman   1952-   US   Crime: *Police work - US*
🏃 *DS Romulus Poe - Las Vegas* ▪ *Lt Pete Decker - Los Angeles*

Jan Burke	Ed McBain	Jefferson Parker
Penelope Evans	Jenny Maxwell	Ridley Pearson
Joy Fielding	Carol O'Connell	

Jonathan Kellerman   1949-   US   Crime: *Police work - US*
www.mysterynet.com/jkellerman/
🏃 *Det Milo Sturgis & Alex Delaware,*
Psychologist - Los Angeles

Mary Higgins Clark	Frances Hegarty	Jefferson Parker
Harlan Coben	Jonnie Jacobs	James Patterson
John Connolly	Russell James	Ridley Pearson
Mo Hayder	John T Lescroart	

Cathy Kelly   *Ire*   *Chick Lit*
www.cathy-kelly.com

Zoë Barnes	Sheila O'Flanagan	*Parker* 2001 ✿
Colette Caddle	Kate O'Riordan	
Claudine Cullimore	Lesley Pearse	
Sarah Harvey	Patricia Scanlan	
Josie Lloyd & Emlyn Rees	Linda Taylor	
Anna Maxted	Kate Thompson	

Nora Kelly   1945-   US   *Crime*
🏃 *Gillian Adams, Academic - USA*

Amanda Cross	Gillian Slovo	Michelle Spring
Sarah Dunant	Joan Smith	

Sheelagh Kelly   *Saga*
🏃 *Feeney Family* ▪ *Prince Family - Yorkshire*

Helen Cannam	Genevieve Lyons	Ann Victoria Roberts
Doreen Edwards	D M Purcell	Liz Ryan
Mary A Larkin	Elvi Rhodes	Patricia Shaw

K

Don't forget lists of: *Genres* * *Characters* * *Literary prizes* * *Further reading* ☞

Susan Kelly   1955-   Crime: Police work - Br
⚕ DCI Nick Trevelyan & DS Angela Hope ▪ Supt Gregory Summers - Thames Valley

Vivien Armstrong	Natasha Cooper	Janet Neel
Joanna Cannan	Colin Dexter	John Sherwood
Paul Charles	Barry Maitland	Veronica Stallwood

James Kelman   1946-   Sco   General
www.JamesKelman.co.uk

Des Dillon	A L Kennedy	Black	1989 ✿
Michel Faber	Carl MacDougall	Booker	1994 ✿
Alasdair Gray	William McIlvanney		
Richard Greensted	Agnes Owens		
Sean Hughes	Irvine Welsh		

Judith Kelman   1945-   US   Adventure/Thriller
www.jkelman.com

Virginia Andrews	Diane Guest	Barbara Michaels
Bethany Campbell	Frances Hegarty	Hilary Norman
Kit Craig	Iris Johansen	Melanie Tem
Joy Fielding		

Thomas Keneally   1935-   Aus   General
also writes as William Coyle

Malcolm Bradbury	Janette Turner Hospital	Booker	1982 ✿
Peter Carey	David Malouf		
E L Doctorow	Brian Moore		
Robert Drewe	Julian Rathbone		
Charles Frazier	Adam Thorpe		
Rodney Hall	Patrick White		

A L Kennedy   1965-   Sco   General
www.al-kennedy.co.uk

Joan Brady	Alasdair Gray	S Maugham	1994 ✿
Amanda Craig	James Kelman	Encore	1996 ✿
Michel Faber	Andrew O'Hagan		
Janice Galloway			

K

Douglas Kennedy   1955-   US   Adventure/Thriller

Peter Blauner	Richard North Patterson	TGR	1998 ✿
Dexter Dias	Paul Watkins		
Patricia Highsmith	Stuart Woods		
Andrew Klavan			

Lena Kennedy   1913- 86   Saga
London

Philip Boast	Marie Joseph	Genevieve Lyons
Patricia Burns	Beryl Kingston	M R O'Donnell
June Francis	Peter Ling	Sally Worboyes
Elizabeth Jeffrey		

William Kennedy   1928-   US   General

Pete Dexter	Peter Matthiessen	Pulitzer	1984 ✿
E L Doctorow	John Steinbeck		
Garrison Keillor			

Alexander Kent   1924-   Sea: Historical
is Douglas Reeman   ☆ Richard Bolitho

Tom Connery	A E Langsford	Marcus Palliser
Bernard Cornwell	Jonathan Lunn	Dan Parkinson
David Donachie	Philip McCutchan	Dudley Pope
C S Forester	Jan Needle	Julian Stockwin

Jack Kerouac   1922-69   US   General
www.cmgww.com/historic/kerouac/

Albert Camus	Jay McInerney	John Steinbeck
Alex Garland	Larry McMurtry	

Katharine Kerr   1944-   US   Fantasy: Myth
Deverry Series

Alice Borchardt	Stephen R Lawhead	Jan Siegel
Mark Chadbourn	Anne McCaffrey	Judith Tarr
Guy Gavriel Kay	Caiseal Mor	J R R Tolkien
Greg Keyes		

K

Philip Kerr *1956- Sco* Adventure/Thriller

Geoffrey Archer
Michael Crichton
David Ignatius
J Robert Janes

Stuart M Kaminsky
Donna Leon
Manuel Vázquez Montalbán

Martin Cruz Smith
Nigel West
Robert Wilson

Valerie Kershaw Crime

🜨 *Mitch Mitchell, Radio presenter - Birmingham*

Marian Babson
John Burns
Denise Danks
Ron Ellis

Janet Evanovich
Jonathan Gash
Alison Joseph

Marianne MacDonald
Claire McNab
Chris Niles

Leo Kessler *1926-* War: Modern

also writes as Duncan Harding & Charles Whiting

Harold Coyle
John Harris

Derek Robinson
Alan Savage

Greg Keyes *1963- US* Fantasy: Epic

James Barclay
L Sprague de Camp
Steven Erikson

Guy Gavriel Kay
Katharine Kerr
Stephen R Lawhead

H G Wells
Tad Williams

Marian Keyes *1963- Ire* Chick Lit

Colette Caddle
Claudine Cullimore
Jane Green
Anna Maxted

Sheila O'Flanagan
Kate O'Riordan
Susan Oudot
Alexandra Potter

Judith Summers
Linda Taylor
Kate Thompson
Grace Wynne-Jones

Paul Kilduff *1965- Ire* Crime: Legal/financial

www.paulkilduff.com

David Baldacci
Harry Bingham
Po Bronson

Colin Harrison
John McLaren

Brad Meltzer
Scott Turow

K

Michael Kimball   US   Adventure/Thriller
www.michaelkimball.com

David Guterson   Colin Harrison   John Sandford

Anna King   1948-   Saga
London

Harry Bowling   Elizabeth Lord   Mary Jane Staples
Helen Carey   Anne Melville   Elizabeth Waite
Harry Cole   Jenny Oldfield   Sally Worboyes
Patricia Grey

Francis King   1923-   General

Dirk Bogarde   Michael Frayn   Stanley Middleton
David Cook   Alan Hollinghurst   Christina Stead
E M Forster   Christopher Hudson   Colm Toibin

Laurie R King   1952-   US   Crime: Police work - US
www.laurieking.com/   ⚐ Det Kate Martinelli & Det Al Hawkin - San Francisco
                                    Sherlock Holmes & Mary Russell - C20th London

Jan Burke   Jeremy Dronfield   Claire McNab
Caleb Carr   Paula Gosling   Anne Perry
Amanda Cross   Richard Grayson   Roberta Rogow
Arthur Conan Doyle   Gillian Linscott   Charles Todd

Ross King   Historical

Umberto Eco   Sheri Holman
Sandra Gulland   Tim Jeal

Stephen King   1947-   US   Horror
also writes as Richard Bachman
www.stephenking.com/

Richard Bachman   Diane Guest   Phil Rickman
Guy Burt   Peter James   John Saul
John Crowley   Jenny Jones   Dan Simmons
John Farris   Stephen Laws   T M Wright

K

Barbara Kingsolver   1955-   US   General
www.kingsolver.com

Gail Anderson-Dargatz	Ellen Gilchrist	Thomas McGuane
Andrea Barrett	Janice Graham	Jacquelyn Mitchard
Louise Erdrich	Kate Grenville	Gloria Naylor
Patricia Gaffney	Jane Hamilton	

Beryl Kingston   1931-   Saga
Easter Empire - London

Philip Boast	Elizabeth Jeffrey	Victor Pemberton
Rose Boucheron	Lena Kennedy	Claire Rayner
Patricia Burns	Anne Melville	Ann Victoria Roberts
Helen Carey	Gilda O'Neill	Malcolm Ross

Sophie Kinsella   Chick Lit

| Francesca Clementis | Serena Mackesy | Alexandra Potter |
| Kathy Lette | Chris Manby | |

Gwen Kirkwood   Saga
'Fiarlyden' Series - Scotland

Doris Davidson	Elisabeth McNeill	Kirsty White
Christine Marion Fraser	Eileen Ramsay	Mary Withall
Evelyn Hood		

Andrew Klavan   1954-   US   Adventure/Thriller:
Psychological
also writes as Keith Peterson
www.twbooks.co.uk/authors/andrewklavan.html

Chaz Brenchley	Sharyn McCrumb	TGR 1996 ✿
Joe Donnelly	Scott Smith	
Thomas Harris	Tim Willocks	
Douglas Kennedy	Stuart Woods	

Ivan Klima   1931-   Cz   General

| Albert Camus | Sue Gee |
| Tibor Fischer | Franz Kafka |

K

Matthew Kneale

Historical

Andrea Barrett	Olivia Manning	*Mail*	*1992* ❀
William Boyd	Evelyn Waugh	*Whitbread*	*2000* ❀

Alanna Knight *1923- Sco*

Crime: *Historical*

DI Jeremy Faro - C19th Edinburgh

Gwendoline Butler	Gillian Linscott	Roberta Rogow
Arthur Conan Doyle	Peter Lovesey	Kate Ross
Richard Grayson	Amy Myers	Norman Russell
Ray Harrison	Anne Perry	

Bernard Knight *1931- Wales*

Crime: *Historical*

Sir John De Wolfe - C12th Devon

Alys Clare	Paul Harding	Ian Morson
Michael Clynes	Michael Jecks	Candace Robb
Paul Doherty	Edward Marston	Kate Sedley
Susanna Gregory	Viviane Moore	

India Knight

General

Raffaella Barker	Anna Maxted	Sue Townsend
Victoria Corby	Claire Naylor	Daisy Waugh
Kathy Lette	Adele Parks	Isabel Wolff

Bill Knox *1928-99 Sco*

Crime: *Police work - Br*

also wrote as Michael Kirk,
Robert MacLeod & Noah Webster

DCI Colin Thane & DI Phil Moss - Glasgow
Webb Garrick, Scottish Fisheries Inspector

Jeffrey Ashford	Joyce Holms	*CWA* *1986* ❀
M C Beaton	Quintin Jardine	
Margaret Duffy	Jim Lusby	
Gerald Hammond	Ian Rankin	
Reginald Hill		

Elizabeth Knox *1959- NZ*

General

www.vuw.ac.nz/nzbookcouncil/writers/knoxelizabeth.htm

Ian McEwan	Haruki Murakami	Salley Vickers
Andrew Miller	Lawrence Norfolk	

K

Dean R Koontz   1945-   US   Horror
www.randomhouse.com/features/koontz/index2.html

Richard Bachman	Richard Laymon	Michael Slade
John Douglas	Robert McCammon	Peter Straub
Stephen Gallagher	Richard Matheson	Whitley Strieber
Stephen Laws	John Saul	Tim Willocks

Judith Krantz   1928-   US   Glitz & Glamour

Lisa Appignanesi	Jude Deveraux	Roberta Latow
Pat Booth	Laramie Dunaway	Johanna Lindsey
Jackie Collins	Julie Ellis	Madge Swindells
Jilly Cooper	Judith Gould	

Jayne Ann Krentz   1948-   US   Glitz & Glamour
also writes as Jayne Castle & Amanda Quick
www.jayneannkrentz.com

Sandra Brown	Judith Gould	Lynne Pemberton
Janet Dailey	Penny Jordan	Nora Roberts
Barbara Delinsky	Judith McNaught	Lavyrle Spencer

Rochelle Krich   1947-   US   Crime: Police work - US
www.rochellekrich.com/   ⚉ Det Jessie Drake - Los Angeles

Patricia D Cornwell	Lynn S Hightower	Irene Lin-Chandler
Jeffery Deaver	Tami Hoag	James Patterson
John Gilstrap	Lynda La Plante	Kathy Reichs

Hanif Kureishi   1954-   General
www.hanifkureishi.com

Armistead Maupin	Zadie Smith	Whitbread 1990 ✸
Gita Mehta	Meera Syal	
Timothy Mo	Louisa Young	
Caryl Phillips		

Katherine Kurtz   1944-   US   Fantasy: Epic
www.deryni.net   Deryni Series

K

Robin Hobb	Mercedes Lackey	Jennifer Roberson
J V Jones	Melanie Rawn	Judith Tarr

Duncan Kyle   *1930-2000*   *Adventure/Thriller*

Desmond Bagley   Clare Francis   Robert Ludlum
John Buchan   Jack Higgins   Alistair MacLean
Jon Cleary   Hammond Innes   Glover Wright

Lynda La Plante   *1946-*   *General*
♣ Dolly Rawlins, Widow - England

Pat Booth   Julie Ellis
Martina Cole   Una-Mary Parker

Lynda La Plante   *1946-*   *Crime: Police work - Br/US*
♣ DCI Jane Tennison • Supt Mike Walker - British
Lorraine Page, PI - Los Angeles

Martina Cole   Rochelle Krich   George P Pelecanos
H R F Keating   Sara Paretsky

Sarah Lacey   *Crime: PI*
is Kay Mitchell   *♣ Leah Hunter, Tax Inspector -*
www.twbooks.co.uk/authors/sarahlacey.html   *'Bramfield', Yorkshire*

Natasha Cooper   Alison Joseph   Annette Roome
Judith Cutler   Janet Laurence   Veronica Stallwood
Anabel Donald   Nancy Livingston

Mercedes Lackey   *1950-*   US   *Fantasy: Epic*
www.dragoncon.org/people/lackeym.html

Barbara Hambly   L E Modesitt Jr   Mickey Zucker Reichert
Katherine Kurtz   Elizabeth Moon   R A Salvatore
Holly Lisle   Melanie Rawn   Margaret Weis
Anne McCaffrey

Deryn Lake   *1937-*   *Crime: Historical*
is Dinah Lampitt   *♣ John Rawlings, Apothecary - C18th London*
www.twbooks.co.uk/authors/derynlake.html

Bruce Alexander   Richard Grayson   Janet Laurence
Stephanie Barron   Ray Harrison   Margaret Lawrence
Gwendoline Butler   Keith Heller   Hannah March

K
L

163

Rosalind Laker   1925-   Historical
is Barbara Douglas & also writes as Barbara Paul

Elizabeth Chadwick   Georgette Heyer   Judith Lennox
Jean Chapman   Pamela Hill   Norah Lofts
Sandra Gulland   Dinah Lampitt   Cynthia S Roberts
Cynthia Harrod-Eagles

Charlotte Lamb   1937-2000   General
also wrote as Sheila Coastes, Laura Hardy, Sheila Holland, Sheila Lancaster & Victoria Woolf

Daphne Du Maurier   Claire Rayner
Sue Gee   Lindsay Townsend

Angela Lambert   1940-   General

Hilary Bailey   Edna O'Brien   *Parker*   *1998* ❀
Kate Hatfield   Kate Saunders
Elizabeth Jane Howard   Magda Sweetland
Angela Huth   Elizabeth Tettmar
Hilary Mantel

Derek Lambert   1929-2001   Adventure/Thriller
also wrote as Richard Falkirk

Jon Cleary   Frederick Forsyth   Craig Thomas
June Drummond   John Lawton   Gordon Thomas
Brendan Dubois   Robert Ludlum

Dinah Lampitt   1937-   Historical
also writes as Deryn Lake
www.twbooks.co.uk/authors/dinahlampitt.html

Philippa Carr   Domini Highsmith   Morgan Llywelyn
Barbara Erskine   Rosalind Laker   Diana Norman
Elizabeth Harris

John Lanchester   1962-   General

Terence Blacker   Mark Wallington   *Betty Trask*   *1996* ❀
Jonathan Coe   Nigel Williams   *Hawthornden* *1997* ❀

Lee Langley 1927- US   General

L

Anita Desai	M M Kaye	Vikram Seth
Elspeth Huxley	Penelope Lively	Reay Tannahill
Ruth Prawer Jhabvala	Paul Scott	

A E Langsford   Sea: Historical

Gerry Carroll	Bart Davis	Alexander Kent
James Cobb	David Donachie	Nicholas Monsarrat
Tom Connery	C S Forester	Peter Tonkin

Joe R Lansdale 1951- US   Crime
www.joerlansdale.com/   ⚘ Hap Collins & Leonard Pine - Texas

Anthony Bourdain	Martin Limon	John Straley
Robert Crais	David Lindsey	Doug J Swanson
Bill Fitzhugh	Kem Nunn	Andrew Vachss
Jon A Jackson	Laurence Shames	Steve Womack

Mary A Larkin 1935- Ire   Saga
is Mary A McNulty   Northern Ireland
www.marylarkin.co.uk

Maeve Binchy	Rose Doyle	Catrin Morgan
Elaine Crowley	Sheelagh Kelly	Joan O'Neill
Frank Delaney	Genevieve Lyons	Liz Ryan

Emma Lathen 1927-97 US   Crime
was Mary J Latsis & Martha Henissart   ⚘ John Putnam Thatcher, Banker - New York
also wrote as R B Dominic

Lilian Jackson Braun	Elizabeth Ferrars	Emma Page
Amanda Cross	Charlotte MacLeod	

Roberta Latow US   Glitz & Glamour

Maria Barrett	Jackie Collins	Fern Michaels
Pat Booth	Shirley Conran	Penny Vincenzi
Sandra Brown	Judith Krantz	

Don't forget lists of: *Genres* * *Characters* * *Literary prizes* * *Further reading* ☞

Janet Laurence   1937-   *Crime*
also writes as Julia Lisle   ⚲ *Darina Lisle, Cook - England* ▪ *Canaletto, Artist - C18th London*

Bruce Alexander	Sarah Lacey	Amy Myers
Stephanie Barron	Deryn Lake	Annette Roome
Keith Heller	Margaret Lawrence	David Williams
Joyce Holms	Roy Lewis	

Stephen R Lawhead   1950-   US   *Fantasy: Myth*
www.stephenlawhead.com

C J Cherryh	Katharine Kerr	Adam Nichols
Helen Hollick	Greg Keyes	Michael Scott Rohan
Guy Gavriel Kay	Valery Leith	Judith Tarr
Paul Kearney	Caiseal Mor	Jane Welch

D H Lawrence   1885-1930   *General*

John Galsworthy	Aldous Huxley	Alan Sillitoe
Thomas Hardy	James Joyce	Christina Stead

Margaret Lawrence   US   *Crime: Historical*
⚲ *Hannah Trevor, Midwife - C18th New England*

Bruce Alexander	Deryn Lake	Hannah March
Gwendoline Butler	Janet Laurence	Derek Wilson
Keith Heller		

Martha Lawrence   1956-   US   *Crime*
is Martha C Lawrence
www.marthalawrence.com/   ⚲ *Elizabeth Chase, Psychic Investigator - California*

Jan Burke	Marcia Muller	Kathy Hogan Trocheck
Sue Grafton	Sara Paretsky	

Stephen Laws   1952-   *Horror*

Jonathan Aycliffe	Stephen King	Christopher Pike
Ramsey Campbell	Dean R Koontz	Phil Rickman
Joe Donnelly	Richard Matheson	Peter Straub
James Herbert	Mark Morris	Tim Wilson

John Lawton

Adventure/Thriller

♟ *Frederick Troy*

James Adams
Ted Allbeury
Francis Bennett
Stephen J Cannell

Jon Cleary
Len Deighton
James Follett

Ken Follett
Joseph Kanon
Derek Lambert

Richard Laymon   *1947-2001   US*

Horror

also wrote as Richard Kelly

Clive Barker
John Douglas
John Farris
Shaun Hutson

Dean R Koontz
Bentley Little
Christopher Pike
Michael Slade

Guy N Smith
Peter Straub
Bernard Taylor
T M Wright

John Le Carré   *1931-*

Adventure/Thriller

is David Cornwell
www.johnlecarre.com

♟ *George Smiley, Spy*

Eric Ambler
Francis Bennett
James Buchan
John Burdett
Bryan Forbes
Brian Freemantle

Alan Judd
Joseph Kanon
Henry Porter
Anthony Price
Daniel Silva
Robert Wilson

CWA   1977 ❁

Ursula K Le Guin   *1929-   US*

Fantasy: Epic

www.ursulakleguin.com

A A Attanasio
Octavia E Butler
C J Cherryh
Ellen Datlow

Mary Gentle
Frank Herbert
C S Lewis
Robert Silverberg

Sheri S Tepper
Vernor Vinge
T H White
Gene Wolfe

Frank Lean   *1942-*

Crime: PI

is Frank Leneghan

♟ *Dave Cunane - Manchester*

Phil Andrews
John Baker
Adam Baron
Jack Harvey

Reginald Hill
Val McDermid
Cath Staincliffe

Mark Timlin
Peter Turnbull
Martyn Waites

Stephen Leather   Adventure/Thriller
www.stephenleather.com

Geoffrey Archer	Gavin Esler	Tim Sebastian
Larry Bond	Frederick Forsyth	Gerald Seymour
Tom Bradby	Jack Higgins	John Trenhaile
Harold Coyle	David Mason	

Ross Leckie   1957-   Sco   Historical
⚘ Hannibal - Carthage

Robert Graves	Colleen McCullough	Allan Massie
Christian Jacq	Valerio Massimo Manfredi	Steven Pressfield

Harper Lee   1926-   US   General

Suzanne Berne	Joyce Carol Oates	Pulitzer	1961 ✾
Pat Conroy	J D Salinger		
David Guterson	John Steinbeck		
Carson McCullers	Meera Syal		
Toni Morrison	Alice Walker		
Stewart O'Nan	Larry Watson		

Maureen Lee   Saga
Pearl Street - Liverpool

Lyn Andrews	Ruth Hamilton	Parker	2000 ✾
Anne Baker	Anna Jacobs		
Jean Chapman	Joan Jonker		
Katie Flynn	Margaret Mayhew		
Helen Forrester	Elizabeth Murphy		
June Francis			

Tanith Lee   1947-   Fantasy: Dark
www.tanithlee.com   ⚘ Venus (Venice)

Peter S Beagle	Ellen Datlow	Terry Pratchett
Marion Zimmer Bradley	Barry Hughart	Freda Warrington

Gordon Legge   1961-   Sco   General

Iain Banks	Nick Hornby	Alan Spence
Des Dillon	Duncan McLean	Alan Warner

Dennis Lehane   1966-   US   Crime: PI
www.dennislehanebooks.com   ⚹ Patrick Kenzie & Angie Gennaro - Boston, Mass

Adam Baron	Stephen Dobyns	James Patterson
Peter Blauner	Jon A Jackson	Chris Petit
Anthony Bourdain	Martin Limon	Robert K Tanenbaum
John Connolly	Reggie Nadelson	Boston Teran

Fritz Leiber   1910-92   US   Fantasy: Epic

Steven Brust	Michael Moorcock	Clifford D Simak
L Sprague de Camp	Martin Scott	Jack Vance
H P Lovecraft	Bob Shaw	

Annie Leith   1937-   General
also writes as Anita Burgh

H E Bates	E F Benson	Kathleen Rowntree
Guy Bellamy	Julia Lisle	Peter Tinniswood

Valery Leith   1968-   Fantasy: Epic
is Tricia Sullivan   Everien

David Gemmell	Paul Kearney
J V Jones	Stephen R Lawhead

J Robert Lennon   General

Carol Clewlow	Connie May Fowler	Anita Shreve
Andre Dubus	Robert Goddard	

Judith Lennox   1953-   Saga

Diana Gabaldon	Sybil Marshall	Mary Stewart
Caroline Harvey	Imogen Parker	Judy Turner
Rosalind Laker	Rosamunde Pilcher	

Don't forget lists of: Genres * Characters * Literary prizes * Further reading ☞

Donna Leon   1942-   US   Crime: Police work - foreign
 Commissario Guido Brunetti - Venice, Italy

David Armstrong	Mark Hebden	Magdalen Nabb
Michael Dibdin	Philip Kerr	Barbara Nadel
Nicolas Freeling	Henning Mankell	Maureen O'Brien
Juliet Hebden	Manuel Vázquez Montalbán	Christopher West

Elmore Leonard   1925-   US   Crime: Modern
www.elmoreleonard.com/

Lawrence Block	George V Higgins	Doug J Swanson
Tim Cockey	Robert B Parker	Peter Tasker
Kinky Friedman	David Peace	Donald E Westlake
Steve Hamilton	John B Spencer	Don Winslow

John T Lescroart   1948-   US   Crime: Legal/financial
www.johnlescroart.com/
 Dismas Hardy, Attorney - San Francisco
Abe Glitsky, Policeman

Harry Bingham	Jonathan Kellerman	John Sandford
Linda Fairstein	Steve Martini	Lisa Scottoline
John Grisham	Nancy Taylor Rosenberg	Robert K Tanenbaum
Jonnie Jacobs		

Doris Lessing   1919-   General
is Doris Tayler & also writes as Jane Somers
http://lessing.redmood.com

J M Coetzee	Pamela Jooste	Joyce Carol Oates
Janet Frame	Candia McWilliam	Paul Scott
Nadine Gordimer	Anne Michaels	Muriel Spark
Elspeth Huxley	Iris Murdoch	

Kathy Lette   1958-   Aus   Chick Lit
www.kathylette.com

Catherine Alliott	Sophie Kinsella	Tyne O'Connell
Sherry Ashworth	India Knight	Susan Oudot
Catherine Feeny	Josie Lloyd & Emlyn Rees	Alexandra Potter
Christina Jones	Melissa Nathan	Sue Townsend

Primo Levi   1919-87   It   *General*

David Grossman   Isaac Bashevis Singer   Alexander Solzhenitsyn

C S Lewis   1898-1963   *Fantasy:* Literary

Ursula K Le Guin   Philip Pullman   Jules Verne
H P Lovecraft   J R R Tolkien   T H White

Roy Lewis   1933-   Wales   *Crime*
also writes as J R Lewis & David Springfield   ⚲ *DI Crow - Northumberland Police*
Arnold Landon, Archaeologist - Newcastle
Eric Ward, Solicitor - Tyneside

Paul Adam   Janet Laurence   Gwen Moffat
David Armstrong   John Malcolm   David Williams
Jeffrey Ashford   Jessica Mann   Derek Wilson
Kate Ellis   M R D Meek

Susan Lewis   *Glitz & Glamour*

Louise Bagshawe   Shirley Conran   Frankie McGowan
Maria Barrett   Judith Gould   Freya North
Sally Beauman   Judi James   Imogen Parker

Freda Lightfoot   *Saga*
also writes as Marion Carr   Manchester
www.fredalightfoot.co.uk

Rita Bradshaw   Ruth Hamilton   Claire Lorrimer
Betty Burton   Evelyn Hood   E V Thompson
Alexandra Connor   Joan Jonker   Margaret Thornton
Elizabeth Gill

Catherine Lim   Sing   *General*

Jung Chang   Arthur Golden   Amy Tan

Don't forget lists of: *Genres * Characters * Literary prizes * Further reading* ☞

Sue Limb 1946- Humour

www.suelimb.com

L

Mavis Cheek	Jane Green	Keith Waterhouse
Kate Fenton	Helen Muir	Arabella Weir
Laurie Graham	Sue Townsend	

Martin Limon 1948- US Crime
♃ Ernie Bascom & George Suenno, US Military police - South Korea

| James Lee Burke | Michael Connelly | Dennis Lehane |
| Lee Child | Joe R Lansdale | David Lindsey |

Irene Lin-Chandler 1965- Tai Crime: PI
♃ Holly-Jean Ho - Chinatown, London

| Liz Evans | Rochelle Krich | Scarlett Thomas |
| Lauren Henderson | Mike Phillips | |

Megan Lindholm 1952- US Fantasy: Epic
also writes as Robin Hobb ♃ The Reindeer People
www.robinhobbonline.com

| Alice Borchardt | Sara Douglass | Sheri S Tepper |
| C J Cherryh | J V Jones | |

Douglas Lindsay 1964- Sco Crime: Humour
www.barney-thomson.com/douglas-lindsay.html ♃ Barney Thomson, Barber - Scotland

| Colin Bateman | Tim Dorsey | Paul Johnston |
| Christopher Brookmyre | Carl Hiaasen | |

Frederic Lindsay 1933- Sco Crime: Police work - Br
www.twbooks.co.uk/authors/fredericlindsay.html ♃ DI Jim Meldrum

Ajay Close	Denise Mina	Ian Rankin
Quintin Jardine	Manda Scott	Peter Turnbull
William McIlvanney		

Don't forget lists of: *Genres * Characters * Literary prizes * Further reading* ☞

David Lindsey 1944- US Adventure/Thriller: Police work - US
www.davidlindsey.com ☆ Det Stuart Haydon, Homicide police intelligence - Houston, Texas

L

Thomas H Cook	Joe R Lansdale	John Sandford
Robert Ferrigno	Martin Limon	Tim Willocks
Thomas Harris	Richard North Patterson	Stuart Woods

Johanna Lindsey 1952- US Glitz & Glamour

Pat Booth	Judith Krantz	Jean Saunders
Jude Deveraux	Fern Michaels	June Flaum Singer

Peter Ling Saga
☆ Judge Family ▪ Minster Family - London

Philip Boast	Lena Kennedy	Alison Stuart
Patricia Burns	Patricia Shaw	Elizabeth Waite
Elizabeth Jeffrey	Mary Jane Staples	Dee Williams

Joan Lingard 1932- Sco General
www.joanlingard.co.uk

Anne Fine	Sue Gee	Bernard MacLaverty
Maureen Freely	Eileen Goudge	Deborah Moggach
Jane Gardam	Jennifer Johnston	

Gillian Linscott 1944- Crime: Historical
www.gillianlinscott.co.uk ☆ Nell Bray, Suffragette

Richard Grayson	Peter Lovesey	CWA 2000 ❀
Martha Grimes	Gwen Moffat	
Ray Harrison	Elizabeth Peters	
Laurie R King	Charles Todd	
Alanna Knight	M J Trow	

Elinor Lipman 1950- US General

Laurie Graham	Anne Tyler
Carol Shields	Rebecca Wells

Laura Lippman 1959- US
www.lauralippman.com

Crime: PI

🏃 Tess Monaghan - Baltimore

Edna Buchanan	Liza Cody	Marcia Muller
Jan Burke	Sue Grafton	Sara Paretsky
Carol Higgins Clark	Margaret Maron	Valerie Wilson Wesley
Tim Cockey		

Holly Lisle 1960- US
www.hollylisle.com

Fantasy: Epic

Alice Borchardt	Kate Elliott	Laurell K Hamilton
Marion Zimmer Bradley	Simon R Green	Mercedes Lackey

Julia Lisle 1937-
also writes as Janet Laurence

General

Hazel Hucker	Annie Leith	Marcia Willett
Erica James	Libby Purves	

Toby Litt 1968-

General

Jake Arnott	Colin Bateman	Ian McEwan

Robert Littell 1935- US

Adventure/Thriller

Eric Ambler	Robert Harris	
Stephen J Cannell	Glenn Meade	CWA 1973 ❀
Alan Furst	Barnaby Williams	

Bentley Little 1960- US
also writes as Phillip Emmons

Horror

Clive Barker	James Herbert	Mark Morris
Simon Clark	Shaun Hutson	Dan Simmons
Muriel Gray	Richard Laymon	

Adam Lively 1961- Wales

General

Julian Barnes	Robert Edric
Peter Benson	Adam Thorpe

Penelope Lively 1933- General

www.penelopelively.net

Nina Bawden	Alice Thomas Ellis
Rachel Billington	Penelope Fitzgerald
Elizabeth Bowen	Susan Hill
Anita Brookner	Lee Langley
A S Byatt	Libby Purves
Isabel Colegate	

Booker   1987 ❀

Nancy Livingston 1935-95 Crime: Humour

🕏 Mr G D H Pringle, HM Tax Inspector, retired

Marian Babson	Michael Pearce
M C Beaton	Laurence Shames
Lilian Jackson Braun	Simon Shaw
Simon Brett	Charles Spencer
Sarah Lacey	

CWA   1988 ❀

Robert Llewellyn Humour

www.llew.co.uk

Guy Bellamy	Tony Parsons
Ben Elton	Peter Tinniswood

Sam Llewellyn 1948- Adventure/Thriller

Gerry Carroll	Mike Lunnon-Wood	Antony Trew
Bernard Cornwell	Philip McCutchan	

Josie Lloyd & Emlyn Rees Chick Lit

Susie Boyt	Kathy Lette	Sue Margolis
Rebecca Campbell	Serena Mackesy	Tyne O'Connell
Lisa Jewell	Chris Manby	Isabel Wolff
Cathy Kelly		

Morgan Llywelyn 1947- Ire Historical

also writes as Shannon Lewis
http://celt.net/Boru/boru1.html

Dinah Lampitt	Edith Pargeter
Diana Norman	Sharon Penman

David Lodge   1935-   *General*
home.freeuk.com/castlegates/lodge.htm

Kingsley Amis	Stanley Middleton	*Hawthornden 1975* ✦
William Boyd	John Mortimer	*Whitbread 1980* ✦
Malcolm Bradbury	Alan Sillitoe	
Colin Douglas	Leslie Thomas	
Michael Frayn	Keith Waterhouse	
Howard Jacobson	Evelyn Waugh	

Norah Lofts   1904-83   *General*
also wrote as Juliet Astley & Peter Curtis

Vanessa Alexander	Georgette Heyer	Rosalind Laker
Elizabeth Chadwick	Pamela Hill	Jean Plaidy
Sandra Gulland	Victoria Holt	

Elizabeth Lord   *Saga*
                                                           London

Harry Bowling	Patricia Grey	Alison Stuart
Patricia Burns	Anna King	Elizabeth Waite
Pamela Evans	Mary Jane Staples	Jeanne Whitmee

Claire Lorrimer   1921-   *Saga*
also writes as Beatrice Coogan & Patricia Robins   ⚶ *Rochford Family*

Charlotte Vale Allen	Victoria Holt	Freda Lightfoot
Domini Highsmith	Sara Hylton	Barbara Whitnell

Tim Lott   1957-   *Lad lit*

Martin Amis	Nick Hornby	*Whitbread 1999* ✦
Mark Barrowcliffe	John McCabe	
Matthew Beaumont	Tony Parsons	
Stephen Fry	Ben Richards	
Alex Garland	Sean Thomas	

*Don't forget lists of: Genres * Characters * Literary prizes * Further reading* ☞

H P Lovecraft 1890-1937 US *Horror*
www.hplovecraft.com

L

Ray Bradbury
Ramsey Campbell
John Farris

Fritz Leiber
C S Lewis
Brian Lumley

S P Somtow
Peter Straub

James Lovegrove 1966- *Science Fiction: Near future*
www.jameslovegrove.com

J G Ballard
Eric Brown
Pat Cadigan

John Meaney
Michael Marshall Smith

Neal Stephenson
Bruce Sterling

Peter Lovesey 1936- *Crime: Historical*
also writes as Peter Lear

Sgt Cribb & PC Thackeray - Historical, C19th England
Peter Diamond, Police - Br, C20th Bath

Arthur Conan Doyle	Kate Ross	CWA	1978 ❀
Ray Harrison	Norman Russell	CWA	1982 ❀
Alanna Knight	Julian Symons	CWA	1995 ❀
Gillian Linscott	M J Trow	CWA	1996 ❀
Amy Myers		CWA	2000 ❀

Sarah Lovett US *Crime*
www.sarahlovett.com

Sylvia Strange, Forensic psychologist - New Mexico

Patricia D Cornwell
Frances Fyfield
Elizabeth George

Lynn S Hightower
Kathy Reichs
Ruth Rendell

Robert W Walker
Minette Walters

Robert Ludlum 1927-2001 US *Adventure/Thriller*
also wrote as Jonathan Ryder
www.robertludlumbooks.com

Tom Bradby
John Burdett
Conor Cregan
Brendan Dubois

Joseph Finder
Greg Iles
Duncan Kyle
Derek Lambert

Matthew Reilly
Kenneth Royce
Lawrence Sanders
Murray Smith

Brian Lumley 1937- Horror
www.brianlumley.com
🏃 Harry Keogh

| Poppy Z Brite | H P Lovecraft | T M Wright |
| Tom Holland | Anne Rice | |

Jonathan Lunn Sea: Historical
is Daniel Hall
🏃 Kit Killigrew - C19th

C S Forester	James L Nelson	Dudley Pope
Alexander Kent	Patrick O'Brian	Julian Stockwin
Philip McCutchan	Marcus Palliser	Richard Woodman

Mike Lunnon-Wood War: Modern

Geoffrey Archer	Andy McNab	Craig Thomas
Frederick Forsyth	John Nichol	Peter Tonkin
Sam Llewellyn		

Alison Lurie 1926- US General

Jane Austen	Louise Erdrich	
Nina Bawden	Lorrie Moore	Pulitzer 1985 ✿
Rachel Billington	Jane Rogers	
Joan Brady	Teresa Waugh	
Agnes Desarthe	Edith Wharton	

Jim Lusby Ire Crime: Police work - foreign
🏃 DI Cal McCadden - Waterford, Ireland

John Brady	John Harvey	Rory McCormac
Bartholomew Gill	Quintin Jardine	Eugene McEldowney
Hugo Hamilton	Bill Knox	

Eric Lustbader 1946- US Adventure/Thriller
also writes as Eric Van Lustbader
🏃 Nicholas Linnear

Bryce Courtenay	Christopher Nicole	Justin Scott
Colin Falconer	Marc Olden	Dov Silverman
David Morrell	Alan Savage	Murray Smith

178

Gavin Lyall   1932-   Adventure/Thriller
♟ Harry Maxim, Spy ▪ Captain Matthew Ranklin, Spy

Jon Cleary	John Francome	A J Quinnell
Len Deighton	John Gardner	Derek Robinson
Ian Fleming	Alistair MacLean	Michael Shea
Dick Francis	Richard Pitman	William Smethurst

Patrick Lynch   1962-   Adventure/Thriller
is Philip Sington

Robin Cook	Daniel Easterman
Bryce Courtenay	Justin Scott

Genevieve Lyons   *Ire*   Historical

Evelyn Anthony	Elaine Crowley	Elisabeth McNeill
Maeve Binchy	Sheelagh Kelly	Anne Melville
Catherine Coulter	Lena Kennedy	Mary Minton
Teresa Crane	Mary A Larkin	M R O'Donnell

Amin Maalouf   1949-   *Lebanon*   Adventure/Thriller

James Clavell	Daniel Easterman	Julian Rathbone
Bryce Courtenay	Lawrence Norfolk	Alan Savage

Paul J McAuley   1955-   Science Fiction: Technical

Gregory Benford	Linda Nagata	*Arthur C Clarke 1996* ✸
Christopher Evans	Richard Powers	
Paul Johnston	Alastair Reynolds	
Jack McDevitt	Ian Watson	
Ian McDonald	David Wingrove	
John Meaney	Jack Womack	

Ed McBain   1926-   US   Crime: Police work - US
is Salvatore Lombino   *♟ Det Steve Carella - 87th Precinct,*
& also writes as Curt Cannon, Hunt Collins,   *'Isola' Police Department*
Evan Hunter & Richard Marsten   *Det Matthew Hope, Attorney*
www.edmcbain.com

K C Constantine	Donald Harstad	Faye Kellerman
John Creasey	Tony Hillerman	Robert B Parker
William Diehl	Jon A Jackson	Joseph Wambaugh
W E B Griffin	J A Jance	

Brenda McBryde

Saga
NE England

Irene Carr
Valerie Georgeson
Una Horne

Sheila Jansen
Wendy Robertson
Sarah Shears

Janet MacLeod Trotter
Dee Williams

M

John McCabe   1967-

Humour

Terence Blacker
Douglas Coupland
Ben Elton

James Hawes
Charles Higson

Nick Hornby
Tim Lott

Patrick McCabe   1955-   Ire

General

Dermot Bolger
Bruce Chatwin
Roddy Doyle
James Hawes

Sean Hughes
Colum McCann
John McGahern
Paul Micou

Joseph O'Connor
David Park
Will Self

Anne McCaffrey   1926-   US   Science Fiction: Space and time

also writes as Elizabeth Moon
www.annemccaffrey.org

Lois McMaster Bujold
Stephen Donaldson
Barbara Hambly
Elizabeth Haydon

Katharine Kerr
Mercedes Lackey
Julian May
Melanie Rawn

Jan Siegel
Sheri S Tepper
Margaret Weis

Robert McCammon   1952-   US

Horror

Douglas Clegg
John Farris
Dean R Koontz
Graham Masterton

Anne Rice
John Saul
Steven Spruill

Peter Straub
Whitley Strieber
T M Wright

Colum McCann   1965-   Ire

General

Dermot Bolger
Patrick McCabe

Brian Moore
Joseph O'Connor

Cormac McCarthy   1933-   US   General
South-West USA

Thomas Eidson	Jim Harrison	Stewart O'Nan
William Faulkner	Stuart Harrison	David Adams Richards
Charles Frazier	Carson McCullers	J D Salinger
David Guterson	Thomas McGuane	Larry Watson

M

Wil McCarthy   1967-   US   Science Fiction: Technical

Stephen Baxter	Michael Moorcock	Robert Charles Wilson
Greg Bear	Linda Nagata	David Wingrove
Gregory Benford	Vernor Vinge	

Geraldine McCaughrean   1951-   General

Dorothy Dunnett	Penelope Fitzgerald	Jill Paton Walsh
Robert Edric	Julian Rathbone	

Ken McClure   Sco   Crime: Medical
also writes as Ken Begg

Paul Adam	Robin Cook	Andrew Puckett
Colin Andrews	Michael Crichton	Claire Rayner
Paul Carson	Tess Gerritsen	Leah Ruth Robinson
Windsor Chorlton	Richard Preston	Stella Shepherd

Rory McCormac   Crime
⚕ *Frank Samson, Veterinary surgeon - Ireland*

John Brady	Bartholomew Gill	Jim Lusby
Ruth Dudley Edwards	Hugo Hamilton	Eugene McEldowney

L McCrossan   Chick Lit

Jenny Colgan	Isla Dewar	Wendy Holden
Claudine Cullimore	Maggie Gibson	Lisa Jewell

Don't forget lists of: *Genres* * *Characters* * *Literary prizes* * *Further reading* ☞

Sharyn McCrumb   1948-   US   Crime: Psychological
www.sharynmccrumb.com/
‡ Sheriff Spenser Arrowood
Elizabeth McPherson, Anthropologist - Appalachians, East Tennessee

Nevada Barr	Andrew Klavan	Ruth Rendell
Caleb Carr	Margaret Maron	Kathy Hogan Trocheck
Tony Hillerman	Carol O'Connell	

M

Carson McCullers   1917-67   US   General
www.carson-mccullers.com
Southern USA

Truman Capote	Connie May Fowler	Cormac McCarthy
William Faulkner	Alice Hoffman	J D Salinger
F Scott Fitzgerald	Harper Lee	Anne Rivers Siddons

Colleen McCullough   1938-   Aus   Historical

Margaret George	Allan Massie	Edward Rutherfurd
Robert Graves	Lynne Pemberton	Simon Scarrow
Christian Jacq	Mary Renault	Patricia Shaw
Ross Leckie	Rosemary Rowe	Wilbur Smith

Philip McCutchan   1920-96   Sea: Historical & Modern
also wrote as
Duncan MacNeil
‡ Donald Cameron & St Vincent Halfhyde - Royal Navy
Commodore Kemp, Merchant Marine

Alexander Fullerton	Sam Llewellyn	Antony Trew
Max Hennessy	Jonathan Lunn	John Winton
Richard Howard	Dudley Pope	Richard Woodman
Alexander Kent	Peter Tonkin	

Val McDermid   1955-   Sco   Crime
www.valmcdermid.com/
‡ DCI Carol Jordan & Dr Tony Hill, Psychologist
Lindsay Gordon, journalist - Glasgow ▪ Kate Brannigan, PI - Manchester
Fiona Cameron, Academic psychologist

Denise Danks	Ellen Hart	CWA 1995 ✿
Stella Duffy	Frank Lean	
Alma Fritchley	Denise Mina	
Joseph Glass	Gemma O'Connor	
Lesley Grant-Adamson	Danuta Reah	
Christine Green	Sally Spencer	

Jack McDevitt 1935- US Science Fiction: Space and time
www.sfwa.org/members/mcdevitt ⚡ Priscilla Hutchins (Hutch)

Poul Anderson	Paul J McAuley	Alastair Reynolds
Stephen Baxter	Ken MacLeod	Clifford D Simak
Arthur C Clarke		

M

Ian McDonald 1960- Science Fiction: Space and time
www.lysator.liu.se/~unicorn/mcdonald/

Stephen Baxter	K W Jeter	Linda Nagata
Pat Cadigan	Gwyneth Jones	Kim Stanley Robinson
Greg Egan	Paul J McAuley	Brian Stableford
Jon Courtenay Grimwood		

John D MacDonald 1916-86 US Crime: PI
⚡ Travis McGee - Florida

Lawrence Block	Erle Stanley Gardner	Lawrence Sanders
Raymond Chandler	James Hall	Donald E Westlake
James Hadley Chase	J A Jance	Charles Willeford

Malcolm Macdonald 1932- Saga
also writes as M R O'Donnell & Malcolm Ross ⚡ Stevenson Family

Gloria Cook	Jenny Glanfield	Janet Tanner
Alexander Cordell	Winston Graham	T R Wilson
R F Delderfield	Caroline Stickland	

Marianne MacDonald 1934- Can Crime
www.malicebooks.com/web_pages/britauth/macdonald.htm ⚡ Dido Hoare, Antiquarian Bookseller - London

Mary Clayton	Hazel Holt	Annette Roome
Natasha Cooper	Alison Joseph	Veronica Stallwood
Alma Fritchley	Morag Joss	Scarlett Thomas
Veronica Heley	Valerie Kershaw	

Ross Macdonald   1915-83   US   Crime: PI

was Kenneth Millar & also wrote as John Macdonald
& John Ross Macdonald   ⅄ Lew Archer - California
www.kirjasto.sci.fi/rossmacd.htm

Lawrence Block	James Crumley	George P Pelecanos
Raymond Chandler	Dashiell Hammett	Sam Reaves
James Hadley Chase	Joseph Hansen	James Sallis

M

Carl MacDougall   1941-   Sco   General

www.sciences.demon.co.uk/r-macdoug-c.htm

Iain Banks	James Kelman	Allan Massie
Alex Benzie	Bernard MacLaverty	Alan Spence
Andrew Greig	Duncan McLean	Alan Warner

Eugene McEldowney   1943-   Ire   Crime: Police work - Br

⅄ Supt Cecil Megarry - RUC

John Brady	Bill James	Ian Rankin
Bartholomew Gill	Jim Lusby	Peter Turnbull
Hugo Hamilton	Rory McCormac	

Ian McEwan   1948-   General

Martin Amis	Esther Freud	Whitbread 1987 ✺
Iain Banks	Elizabeth Knox	Booker 1998 ✺
David Cook	Toby Litt	W H Smith 2001 ✺
Jeremy Dronfield	Julie Myerson	
Michel Faber	David Park	
Tibor Fischer	Tim Parks	

John McGahern   1934-   Ire   General

John Banville	Brian Moore	V S Pritchett
James Joyce	Ardal O'Hanlon	Colm Toibin
Patrick McCabe	David Park	William Trevor

Michael McGarrity   US   Crime: PI

⅄ Kevin Kearney, retired policeman - New Mexico

Ace Atkins	Steve Hamilton	Tony Hillerman
Nevada Barr	Donald Harstad	J A Jance
Robert Ferrigno		

Frankie McGowan

Glitz & Glamour

Barbara Taylor Bradford	Susan Lewis
Shirley Conran	Penny Vincenzi

Jill McGown   1947-   Sco

www.jillmcgown.com

Crime: Police work - Br

🏃 DCI Lloyd & DI Judy Hill - 'Stansfield'

Jo Bannister	Barry Maitland	Ann Quinton
Stephen Booth	Priscilla Masters	Staynes & Storey
Linda Davies	Jennie Melville	Julian Symons
Paula Gosling	Janet Neel	Rebecca Tope

Elizabeth McGregor

Crime: Psychological

also writes as Holly Fox
www.bookreporter.com/authors/au-mcgregor-elizabeth.asp

Penelope Evans	J Wallis Martin	Melanie Tem
Nicci French	Carol Smith	Barbara Vine

Thomas McGuane   1939-   US

General

Martin Amis	Jim Harrison	Larry McMurtry
Pete Dexter	Barbara Kingsolver	Thomas Pynchon
Richard Ford	Cormac McCarthy	Tom Robbins

William McIlvanney   1936-   Sco

Crime: Police work - Br

🏃 DI Jack Laidlaw - Glasgow

John Harvey	Frederic Lindsay	Whitbread	1975 ✹
Quintin Jardine	Ian Rankin	CWA	1977 ✹
James Kelman	Peter Turnbull	CWA	1983 ✹

Jay McInerney   1955-   US

General

www.jaymcinerney.com

Dominick Dunne	Armistead Maupin	Matt Thorne
Bret Easton Ellis	Philip Roth	Tom Wolfe
Jack Kerouac	J D Salinger	

Shena Mackay 1944- Sco General
www.nls.uk/writestuff/heads/wee-mackay.html

Jane Asher	Esther Freud	Candia McWilliam
Kate Atkinson	Jane Hamilton	Marge Piercy
Pat Barker	Angela Huth	Muriel Spark
Mavis Cheek	Jennifer Johnston	

M

Walter Macken 1915-67 Ire General
www.irishwriters-online.com/waltermacken.html

Christine Marion Fraser	Miss Read	Rebecca Shaw
Mary E Pearce	Pam Rhodes	Sarah Shears

Juliet E McKenna 1965- Fantasy: Epic

James Barclay	Elizabeth Haydon	K J Parker
Steven Erikson	Kate Jacoby	Freda Warrington
David Farland	George R R Martin	

Hilda McKenzie Wales Saga
Wales

Catrin Collier	Catrin Morgan	Rosie Thomas
Mary Minton	Cynthia S Roberts	Grace Thompson

Serena Mackesy Chick Lit

Zoë Barnes	Sophie Kinsella	Sue Margolis
Anna Davis	Josie Lloyd & Emlyn Rees	Tyne O'Connell
Helen Fielding	Chris Manby	

Mary Mackie Saga
also writes as Alex Andrews, Caroline Charles, Lincolnshire ▪ Norfolk
Cathy Christopher, Mary Christopher & Susan Stevens

Margaret Dickinson	Connie Monk	Judith Saxton
Helen Forrester	Elizabeth Murphy	Sue Sully
Jonathan Grant	Pamela Pope	T R Wilson
Elizabeth Jeffrey		

John McLaren   1951-   Sco   *Crime: Legal/financial*

Harry Bingham
Paul Erdman
Stephen Frey

John Grisham
Paul Kilduff

Brad Meltzer
Scott Turow

Bernard MacLaverty   1942-   Ire   *General*
www.imsa.edu/~paulb/irish/literature/maclaverty.html

Dermot Bolger
David Cook
Ronald Frame
Joan Lingard

Carl MacDougall
Allan Massie
Joseph O'Connor
Julian Rathbone

Piers Paul Read
Adam Thorpe
Colm Toibin
Niall Williams

Alistair MacLean   1922-87   Sco   *Adventure/Thriller*
also wrote as Ian Stuart
www.kirjasto.sci.fi/maclean.htm

Desmond Bagley
Gerry Carroll
Ian Fleming
James Follett

Hammond Innes
Geoffrey Jenkins
Duncan Kyle
Gavin Lyall

Nicholas Monsarrat
A J Quinnell
William Smethurst
Peter Tonkin

Duncan McLean   1964-   Sco   *General*

Iain Banks
Guy Burt
Des Dillon
Michel Faber
Gordon Legge

Carl MacDougall
Andrew O'Hagan
Paul Sayer
Alan Spence
Alan Warner

S Maugham   1993 ❀

Alison McLeay   d 1998   Sco   *Saga*

Inga Dunbar
Barbara Erskine
Diana Gabaldon

Judith Glover
Philippa Gregory
Rosamunde Pilcher

Reay Tannahill
Eileen Townsend

Don't forget lists of: *Genres * Characters * Literary prizes * Further reading* ☞

Charlotte MacLeod 1922- Can   Crime: Humour

also writes as Ailsa Craig   ⚘ Madoc Rhys ▪ Prof Peter Shandy, PI
www.twbookmark.com/authors/62/260/   Max Bittersohn & Sarah Kelling, Amateur PI
                                                            New England

M

Marian Babson	Emma Lathen	John Sherwood
Lilian Jackson Braun	Margaret Maron	Kathy Hogan Trocheck
Edmund Crispin	Gwen Moffat	David Williams

Ken MacLeod 1954- Sco   Science Fiction: Space and time

Steve Aylett	Jack McDevitt	BSFA 1999 ✹
Iain M Banks	John Meaney	
Ray Bradbury	China Miéville	
Octavia E Butler	Alastair Reynolds	
Greg Egan	Adam Roberts	
Christopher Evans	Mary Doria Russell	

Pauline McLynn Ire   Crime: Humour

⚘ Leo Street - Dublin

John Brady	Sparkle Hayter	Ardal O'Hanlon
Janet Evanovich	Lauren Henderson	Susan Sussman with
Liz Evans	Susan Isaacs	Sarajane Avidon
Maggie Gibson		

Katharine McMahon   General

www.sciences.demon.co.uk/r-mcmahon-k.htm

Tracy Chevalier	Marianne Fredriksson
Stevie Davies	Salley Vickers

Terry McMillan 1951- US   General

http://voices.cla.umn.edu/authors/TerryMcMillan.html

Esther Freud	Toni Morrison	Alice Walker
John Irving	Gloria Naylor	Valerie Wilson Wesley

Don't forget lists of: *Genres * Characters * Literary prizes * Further reading* ☞

Larry McMurtry   1936-   US   General
www.bookreporter.com/authors/au-mcmurtry-larry.asp

Pat Conroy   Jack Kerouac   Pulitzer   1986 ✵
Barbara Esstman   Thomas McGuane
Nicholas Evans   James A Michener   **M**
Charles Frazier   Marge Piercy
Jim Harrison   John Steinbeck
John Irving

Andy McNab   1960-   *War:* Modern

Peter Cave   Frederick Forsyth   John Nichol
Shaun Clarke   Alan Judd   Chris Ryan
Murray Davies   Mike Lunnon-Wood   Gordon Stevens

Claire McNab   1940-   Aus   *Crime:* Police work - foreign
also writes as Clare Carmichael   ⚐ *DI Carol Ashton - Sydney*
                            Denise Cleever, Intelligence Agent - Australia

Jan Burke   Peter Guttridge   Laurie R King
John Burns   Ellen Hart   Margaret Maron
Jon Cleary   J A Jance   Chris Niles
Stella Duffy   Valerie Kershaw   Carol O'Connell

Judith McNaught   1944-   US   General
www.judithmcnaught.com

Elizabeth Boyle   Judith Gould   Amanda Quick
Catherine Coulter   Penny Jordan   Lavyrle Spencer
Barbara Delinsky   Jayne Ann Krentz   Danielle Steel

Elisabeth McNeill   1931-   Sco   *Saga*
                                                           Scotland

Emma Blair   Genevieve Lyons   Sarah Shears
Teresa Crane   Anne Melville   Agnes Short
Doris Davidson   Elvi Rhodes   Kirsty White
Gwen Kirkwood

189

Candia McWilliam 1955- Sco General

Nicola Barker	Allan Massie	*Guardian* 1994 ✹
Elizabeth Bowen	Iris Murdoch	
A S Byatt	Jane Rogers	
Sally Emerson	Muriel Spark	
Doris Lessing	Jill Paton Walsh	
Shena Mackay	Marina Warner	

Norman Mailer 1923- US General
www.normanmailerworksanddays.com

Don DeLillo	William Styron	*Pulitzer* 1980 ✹
Joseph Heller	John Updike	
Ernest Hemingway	Gore Vidal	
John Steinbeck	Tom Wolfe	

Barry Maitland 1941- Sco Crime: Police work - Br
www.malicebooks.com/web_pages/britauth/maitland.htm

ꙮ DCI David Brock &
DS Kathy Kolla - London

David Armstrong	Kate Ellis	Jill McGown
Jo Bannister	Elizabeth George	Maureen O'Brien
Stephen Booth	Cynthia Harrod-Eagles	Mike Phillips
Ann Cleeves	Susan Kelly	Alan Scholefield

Sara Maitland 1950- Sco General
http://trace.ntu.ac.uk/voices/maitland.htm

Beryl Bainbridge	Zoe Fairbairns	Emma Tennant
Margaret Drabble	Catherine Fox	Fay Weldon
Alice Thomas Ellis	Michele Roberts	

Maggie Makepeace Saga

Anne Atkins	Katie Fforde	Titia Sutherland
Nina Dufort	Rosamunde Pilcher	Ann Swinfen
Kate Fenton	Jill Roe	Marcia Willett

Don't forget lists of: *Genres* * *Characters* * *Literary prizes* * *Further reading* ☞

John Malcolm 1936-   *Crime*

♁ Tim Simpson, Art investment advisor

William Ardin	Philip Hook	Iain Pears
Jonathan Gash	Roy Lewis	Derek Wilson

M

Allan Mallinson   *War: Historical*

♁ Matthew Hervey, Captain - C19th Light Dragoons

Nicholas Carter	Garry Douglas	Patrick O'Brian
Tom Connery	Richard Howard	Dan Parkinson
Bernard Cornwell	Christopher Nicole	

David Malouf 1934- Aus   *General*

www.middlemiss.org/lit/authors/maloufd/maloufd.html

Peter Carey	Elizabeth Jolley	Commonwealth 1991 ✹
James Clavell	Thomas Keneally	IMPAC 1996 ✹
Robert Drewe	Ben Okri	
Rodney Hall	Morris West	
Janette Turner Hospital	Patrick White	

David Mamet 1947- US   *General*

Paul Auster	Don DeLillo
Raymond Carver	Jim Harrison

Chris Manby 1972-   *Chick Lit*

Jessica Adams	Josie Lloyd & Emlyn Rees	Tyne O'Connell
Faith Bleasdale	Serena Mackesy	Alexandra Potter
Sarah Harris	Sue Margolis	Linda Taylor
Sophie Kinsella	Helen Muir	Arabella Weir

Valerio Massimo Manfredi 1943- It   *Historical*

♁ Alexander the Great

Robert Graves	Allan Massie	Mary Renault
Christian Jacq	Steven Pressfield	Wilbur Smith
Ross Leckie		

Henning Mankell 1948- Swe Crime: Police work - foreign

Insp Kurt Wallander - Ystad, Sweden

Colin Dexter	Donna Leon	CWA 2001 ❁
Kerstin Ekman	Barbara Nadel	
Nicolas Freeling	Alexander McCall Smith	
Peter Hoeg	Janwillem van de Wetering	

M

Jessica Mann 1937- Crime

www.jessicamann.net

Tamara Hoyland, Archaeologist
Thea Crawford, Professor ▪ Dr Fidelis Berlin, Psychiatrist

Kate Ellis	Susan Moody	Margaret Yorke
Roy Lewis	Alison Taylor	

Olivia Manning 1908-80 General

Lynne Reid Banks	Robert Graves	Tom-Gallon 1949 ❁
Elizabeth Bowen	Matthew Kneale	
Lawrence Durrell	Paul Scott	
Rumer Godden	Evelyn Waugh	

Jill Mansell Chick Lit

http://authorpages.hoddersystems.com/jillmansell

Catherine Alliott	Jilly Cooper	Melissa Nathan
Zoë Barnes	Sarah Harris	Victoria Routledge
Francesca Clementis	Christina Jones	Penny Vincenzi
Jenny Colgan		

Hilary Mantel 1952- General

www.complete-review.com/authors/mantelh.htm

Hilary Bailey	Carole Morin	Holtby 1990 ❁
Candida Crewe	Julie Myerson	Hawthornden 1996 ❁
Joanne Harris	Jane Rogers	
Elizabeth Jolley	Muriel Spark	
Angela Lambert	Harriet Waugh	
Deborah Moggach		

Don't forget lists of: *Genres * Characters * Literary prizes * Further reading* ☞

Lindsay Maracotta US   Crime
⚲ Lucy Freers, Animated film maker - California

Marian Babson
Jeffery Deaver
Janet Evanovich

Sparkle Hayter
Susan Isaacs

Donald Rawley
Kathy Hogan Trocheck

Hannah March   Crime: Historical
⚲ Robert Fairfax - C18th England

Bruce Alexander
Stephanie Barron
Gwendoline Butler

Keith Heller
Deryn Lake
Margaret Lawrence

Fidelis Morgan
Derek Wilson

John Marco US   Fantasy: Epic
www.tyrantsandkings.com/

James Barclay
Terry Brooks
Chris Bunch

Stephen Donaldson
Steven Erikson

Raymond E Feist
Robert Jordan

Phillip M Margolin 1944- US   Crime: Legal/financial
www.phillipmargolin.com

William Diehl
Stephen Frey
Thomas Harris
Colin Harrison

Steve Martini
Richard North Patterson
Nancy Taylor Rosenberg

John Sandford
Lisa Scottoline
Scott Turow

Sue Margolis   Chick Lit

Catherine Alliott
Zoë Barnes
Josie Lloyd & Emlyn Rees

Serena Mackesy
Chris Manby

Sheila O'Flanagan
Isabel Wolff

Juliet Marillier NZ   Fantasy: Myth
www.julietmarillier.com   *Sevenwaters Trilogy ▪ Saga of the Light Isles*

Alice Borchardt
Marion Zimmer Bradley
Storm Constantine

Charles de Lint
Robin Hobb
George R R Martin

Caiseal Mor
Catrin Morgan
Jan Siegel

Margaret Maron 1959- US

Crime: Police work - US

⚑ *Deborah Knott, Judge - North Carolina*
Sigrid Harald - New York Police

www.margaretmaron.com/

M

Nevada Barr	W E B Griffin	Charlotte MacLeod
Lilian Jackson Braun	Ellen Hart	Claire McNab
Jan Burke	Laura Lippman	Kathy Hogan Trocheck
Carol Higgins Clark	Sharyn McCrumb	Robert W Walker

Adam Mars-Jones 1954-

General

Michael Carson	Armistead Maupin	*S Maugham 1982* ✿
Philip Hensher	Edmund White	
Alan Hollinghurst		

Ngaio Marsh 1899-1982 NZ

Crime: Police work - Br

⚑ *DI Roderick Alleyn*

Margery Allingham	Elizabeth Ferrars	Dorothy L Sayers
Joanna Cannan	Janet Harward	Dorothy Simpson
John Dickson Carr	Emma Page	Josephine Tey
Agatha Christie	David Roberts	Patricia Wentworth

Sybil Marshall 1913-

General

'Old Swithinford'

Caroline Bridgwood	Pamela Oldfield	Miss Read
Margaret Dickinson	Mary E Pearce	Pam Rhodes
Judith Lennox	Ann Purser	Susan Sallis
Nora Naish		

Edward Marston 1940- Wales

Crime: Historical

also writes as Martin Inigo,
A E Marston, Kenneth Miles
& Christopher Mountjoy

⚑ *Nicholas Bracewell, Theatre - C16th*
Ralph Delchard & Gervase Bret - C11th ⎫ *England*
Christopher Redmayne & Jonathan Bale - C17th ⎭

Fiona Buckley	Paul Doherty	Viviane Moore
P F Chisholm	Susanna Gregory	Fidelis Morgan
Michael Clynes	Michael Jecks	Kate Sedley
Judith Cook	Bernard Knight	Peter Tonkin

*Don't forget lists of: Genres * Characters * Literary prizes * Further reading* ☞

David Martin   1946-   US   Horror

Chaz Brenchley   Jack Harvey   Graham Masterton
Philip Caveney   Graham Joyce   Michael Stewart

David Ralph Martin   Crime: Police work - Br **M**
                                    ⚑ DS Vic Hallam & DC John Cromer - Bristol

Ken Bruen   Bill James   Martyn Waites
Paul Charles   David Peace

George R R Martin   1948-   US   Fantasy: Epic
www.georgerrmartin.com

James Barclay   Maggie Furey   Tim Powers
C J Cherryh   Jan Siegel   Robert Silverberg
David A Drake   Juliet E McKenna   Roger Taylor
Steven Erikson   Juliet Marillier   Harry Turtledove

J Wallis Martin   Adventure/Thriller: Psychological

Nicci French   Maureen O'Brien   Minette Walters
Elizabeth McGregor   Ruth Rendell   Robert Wilson
Janet Neel

Steve Martini   1946-   US   Crime: Legal/financial
www.stevemartini.com/   ⚑ Paul Madriani, Lawyer - San Diego

Catherine Arnold   Philip Friedman   Richard North Patterson
Harry Bingham   John T Lescroart   Nancy Taylor Rosenberg
Alan M Dershowitz   Phillip M Margolin   Lisa Scottoline
Linda Fairstein   Brad Meltzer   Robert K Tanenbaum

David Mason   1951-   US   Adventure/Thriller

Jeffrey Archer   Frederick Forsyth   John Nichol
Stephen J Cannell   Johnny 'Two Combs' Howard   Chris Ryan
Tom Clancy   Stephen Leather
Conor Cregan

Allan Massie   *1938-*   *Sco*   *General*

Alex Benzie	Bernard MacLaverty	Piers Paul Read
Ronald Frame	Candia McWilliam	William Rivière
Carl MacDougall	Frederic Raphael	

Allan Massie   *1938-*   *Sco*   *Historical*

Lindsey Davis	Valerio Massimo Manfredi	Steven Saylor
Robert Graves	Robert Nye	Simon Scarrow
Ross Leckie	Mary Renault	Marilyn Todd
Colleen McCullough	Rosemary Rowe	David Wishart

John Masters   *1914-83*   *US*   *General*

Amit Chaudhuri	M M Kaye	R K Narayan
James Clavell	James A Michener	Paul Scott
Rumer Godden	Nicholas Monsarrat	Morris West
Ruth Prawer Jhabvala	V S Naipaul	

Priscilla Masters   *1952-*   *Crime: Police work - Br*
www.joannapiercy.com/PriscillaMasters.htm   ♁ DI Joanna Piercy & DS Mike Korpanski
'Moorlands', Staffordshire

Jo Bannister	Deborah Crombie	Marjorie Eccles
Brian Battison	Judith Cutler	H R F Keating
Stephen Booth	Margaret Duffy	Jill McGown

Graham Masterton   *1946-*   *Sco*   *Horror*

John Farris	Robert McCammon	John Saul
Christopher Fowler	David Martin	Michael Stewart
Stephen Gallagher	Kim Newman	Whitley Strieber
Shaun Hutson		

Ángeles Mastretta   *1949-*   *Mex*   *General*
www.lasmujeres.com/angelesmastretta/

Isabel Allende	Laura Esquivel
Mário de Carvalho	Gabriel Garcia Márquez

Richard Matheson 1926- US *Horror*
also writes as Logan Swanson

Jonathan Aycliffe
Dennis Etchison

Robert Girardi
Dean R Koontz

Stephen Laws
Peter Straub

Carole Matthews *Chick Lit*
www.carolematthews.co.uk

Catherine Alliott
Zoë Barnes

Francesca Clementis
Isla Dewar

Julie Ellis
Sue Welfare

Peter Matthiessen 1927- US *General*

Dennis Bock
Jim Crace
Pete Dexter

Jim Harrison
Joseph Kanon
William Kennedy

Annie Proulx
William Rivière
Larry Watson

Somerset Maugham 1874-1965 *General*

Joseph Conrad
Charles Dickens
Michel Faber

Christopher Hudson
J B Priestley
V S Pritchett

Barbara Pym
Morris West

Armistead Maupin 1944- US *General*

Truman Capote
Michael Carson
Patrick Gale

Alan Hollinghurst
Hanif Kureishi

Jay McInerney
Adam Mars-Jones

John R Maxim US *Adventure/Thriller*
⚐ *Paul Bannerman, US Intelligence - Connecticut*

Tom Clancy
Stephen Coonts

Patricia D Cornwell
Daniel Easterman

Stephen Hunter
James Patterson

Anna Maxted *Chick Lit*

Geraldine Bedell
Martina Devlin
Isla Dewar

Lisa Jewell
Cathy Kelly
Marian Keyes

India Knight
Claire Naylor
Adele Parks

Jenny Maxwell   *Sco*   *Adventure/Thriller*

Louise Doughty   Faye Kellerman   Peter Robinson
Penelope Evans   James Patterson   Carol Smith

M Robin Maxwell   *Historical*

Philippa Gregory   Maureen Peters   Anya Seton
Sandra Gulland   Jean Plaidy

Julian May   *1931- US*   *Fantasy: Epic*
Pliocene Saga

A A Attanasio   Stephen Donaldson   Michael Moorcock
Marion Zimmer Bradley   Barbara Hambly   Robert Silverberg
Ellen Datlow   Anne McCaffrey   Gene Wolfe

Peter May   *Sco*   *Crime: Police work - foreign*
⚗ Det Li Yan, PR - China ▪ Margaret Campbell, Pathologist - Chicago

Martin Booth   Patricia D Cornwell   Martin Cruz Smith
Lee Child   Kathy Reichs   Christopher West
Martina Cole

Margaret Mayhew   *Saga*

Anne Baker   Lilian Harry   Maureen Lee
Helen Carey   Angela Huth   Victor Pemberton
Elizabeth Elgin   Joan Jonker

J K Mayo   *1914-*   *Adventure/Thriller*
⚗ Col Harry Seddall

Eric Ambler   Ian Fleming   A J Quinnell
Peter Driscoll   John Gardner

Juliette Mead   *1960-*   *General*

Kate Alexander   Elizabeth Darrell   Kate Sharam
Elizabeth Buchan   Sebastian Faulks

Glenn Meade   Ire   Adventure/Thriller

Campbell Armstrong   Robert Harris   Donald James
Lionel Davidson   Greg Iles   Robert Littell
Frederick Forsyth

John Meaney   Science Fiction: Technical

Greg Bear   Jon Courtenay Grimwood   Ken MacLeod
Gene Brewer   James Lovegrove   Alastair Reynolds
Greg Egan   Paul J McAuley   Adam Roberts

M R D Meek   1918-   Sco   Crime
♁ Lennox Kemp, Solicitor - London

Colin Dexter   Joyce Holms   Roy Lewis
Martin Edwards   P D James   R D Wingfield
Frances Fyfield

Gita Mehta   1943-   Ind   General

Amit Chaudhuri   Hanif Kureishi   Michael Ondaatje
Anita Desai   R K Narayan   Salman Rushdie
M M Kaye

Brad Meltzer   1970-   US   Adventure/Thriller: Legal/financial
www.bradmeltzer.com

David Baldacci   Paul Kilduff   Christopher Reich
Po Bronson   John McLaren   Michael Ridpath
Stephen Frey   Steve Martini

Anne Melville   1926-98   Saga
♁ Lorimer Family ▪ Hardie Family

Judith Glover   Genevieve Lyons   Pamela Oldfield
Anna King   Elisabeth McNeill   Claire Rayner
Beryl Kingston   Mary Minton   Sarah Shears

Don't forget lists of: *Genres* * *Characters* * *Literary prizes* * *Further reading* ☞

Jennie Melville 1922-

also writes as Gwendoline Butler

Crime: *Police work - Br*
⚥ DI Charmian Daniels - Windsor

Natasha Cooper	Jill McGown	Ann Quinton
Paula Gosling	Iain Pears	Patricia Wentworth

M

Pauline Melville 1941- Guy

General

Fred D'Aguiar	Bernice Rubens	*Guardian*	1990 ❀
Lucy Ellman	Evelyn Waugh	*Whitbread*	1997 ❀
Graham Greene	Harriet Waugh		

Catherine Merriman 1949- Wales

General

Carol Birch	Helen Dunmore	Julia Hamilton
Melvyn Bragg	Lesley Glaister	

Judith Michael 1934- US

is Judith Barnard & Michael Fain

Glitz & Glamour

Sally Beauman	Jackie Collins	Judith Gould
Celia Brayfield	Lucinda Edmonds	Judi James

Anne Michaels 1958- Can

General

Julia Blackburn	Bernhard Schlink	*Guardian*	1997 ❀
Dennis Bock	Carol Shields	*Orange*	1997 ❀
Doris Lessing	Madeleine St John	*Wingate*	1997 ❀
Caryl Phillips	Jane Urquhart		
Michele Roberts			

Barbara Michaels 1927- US

is Barbara Mertz & also writes as Elizabeth Peters
www.mpmbooks.com

General

Jane Brindle	Elizabeth Harris	Mary Stewart
June Drummond	Jane Aiken Hodge	Madge Swindells
Diane Guest	Judith Kelman	Daoma Winston

Don't forget lists of: *Genres* * *Characters* * *Literary prizes* * *Further reading* ☞

Fern Michaels   1933-   US   Glitz & Glamour

is Mary Kuczkir
www.fernmichaels.com/

Jackie Collins   Roberta Latow   June Flaum Singer
Jude Deveraux   Johanna Lindsey   Lavyrle Spencer
Julie Ellis

James A Michener   1907-97   US   General

www.jamesmichener.com

Howard Fast   John Masters   Leon Uris
Larry McMurtry   Edward Rutherfurd   Gore Vidal

Paul Micou   1959-   US   General

William Boyd   Patrick McCabe   Evelyn Waugh
Ronald Frame   J D Salinger   Tom Wolfe
Patrick Gale

Stanley Middleton   1919-   General

Kingsley Amis   David Lodge   Booker   1974 ✹
Melvyn Bragg   Alan Sillitoe
Francis King   Tony Warren

China Miéville   Science Fiction: Space and time

Stephen Baxter   Philip Pullman   Arthur C Clarke 2001 ✹
Orson Scott Card   Alastair Reynolds
Mary Gentle   Adam Roberts
Ken MacLeod   Kim Stanley Robinson
Michael Moorcock   Michael Marshall Smith
Larry Niven

Rosalind Miles   Historical

www.rosalind.net

Margaret George   Sharon Penman
Helen Hollick   Mary Stewart

Andrew Miller   1960-   Historical

Elizabeth Knox   Iain Pears   Black   1997 ❀
Lawrence Norfolk   Rose Tremain   IMPAC   1999 ❀
Charles Palliser   Barry Unsworth

M

Sue Miller   1943-   US   General

Ethan Canin   Jane Hamilton   Marge Piercy
Patricia Gaffney   Lorrie Moore   Mona Simpson
Ellen Gilchrist   Mary McGarry Morris   Amy Tan

Magnus Mills   1954-   Humour

Jonathan Coe   Graham Swift   McKitterick   1999 ❀
Roddy Doyle   Rupert Thomson
Michel Faber   Keith Waterhouse

Denise Mina   1966-   Sco   Crime
⚇ Maureen O'Donnell - Glasgow & London

Ajay Close   Val McDermid   CWA   1998 ❀
Quintin Jardine   Ian Rankin
Frederic Lindsay   Manda Scott

Mary Minton   Saga

Anne Bennett   Penny Jordan   Anne Melville
Brenda Clarke   Marie Joseph   M R O'Donnell
Lilian Harry   Genevieve Lyons   Pamela Pope
Anna Jacobs   Hilda McKenzie   Alexandra Raife

Rohinton Mistry   1952-   Can   General

Anita Rau Badami   V S Naipaul   Commonwealth 1992 ❀
Amit Chaudhuri   R K Narayan   Commonwealth 1996 ❀
Anita Desai   Paul Scott   Holtby   1996 ❀
Charles Dickens   Vikram Seth
Abdulrazak Gurnah

Jacquelyn Mitchard   1953-   US   General

David Guterson   Barbara Kingsolver   Jane Smiley
Alice Hoffman   Anita Shreve

Gladys Mitchell   1901-83   Crime **M**
also wrote as Stephen Hocaby & Malcolm Torrie
www.gladysmitchell.com   ⚘ *Dame Beatrice Bradley, Psychiatrist*

Catherine Aird   Edmund Crispin   Gwen Moffat
Joanna Cannan   Janet Harward   David Roberts
John Dickson Carr   Georgette Heyer   John Sherwood
Agatha Christie   Michael Innes   Patricia Wentworth

Kay Mitchell   Crime: Police work - Br
also writes as Sarah Lacey
www.twbooks.co.uk/authors/kaymitchell.html   *CI John Morrissey - 'Malminster', Yorkshire*

Agatha Christie   J M Gregson   Janet Neel
Caroline Graham   Martha Grimes

Timothy Mo   1953-   General
www.timothymo.com

Jung Chang   Hanif Kureishi | Faber | 1979 ❀ |
Alex Garland   Caryl Phillips | Hawthornden | 1982 ❀ |
Arthur Golden   William Rivière | Black | 1999 ❀ |
James Hamilton-Paterson Amy Tan
Kazuo Ishiguro

L E Modesitt Jr   1943-   US   Fantasy: Epic
                                                          ⚘ *Anna Marshall - Erde*

C J Cherryh   Mercedes Lackey   Linda Lay Shuler
Louise Cooper   Elizabeth Moon   Margaret Weis
David A Drake   Mickey Zucker Reichert Janny Wurts
Simon R Green   R A Salvatore   Jonathan Wylie

Gwen Moffat   1924-   Crime
www.twbooks.co.uk/authors/gmoffat.html   ⚘ *Melinda Pink, Travel writer*

Roy Lewis   Gladys Mitchell   John Sherwood
Gillian Linscott   Betty Rowlands   Patricia Wentworth
Charlotte MacLeod

M

Deborah Moggach *1948-* *General*

Jane Asher
Carol Birch
Tracy Chevalier
Candida Crewe
Jill Dawson
Catherine Feeny
Sue Gee
Angela Huth
Joan Lingard
Hilary Mantel
Rose Tremain
Gillian White

Connie Monk *Saga*

West Country

Brenda Clarke
Jonathan Grant
Elizabeth Ann Hill
Mary Mackie
Eileen Stafford
Jessica Stirling
Janet Tanner
Elizabeth Warne
Dee Williams

Nicholas Monsarrat *1910-79* *Sea: Modern*

John Harris
Hammond Innes
A E Langsford
Alistair MacLean
John Masters
Nevil Shute
Peter Tonkin
Antony Trew

Manuel Vázquez Montalbán *1939-* *Spain* *Crime: PI*

Pepe Carvalho - Barcelona

Michael Dibdin
Roderic Jeffries
Philip Kerr
Donna Leon
Barbara Nadel
Daniel Pennac
Christopher West

Rick Moody *1961-* *US* *General*

John Irving
Lorrie Moore
Philip Roth
John Updike

Susan Moody *1940-* *Crime: PI*

also writes as Susannah James

Penny Wanawake, PI - London
Cassie Swann, Bridge player

Linda Barnes
Liza Cody
Lauren Henderson
Jessica Mann
Marcia Muller
Mike Ripley
Barbara Vine

Elizabeth Moon   1945-   US   Fantasy: Epic
is Anne McCaffrey

Terry Brooks
Lois McMaster Bujold
Kate Elliott
Barbara Hambly

Mercedes Lackey
L E Modesitt Jr
Mickey Zucker Reichert

R A Salvatore
Margaret Weis
Janny Wurts

Bel Mooney   1946-   General
www.bel-mooney.co.uk

Nina Bawden
Kate Bingham
Valerie Blumenthal

Margaret Drabble
Helen Dunmore
Sue Gee

Sian James
Bernice Rubens
Fay Weldon

Michael Moorcock   1939-   Fantasy: Epic
www.eclipse.co.uk/sweetdespise/moorcock

Jonathan Carroll
Louise Cooper
Philip K Dick
Mary Gentle
Fritz Leiber
Wil McCarthy

Julian May
China Miéville
Linda Nagata
Rachel Pollack
Kristine Kathryn Rusch
Jack Vance

Guardian   1977 ✸

Brian Moore   1921-99   Can   General

Martin Amis
Dermot Bolger
David Cook
Graham Greene

Thomas Keneally
Colum McCann
John McGahern
Joseph O'Connor

Colm Toibin
William Trevor
Morris West
Tim Winton

Charlotte Moore   Aga Saga
also writes as Charlotte McKay

Judy Astley
Anne Atkins

Elizabeth Jane Howard
Kathleen Rowntree

Rebecca Shaw
Willow Tickell

Lorrie Moore   1957-   US   General

Judy Budnitz
Suzannah Dunn
Louise Erdrich
Ellen Gilchrist

Alison Lurie
Sue Miller
Rick Moody

Mary McGarry Morris
Anna Quindlen
Paul Sayer

Viviane Moore   1960-   Crime: Historical
♁ Chevalier Galeran de Lesnevan - C12th France

Alys Clare	Michael Jecks	Ellis Peters
Paul Doherty	Bernard Knight	Candace Robb
Susanna Gregory	Edward Marston	Kate Sedley
Paul Harding	Ian Morson	

Caiseal Mor   Aus   Fantasy: Myth

James Barclay	Robin Hobb	Stephen R Lawhead
Marion Zimmer Bradley	Katharine Kerr	Juliet Marillier
Charles de Lint		

Catrin Morgan   Wales   Saga
♁ Lily Walters - Wales

Catrin Collier	Mary A Larkin	Grace Thompson
Margaret Dickinson	Hilda McKenzie	Juliet Marillier
Iris Gower	Cynthia S Roberts	

Fidelis Morgan   1952-   Crime: Historical
also writes as Morgan Benedict
www.fidelismorgan.com   ♁ Countess of Ashby-de-la-Zouche - C17th London

Bruce Alexander	P F Chisholm	Hannah March
Stephanie Barron	Michael Clynes	Edward Marston
Fiona Buckley	Judith Cook	Iain Pears
Gwendoline Butler	Ruth Dudley Edwards	

Carole Morin   Sco   General

Carol Birch	Jenn Crowell	Hilary Mantel
Ajay Close	Helen Dunmore	

David Morrell   1943-   Can   Adventure/Thriller
♁ Rambo

Campbell Armstrong	Eric Lustbader	Alan Savage
David Baldacci	James Patterson	Dov Silverman
William Diehl	A J Quinnell	Douglas Terman
John Douglas		

Mark Morris *1963-* *Horror*

Richard Bachman
Simon Clark
Joe Donnelly
Stephen Gallagher

Muriel Gray
Shaun Hutson
Graham Joyce
Stephen Laws

Bentley Little
Jim Newman
Tim Wilson

Mary McGarry Morris *1947- US* *General*

Joan Brady
Ethan Canin

Sue Miller
Lorrie Moore

Toni Morrison *1931- US* *General*
is Chloe Anthony Wofford

Lisa Alther
William Faulkner
Janette Turner Hospital
Elspeth Huxley

Harper Lee
Terry McMillan
Gloria Naylor
Alice Walker

Pulitzer   1988 ✹

Mary Morrissy *1957- Ire* *General*

Kate Atkinson
Beryl Bainbridge

Pat Barker
Margaret Forster

Linda Grant
Tim Parks

Ian Morson *1947-* *Crime: Historical*
🏃 *Master William Falconer - C13th Oxford*

Alys Clare
Paul Doherty
Susanna Gregory
Paul Harding

Michael Jecks
Bernard Knight
Viviane Moore

Ellis Peters
Candace Robb
Kate Sedley

John Mortimer *1923-* *Humour*
🏃 *Horace Rumpole, Barrister - London* ▪ *Leslie Titmus - 'Rapstone Valley'*

Malcolm Bradbury
Caro Fraser
Roy Hattersley

David Lodge
Frederic Raphael
Peter Rawlinson

Keith Waterhouse
P G Wodehouse

Don't forget lists of: *Genres* ✳ *Characters* ✳ *Literary prizes* ✳ *Further reading* ☞

Walter Mosley   1952-   US   Crime
www.waltermosley.com   ⚇ Socrates Fortlow ▪ Easy Rawlins - Los Angeles

Ace Atkins
Stephen Donaldson
Steve Hamilton
Dashiell Hammett
Mike Phillips
James Sallis

Alexander McCall Smith
Cath Staincliffe
Peter Tasker
Hillary Waugh
Charles Willeford

CWA   1991 ✿

M

Helen Muir   1937-   Humour

Mavis Cheek
Laurie Graham

Sue Limb
Chris Manby

Sue Townsend
Nigel Williams

Marcia Muller   1944-   US   Crime: PI
⚇ Sharon McCone - San Francisco

Nicola Barker
Linda Barnes
Carol Higgins Clark
Liza Cody

Stella Duffy
Joseph Hansen
Jonnie Jacobs
Martha Lawrence

Laura Lippman
Susan Moody
Alexander McCall Smith
Mary Wings

Alice Munro   1931-   Can   General

Gail Anderson-Dargatz
Andrea Barrett
Raymond Carver
Jane Hamilton

Elizabeth Jolley
Edna O'Brien
Mona Simpson

Lisa St Aubin de Terán
Marly Swick
Amy Tan

Haruki Murakami   1949-   Ja   General

Don DeLillo
Bret Easton Ellis

Peter Hoeg
Kazuo Ishiguro

Elizabeth Knox

Don't forget lists of: *Genres* * *Characters* * *Literary prizes* * *Further reading* ☞

Iris Murdoch 1919-99   General
www.irismurdoch.plus.com/

Joan Aiken
Elizabeth Bowen
Jostein Gaarder
Sue Gee
Jennifer Johnston
Doris Lessing

Candia McWilliam
Bernice Rubens
Muriel Spark
Emma Tennant
A N Wilson
Virginia Woolf

| Whitbread | 1974 ❋ |
| Booker | 1978 ❋ |

M

Elizabeth Murphy   Saga
🏃 Ward Family

Lyn Andrews
Anne Baker
Katie Flynn

Helen Forrester
Ruth Hamilton
Maureen Lee

Mary Mackie
Margaret Thornton

Gloria Murphy US   Horror

Bethany Campbell
Mary Higgins Clark
Kit Craig

Joy Fielding
Clare Francis
Frances Galleymore

Frances Hegarty
Iris Johansen

Margaret Murphy 1959-   Crime: Psychological
www.margaretmurphy.co.uk/

Patricia D Cornwell
Joy Fielding
Frances Fyfield

Ridley Pearson
Aline Templeton
Barbara Vine

Minette Walters
Laura Wilson

Annie Murray   Saga
Birmingham

Donna Baker
Rita Bradshaw
Jean Chapman
Alexandra Connor

Sara Fraser
Judith Glover
Roy Hattersley

Meg Hutchinson
Lynda Page
Harriet Smart

Amy Myers 1938-
also writes as Laura Daniels & Harriet Hudson

Crime: Historical
🕅 Auguste Didier, Chef - C19th Europe

Richard Grayson	Peter Lovesey	Kate Ross
Ray Harrison	Anne Perry	Julian Symons
Alanna Knight	Elizabeth Peters	M J Trow
Janet Laurence		

Julie Myerson 1960-

General

Lesley Glaister	Hilary Mantel
Ian McEwan	Muriel Spark

Magdalen Nabb 1947-

Crime: Police work - foreign
🕅 Marshal Guarnaccia - Florence, Italy

Michael Dibdin	Roderic Jeffries	Michael Pearce
Juliet Hebden	H R F Keating	Georges Simenon
Mark Hebden	Donna Leon	

Vladimir Nabokov 1899-1977 Rus

General

Martin Amis	Kazuo Ishiguro	Alexander Solzhenitsyn
John Banville	James Joyce	John Updike
Anthony Burgess	Thomas Pynchon	

Barbara Nadel

Crime: Police work - foreign
🕅 Cetin Ikmen - Istanbul

Michael Dibdin	Henning Mankell	Michael Pearce
Nicolas Freeling	Manuel Vázquez Montalbán	Christopher West
Donna Leon		

Reggie Nadelson US

Crime: PI
🕅 Artie Cohen, ex-detective - New York

Lawrence Block	Loren D Estleman	Martin Cruz Smith
Raymond Chandler	Donald James	Charles Willeford
Michael Connelly	Dennis Lehane	Steve Womack
Robert Crais		

Linda Nagata　1960-　US　Science Fiction: Technical
www.maui.net/~nagata/

Paul J McAuley
Wil McCarthy
Ian McDonald

Michael Moorcock
Kim Stanley Robinson

Vernor Vinge
Robert Charles Wilson

V S Naipaul　1932-　Carib　General

Joseph Conrad
David Dabydeen
Chitra Banerjee Divakaruni
Graham Greene
Abdulrazak Gurnah
Ruth Prawer Jhabvala

Elizabeth Jolley
John Masters
Rohinton Mistry
Vikram Seth
Paul Theroux
Patrick White

Booker　1971 ❀ **N**

Nora Naish　Aga Saga

Anna Barrie
Marika Cobbold
Fanny Frewen
Sybil Marshall

Elizabeth Pewsey
Ann Purser
Jill Roe

Kathleen Rowntree
Mary Sheepshanks
Mary Wesley

R K Narayan　1906-2001　Ind　General

Amit Chaudhuri
Anita Desai
Rumer Godden

John Masters
Gita Mehta
Rohinton Mistry

Arundhati Roy
Vikram Seth

Melissa Nathan　Chick Lit

Catherine Alliott
Francesca Clementis
Jenny Colgan
Victoria Corby

Kate Fenton
Wendy Holden
Erica James
Kathy Lette

Jill Mansell
Freya North
Victoria Routledge

Claire Naylor　Chick Lit

Martina Devlin
Sarah Harris
Lisa Jewell

India Knight
Anna Maxted

Adele Parks
Daisy Waugh

Gloria Naylor   1950-   US   *General*

Barbara Kingsolver   Toni Morrison   Alice Walker
Terry McMillan   Amy Tan

Jan Needle   1943-   *Sea: Historical*
also writes as Frank Kippax   ⚕ *William Bentley, Sea Officer - C18th British Navy*

N

William Bedford   C S Forester   Dan Parkinson
Tom Connery   Alexander Kent   Dudley Pope
David Donachie   Patrick O'Brian   Richard Woodman

Janet Neel   1940-   *Crime: Police work - Br*
also writes as Janet Cohen   ⚕ *DCI John McLeish & Francesca Wilson, Civil servant*
                                                       City of London

David Armstrong   J Wallis Martin   *CWA*   1988 ❀
Natasha Cooper   Kay Mitchell
Ruth Dudley Edwards   Elizabeth Peters
Susan Kelly   Michael Ridpath
Jill McGown   Dorothy Simpson

Barbara Neil   *General*

Dirk Bogarde   Helen Dunmore   Barbara Trapido
A S Byatt   Jane Smiley

Isobel Neill   Sco   *Saga*
                                                       Scotland

Tessa Barclay   Evelyn Hood   Eileen Ramsay
Emma Blair   Nora Kay   Jessica Stirling
Margaret Thomson Davis   Frances Paige   Kirsty White
Christine Marion Fraser

James L Nelson   US   *Sea: Historical*
www.jameslnelson.com   ⚕ *Thomas Marlowe, ex Pirate - USA ▪ Brethren of the Coast Trilogy*

David Donachie   Patrick O'Brian   Dan Parkinson
C S Forester   Marcus Palliser   Julian Stockwin
Jonathan Lunn

Karen Nelson
also writes as Karen Hayes

General

Amanda Brookfield
Victoria Clayton
Karen Hayes

Mary Selby
Peta Tayler
Joanna Trollope

Mary Wesley
Marcia Willett

Andrea Newman   *1938-*

General

Sarah Harrison
Josephine Hart

Kate Hatfield
Ann Oakley

Wendy Perriam
Fay Weldon

N

Kim Newman   *1959-*
http://www.johnnyalucard.com/

Horror
Anno Dracula Series

Jonathan Aycliffe
Anne Billson
Poppy Z Brite

Joe Donnelly
Christopher Fowler
Laurell K Hamilton

Tom Holland
Graham Masterton
Mark Morris

John Nichol   *1963-*
www.johnnichol.com

Adventure/Thriller

Peter Cave
Tom Clancy
Shaun Clarke
Murray Davies

Richard Herman
Johnny 'Two Combs' Howard
Mike Lunnon-Wood

Andy McNab
David Mason
Chris Ryan

Adam Nichols
www.twbooks.co.uk/authors/adamnichols.html#author

Fantasy: Epic
⚘ *Elinor Whiteblade*

David Gemmell
Julia Gray
Simon R Green

Stephen R Lawhead
Michael Scott Rohan

Jane Welch
Tad Williams

Geoff Nicholson   *1953-*

Humour

Terence Blacker
Jonathan Coe
Joseph Connolly

Neil Ferguson
Stephen Fry
Tom Sharpe

Iain Sinclair
Leslie Thomas
Nigel Williams

Don't forget lists of: *Genres * Characters * Literary prizes * Further reading* ☞

Christopher Nicole 1930-
also writes as Alan Savage

Adventure/Thriller
Arms Trade Series

James Clavell
Colin Falconer
Eric Lustbader

Allan Mallinson
Marc Olden

Nick Nielsen

Fantasy: *Humour*

Tom Arden
Gene Brewer

Tom Holt
Jeff Noon

Robert Rankin
Michael Marshall Smith

Chris Niles   NZ

Crime
🏃 *Sam Ridley, Radio journalist - Sydney*

Phil Andrews
Marc Blake
Jan Burke

John Burns
Ron Ellis
Peter Guttridge

Valerie Kershaw
Claire McNab

Larry Niven   1938-   US

Science Fiction: *Space and time*

Isaac Asimov
Ben Bova
David Brin
Peter F Hamilton

Harry Harrison
Frank Herbert
China Miéville
Kim Stanley Robinson

Robert Silverberg
Vernor Vinge
Ian Watson
Roger Zelazny

David Nobbs   1935-

Humour

Kingsley Amis
H E Bates
Colin Douglas
Roddy Doyle

Stephen Fry
Tom Holt
Leslie Thomas
Peter Tinniswood

Alan Titchmarsh
Mark Wallington
Nigel Williams

Jeff Noon   1957-
www.jeffnoon.com

Science Fiction: *Near future*

Steve Aylett
Alexander Besher
Gene Brewer
Pat Cadigan
Philip K Dick
Thomas M Disch

Jon Courtenay Grimwood
Nick Nielsen
Rachel Pollack
Michael Marshall Smith
Neal Stephenson
Kurt Vonnegut

Arthur C Clarke 1994 ✺

Lawrence Norfolk   1963-

General

♁ *John Lempriere - C17th London*

Jim Crace	Amin Maalouf	Graham Swift
Umberto Eco	Andrew Miller	Adam Thorpe
Elizabeth Knox	Charles Palliser	

Diana Norman   1935-

Historical

Evelyn Anthony	Dinah Lampitt	Jean Plaidy
Philippa Carr	Morgan Llywelyn	Connie Willis
Georgette Heyer	Maureen Peters	

N

Geoffrey Norman   US

Crime: PI

♁ *Morgan Hunt - Florida*

Edna Buchanan	Stephen Hunter	Laurence Shames
James Hall	Robert B Parker	Les Standiford

Hilary Norman
also writes as Alexandra Henry

General

Sally Beauman	Josephine Hart	Arabella Seymour
Celia Brayfield	Lesley Pearse	

Hilary Norman
also writes as Alexandra Henry

Adventure/Thriller

Mary Higgins Clark	Clare Francis
Martina Cole	Judith Kelman

Freya North   1968-
www.freyanorth.co.uk

Chick Lit

Zoë Barnes	Elizabeth Gage	Susan Oudot
Susie Boyt	Lisa Jewell	Lesley Pearse
Victoria Colby	Susan Lewis	Fiona Walker
Jenn Crowell	Melissa Nathan	Daisy Waugh

Don't forget lists of: *Genres * Characters * Literary prizes * Further reading* ☞

Kem Nunn   US

Crime
Surfing - California

Raymond Chandler	Vicki Hendricks	George P Pelecanos
Robert Crais	Joe R Lansdale	Donald Rawley
James Crumley	Jefferson Parker	

Robert Nye   1939-

General

Peter Ackroyd	Iain Sinclair	*Guardian* 1976 ❀
Bruce Chatwin	Rose Tremain	*Hawthornden* 1976 ❀
John Fowles	Barry Unsworth	
Allan Massie		

Patrick O'Brian   1914-2000

Sea: *Historical*
www.wwnorton.com/pob/   ⚲ *Jack Aubrey & Stephen Maturin - C18th/19th*

Tom Connery	Jonathan Lunn	Marcus Palliser
David Donachie	Allan Mallinson	Dan Parkinson
C S Forester	Jan Needle	Showell Styles
Richard Howard	James L Nelson	Victor Suthren

Edna O'Brien   1932-   Ire

General

www.kirjasto.sci.fi/eobrien.htm

Lynne Reid Banks	Angela Lambert	J D Salinger
Clare Boylan	Alice Munro	Fay Weldon
Alice Thomas Ellis	Joyce Carol Oates	Niall Williams
Jennifer Johnston		

Maureen O'Brien

Crime: *Police work - Br*
⚲ *Insp John Bright - London*

Paul Charles	Elizabeth George	Barry Maitland
Elizabeth Ferrars	Martha Grimes	J Wallis Martin
Frances Fyfield	Donna Leon	Ruth Rendell

Tim O'Brien   1946-   US

General

www.illyria.com/tobhp.html

Michael Collins	Joseph Heller
Richard Ford	John Irving

216

Carol O'Connell   1947-   US

Crime: Police work - US
⚹ Sgt Kathleen Mallory - New York

Denise Danks	Sue Grafton	Sharyn McCrumb
Linda Davies	Ellen Hart	Claire McNab
Robert Ferrigno	Faye Kellerman	Kathy Reichs
Frances Galleymore		

Tyne O'Connell   Aus   Chick lit
www.tyneoconnell.com

Zoë Barnes	Kathy Lette	Alistair MacLean
Claire Calman	Josie Lloyd & Emlyn Rees	Yvonne Roberts
Jenny Colgan	Serena Mackesy	

O

Gemma O'Connor   Ire   Crime: Psychological

Patricia D Cornwell	Lesley Grant-Adamson	Carol Smith
Nicci French	Morag Joss	Laura Wilson
Robert Goddard	Val McDermid	

Joseph O'Connor   1963-   Ire   Humour
www.irishwriters-online.com/josephoconnor.html

Dermot Bolger	Colum McCann	Brian Moore
Roddy Doyle	Bernard MacLaverty	Niall Williams
Patrick McCabe		

M R O'Donnell   1932-   Saga
also writes as Malcolm Macdonald & Malcolm Ross

Elaine Crowley	Marie Joseph	Mary Minton
Frank Delaney	Lena Kennedy	T R Wilson
Susan Howatch	Genevieve Lyons	

Sheila O'Flanagan   1962-   Ire   Chick Lit

Jenn Crowell	Cathy Kelly	Lesley Pearse
Claudine Cullimore	Marian Keyes	Patricia Scanlan
Martina Devlin	Sue Margolis	Kate Thompson

Andrew O'Hagan   *1968-   Sco*   *General*

Melvyn Bragg
Janice Galloway
Andrew Greig
A L Kennedy

Duncan McLean
Tim Pears
Alan Spence

Holtby   *1999* ❁

Ardal O'Hanlon   *1965-*   *Humour*
www.ardalohanlon.co.uk

Colin Bateman
Roddy Doyle
Nick Hornby

Sean Hughes
John McGahern

Pauline McLynn
Tony Parsons

O

Stewart O'Nan   *US*   *General*
www.stewart-onan.com

Lauren Belfer
Caleb Carr
Thomas Eidson

Louise Erdrich
Charles Frazier
Harper Lee

Cormac McCarthy
Larry Watson

Gilda O'Neill   *Saga*
East End of London

Emma Dally
June Francis
Meg Henderson
Beryl Kingston

Pamela Oldfield
Victor Pemberton
Sally Spencer
Alison Stuart

Jeanne Whitmee
Dee Williams
Audrey Willsher
Sally Worboyes

Joan O'Neill   *Ire*   *Saga*
Ireland

Josephine Cox
Elaine Crowley
Frank Delaney

Rose Doyle
Catherine Dunne
Iris Gower

Mary A Larkin
Liz Ryan
Mary Ryan

Kate O'Riordan   *Ire*   *Humour*

Sherry Ashworth
Colette Caddle

Martina Devlin
Cathy Kelly

Marian Keyes

Ann Oakley 1944-   General
also writes as Rosamund Clay

Lisa Alther
Lisa Appignanesi
Guy Bellamy
Candida Clark

Lucy Ellman
Jill Gascoine
Maeve Haran

Josephine Hart
Andrea Newman
Libby Purves

Joyce Carol Oates 1938- US   General
also writes as Rosamond Smith

Judy Budnitz
Raymond Carver
Jenny Diski
William Faulkner

Connie May Fowler
Harper Lee
Doris Lessing

Edna O'Brien
V S Pritchett
Edith Wharton

O

Ben Okri 1959- Nigeria   General
www.uweb.ucsb.edu/~rbb0/academic/projects/okri/okri.html

Angela Carter
David Dabydeen
Gabriel Garcia Márquez

David Malouf
Caryl Phillips

Booker   1991 ❀

Marc Olden US   Adventure/Thriller

Martin Booth
Eric Lustbader

Christopher Nicole
Alan Savage

Justin Scott

Jenny Oldfield 1949-   Saga
also writes as Kate Fielding   ☂ *Parsons Family - London*

Anna King
Victor Pemberton
Sally Spencer

Sally Stewart
Willow Tickell

Jeanne Whitmee
Sally Worboyes

Pamela Oldfield 1931-   Saga
                            Heron Saga • Foxearth Trilogy - Kent

Tessa Barclay
Betty Burton
Christine Marion Fraser
Valerie Georgeson

Judith Glover
Sybil Marshall
Anne Melville
Gilda O'Neill

Pamela Pope
Jeanne Whitmee
Sarah Woodhouse

Nick Oldham 1956-   Crime: Police work - Br
⅄ DI Henry Christie - Blackpool

Nicholas Blincoe	Raymond Flynn	Leslie Thomas
Judith Cutler	Frank Palmer	Mark Timlin

Michael Ondaatje 1943- Sri Lan   General

Murray Bail	William Rivière	Booker 1992 ❀
Dennis Bock	Salman Rushdie	
James Bradley	Colin Thubron	
Kazuo Ishiguro	Paul Watkins	
Gita Mehta	Marianne Wiggins	
David Adams Richards		

O

Roger Ormerod 1920-   Crime
⅄ Richard Patton, ex policeman & Amelia - England

W J Burley	Elizabeth Ferrars
Colin Dexter	Nicholas Rhea

George Orwell 1903-50   General
was Eric Blair
www.k-1.com/Orwell/

Ray Bradbury	Graham Greene	Franz Kafka
Anthony Burgess	Aldous Huxley	

Susan Oudot   General

Susie Boyt	Freya North	Barbara Trapido
Marian Keyes	Lesley Pearse	Grace Wynne-Jones
Kathy Lette	Judith Summers	

Agnes Owens 1926- Sco   General

Isla Dewar	Janice Galloway	James Kelman
Sally Emerson	Alasdair Gray	Alan Spence

Amos Oz   1939-   Isr   General

Lynne Reid Banks	David Grossman	Howard Jacobson
Saul Bellow	Christopher Hope	Isaac Bashevis Singer
William Faulkner	Alan Isler	Alexander Solzhenitsyn

Emma Page   1921-   Crime: Police work - Br
is Honaria Tirbutt   ☂ DCI Kelsey & DS Lambert - Worcestershire

Margery Allingham	Ngaio Marsh	Barbara Whitehead
Reginald Hill	Dorothy Simpson	R D Wingfield
Emma Lathen		

O
P

Lynda Page   Saga
Leicester

Margaret Dickinson	Sheila Jansen	Kay Stephens
Sara Fraser	Annie Murray	Margaret Thornton
Meg Hutchinson	Sally Spencer	Audrey Willsher

Frances Paige   Sco   Saga
☂ MacKintosh Sisters • McGrath Family - Scotland

Tessa Barclay	Christine Marion Fraser	Eileen Ramsay
Doris Davidson	Meg Henderson	Alison Skelton
Margaret Thomson Davis	Nora Kay	Anne Vivis
Inga Dunbar	Isobel Neill	Kirsty White

Chris Paling   1956-   Adventure/Thriller

Robert Edric	John Harvey	Nicholas Royle
Sebastian Faulks	Ian Rankin	Martyn Waites

Charles Palliser   1947-   US   Historical

Peter Carey	Susan Hill	Iain Pears
Caleb Carr	Andrew Miller	Barry Unsworth
Robert Goddard	Lawrence Norfolk	

Don't forget lists of: *Genres * Characters * Literary prizes * Further reading* ☞

Marcus Palliser

Sea: *Historical*
⚡ Matthew Loftus

C S Forester
Alexander Kent
Jonathan Lunn

James L Nelson
Patrick O'Brian

Dan Parkinson
Julian Stockwin

Elizabeth Palmer   *1942-*

Aga Saga

Amanda Brookfield
Katie Fforde
Libby Purves

Barbara Pym
Mary Selby
Henrietta Soames

Titia Sutherland
Sarah Woodhouse

Frank Palmer   *1933-2000*

Crime: *Police work - Br*
⚡ Asst CC Phil 'Sweeney' Todd ▪ DI 'Jacko' Jackson - East Midlands

David Armstrong
Jon Cleary
Raymond Flynn

Reginald Hill
Nick Oldham

Peter Turnbull
Eric Wright

P

Michael Palmer   *US*

Adventure/Thriller: *Medical*
www.michaelpalmerbooks.com/

Colin Andrews
Paul Carson
Robin Cook

Tess Gerritsen
Mo Hayder
Richard Preston

Andrew Puckett
Claire Rayner
Leah Ruth Robinson

Sara Paretsky   *1947-   US*

Crime: *PI*
http://saraparetsky.com/
⚡ V I Warshawski - Chicago

Linda Barnes
Edna Buchanan
Charlotte Carter
Carol Higgins Clark
Stephen Dobyns
Joseph Hansen

Lynda La Plante
Martha Lawrence
Laura Lippman
Sam Reaves
Sandra Scoppettone
Gillian Slovo

CWA	*1988* ✹
CWA	*2002* ✹

Edith Pargeter   *1913-95*

Historical
also wrote as Ellis Peters

Nicholas Carter
Margaret George
Pamela Hill

Morgan Llywelyn
Sharon Penman

Jean Plaidy
Nigel Tranter

David Park   Ire   General

Patrick McCabe   John McGahern   William Trevor
Ian McEwan   Colm Toibin

Imogen Parker   1958-   General

Maeve Binchy   Judith Lennox
Victoria Clayton   Susan Lewis

Jefferson Parker   US   Crime: Modern
also writes as T Jefferson Parker   California
www.tjeffersonparker.com/

Mark Burnell   Faye Kellerman   Chris Petit
John Connolly   Jonathan Kellerman   Joseph Wambaugh
Stephen Dobyns   Kem Nunn   Stuart Woods
John Gilstrap   Ridley Pearson

P

K J Parker   Fantasy: Epic
                                          The Fencer Trilogy

Tom Arden   Juliet E McKenna   Freda Warrington
Chaz Brenchley   Tim Powers   Jane Welch
Kate Jacoby

Robert B Parker   1932-   US   Crime
www.mindspring.com/~boba4   Jesse Stone, Police - US
                     Spenser, PI • PI Sunny Randall - Boston   Massachusetts

Lawrence Block   Kinky Friedman   Geoffrey Norman
James Hadley Chase   J A Jance   Sam Reaves
Harlan Coben   Elmore Leonard   Peter Tasker
K C Constantine   Ed McBain   Donald E Westlake

Una-Mary Parker   1930-   Glitz & Glamour

Maria Barrett   Julie Ellis   Lynda La Plante
Sally Beauman   Judi James   Lavyrle Spencer
Barbara Taylor Bradford Penny Jordan   Danielle Steel
Barbara Delinsky

Dan Parkinson

Sea: Historical
🏃 *Patrick Dalton*

Tom Connery	Allan Mallinson	Patrick O'Brian
David Donachie	Jan Needle	Marcus Palliser
C S Forester	James L Nelson	Julian Stockwin
Alexander Kent		

Adele Parks

Chick Lit

Victoria Corby	Lisa Jewell	Claire Naylor
Martina Devlin	India Knight	Daisy Waugh
Sarah Harris	Anna Maxted	

Tim Parks   1954-

General

http://www.timparks.co.uk

P

Pat Barker	Ian McEwan	*S Maugham 1986* ✿
Julian Barnes	Mary Morrissy	*Betty Trask 1986* ✿
William Boyd	Amanda Prantera	
Bret Easton Ellis	Barbara Trapido	

Julie Parsons   *Ire*

Adventure/Thriller: Psychological

Ruth Rendell	Minette Walters
Barbara Vine	Margaret Yorke

Tony Parsons

Lad Lit

David Baddiel	Alex George	Ardal O'Hanlon
Mark Barrowcliffe	Robert Llewellyn	Ben Richards
Ben Elton	Tim Lott	Sean Thomas
Mike Gayle		

Ann Patchett   1963-   *US*

General

Barbara Esstman	Carol Shields	*Orange 2002* ✿
Jane Hamilton	Jane Urquhart	
Susan Hill		

James Patterson   1947-   US   Crime: Psychological

www.jamespatterson.com
ᵗ Det Alex Cross - Washington DC
'Women's Murder Club' - San Francisco

Adam Baron	Jonathan Kellerman	Jenny Maxwell
Jeffery Deaver	Rochelle Krich	David Morrell
Mo Hayder	Dennis Lehane	Chris Petit
Tami Hoag	John R Maxim	Robert W Walker

Richard North Patterson   1947- US   Crime: Legal/financial

ᵗ Christopher Paget, Attorney - San Francisco

Dexter Dias	David Lindsey	Michael Ridpath
William Diehl	Phillip M Margolin	Nancy Taylor Rosenberg
Philip Friedman	Steve Martini	Lisa Scottoline
Douglas Kennedy		

James Pattinson   Adventure/Thriller **P**

Brian Callison	Clive Cussler	Hammond Innes
James Cobb	Alexander Fullerton	Douglas Reeman

Stewart Pawson   1940-   Crime: Police work - Br

ᵗ DI Charlie Priest - Yorkshire

David Armstrong	Raymond Flynn	Peter Robinson
Robert Barnard	Patricia Hall	Peter Turnbull
Pauline Bell	Nicholas Rhea	Barbara Whitehead

David Peace   1967-   Crime: Police work - Br

ᵗ Red Riding Quartet - Yorkshire

Christopher Brookmyre	Bill James	Ian Rankin
Ken Bruen	Elmore Leonard	Danuta Reah
James Ellroy	David Ralph Martin	

Mary E Pearce   1932-   Saga

Appletree Saga ▪ Wayman Family - Worcestershire

Margaret Dickinson	Kitty Ray	Margaret Sunley
Walter Macken	Miss Read	Anne Worboys
Sybil Marshall	Sarah Shears	

Michael Pearce
www.twbooks.co.uk/authors/mpearce.html

Crime: Historical
🏃 *Dmitri Kameron, Lawyer - Tsarist Russia*
The Mamur Zapt (Gareth Owen), Secret police -
early C20th Egypt

Roderic Jeffries	Barbara Nadel	*CWA* 1993 ✹
H R F Keating	Elizabeth Peters	
Nancy Livingston	Laura Joh Rowland	
Magdalen Nabb		

Iain Pears   1955-

Crime
🏃 *Jonathan Argyll, Art historian*

William Ardin	Jonathan Gash	Andrew Miller
Gwendoline Butler	Philip Hook	Fidelis Morgan
Caleb Carr	John Malcolm	Charles Palliser
Umberto Eco	Jennie Melville	Derek Wilson

P

Tim Pears   1956-

General

Tim Binding	Neil Ferguson	*Hawthornden 1994* ✹
Jonathan Coe	Andrew O'Hagan	
Robert Edric	Paul Sayer	

Lesley Pearse   1945-

General

Zoë Barnes	Hilary Norman	Susan Oudot
Susie Boyt	Freya North	Claire Rayner
Jilly Cooper	Sheila O'Flanagan	Arabella Seymour
Cathy Kelly		

Ridley Pearson   1953-   US
www.ridleypearson.com/

Crime: Police work - US
🏃 *Sgt Lou Boldt - Seattle*

Jon Cleary	Jon A Jackson	Eric Wright
Jeffery Deaver	J A Jance	Margaret Murphy
W E B Griffin	Faye Kellerman	Jefferson Parker
Donald Harstad	Jonathan Kellerman	John Sandford

Don't forget lists of: *Genres * Characters * Literary prizes * Further reading* ☞

George P Pelecanos 1957- US — Crime: PI

Nick Stefanos ▪ Derek Strange & Terry Quinn - Washington DC

Lawrence Block
James Lee Burke
Raymond Chandler
James Crumley
Lynda La Plante
Ross Macdonald
Kem Nunn
Donald Rawley
Jim Thompson

Lynne Pemberton — General

Maria Barrett
Sally Beauman
Maeve Binchy
Jayne Ann Krentz
Colleen McCullough
Belva Plain
Nora Roberts
Lavyrle Spencer
Rosie Thomas

Margaret Pemberton 1943- — Historical

also writes as Maggie Hudson

London Sequence

Harry Bowling
Emma Dally
Harriet Hudson
Sara Hylton
Judith Saxton
Danielle Steel
Nicola Thorne

P

Victor Pemberton — Saga

London

Philip Boast
Harry Bowling
Pamela Evans
Lilian Harry
Beryl Kingston
Margaret Mayhew
Jenny Oldfield
Gilda O'Neill
Sally Spencer
Mary Jane Staples
Sally Worboyes

Sharon Penman US — Historical

Elizabeth Chadwick
Dorothy Dunnett
Helen Hollick
Morgan Llywelyn
Rosalind Miles
Edith Pargeter
Mary Stewart
Nigel Tranter

John Penn — Crime: Police work - Br

is Palma Harcourt
also writes as Jack H Trotman

DCI Tansey - 'Columbury'
Insp Thorne & Sgt Abbot

Catherine Aird
John Brady
W J Burley
Agatha Christie
Elizabeth Ferrars
Ann Quinton

Daniel Pennac   1944-   Fr   Crime: Humour
♂ Benjamin Malaussène - Paris, France

| Michael Dibdin | H R F Keating | Georges Simenon |
| Nicolas Freeling | Manuel Vázquez Montalbán | Janwillem van de Wetering |

Wendy Perriam   1940-   General

| Clare Boylan | Sarah Harrison | Fay Weldon |
| Carol Clewlow | Andrea Newman | |

Anne Perry   1938-   NZ   Crime: Historical
www.anneperry.net
♂ Insp Thomas & Charlotte Pitt ⎱ C19th England
Insp William & Hester Monk ⎰

Caleb Carr	Ray Harrison	Roberta Rogow
Arthur Conan Doyle	Laurie R King	Kate Ross
Paula Gosling	Alanna Knight	Norman Russell
Richard Grayson	Amy Myers	M J Trow

Elizabeth Peters   1927-   US   Crime: Historical
is Barbara Mertz & also writes as Barbara Michaels   ♂ Amelia Peabody, C19th Egyptologist
http://www.mpmbooks.com/

| Gillian Linscott | Janet Neel |
| Amy Myers | Michael Pearce |

Ellis Peters   1913-95   Crime: Historical
was Edith Pargeter   ♂ Brother Cadfael - C13th Shropshire ▪ CI George Felse - Police Br

Alys Clare	Viviane Moore		
Paul Doherty	Ian Morson	CWA	1980 ❁
Susanna Gregory	Candace Robb		
Paul Harding	Kate Sedley		
Michael Jecks	Peter Tremayne		

Maureen Peters   1935-   Wales   Historical
also writes as Veronica Black & Catherine Darby

| Tracy Chevalier | Robin Maxwell | Jean Plaidy |
| Pamela Hill | Diana Norman | Jean Stubbs |

Chris Petit

Mark Burnell	Dennis Lehane	James Patterson
Thomas Harris	Jefferson Parker	

Elizabeth Pewsey   1948-

General

Nina Bawden	Elizabeth Falconer	Nora Naish
Amanda Brookfield	Catherine Feeny	Kate Pullinger
Clare Chambers	Kate Fielding	Kitty Ray
Jill Dawson	Fanny Frewen	Sophia Watson

Caryl Phillips   1958-   Carib

General

Fred D'Aguiar	Anne Michaels	*Sunday Times* 1992 ✹
David Dabydeen	Timothy Mo	*Black* 1993 ✹
Hanif Kureishi	Ben Okri	

Mike Phillips   1946-   Guy

Crime

⚲ *Sam Dean, Journalist - London*

Lauren Henderson	Mike Ripley	*CWA* 1990 ✹
Irene Lin-Chandler	James Sallis	
Barry Maitland	Cath Staincliffe	
Walter Mosley	Mark Timlin	

Marge Piercy   1936-   US
http://archer-books.com/Piercy/

General

Lisa Alther	Larry McMurtry	*Arthur C Clarke* 1993 ✹
Maureen Duffy	Sue Miller	
Dominick Dunne	Erin Pizzey	
Shena Mackay	Jane Smiley	

Christopher Pike   US

Horror

Shaun Hutson	Richard Laymon	Guy N Smith
Stephen Laws	John Saul	

Don't forget lists of: *Genres* * *Characters* * *Literary prizes* * *Further reading* ☞

Rosamunde Pilcher   1924-   Aga Saga

Victoria Clayton   Alexandra Raife   Parker   1996 ❀
Jenny Glanfield   Jean Saunders
Judith Glover   Sally Stewart
Judith Lennox   Magda Sweetland
Alison McLeay   Ann Swinfen
Maggie Makepeace   Eileen Townsend

Richard Pitman   Crime
                                                           Horse racing

David Brierley   John Francome
Dick Francis   Gavin Lyall

Erin Pizzey   1939-   General

P Charlotte Bingham   Shirley Conran   Patricia Scanlan
Anita Burgh   Marge Piercy

Jean Plaidy   1906-93   Historical
also wrote as Philippa Carr & Victoria Holt

Evelyn Anthony   Jane Aiken Hodge   Maureen Peters
Dorothy Dunnett   Robin Maxwell   Jean Stubbs
Margaret George   Diana Norman   Nigel Tranter
Sandra Gulland   Edith Pargeter

Belva Plain   1918-   US   Saga
                                                  ⚐ Werner Family - USA

Teresa Crane   Lynne Pemberton   Sue Sully
Janet Dailey   Anne Rivers Siddons   Rosie Thomas
Barbara Delinsky   Lavyrle Spencer   Nora Roberts
Jude Deveraux   Danielle Steel

Rachel Pollack   1945-   US   Science Fiction: Near future

Alexander Besher   Michael Moorcock   Arthur C Clarke 1989 ❀
Pat Cadigan   Jeff Noon
William Gibson   Michael Marshall Smith
Jon Courtenay Grimwood   Neal Stephenson

Dudley Pope 1925-97   Sea: Historical & Modern

Tom Connery
David Donachie
C S Forester

Alexander Kent
Jonathan Lunn
Philip McCutchan

Jan Needle
Showell Styles
Richard Woodman

Pamela Pope   Saga
London ▪ East Anglia

Margaret Dickinson
Margaret Graham
Jonathan Grant

Mary Mackie
Mary Minton
Pamela Oldfield

Jeanne Whitmee
Barbara Whitnell
T R Wilson

Henry Porter   Adventure/Thriller

Tom Clancy
Robert Harris

John Le Carré
Gerald Seymour

Robert Wilson

P

Alexandra Potter   Chick Lit

Jessica Adams
Jenny Colgan
Helen Fielding

Marian Keyes
Sophie Kinsella
Kathy Lette

Chris Manby
Fiona Walker

Anthony Powell 1905-2000   General
www.anthonypowell.org.uk

Isabel Colegate
E M Forster
Graham Greene

Aldous Huxley
J B Priestley
Evelyn Waugh

Henry Williamson
A N Wilson

Richard Powers 1957- US   Science Fiction: Near future

Jonathan Franzen
Paul J McAuley

Neal Stephenson
Bruce Sterling

Tim Powers 1952- US   Fantasy: Contemporary

Philip K Dick
Neil Gaiman
Mary Gentle
Barbara Hambly

Robert Holdstock
George R R Martin
K J Parker
Philip Pullman

Michael Scott Rohan
H G Wells
Connie Willis
Gene Wolfe

Amanda Prantera   1942-   General

J M Coetzee	Tim Parks	Barbara Trapido
Amanda Craig	Anita Shreve	Barry Unsworth
Maureen Duffy	Rupert Thomson	Marina Warner
Elizabeth Falconer		

Terry Pratchett   1948-   Fantasy: Humour
Discworld Series

Douglas Adams	Andrew Harman	BSFA	1989 ✷
Piers Anthony	Tom Holt		
Robert Asprin	Barry Hughart		
Craig Shaw Gardner	Tanith Lee		
Rob Grant	Robert Rankin		
Simon R Green	Martin Scott		

P Steven Pressfield   Historical
Ancient Greece

Bernard Cornwell	Ross Leckie	Mary Renault
Robert Graves	Valerio Massimo Manfredi	

Richard Preston   Crime

Colin Andrews	Ken McClure	Andrew Puckett
Robin Cook	Michael Palmer	Leah Ruth Robinson
Michael Crichton		

Anthony Price   1928-   Adventure/Thriller
🏃 Dr David Audley

Lionel Davidson	John Le Carré	CWA	1970 ✷
Len Deighton	A J Quinnell	CWA	1974 ✷
Clive Egleton	Julian Rathbone		
Brian Freemantle			

Robert T Price   Sco   Crime
🏃 Kenny Madigan, ex Car thief - Stratford-upon-Avon

Ron Ellis	Mike Ripley
Bill James	Mark Timlin

J B Priestley   *1894-1984*   *General*

A J Cronin
R F Delderfield
John Galsworthy

W Somerset Maugham
Tim Pears

Anthony Powell
Angus Wilson

V S Pritchett   *1900-97*   *General*

Elizabeth Bowen
John McGahern

W Somerset Maugham
Joyce Carol Oates

William Trevor

Annie Proulx   *1935-   US*   *General*
previously wrote as E Annie Proulx

Margaret Atwood
Andrea Barrett
Lauren Belfer
Suzanne Berne
Joan Brady

Thomas Eidson
Louise Erdrich
Jonathan Franzen
Peter Hoeg
Peter Matthiessen

Irish Times	*1993* ❋
Pulitzer	*1994* ❋

P

Andrew Puckett   *Crime: Medical*
🏃 Sister Jo Farwell & Insp Tom Jones

Anthea Cohen
Christine Green

Ken McClure
Michael Palmer

Richard Preston
Leah Ruth Robinson

Kate Pullinger   *Can*   *General*

Hilary Bailey
Nina Bawden
Mavis Cheek

Jill Dawson
Jane Gardam
Susan Hill

Elizabeth Pewsey
Gillian White

Philip Pullman   *1946-*   *Fantasy*
www.randomhouse.com/features/pullman/philippullman/   *Dark Materials Trilogy*

Stephen Donaldson
Neil Gaiman
Mary Gentle
C S Lewis

China Miéville
Tim Powers
Michael Scott Rohan
J R R Tolkien

Whitbread   2002 ❋

D M Purcell
previously wrote as Deirdre Purcell

Saga
Ireland

Maeve Binchy	Rose Doyle	Mary Ryan
Elaine Crowley	Sheelagh Kelly	Susan Sallis
Frank Delaney	Liz Ryan	Patricia Scanlan

Ann Purser

General
'Round Ringford'

Anne Atkins	Jan Karon	Kitty Ray
Anna Barrie	Sybil Marshall	Miss Read
Marika Cobbold	Nora Naish	Willow Tickell
Erica James		

Libby Purves   1950-

General

P

Valerie Blumenthal	Julia Lisle	Jill Roe
Candida Clark	Penelope Lively	Kate Sharam
Patricia Gaffney	Ann Oakley	Robyn Sisman
Sian James	Elizabeth Palmer	Marcia Willett

Mario Puzo   1920-99   US
www.jgeoff.com/puzo

General
🏃 The Godfather

Lorenzo Carcaterra	James Ellroy	Harold Robbins
Richard Condon	George V Higgins	Joseph Wambaugh

Marc Pye   Sco

Crime: Modern
Glasgow

Jake Arnott	Alan Warner
Jerry Raine	Irvine Welsh

Barbara Pym   1913-80

General

Jane Austen	Elizabeth Jolley	Emma Tennant
Anita Brookner	W Somerset Maugham	Salley Vickers
Isabel Colegate	Elizabeth Palmer	A N Wilson
Alice Thomas Ellis	Madeleine St John	

Thomas Pynchon   1937-   US   *General*

Paul Auster
Saul Bellow
Richard Condon
Don DeLillo

Lawrence Durrell
Joseph Heller
John Irving
Thomas McGuane

Vladimir Nabokov
Tom Robbins
Tom Wolfe

Amanda Quick   1948-   US   *Historical*
is Jayne Ann Krentz and also writes as Jayne Castle
www.krentz-quick.com

Elizabeth Boyle
Marion Chesney

Catherine Coulter
Georgette Heyer

Judith McNaught
Joan Smith

Anna Quindlen   1953-   US   *General*

Margaret Forster
Linda Grant

Elizabeth Jane Howard
Susan Isaacs

Lorrie Moore
Jane Smiley

A J Quinnell   1939-   *Adventure/Thriller*
♁ Creasy, ex mercenary

Tom Bradby
Gavin Lyall
Alistair MacLean
J K Mayo

David Morrell
Anthony Price
Michael Shea

Dov Silverman
William Smethurst
Wilbur Smith

Ann Quinton   *Crime:* Police work - Br
♁ DI James Roland & DS Patrick Mansfield - Suffolk ▪ DI Nick Holroyd - 'Casterford'

Vivien Armstrong
M C Beaton
Brian Cooper
Clare Curzon

Eileen Dewhurst
Marjorie Eccles
Malcolm Forsythe
Caroline Graham

J M Gregson
Jill McGown
Jennie Melville
John Penn

Don't forget lists of: *Genres* * *Characters* * *Literary prizes* * *Further reading* ☞

Alexandra Raife

Saga
Scotland

Jay Allerton
Margaret Thomson Davis
Elizabeth Falconer

Mary Minton
Rosamunde Pilcher

Liz Ryan
Anne Vivis

Jerry Raine 1955-

Crime: Modern

Jake Arnott
Philip Caveney
Jeff Gulvin

Bill James
Marc Pye

Mike Ripley
Mark Timlin

Eileen Ramsay Sco

Saga
Scotland

Jay Allerton
Emma Blair
Jessica Blair
Doris Davidson

Nora Kay
Gwen Kirkwood
Isobel Neill
Frances Paige

Harriet Smart
Anne Vivis
Mary Withall

R Ian Rankin 1960- Sco

Crime: Police work - Br

also writes as Jack Harvey
www.ianrankin.com/

⚐ DI John Rebus & DC Siobhan Clarke - Edinburgh

Jeffrey Ashford
Bartholomew Gill
Paul Johnston
Bill Knox
Frederic Lindsay
Eugene McEldowney

William McIlvanney
Denise Mina
Chris Paling
David Peace
Nicholas Royle
Martyn Waites

CWA   1997 ✹

Robert Rankin 1949-

Science Fiction: Humour

Douglas Adams
L Sprague de Camp
Rob Grant
Andrew Harman

Harry Harrison
Tom Holt
Nick Nielsen

Terry Pratchett
Martin Scott
Bob Shaw

Frederic Raphael 1931- US

General

Saul Bellow
Dirk Bogarde

Howard Jacobson
Allan Massie

John Mortimer
Piers Paul Read

Julian Rathbone 1935-   Adventure/Thriller

www.julianrathbone.com

         ⃛ Comm Jan Argand

John Gardner	Russell James	Anthony Price
Palma Harcourt	Amin Maalouf	Craig Thomas
John Harris	Bernard MacLaverty	

Julian Rathbone 1935-   Historical

Philippa Gregory	Geraldine McCaughrean
Thomas Keneally	Barry Unsworth

Donald Rawley 1957-98   US   Crime

Hollywood

Raymond Chandler	Kem Nunn
Lindsay Maracotta	George P Pelecanos

Peter Rawlinson 1919-   General

Jeffrey Archer	Philip Hensher	John Mortimer
Michael Dobbs	Gwen Hunter	Michael Shea

R

Melanie Rawn 1954-   US   Fantasy: Epic

www.melanierawn.com

Marion Zimmer Bradley	Barbara Hambly	Jennifer Roberson
Allan Cole	Katherine Kurtz	Jan Siegel
Louise Cooper	Mercedes Lackey	Margaret Weis
Kate Elliott	Anne McCaffrey	

Kitty Ray   Saga

Mary E Pearce	Ann Purser	Sarah Shears
Elizabeth Pewsey	Miss Read	

Don't forget lists of: *Genres* * *Characters* * *Literary prizes* * *Further reading* ☞

Claire Rayner *1931-*   *Saga*

www.twbooks.co.uk/authors/crayner.html

🏃 Tilly Quentin
Performers Series ▪ Poppy Chronicles

Winston Graham	Charlotte Lamb	Lesley Pearse
Christine Green	Anne Melville	Judith Saxton
Beryl Kingston		

Claire Rayner *1931-*   *Crime*

also writes as Sheila Brandon
www.twbooks.co.uk/authors/crayner.html

🏃 *Dr George Barnabas, female pathologist*

Christine Green	Michael Palmer	Leah Ruth Robinson
Ken McClure	Kathy Reichs	Robert W Walker

Miss Read *1913-*   *Saga*

Fairacre ▪ Thrush Green

Jan Karon	Mary E Pearce	Pam Rhodes
Walter Macken	Ann Purser	Rebecca Shaw
Sybil Marshall	Kitty Ray	Sarah Shears

R

Piers Paul Read *1941-*   *General*

Sebastian Faulks	Frederic Raphael	Hawthornden	1970 ✸
Graham Greene	Paul Theroux	Black	1988 ✸
Bernard MacLaverty	Colin Thubron		
Allan Massie	Angus Wilson		

Danuta Reah   *Crime: Psychological*

Jane Adams	David Peace	Aline Templeton
Stephen Booth	Alison Taylor	Margaret Yorke
Val McDermid		

Sam Reaves *1954- US*   *Crime: PI*

also writes as Dominic Martell
www.martell-reaves.com

🏃 *Cooper MacLeish, Taxi driver - Chicago*

Charlotte Carter	Ross Macdonald	Jim Thompson
Steve Hamilton	Sara Paretsky	Andrew Vachss
Dashiell Hammett	Robert B Parker	

Douglas Reeman   1924-   Sea
also writes as Alexander Kent   🏃 Mike Blackwood

Brian Callison	Geoffrey Jenkins	Antony Trew
Gerry Carroll	James Pattinson	Charles Whiting
James Cobb	Patrick Robinson	John Winton
Hammond Innes		

Christopher Reich   1961-   US   Crime: Legal/financial

Harry Bingham	Brad Meltzer
John Grisham	Scott Turow

Mickey Zucker Reichert   1962-   US   Fantasy: Epic
Last of the Renshai Series

Terry Brooks	Mercedes Lackey	R A Salvatore
David Eddings	L E Modesitt Jr	Margaret Weis
Raymond E Feist	Elizabeth Moon	Janny Wurts
Terry Goodkind		

R

Kathy Reichs   1950-   Can   Crime
http://literati.net/Reichs/   🏃 Dr Temperance Brennan, Pathologist - Montreal

Harlan Coben	John Farrow	Sarah Lovett
Patricia D Cornwell	Joseph Glass	Peter May
Jeffery Deaver	Lynn S Hightower	Carol O'Connell
Linda Fairstein	Rochelle Krich	Claire Rayner

Matthew Reilly   1974-   Aus   Adventure/Thriller
www.matthewreilly.com   🏃 Capt Shane Schofield - US Marine Corps

Stephen Coonts	James Follett	Robert Ludlum
Harold Coyle	W E B Griffin	Craig Thomas
Clive Cussler		

Audrey Reimann   Saga
Lancashire • Yorkshire

Charlotte Vale Allen	Doreen Edwards	Kay Stephens
Aileen Armitage	Audrey Howard	Margaret Sunley
Donna Baker	Elvi Rhodes	Elizabeth Walker
Jessica Blair		

Erich Maria Remarque *1898-1970* *Ger* *General*

Pat Barker	Robert Graves	Henry Williamson
Sebastian Faulks	Paul Watkins	

Mary Renault *1905-83* *Historical*

Dorothy Dunnett	Colleen McCullough	Steven Pressfield
Howard Fast	Valerio Massimo Manfredi	Simon Scarrow
Robert Graves	Allan Massie	Gore Vidal

Ruth Rendell *1930-* *Crime: Police work - Br*

also writes as Barbara Vine ⚥ *DCI George Wexford - 'Kingsmarkham'*
www.twbooks.co.uk/authors/rendell.html

Penelope Evans	Maureen O'Brien	CWA	*1976* ✿
Malcolm Forsythe	Julie Parsons	CWA	*1984* ✿
Morag Joss	Peter Robinson	CWA	*1986* ✿
Sarah Lovett	Aline Templeton		
Sharyn McCrumb	June Thomson		
J Wallis Martin	Laura Wilson		

R

Alastair Reynolds *1966-* **Science Fiction:** *Space opera*

Stephen Baxter	Ken MacLeod	BSFA	*2001* ✿
William Gibson	John Meaney		
Peter F Hamilton	China Miéville		
Paul J McAuley	Adam Roberts		
Jack McDevitt	Kim Stanley Robinson		

Nicholas Rhea *1936-* **Crime:** *Police work - Br*

is Peter Norman Walker & also writes as Andrew Arncliffe, ⚥ *DI Montague Pluke*
Christopher Coram, James Ferguson & Tom Ferris *DS Mark Pemberton*
www.heartbeat.demon.co.uk *PC Nick Parish - 'Adensfield' Yorkshire*

Robert Barnard	Alan Hunter	Stewart Pawson
Caroline Graham	Roger Ormerod	M J Trow
J M Gregson		

Don't forget lists of: *Genres * Characters * Literary prizes * Further reading* ☞

Elvi Rhodes   c 1930-

Saga
Yorkshire

Helen Cannam
Joan Eadith
Elizabeth Gill
Suzanne Goodwin

Sheelagh Kelly
Elisabeth McNeill
Audrey Reimann

Ann Victoria Roberts
Susan Sallis
Margaret Sunley

Pam Rhodes

Saga

Anne Atkins
Walter Macken

Sybil Marshall
Miss Read

Rebecca Shaw
Joanna Trollope

Anne Rice   1941-   US

Horror

also writes as Anne Rampling
www.annerice.com/

Jonathan Aycliffe
Anne Billson
Poppy Z Brite
Nancy Collins

Storm Constantine
John Farris
Laurell K Hamilton
Tom Holland

Jeanne Kalogridis
Brian Lumley
Robert McCammon
Dan Simmons

R

Ben Richards   1964-

General

Martyn Bedford
Mavis Cheek
Douglas Coupland

Laurie Graham
Nick Hornby
Tim Lott

Tony Parsons
Will Self

David Adams Richards   1950-   Can

General

Margaret Atwood
Cormac McCarthy

Michael Ondaatje
Carol Shields

Jo-Anne Richards   SA

General

Bryce Courtenay

Pamela Jooste

Zadie Smith

Phil Rickman

Horror

Campbell Black
David Bowker
Steve Harris

James Herbert
Shaun Hutson
Graham Joyce

Stephen King
Stephen Laws
Tim Wilson

Michael Ridpath   *1961-   Adventure/Thriller: Legal/financial*

David Baldacci   Linda Davies   Brad Meltzer
Harry Bingham   Rankin Davis   Janet Neel
Po Bronson   Paul Erdman   Richard North Patterson
Jonathan Davies   Stephen Frey

Mike Ripley   *1952-*   *Crime*

🏃 *Fitzroy MacLean Angel, Taxi driver - London*

Colin Bateman   Mike Phillips | CWA | 1989 ❀ |
John Brady   Robert T Price | CWA | 1991 ❀ |
John Burns   Jerry Raine
Susan Moody   Mark Timlin

William Rivière   *1954-*   *General*

Martin Booth   Allan Massie   Timothy Mo
James Hamilton-Paterson   Peter Matthiessen   Michael Ondaatje

R Candace Robb   *1950-   US*   *Crime: Historical*
www.candacerobb.com   🏃 *Owen Archer - C14th York ▪ Margaret Kerr - C13th Scotland*

Alys Clare   Paul Harding   Ian Morson
Paul Doherty   Bernard Knight   Ellis Peters
Susanna Gregory   Viviane Moore   Kate Sedley

Harold Robbins   *1912-97   US*   *Glitz & Glamour*

Sandra Brown   Joan Collins   Mario Puzo
Jackie Collins   Arthur Hailey

Tom Robbins   *1936-   US*   *General*

Lisa Alther   John Irving   Thomas Pynchon
Joseph Heller   Thomas McGuane

---

*Don't forget lists of: Genres * Characters * Literary prizes * Further reading* ☞

Jennifer Roberson 1953- US

Fantasy: Epic
Cheysuli Series

Robin Hobb   Katherine Kurtz   Judith Tarr
J V Jones   Melanie Rawn

Adam Roberts 1967-

Science Fiction: Space opera

Iain M Banks   Ken MacLeod   Alastair Reynolds
Gene Brewer   John Meaney   Mary Doria Russell
Eric Brown   China Miéville   Gene Wolfe
Frank Herbert

Ann Victoria Roberts

Saga
York

Aileen Armitage   Sheelagh Kelly
Doreen Edwards   Elvi Rhodes

Cynthia S Roberts

Historical

R

Catrin Collier   Rosalind Laker   Grace Thompson
Gloria Cook   Hilda McKenzie   Barbara Whitnell
Iris Gower   Catrin Morgan   Sarah Woodhouse
Winston Graham   Agnes Short

David Roberts

Crime
⅄ *Lord Edward Corinth & Verity Browne - 1930s England*

Joanna Cannan   Ngaio Marsh   Dorothy L Sayers
Agatha Christie   Gladys Mitchell   Stella Whitelaw
Georgette Heyer

Michele Roberts 1949- Fr

General

Angela Carter   Maureen Freely   Anne Michaels
Carol Clewlow   Joanne Harris   Jeanette Winterson
Emma Donoghue   Janette Turner Hospital Virginia Woolf
Elaine Feinstein   Sara Maitland

Nora Roberts   1950-   US   General
is Elly Wilder and also writes as J D Robb
www.noraroberts.com/

Virginia Andrews	Jude Deveraux	Belva Plain
Catherine Coulter	Jayne Ann Krentz	Nicholas Sparks
Janet Dailey	Lynne Pemberton	Danielle Steel

Yvonne Roberts   General

Helen Fielding	Wendy Holden	Arundhati Roy
Laurie Graham	Tyne O'Connell	

Denise Robertson   Saga
Beloved People Trilogy - NE England

Irene Carr	Margaret Graham	Eileen Stafford
Jean Chapman	Sheila Jansen	Janet MacLeod Trotter
Catherine Cookson	Wendy Robertson	Judy Turner

R Wendy Robertson   Saga
'Priorton', NE England

Irene Carr	Elizabeth Elgin	Denise Robertson
Jean Chapman	Una Horne	Janet MacLeod Trotter
Catherine Cookson	Sheila Jansen	Valerie Wood
Josephine Cox	Brenda McBryde	

Derek Robinson   1932-   War: Modern

W E B Griffin	Max Hennessy	Gavin Lyall
John Harris	Robert Jackson	Chris Ryan
Joseph Heller	Leo Kessler	Paul Watkins

Kim Stanley Robinson   1952-   US   Science Fiction:
Near future

Greg Bear	Linda Nagata	BSFA 1992 ✿
Ben Bova	Larry Niven	
Ray Bradbury	Alastair Reynolds	
Ian McDonald	Brian Stableford	
China Miéville	Sheri S Tepper	

Leah Ruth Robinson   US

is Leah Robinson Rousmaniere
http://leahruthrobinson.com/index_flash.htm

Crime: Medical
🏃 *Dr Evelyn Sutcliffe - New York*

Paul Adam	Tess Gerritsen	Richard Preston
Paul Carson	Ken McClure	Andrew Puckett
Robin Cook	Michael Palmer	Claire Rayner

Patrick Robinson

Sea: Modern

Dale Brown	Bart Davis	Douglas Reeman
Gerry Carroll	P T Deutermann	Peter Tonkin
James Cobb		

Peter Robinson   1950-

www.inspectorbanks.com/

Crime: Police work - Br
🏃 *CI Alan Banks - Yorkshire*

Robert Barnard	Graham Hurley	Dorothy Simpson
Pauline Bell	Jenny Maxwell	Andrew Taylor
Janie Bolitho	Stewart Pawson	R D Wingfield
Colin Dexter	Ruth Rendell	

R

Jill Roe

General

Judy Astley	Patricia Fawcett	Nora Naish
Amanda Brookfield	Sarah Harrison	Libby Purves
Lucy Clare	Karen Hayes	Kathleen Rowntree
Marika Cobbold	Maggie Makepeace	Mary Sheepshanks

Jane Rogers   1952-

General

Margaret Atwood	Candia McWilliam	*S Maugham 1985* ✿
Sally Emerson	Hilary Mantel	
Jane Gardam	Marina Warner	
Alison Lurie		

Roberta Rogow   1942-   US

Crime: Historical
🏃 *Arthur Conan Doyle, Doctor - Victorian England*

Stephanie Barron	Morag Joss	Anne Perry
Arthur Conan Doyle	Laurie R King	Norman Russell
Ray Harrison	Alanna Knight	

Michael Scott Rohan   1951-   Sco   Fantasy
www.users.zetnet.co.uk/mike.scott.rohan/   *Anvil of the World Series*

David Gemmell	Tim Powers	J R R Tolkien
Guy Gavriel Kay	Philip Pullman	Tad Williams
Stephen R Lawhead	Kristine Kathryn Rusch	Jonathan Wylie
Adam Nichols	Judith Tarr	

Annette Roome   1946-   Crime
Chris Martin, Journalist - 'Tipping'

Veronica Heley	Janet Laurence	CWA 1989 ❀
Morag Joss	Marianne MacDonald	
Sarah Lacey	John Sherwood	

Nancy Taylor Rosenberg   1946-   US   Crime: Legal/financial
www.nancytrosenberg.com

Carol Higgins Clark	Tami Hoag	Steve Martini
Alan M Dershowitz	John T Lescroart	Richard North Patterson
Linda Fairstein	Phillip M Margolin	Scott Turow
Philip Friedman		

R

Kate Ross   1956-98   US   Crime: Historical
Julian Kestral, Dandy - Regency England

Stephanie Barron	Georgette Heyer	Amy Myers
Elizabeth Chadwick	Alanna Knight	Anne Perry
Ray Harrison	Peter Lovesey	M J Trow

Malcolm Ross   1932-   Saga
also writes as Malcolm Macdonald & M R O'Donnell   Cornwall

Rosemary Aitken	Jonathan Grant	Beryl Kingston
Gloria Cook	Elizabeth Ann Hill	Sue Sully
Anne Goring	Evelyn Hood	Barbara Whitnell
Winston Graham		

Philip Roth   1933-   US   General

Saul Bellow	Howard Jacobson	Pulitzer 1998 ❀
Joseph Heller	Jay McInerney	W H Smith 2000 ❀
Alan Isler	Rick Moody	

Victoria Routledge 1975-   Chick Lit

Celia Brayfield	Lisa Jewell	Robyn Sisman
Victoria Colby	Jill Mansell	Linda Taylor
Sarah Harvey	Melissa Nathan	Fiona Walker

Rosemary Rowe   Crime: Historical
is Rosemary Aitken   🏃 *Libertus, Mosaicist - Roman Britain*

Lindsey Davis	Allan Massie	Marilyn Todd
Colleen McCullough	Steven Saylor	David Wishart

Laura Joh Rowland 1954- US   Crime: Historical
🏃 *Sano Ichiro - C17th Japan*

James Clavell	Michael Pearce	Christopher West
Lindsey Davis	Peter Tasker	

Betty Rowlands   Crime
🏃 *Melissa Craig, Writer - Cotswolds ▪ Sukey Reynolds, Scene of Crime Officer*

Janie Bolitho	Marjorie Eccles	Hazel Holt
Lizbie Brown	Ann Granger	Graham Hurley
Mary Clayton	Veronica Heley	Gwen Moffat
Natasha Cooper	Joyce Holms	Rebecca Tope

Kathleen Rowntree   General

Anna Barrie	Annie Leith	Jill Roe
Caroline Bridgwood	Charlotte Moore	Mary Selby
Fanny Frewen	Nora Naish	Peta Tayler
Maeve Haran		

Arundhati Roy 1961- Ind   General

Amit Chaudhuri	Yvonne Roberts
R K Narayan	Vikram Seth

R

Don't forget lists of: *Genres * Characters * Literary prizes * Further reading* ☞

Kenneth Royce 1920- Adventure/Thriller
also writes as Oliver Jacks

Clive Egleton
Gavin Esler

Robert Ludlum
Lawrence Sanders

Glover Wright

Nicholas Royle 1957- Crime

Martyn Bedford
Robert Girardi
John Harvey

Quintin Jardine
Chris Paling

Ian Rankin
Martyn Waites

Bernice Rubens 1928- General

Beryl Bainbridge
Anita Brookner
Margaret Drabble
Alice Thomas Ellis
Pauline Melville

Bel Mooney
Iris Murdoch
A N Wilson
Jeanette Winterson

Booker	*1970* ✿

R Kristine Kathryn Rusch 1960- US Science Fiction
also writes as Sandy Schofield

Brian Herbert
Robin Hobb

J V Jones
Michael Moorcock

Michael Scott Rohan
R A Salvatore

Salman Rushdie 1947- General

Anthony Burgess
Amit Chaudhuri
Anita Desai
David Grossman
Janette Turner Hospital

Gita Mehta
Michael Ondaatje
Vikram Seth
Marianne Wiggins

Black	*1981* ✿
Booker	*1981* ✿
Whitbread	*1988* ✿
Whitbread	*1995* ✿

Mary Doria Russell 1950- US Science Fiction
www.literati.net/Russell/

Greg Bear
Orson Scott Card
Gwyneth Jones

Ken MacLeod
Adam Roberts

BSFA	*1997* ✿
Arthur C Clarke	*1998* ✿

Norman Russell
Crime: Historical

⚐ DI Saul Jackson & Sgt Bottomley - C19th Warwickshire, England

Arthur Conan Doyle
Ray Harrison
Morag Joss

Alanna Knight
Peter Lovesey
Anne Perry

Roberta Rogow
M J Trow

Edward Rutherfurd   1948-
Historical

is Francis E Wintle

Jean M Auel
Bernard Cornwell
Dorothy Dunnett

Philippa Gregory
Colleen McCullough

James A Michener
Leon Uris

Chris Ryan   1961-
Adventure/Thriller

Geoffrey Archer
Peter Cave
Shaun Clarke
Conor Cregan

Murray Davies
Johnny 'Two Combs' Howard
Stephen Hunter
Graham Hurley

Andy McNab
David Mason
John Nichol
Derek Robinson

R

Liz Ryan
Saga

Ireland

Maeve Binchy
Elaine Crowley
Frank Delaney

Sheelagh Kelly
Mary A Larkin
Joan O'Neill

D M Purcell
Alexandra Raife

Mary Ryan   *Ire*
General

Maeve Binchy
Clare Boylan
Elaine Crowley

Frank Delaney
Caro Fraser
Joan O'Neill

Marjorie Quarton
Patricia Scanlan

Don't forget lists of: *Genres * Characters * Literary prizes * Further reading* ☞

Lisa St Aubin de Terán   1953-   General

| Isabel Allende | Louis de Bernières | Mail | 1983 ❀ |
| Gail Anderson-Dargatz | Alice Munro | S Maugham | 1983 ❀ |

Madeleine St John   Aus   General

Margaret Drabble   Anne Michaels
Helen Dunmore   Barbara Pym

J D Salinger   1919-   US   General

Truman Capote	Carson McCullers	Paul Micou
Harper Lee	Jay McInerney	Edna O'Brien
Cormac McCarthy		

James Sallis   1944-   US   Crime
⚐ Lew Griffin, Academic - New Orleans

Ace Atkins	Raymond Chandler	Mike Phillips
James Lee Burke	Ross Macdonald	Cath Staincliffe
Charlotte Carter	Walter Mosley	

S Susan Sallis   1929-   Saga
⚐ Rising Family - West Country

Rosemary Aitken	Elizabeth Elgin	D M Purcell
Donna Baker	Anne Goring	Elvi Rhodes
Louise Brindley	Elizabeth Ann Hill	Arabella Seymour
Gloria Cook	Sybil Marshall	Sally Stewart

R A Salvatore   1959-   US   Fantasy: Epic
www.rasalvatore.com

David A Drake	Elizabeth Moon	J R R Tolkien
Mercedes Lackey	Mickey Zucker Reichert	Margaret Weis
L E Modesitt Jr	Kristine Kathryn Rusch	

Don't forget lists of: *Genres * Characters * Literary prizes * Further reading* ☞

Kevin Sampson

Lad Lit
Liverpool

Nicholas Blincoe
Christopher Brookmyre
Philip Caveney

Mike Gayle
Nick Hornby
William Sutcliffe

Matt Thorne
Irvine Welsh

Polly Samson *1962-*

General

www.red-umbrella.co.uk

Raffaella Barker
Esther Freud

Joanne Harris
Nick Hornby

Barbara Trapido

Lawrence Sanders *1920-98* *US*

Adventure/Thriller

Jeffrey Archer
Brendan Dubois
Colin Harrison

Robert Ludlum
John D MacDonald
Kenneth Royce

Sidney Sheldon
Doug J Swanson
John Trenhaile

John Sandford *1944-* *US*

Crime: Police work - US
🏃 Lucas Davenport - Minneapolis

is John R Camp
www.johnsandford.org

James Lee Burke
Michael Connelly
Thomas H Cook

Thomas Harris
Stephen Hunter
Michael Kimball

John T Lescroart
Phillip M Margolin
Ridley Pearson

S

John Saul *1942-* *US*

Horror

www.johnsaul.com/

Steve Harris
Shaun Hutson
Stephen King

Dean R Koontz
Robert McCammon
Graham Masterton

Christopher Pike
Guy N Smith

Jean Saunders *1932-*

Aga Saga

also writes as Rowena Summers

Anna Cheska
Johanna Lindsey

Rosamunde Pilcher
Madeleine Wickham

Kate Saunders · Aga Saga

Claire Calman
Zoe Fairbairns
Philippa Gregory

Kate Hatfield
Angela Lambert

Robyn Sisman
Mary Wesley

Alan Savage · 1930- · War: Modern
is Christopher Nicole

James Clavell
Leo Kessler

Eric Lustbader
Amin Maalouf

David Morrell
Marc Olden

Julian Jay Savarin · Adventure/Thriller

Geoffrey Archer
Campbell Armstrong
Dale Brown

Stephen Coonts
Clive Cussler
Robert Jackson

Wilbur Smith
Douglas Terman
Craig Thomas

Diana Saville · 1943- · Aga Saga

Anne Atkins
Clare Boylan

Sarah Harrison
Mary Wesley

S Judith Saxton · 1936- · Saga
is Judy Turner & also writes as Kate Flynn   ⚘ Neyler Family

Teresa Crane
Janet Dailey
Judith Glover
Sara Hylton

Mary Mackie
Margaret Pemberton
Claire Rayner

Danielle Steel
Janet Tanner
Nicola Thorne

Paul Sayer · 1955- · General

David Cook
Janet Frame
Duncan McLean

Lorrie Moore
Tim Pears
Alan Warner

Whitbread 1988 ✹

Don't forget lists of: *Genres* * *Characters* * *Literary prizes* * *Further reading* ☞

Dorothy L Sayers   1893-1957   *Crime*
www.sayers.org.uk   ⚲ *Lord Peter Wimsey*

Margery Allingham   Agatha Christie   Ngaio Marsh
Joanna Cannan   Martha Grimes   David Roberts
John Dickson Carr   Georgette Heyer   Rex Stout
Kate Charles   Michael Innes   Patricia Wentworth

Steven Saylor   1956-   US   *Crime:* Historical
www.stevensaylor.com   ⚲ *Gordianus The Finder - Ancient Rome*

Lindsey Davis   Rosemary Rowe   David Wishart
Allan Massie   Marilyn Todd

Patricia Scanlan   *Ire*   *Chick Lit*

Clare Boylan   Sheila O'Flanagan   Robyn Sisman
Colette Caddle   Erin Pizzey   Alice Taylor
Martina Devlin   D M Purcell   Fiona Walker
Cathy Kelly   Mary Ryan

Simon Scarrow   *Historical*
www.scarrow.fsnet.co.uk/author.htm   ⚲ *Quintus Licinius Cato - C1st AD Roman Europe*

Bernard Cornwell   Pauline Gedge   Allan Massie   **S**
Lindsey Davis   Colleen McCullough   Mary Renault

Bernhard Schlink   1944-   Ger   *General*

Pat Barker   Anne Michaels
Alan Isler   William Styron

Alan Scholefield   1931-   SA   *Crime:* Police work - Br
also writes as Lee Jordan   ⚲ *Det Supt George Macrae & DS Silver - London*

Hilary Bonner   Cynthia Harrod-Eagles   Andrew Taylor
W J Burley   Barry Maitland   R D Wingfield
June Drummond

Sandra Scoppettone   1936-   US   Crime: PI

also writes as Jack Early   🏃 Lauren Laurano - New York
www.imt.net/~gedison/scoppett.html

Linda Barnes	Sara Paretsky	Michelle Spring
Sue Grafton	Manda Scott	Mary Wings
Lynn S Hightower		

Justin Scott   1944-   US   Sea: Modern

🏃 Ben Abbott

Clive Cussler	Richard Herman	Patrick Lynch
James Follett	Eric Lustbader	Marc Olden

Manda Scott   Sco   Crime

www.mandascott.co.uk   🏃 Dr Kellen Stewart, Therapist - Glasgow

Ajay Close	Alma Fritchley	Sandra Scoppettone
Judith Cutler	Ellen Hart	Joan Smith
Stella Duffy	Frederic Lindsay	Michelle Spring
Sarah Dunant	Denise Mina	Mary Wings

Martin Scott   Fantasy: Humour

is Martin Millar

S

Robert Asprin	Andrew Harman	Fritz Leiber
Neil Gaiman	Harry Harrison	Terry Pratchett
Simon R Green	Tom Holt	Robert Rankin

Paul Scott   1920-78   General

E M Forster	Doris Lessing	*Booker* 1977 ❀
Nadine Gordimer	Olivia Manning	
Graham Greene	John Masters	
Ruth Prawer Jhabvala	Rohinton Mistry	
M M Kaye	Vikram Seth	
Lee Langley		

Don't forget lists of: *Genres * Characters * Literary prizes * Further reading* ☞

Lisa Scottoline   1955-   US

www.scottoline.com

Crime: Legal/financial
⚘ Rosato & Associates - Philadelphia

Catherine Arnold
Linda Fairstein
Erle Stanley Gardner
John Grisham

Craig Holden
Jonnie Jacobs
John T Lescroart
Phillip M Margolin

Steve Martini
Richard North Patterson
Robert K Tanenbaum

Tim Sebastian   1952-

Adventure/Thriller

Geoffrey Archer
Campbell Armstrong
Tom Bradby
Lionel Davidson

Gavin Esler
Bryan Forbes
Humphrey Hawksley
Stephen Leather

Gerald Seymour
Gordon Stevens
Nigel West

Kate Sedley   1926-

is Brenda Clarke

Crime: Historical
⚘ Roger The Chapman - C15th England

P F Chisholm
Alys Clare
Judith Cook
Susanna Gregory

Michael Jecks
Bernard Knight
Edward Marston
Viviane Moore

Ian Morson
Ellis Peters
Candace Robb

Mary Selby

General

Faith Bleasdale
Jill Dawson
Erica James
Karen Nelson

Elizabeth Palmer
Kathleen Rowntree
Sue Sully
Ann Swinfen

Peta Tayler
Willow Tickell
Marcia Willett

Will Self   1961-

www.willself.org.uk

General

Martin Amis
Nicola Barker
Bret Easton Ellis
Anne Fine
Sean Hughes

Patrick McCabe
Ben Richards
Patrick Süskind
Matt Thorne
Irvine Welsh

Faber   1993 ✿

Vikram Seth   1952-   Ind   *General*

Amit Chaudhuri	R K Narayan	
Rumer Godden	Arundhati Roy	
Lee Langley	Salman Rushdie	
Rohinton Mistry	Paul Scott	
V S Naipaul		

Anya Seton   1916-90   *Historical*

Daphne Du Maurier	Victoria Holt	Jean Stubbs
Domini Highsmith	Robin Maxwell	

Arabella Seymour   1948-   *Saga*

Audrey Howard	Lesley Pearse
Hilary Norman	Susan Sallis

Gerald Seymour   1941-   *Adventure/Thriller*

Tom Bradby	Bryan Forbes	Daniel Silva
James Buchan	Stephen Leather	Gordon Thomas
John Burdett	Henry Porter	Nigel West
Gavin Esler	Tim Sebastian	Barnaby Williams

S

Nicholas Shakespeare   1957-   *General*
www.randomhouse.com/boldtype/0200/shakespeare/

Malcolm Bradbury	James Hamilton-Paterson	
Louis de Bernières	Mario Vargas Llosa	*S Maugham 1990* ❀
Graham Greene		

Laurence Shames   1951-   US   *Crime:* Humour
🕴 Peter Amsterdam, PI - Key West, Florida

Anthony Bourdain	James Hall	
Edna Buchanan	Joe R Lansdale	CWA 1995 ❀
Tim Dorsey	Nancy Livingston	
Bill Fitzhugh	Geoffrey Norman	
Kinky Friedman	Doug J Swanson	
Peter Guttridge		

Kate Sharam
General

Elizabeth Buchan
Kate Fenton

Margaret Forster
Juliette Mead

Libby Purves

Tom Sharpe   1928-
Humour

Joseph Connolly
Ruth Dudley Edwards
George MacDonald Fraser
James Hawes

Philip Hensher
Tom Holt
Alan Isler
Howard Jacobson

Geoff Nicholson
Peter Tinniswood
Alan Titchmarsh

Bob Shaw   1931-   Ire
Science Fiction: Humour

Douglas Adams
John Brunner
Rob Grant
Harry Harrison
Tom Holt

Fritz Leiber
Robert Rankin
Clifford D Simak
Ian Watson
Robert Charles Wilson

BSFA	1975 ✿
BSFA	1986 ✿

Patricia Shaw   Aus
Historical

Emma Drummond
Sheelagh Kelly

Peter Ling
Colleen McCullough

E V Thompson
Eileen Townsend

S

Rebecca Shaw
General

Barleybridge Series ▪ Turnham Malpas Series

Anne Atkins
Patricia Fawcett
Kate Fielding
Fanny Frewen

Karen Hayes
Hazel Hucker
Erica James
Jan Karon

Walter Macken
Charlotte Moore
Miss Read
Pam Rhodes

Simon Shaw
Crime: Humour

🚶 Philip Fletcher, Theatre ▪ Grace Cornish, PI - London

Marian Babson
Robert Barnard
Simon Brett
Anthea Cohen
Patricia Highsmith

Nancy Livingston
Charles Spencer
Susan Sussman with
   Sarajane Avidon

CWA	1990 ✿
CWA	1994 ✿

Michael Shea 1938- Sco   General
also writes as Michael Sinclair

Jeffrey Archer	Robert Harris	Peter Rawlinson
Michael Dobbs	Gavin Lyall	Peter Tasker
Ken Follett	A J Quinnell	

Sarah Shears   Saga
♁ Annie Parsons ▪ Franklin Family

Catrin Collier	Elisabeth McNeill	Kitty Ray
Elizabeth Jeffrey	Anne Melville	Miss Read
Brenda McBryde	Mary E Pearce	Barbara Whitnell
Walter Macken		

Mary Sheepshanks   General

Diana Appleyard	Karen Hayes	Jill Roe
Cindy Blake	Hazel Hucker	Peta Tayler
Lucy Clare	Nora Naish	Willow Tickell
Kate Fenton		

Sidney Sheldon 1917- US   Adventure/Thriller
www.sidneysheldon.com

Elizabeth Adler	Richard Condon	Lawrence Sanders
Jeffrey Archer	Arthur Hailey	Wilbur Smith
Lorenzo Carcaterra		

Lucius Shepard 1947- US   Science Fiction: Near future

William Gibson	Dan Simmons
Joe Haldeman	Bruce Sterling

Stella Shepherd 1953-   Crime
♁ DI Richard Montgomery & Sgt William Bird - Police Br ▪ Rowena Kemp, Journalist

Paul Adam	Ann Granger	Ken McClure
Colin Dexter	Alison Joseph	R D Wingfield
Caroline Graham		

John Sherwood 1913-   Crime
🏃 Celia Grant - Horticulture

D M Greenwood   Susan Kelly   Gwen Moffat
Gerald Hammond   Charlotte MacLeod   Annette Roome
Hazel Holt   Gladys Mitchell   Staynes & Storey

Carol Shields 1935- Can   General

Kate Atkinson   Anne Michaels   Pulitzer   1995 ✾
Margaret Atwood   Ann Patchett   Orange   1998 ✾
Kate Bingham   David Adams Richards
Dennis Bock   Jane Urquhart
Joan Brady   Marina Warner
Elinor Lipman   Marianne Wiggins

Agnes Short Sco   Historical
also writes as Rose Shipley

Emma Blair   Elisabeth McNeill   Anne Vivis
Doris Davidson   Cynthia S Roberts

Anita Shreve 1946- US   General

Andrea Barrett   Connie May Fowler   Jacquelyn Mitchard
Suzanne Berne   Patricia Gaffney   Amanda Prantera   S
Carol Clewlow   Jane Hamilton   Nicholas Sparks
Andre Dubus   J Robert Lennon   Robert James Waller

Linda Lay Shuler US   Historical

Jean M Auel   Christian Jacq   L E Modesitt Jr

Nevil Shute 1899-1960   Adventure/Thriller

Jon Cleary   Hammond Innes   Nicholas Monsarrat
Ernest Hemingway   Geoffrey Jenkins   Morris West

Don't forget lists of: *Genres* * *Characters* * *Literary prizes* * *Further reading* ☞

Anne Rivers Siddons   1936-   US   Saga

Pat Conroy   Carson McCullers   Rosie Thomas
Janet Dailey   Belva Plain   Rebecca Wells
Olivia Goldsmith

Jan Siegel   Fantasy: Epic

Marion Zimmer Bradley   Katharine Kerr   Melanie Rawn
Mark Chadbourn   Anne McCaffrey   Margaret Weis
Robin Hobb   Juliet Marillier   Connie Willis
Robert Holdstock   George R R Martin

Sheldon Siegel   Crime: Legal/financial
www.sheldonsiegel.com

David Baldacci   Linda Davies   Jonnie Jacobs
Anthony Bourdain   Rankin Davis   Scott Turow
Po Bronson   John Grisham

Alan Sillitoe   1928-   General

D H Lawrence   Stanley Middleton
David Lodge   Tony Warren

S

Daniel Silva   US   Adventure/Thriller
⚐ Michael Osbourne - CIA

Victor Davis   Frederick Forsyth   John Le Carré
Ian Fleming   Alan Judd   Gerald Seymour

Robert Silverberg   1935-   US   Science Fiction: Space and time

A A Attanasio   Ursula K Le Guin   Larry Niven
Arthur C Clarke   George R R Martin   Freda Warrington
David Eddings   Julian May   Roger Zelazny
Joe Haldeman

Don't forget lists of: *Genres * Characters * Literary prizes * Further reading* ☞

Dov Silverman   1933-   US   Adventure/Thriller

Eric Lustbader   A J Quinnell
David Morrell   Douglas Terman

Clifford D Simak   1904-88   US   Science Fiction: Space and time

Isaac Asimov   Jack McDevitt   Robert Charles Wilson
Ray Bradbury   Bob Shaw   John Wyndham
Fritz Leiber

Georges Simenon   1903-89   Belg   Crime: Police work - foreign
Commissaire Jules Maigret - Paris, France

John Brady   Mark Hebden   Daniel Pennac
John Creasey   J Robert Janes   Rex Stout
Nicolas Freeling   H R F Keating   Janwillem van de Wetering
Juliet Hebden   Magdalen Nabb

Dan Simmons   1948-   US   Science Fiction: Space opera
www.levity.com/corduroy/simmons.htm   Hyperion Series

David Brin   Peter F Hamilton | BSFA   1991 ❀ |
Orson Scott Card   Lucius Shepard
Arthur C Clarke   Vernor Vinge
Joe Haldeman

S

Dan Simmons   1948-   US   Horror
www.levity.com/corduroy/simmons.htm

Richard Bachman   Nancy Collins   Bentley Little
Clive Barker   Stephen King   Anne Rice

Paullina Simons   1963-   US   Adventure/Thriller

Alice Blanchard   John Gilstrap   Stephen Hunter
Pat Conroy   Gwen Hunter   Scott Smith
Jeffery Deaver

Dorothy Simpson   1933-   Crime: Police work - Br
🏃 DI Luke Thanet & DS Lineham - 'Sturrenden', Kent

Brian Battison   Janet Neel   CWA   1985 ✱
Clare Curzon   Emma Page
Caroline Graham   Peter Robinson
Hazel Holt   Staynes & Storey
Ngaio Marsh   Barbara Whitehead

Mona Simpson   1957-   US   General

Ellen Gilchrist   Alice Hoffman   Alice Munro
Jane Hamilton   Sue Miller   Anne Tyler

Iain Sinclair   1943-   General

Peter Ackroyd   Tom Holland   Black   1991 ✱
Angela Carter   Geoff Nicholson   Encore   1992 ✱
Charles Dickens   Robert Nye
Alasdair Gray

Isaac Bashevis Singer   1904-91   US   General

Saul Bellow   Primo Levi   Alexander Solzhenitsyn
David Grossman   Amos Oz   Leon Uris
Alan Isler

June Flaum Singer   US   Glitz & Glamour

Jackie Collins   Judi James   Danielle Steel
Julie Ellis   Johanna Lindsey   Caroline Upcher
Elizabeth Gage   Fern Michaels

Robyn Sisman   US   General

Louise Bagshawe   Libby Purves   Kate Saunders
Olivia Goldsmith   Victoria Routledge   Patricia Scanlan
Jane Gordon

Don't forget lists of: *Genres* * *Characters* * *Literary prizes* * *Further reading* ☞

Alison Skelton   *Saga*

Emma Blair   Inga Dunbar   Frances Paige
Margaret Thomson Davis   Evelyn Hood

Michael Slade   *Can*   *Horror*

Ramsey Campbell   Dean R Koontz   Guy N Smith
John Douglas   Richard Laymon

John Sladek   *1937-2000   US*   *Science Fiction:* Technical

J G Ballard   Philip K Dick   Bruce Sterling
Ben Bova   Thomas M Disch   Kurt Vonnegut

Gillian Slovo   *1952-   SA*   *Crime:* PI
                                                      ⚵ *Kate Baeier - London*

Denise Danks   Lauren Henderson   Joan Smith
Sarah Dunant   Nora Kelly   Michelle Spring
Martin Edwards   Sara Paretsky

Harriet Smart   *Saga*

Jay Allerton   Nora Kay   Eileen Ramsay
Emma Blair   Annie Murray   Jessica Stirling
Sara Fraser

William Smethurst   *Adventure/Thriller*

Desmond Bagley   Gavin Lyall   A J Quinnell
Clive Cussler   Alistair MacLean   Wilbur Smith
Ken Follett

Jane Smiley   *1949-   US*   *General*

Joan Brady   Peter Hoeg   *Pulitzer   1992* ⚙
Thomas Eidson   Jacquelyn Mitchard
Louise Erdrich   Barbara Neil
Ellen Gilchrist   Marge Piercy
Kate Grenville   Anna Quindlen
Jane Hamilton   Robert James Waller

Alexander McCall Smith   *Zim*   *Crime: PI*
♢ Precious Ramotswe - Botswana

Janie Bolitho	Veronica Heley	Walter Mosley
Charlotte Carter	Tony Hillerman	Marcia Muller
Sue Grafton	Henning Mankell	Valerie Wilson Wesley

Carol Smith   *Crime: Psychological*

Elizabeth McGregor	Alison Taylor	Laura Wilson
Jenny Maxwell	Minette Walters	Margaret Yorke
Gemma O'Connor		

Guy N Smith   *1939-*   *Horror*

Shaun Hutson	Christopher Pike	Michael Slade
Richard Laymon	John Saul	

Joan Smith   *1953-*   *Crime*
♢ Loretta Lawson, Academic - London

Amanda Cross	Lesley Grant-Adamson	Manda Scott
Anabel Donald	Nora Kelly	Gillian Slovo
Sarah Dunant	Amanda Quick	Michelle Spring

S

Martin Cruz Smith   *1942-*   *US*   *Crime: Police work - foreign*
also writes as Martin Quinn & Simon Quinn   *♢ Insp Arkady Renko - USSR & Cuba*

David Brierley	Philip Kerr	*CWA* *1981* ❀
Stephen J Cannell	Peter May	
Robert Harris	Reggie Nadelson	
David Ignatius	Gordon Stevens	
Donald James		

Michael Marshall Smith   *1965-*   *Science Fiction: Near future*

Alexander Besher	William Gibson	Jeff Noon
Gene Brewer	James Lovegrove	Rachel Pollack
John Crowley	China Miéville	Neal Stephenson
Christopher Fowler	Nick Nielsen	

Murray Smith

Adventure/Thriller

♁ David Jardine

Stephen Coonts	Clive Egleton	Eric Lustbader
Daniel Easterman	Robert Ludlum	John Trenhaile

Scott Smith   1965-   US

Adventure/Thriller

Alice Blanchard	Donald Harstad	Andrew Klavan
John Gilstrap	Tami Hoag	Paullina Simons

Wilbur Smith   1933-

Adventure/Thriller

Bryce Courtenay	June Drummond	Julian Jay Savarin
John Gordon Davis	Arthur Hailey	Sidney Sheldon
Nelson DeMille	Geoffrey Jenkins	William Smethurst
Peter Driscoll	A J Quinnell	

Wilbur Smith   1933-

Historical

Joy Chambers	Margaret George	Colleen McCullough
Pauline Gedge	Christian Jacq	Valerio Massimo Manfredi

Zadie Smith   1975-

General **S**

http://www.penguin.co.uk/static/packages/uk/articles/smith/smith2.html

Amit Chaudhuri	Black	2000 ❀	W H Smith	2000 ❀
Hanif Kureishi	Guardian	2000 ❀	Sunday Times	2001 ❀
Jo-Anne Richards	Whitbread	2000 ❀	Betty Trask	2001 ❀
Meera Syal				
Louisa Young				

Henrietta Soames   1958-

Aga Saga

Anna Barrie	Elizabeth Palmer
Katie Fforde	Titia Sutherland

Don't forget lists of: *Genres * Characters * Literary prizes * Further reading* ☞

Linda Sole   *Saga*

also writes as Lynn Granville, Anne Herries & Emma Quincey
www.lindasole.co.uk   *Rose Saga*

Evelyn Hood   Grace Thompson   Anne Vivis
E V Thompson   Kate Tremayne

Alexander Solzhenitsyn   *1918-   Rus*   *General*

Primo Levi   Amos Oz
Vladimir Nabokov   Isaac Bashevis Singer

S P Somtow   *Horror*

www.somtow.com

Anne Billson   Poppy Z Brite   Tom Holland
Alice Borchardt   Nancy Collins   H P Lovecraft

Muriel Spark   *1918-   Sco*   *General*

Lynne Reid Banks   Doris Lessing   Iris Murdoch
Nina Bawden   Shena Mackay   Julie Myerson
Isabel Colegate   Candia McWilliam   William Trevor
Agnes Desarthe   Hilary Mantel

S

Nicholas Sparks   *US*   *General*

www.nicholassparks.com

Nicholas Evans   Nora Roberts   Rosie Thomas
Alice Hoffman   Anita Shreve   Robert James Waller

Alan Spence   *1947-   Sco*   *General*

Des Dillon   Gordon Legge   Andrew O'Hagan
Janice Galloway   Carl MacDougall   Agnes Owens
Andrew Greig   Duncan McLean

Charles Spencer *1955-* — *Crime: Humour*

Will Benson, Showbiz writer

Marian Babson
Simon Brett
Jonathan Gash
Peter Guttridge
Nancy Livingston
Simon Shaw
Susan Sussman with Sarajane Avidon
Donald E Westlake

John B Spencer *1944-2002* — *Crime*

Colin Bateman
James Ellroy
Carl Hiaasen
George V Higgins
Elmore Leonard

Lavyrle Spencer *1943- US* — *Saga*

also writes as Elizabeth Gage

Charlotte Vale Allen
Janet Dailey
Barbara Delinsky
Jayne Ann Krentz
Judith McNaught
Fern Michaels
Una-Mary Parker
Lynne Pemberton
Belva Plain
Danielle Steel
Elizabeth Villars

Sally Spencer — *Saga*

www.arrakis.es/~sspencer/

Becky Worrell - London ▪ Taylor Family - Midlands

Donna Baker
Charlotte Bingham
Helen Carey
Pamela Evans
June Francis
Judith Glover
Iris Gower
Jenny Oldfield
Gilda O'Neill
Lynda Page
Victor Pemberton

Sally Spencer — *Crime: Police work - Br*

www.arrakis.es/~sspencer/

CI Charlie Woodend - Lancashire, England

Janie Bolitho
Colin Dexter
Caroline Graham
Ann Granger
J M Gregson
John Harvey
Val McDermid
June Thomson
R D Wingfield

Michelle Spring *Can* — *Crime: PI*

www.unusualsuspects.co.uk

Laura Principal - Oxford

Judith Cutler
Alma Fritchley
Graham Hurley
Nora Kelly
Sandra Scoppettone
Manda Scott
Gillian Slovo
Joan Smith
Veronica Stallwood
Mary Wings

Steven Spruill   1946-   US   *Horror*

Anne Billson   Thomas Harris   Jeanne Kalogridis
Douglas Clegg   James Herbert   Robert McCammon
Laurell K Hamilton

Brian Stableford   1948-   *Science Fiction:* Technical
also writes as Francis Amery & Brian Craig

Gregory Benford   Ian McDonald   Ian Watson
Christopher Evans   Kim Stanley Robinson   David Zindell
Colin Greenland

Eileen Stafford   *Saga*
Bristol

Brenda Clarke   Denise Robertson   Janet Tanner
Elizabeth Ann Hill   Sue Sully   Elizabeth Warne
Connie Monk

Cath Staincliffe   1956-   *Crime:* PI
www.twbooks.co.uk/authors/cstaincliffe.html   ⚐ *Sal Kilkenny - Manchester*

John Baker   Frank Lean   James Sallis
Ron Ellis   Walter Mosley   Stella Whitelaw
Alma Fritchley   Mike Phillips

Diana Stainforth   *Saga*

Sally Brampton   Suzanne Goodwin   Rosie Thomas
Janet Dailey   Maeve Haran

Veronica Stallwood   *Crime*
⚐ *Kate Ivory, Writer - Oxford*

Natasha Cooper   Susan Kelly   Michelle Spring
Colin Dexter   Sarah Lacey   Laura Wilson
Anabel Donald   Marianne MacDonald

Don't forget lists of: *Genres* * *Characters* * *Literary prizes* * *Further reading* ☞

Les Standiford   1945-   US   _Crime_
                              ⚹ John Deal, Builder - Florida

Edna Buchanan	Charlotte Carter	Steve Hamilton
James Lee Burke	James Hall	Geoffrey Norman

Mary Jane Staples   1911-   _Saga_
also writes as James Sinclair & Reginald Staples   _⚹ Staples Family - London_
Adams Family

Kate Alexander	Pamela Evans	Victor Pemberton
Harry Bowling	Anna King	Alison Stuart
Helen Carey	Peter Ling	Dee Williams
Harry Cole	Elizabeth Lord	Audrey Willsher

Staynes & Storey   _Crime: Police work - Br_
also writes as Elizabeth Eyre   _⚹ Supt Bone_

D M Greenwood	Jill McGown	Dorothy Simpson
Hazel Holt	John Sherwood	

Christina Stead   1902-83   NZ   _General_

John Galsworthy	D H Lawrence
Francis King	Patrick White

S

Danielle Steel   1947-   US   _Saga_
www.daniellesteel.com

Charlotte Vale Allen	Judith McNaught	Nora Roberts
Barbara Taylor Bradford	Una-Mary Parker	Judith Saxton
Barbara Delinsky	Margaret Pemberton	June Flaum Singer
Jude Deveraux	Belva Plain	Lavyrle Spencer

John Steinbeck   1902-68   US   _General_

F Scott Fitzgerald	Jack Kerouac	Norman Mailer
Richard Ford	Harper Lee	William Styron
Ernest Hemingway	Larry McMurtry	Leon Uris
William Kennedy		

Kay Stephens

Saga
Stonemoor Series - Yorkshire

Aileen Armitage	Inga Dunbar	Margaret Sunley
Anne Bennett	Elizabeth Elgin	Kate Tremayne
Helen Cannam	Lynda Page	Elizabeth Walker
Alexandra Connor	Audrey Reimann	Valerie Wood

Neal Stephenson   1959-   US   *Science Fiction: Near future*

Steve Aylett	Greg Egan	Jeff Noon
John Barnes	Jon Courtenay Grimwood	Rachel Pollack
Alexander Besher	Gwyneth Jones	Richard Powers
Eric Brown	James Lovegrove	Michael Marshall Smith

Bruce Sterling   1954-   US   *Science Fiction: Near future*

Steve Aylett	Richard Powers
John Barnes	Lucius Shepard
Alexander Besher	John Sladek
Eric Brown	Tad Williams
Jon Courtenay Grimwood	David Wingrove
James Lovegrove	Jack Womack

Arthur C Clarke 2000 ✸

S Gordon Stevens   1945-   *Adventure/Thriller*

David Brierley	Andy McNab	Terence Strong
Alan Furst	Tim Sebastian	Gordon Thomas
David Ignatius	Martin Cruz Smith	

Jane Stevenson   1959-   Sco   *Historical*

Tracy Chevalier	Rose Tremain
Dorothy Dunnett	Sarah Waters

Grant Stewart   1967-   Sco   *Adventure/Thriller*

Marc Blake	Stuart Harrison
Tim Dorsey	James Hawes

Mary Stewart   *1916-   Sco*   *General*

Daphne Du Maurier   Judith Lennox   Sharon Penman
Helen Hollick   Barbara Michaels   Lindsay Townsend
M M Kaye   Rosalind Miles   Anne Worboys
Susanna Kearsley

Michael Stewart   *1945-*   *Horror*

Robin Cook   Graham Joyce   Graham Masterton
Richard Greensted   David Martin

Sally Stewart   *Saga*

Betty Burton   Rosamunde Pilcher   Judith Summers
Jenny Oldfield   Susan Sallis

Caroline Stickland   *Saga*
                                                                    Dorset

Brenda Clarke   Malcolm Macdonald   Patricia Wendorf
Harriet Hudson   Janet Tanner   T R Wilson

Jessica Stirling   *1935-   Sco*   *Saga* **S**
also writes as Caroline Crosby   🏃 *Clare Kelso* ⎫
& Hugh C Rae   *Holly Beckman - Glasgow* ⎬ *Scotland*
                           Conway, Nicholson & Patterson Families ⎭

Emma Blair   Meg Hutchinson   Harriet Smart
Doris Davidson   Nora Kay   Kirsty White
Margaret Thomson Davis   Connie Monk   Mary Withall
Christine Marion Fraser Isobel Neill

Julian Stockwin   *1944-*   *Sea: Historical*
www.julianstockwin.com   🏃 *Thomas Paine Kydd - C18th/19th England*

Alexander Kent   Marcus Palliser   Showell Styles
Jonathan Lunn   Dan Parkinson   Richard Woodman
James L Nelson

Rex Stout   1886-1975   US   Crime: PI
⚹ Nero Wolfe & Archie Goodwin - New York

John Dickson Carr   Jeffery Deaver   Dorothy L Sayers
James Hadley Chase   Erle Stanley Gardner   Georges Simenon
K C Constantine

John Straley   US   Crime: PI
⚹ Cecil Younger - Alaska

Nevada Barr   Steve Hamilton   Joe R Lansdale
Robert Crais   Tony Hillerman

Joyce Stranger   1921-   General
www.k9phoenix.freeserve.co.uk/aboutjoyce.htm

Richard Adams   William Horwood
Nicholas Evans   Henry Williamson

Peter Straub   1943-   US   Horror
www.net-site.com/straub

Richard Bachman   John Farris   H P Lovecraft
Jonathan Carroll   Dean R Koontz   Robert McCammon
Douglas Clegg   Stephen Laws   Richard Matheson
Dennis Etchison   Richard Laymon   T M Wright

Whitley Strieber   US   Horror

Ramsey Campbell   Shaun Hutson   Robert McCammon
John Farris   Dean R Koontz   Graham Masterton

Terence Strong   1946-   War: Modern

James Adams   W E B Griffin   Gordon Stevens
Gavin Esler   Jack Harvey   Gordon Thomas

Don't forget lists of: *Genres * Characters * Literary prizes * Further reading* ☞

Tony Strong 1962-   Crime: Psychological

Martyn Bedford   Scott Turow   Minette Walters
Robert Goddard   Barbara Vine

Alison Stuart   Saga
                                                   London

Betty Burton   Peter Ling   Mary Jane Staples
Pamela Evans   Elizabeth Lord   Dee Williams
Sara Fraser   Gilda O'Neill   Audrey Willsher
Harriet Hudson

Jean Stubbs 1926-   Saga
                                          ⚘ Howarth Chronicles

Winston Graham   Jean Plaidy   Tom-Gallon   1964 ✿
Susan Howatch   Anya Seton
Maureen Peters   Reay Tannahill

Showell Styles 1908-   Sea: Historical
                                              ⚘ Mr Fitton

C S Forester   Dudley Pope   Richard Woodman
Patrick O'Brian   Julian Stockwin

S

William Styron 1925- US   General

Saul Bellow   Richard Ford   Bernhard Schlink
Pat Conroy   Ernest Hemingway   John Steinbeck
Don DeLillo   Norman Mailer   Alice Walker
William Faulkner

Sue Sully   Saga
                                               West Country

Donna Baker   Audrey Howard   Malcolm Ross
Anita Burgh   Susan Howatch   Mary Selby
Daphne Du Maurier   Mary Mackie   Eileen Stafford
Rosemary Enright   Belva Plain

Judith Summers 1953-   *General*

Marian Keyes   Sally Stewart
Susan Oudot   Grace Wynne-Jones

Margaret Sunley   *Saga*
⚐ Oak Family - Yorkshire

Aileen Armitage   Mary E Pearce   Elvi Rhodes
Elizabeth Elgin   Audrey Reimann   Kay Stephens

Patrick Süskind 1949- *Ger*   *General*

Umberto Eco   Will Self
Franz Kafka   Virginia Woolf

Susan Sussman with Sarajane Avidon *US* *Crime*
⚐ Morgan Taylor, Actress - Chicago

Marian Babson   Sue Grafton   Pauline McLynn
Lilian Jackson Braun   Sparkle Hayter   Simon Shaw
Liz Evans   Susan Isaacs   Charles Spencer

S William Sutcliffe 1971-   *Humour*

Mark Barrowcliffe   Alex Garland   Sean Thomas
Matthew Branton   Nick Hornby   Matt Thorne
Anna Davis   Kevin Sampson   Evelyn Waugh

Titia Sutherland   *General*

Louise Brindley   Fanny Frewen   Elizabeth Palmer
Amanda Brookfield   Maggie Makepeace   Henrietta Soames
Zoe Fairbairns

Victor Suthren   *Sea: Historical*

Tom Connery   Patrick O'Brian   Richard Woodman
C S Forester   Antony Trew

Doug J Swanson
1953- US   **Crime:** PI

www.dougswanson.com   🏃 *Jack Flippo - Dallas, Texas*

Harlan Coben	Joe R Lansdale	*CWA*	*1994* ✿
Robert Crais	Elmore Leonard		
Kinky Friedman	Lawrence Sanders		
Carl Hiaasen	Laurence Shames		

Magda Sweetland
1943- *Sco*   *General*

Barbara Erskine	Angela Lambert	*Authors*	*1985* ✿
Diana Gabaldon	Rosamunde Pilcher		

Marly Swick
1949- US   *General*

Nicholas Evans	Anne Tyler
Alice Munro	Rebecca Wells

Graham Swift
1949-   *General*

Julian Barnes	Magnus Mills	*Faber*	*1983* ✿
Peter Benson	Lawrence Norfolk	*Guardian*	*1983* ✿
Neil Ferguson	Rose Tremain	*Holtby*	*1983* ✿
John Fowles	Marina Warner	*Black*	*1996* ✿
Maggie Gee	Gillian White	*Booker*	*1996* ✿
Kazuo Ishiguro	T R Wilson		

S

Madge Swindells
Glitz & Glamour

Alexandra Campbell	Judith Krantz	Phyllis A Whitney
Jackie Collins	Barbara Michaels	Daoma Winston

Ann Swinfen
Aga Saga

Katie Fforde	Maggie Makepeace	Mary Selby
Elizabeth Jane Howard	Rosamunde Pilcher	

Meera Syal   1962-   Ind   General

Chitra Banerjee Divakaruni   Hanif Kureishi   Zadie Smith
Maureen Freely   Harper Lee   Louisa Young
Esther Freud

Julian Symons   1912-94   Crime: Police work - Br
                                                              ♂ Insp Bland

Agatha Christie   Patricia Highsmith   Peter Lovesey
John Creasey   P D James   Jill McGown
B M Gill   Roderic Jeffries   Amy Myers
Ray Harrison

Amy Tan   1952-   US   General

Anita Rau Badami   Kerstin Ekman   Timothy Mo
Andrea Barrett   Arthur Golden   Alice Munro
Jung Chang   Catherine Lim   Gloria Naylor
Anita Desai   Sue Miller   Jane Urquhart

Robert K Tanenbaum   US   Crime: Legal/financial
                                ♂ Roger 'Butch' Karp, Asst Chief DA - New York

Lawrence Block   Frances Fyfield   John T Lescroart
Loren D Estleman   Steve Hamilton   Steve Martini
Linda Fairstein   Dennis Lehane   Lisa Scottoline

Reay Tannahill   1929-   Sco   Saga

Inga Dunbar   Cynthia Harrod-Eagles   *Parker*   1990 ❀
Dorothy Dunnett   Lee Langley
Barbara Erskine   Alison McLeay
Diana Gabaldon   Jean Stubbs
Philippa Gregory   Anne Vivis

Janet Tanner   Saga
                                              ♂ Hillsbridge Family - Somerset

Sara Fraser   Judith Saxton   Elizabeth Villars
Malcolm Macdonald   Eileen Stafford   Elizabeth Warne
Connie Monk   Caroline Stickland

Judith Tarr   1955-   US

Fantasy: Epic
Hound and the Falcon Trilogy

Alice Borchardt
Storm Constantine
Sara Douglass
Laurell K Hamilton

Robert Holdstock
Katharine Kerr
Katherine Kurtz

Stephen R Lawhead
Jennifer Roberson
Michael Scott Rohan

Peter Tasker

Crime: PI
≛ Kazuo Mori - Tokyo, Japan

Robert Crais
James Ellroy
Elmore Leonard

Walter Mosley
Robert B Parker
Laura Joh Rowland

Michael Shea
Christopher West

Peta Tayler

General

Amanda Brookfield
Marika Cobbold
Patricia Fawcett
Karen Hayes

Karen Nelson
Kathleen Rowntree
Mary Selby
Mary Sheepshanks

Willow Tickell
Mary Wesley
Madeleine Wickham

Alice Taylor   Ire

Saga

Maeve Binchy
Clare Boylan

Kathleen Conlon
Patricia Scanlan

Alison Taylor
also writes as Alison G Taylor

Crime: Police work - Br
≛ DCI Michael McKenna - North Wales

T

Jane Adams
Janie Bolitho
Hilary Bonner
Stephen Booth

Jessica Mann
Danuta Reah
Carol Smith

Aline Templeton
Minette Walters
Margaret Yorke

Don't forget lists of: *Genres* * *Characters* * *Literary prizes* * *Further reading* ☞

Andrew Taylor 1951-

also writes as John Robert Taylor
www.lydmouth.demon.co.uk

Crime: *Police work - Br*

♁ *Jill Francis & DI Richard Thornhill - 'Lydmouth',*
1950s Welsh Borders • Roth Trilogy - North London

Hilary Bonner	Alan Scholefield	
Ann Cleeves	Aline Templeton	
Richard Greensted	David Williams	
Gregory Hall	Laura Wilson	
Elizabeth Ironside	R D Wingfield	
Peter Robinson		

CWA	1982 ❀
CWA	2001 ❀

Bernard Taylor

Horror

Campbell Black	James Herbert	Richard Laymon
David Bowker	Peter James	Gillian White

Linda Taylor

Humour

Jane Green	Marian Keyes	Victoria Routledge
Cathy Kelly	Chris Manby	

Roger Taylor 1938-

Fantasy: Epic

Maggie Furey	George R R Martin	Harry Turtledove
Paul Kearney	J R R Tolkien	

Melanie Tem

Adventure/Thriller: Psychological

Mary Higgins Clark	Jenny Jones	Elizabeth McGregor
Joy Fielding	Judith Kelman	Gillian White
Laurell K Hamilton		

Aline Templeton

Crime: *Psychological*
♁ *DS Tom Ward - Derbyshire*

Jane Adams	Margaret Murphy	Alison Taylor
Stephen Booth	Danuta Reah	Andrew Taylor
Deborah Crombie	Ruth Rendell	Minette Walters
Reginald Hill		

Emma Tennant *1937-* Sco   *General*
also writes as Catherine Aydy

Joan Aiken	Penelope Fitzgerald	Iris Murdoch
Jane Austen	Esther Freud	Barbara Pym
Hilary Bailey	Sara Maitland	Fay Weldon

Sheri S Tepper *1929-* US   *Fantasy: Epic*
also writes as B J Oliphant & A J Orde

Marion Zimmer Bradley	Mary Gentle	Ursula K Le Guin
Octavia E Butler	Barbara Hambly	Megan Lindholm
Jonathan Carroll	Frank Herbert	Anne McCaffrey
C J Cherryh	Gwyneth Jones	Kim Stanley Robinson

Boston Teran US   *Crime: Modern*
www.bostonteran.com   *♁ Sheriff John Victor Sully - California*

Alice Blanchard	Robert Ferrigno	*CWA* 2000 ❀
Michael Connelly	Thomas Harris	
James Crumley	Donald Harstad	
James Ellroy	Dennis Lehane	

Douglas Terman *1933-* US   *Adventure/Thriller*

Dale Brown	Jack Harvey	Julian Jay Savarin
Tom Clancy	Richard Herman	Dov Silverman
Stephen Coonts	David Morrell	

Elizabeth Tettmar   *General*

Margaret Forster	Angela Huth
Elizabeth Jane Howard	Angela Lambert

Josephine Tey *1897-1952* Sco   *Crime: Police work - Br*
was Elizabeth Macintosh   *♁ DI Alan Grant - London*

Margery Allingham	Michael Innes
Patricia Highsmith	Ngaio Marsh

James Thayer   US   Adventure/Thriller

Larry Bond   Clive Cussler   Richard Herman
Tom Clancy   Frederick Forsyth   Jack Higgins
Harold Coyle

Stephanie Theobald   Chick Lit

Geraldine Bedell   Helen Fielding
Jenny Colgan   Amy Jenkins

Paul Theroux   1941-   US   General

Joseph Conrad   Sebastien Japrisot | Whitbread | 1978 ❀ |
Pat Conroy   V S Naipaul | Black | 1981 ❀ |
Giles Foden   Piers Paul Read | S Maugham | 2002 ❀ |
Alex Garland   Adam Thorpe
Abdulrazak Gurnah   Colin Thubron
Ernest Hemingway   John Updike

Craig Thomas   1942-   Adventure/Thriller

Geoffrey Archer   James Follett   Julian Rathbone
Dale Brown   Jack Higgins   Matthew Reilly
Harold Coyle   Derek Lambert   Julian Jay Savarin
Clive Cussler   Mike Lunnon-Wood

T Gordon Thomas   Adventure/Thriller

Ken Follett   Derek Lambert   Gordon Stevens
Graham Hurley   Gerald Seymour   Terence Strong

Leslie Thomas   1931-   General

George MacDonald Fraser   Geoff Nicholson   Alan Titchmarsh
Joseph Heller   David Nobbs   Keith Waterhouse
David Lodge   Peter Tinniswood

Don't forget lists of: *Genres * Characters * Literary prizes * Further reading* ☞

Leslie Thomas 1931-

Crime: PI
♁ 'Dangerous' Davies

Natasha Cooper
Anabel Donald

Raymond Flynn
Nick Oldham

Rosie Thomas 1947- Wales

Saga

also writes as Jancy King

Barbara Taylor Bradford
Sally Brampton
Candida Clark
Jill Gascoine
Josephine Hart
Hilda McKenzie

Lynne Pemberton
Belva Plain
Anne Rivers Siddons
Nicholas Sparks
Diana Stainforth
Sophia Watson

Parker   1985 ✿

Scarlett Thomas 1973-

Crime
♁ Lily Pascale - Devon

Judith Cutler
Janet Evanovich
Liz Evans
Sparkle Hayter

Lauren Henderson
Joyce Holms
Irene Lin-Chandler

Marianne MacDonald
Rebecca Tope
Stella Whitelaw

Sean Thomas 1963-

Lad Lit

David Baddiel
Nick Hornby

Tim Lott
Tony Parsons

William Sutcliffe

T

E V Thompson 1931-

Historical
♁ Retallick Family

Gloria Cook
Alexander Cordell
R F Delderfield
Anne Goring

Cynthia Harrod-Eagles
Elizabeth Ann Hill
Barbara Wood
Freda Lightfoot

Kate Tremayne
Patricia Shaw
Linda Sole
Barbara Whitnell

Grace Thompson Wales

Saga

also writes as Kay Christopher

Valley Series - Wales ▪ Pendragon Island Series

Catrin Collier
Catherine Cookson
Iris Gower

Hilda McKenzie
Catrin Morgan

Cynthia S Roberts
Linda Sole

Jim Thompson   1906-77   US   Crime

James Crumley   Russell James   Andrew Vachss
James Ellroy   George P Pelecanos   Charles Willeford
George V Higgins   Sam Reaves

Kate Thompson   1956-   General
                                                                        Ireland

Maeve Binchy   Martina Devlin   Marian Keyes
Colette Caddle   Cathy Kelly   Sheila O'Flanagan
Jenny Colgan

June Thomson   1930-   Crime: Police work - Br
                                                  ⚐ DCI Jack Finch - Essex

Brian Battison   Arthur Conan Doyle   Ruth Rendell
Ken Bruen   Elizabeth Ferrars   Sally Spencer
W J Burley   Anthea Fraser   Barbara Whitehead
Agatha Christie

Rupert Thomson   1955-   General

Douglas Coupland   Michel Faber   Magnus Mills
Jim Crace   John Fowles   Amanda Prantera

Matt Thorne   1974-   Lad Lit

David Baddiel   Kevin Sampson   Encore   2000 ❀
Bret Easton Ellis   Will Self
Jay McInerney   William Sutcliffe

Nicola Thorne   Saga
is Rosemary Ellerbeck & also writes as Katherine Yorke   ⚐ Askham Family ▪ Champagne Series

Charlotte Vale Allen   Margaret Pemberton   Barbara Whitnell
Tessa Barclay   Judith Saxton   Barbara Wood
Barbara Taylor Bradford   Elizabeth Villars

Margaret Thornton 1934-

Saga
Blackpool

Lyn Andrews	Rosemary Enright	Elizabeth Murphy
Jessica Blair	June Francis	Lynda Page
Louise Brindley	Ruth Hamilton	Tony Warren
Alexandra Connor	Freda Lightfoot	

Adam Thorpe 1956-

General

Paul Auster	Adam Lively	Holtby 1993 ✾
William Boyd	Bernard MacLaverty	
Thomas Hardy	Lawrence Norfolk	
Kazuo Ishiguro	Paul Theroux	
Thomas Keneally	Henry Williamson	

Colin Thubron 1939-

General

Michael Ondaatje	Paul Theroux
Piers Paul Read	Jeanette Winterson

Jane Thynne 1961-

General

Robert Edric	Sue Gee
Sebastian Faulks	Andrew Greig

Willow Tickell

General

Marika Cobbold	Jenny Oldfield	Mary Sheepshanks
Karen Hayes	Ann Purser	Peta Tayler
Charlotte Moore	Mary Selby	Madeleine Wickham

T

Mark Timlin 1950-
also writes as Johnny Angelo, Jim Ballantyne & Tony Williams
www.users.totalise.co.uk/~slider

Crime: PI

🏃 *Nick Sharman - London*

Jake Arnott	Frank Lean	Robert T Price
Nicholas Blincoe	Nick Oldham	Jerry Raine
Jeremy Cameron	Mike Phillips	Mike Ripley
Bill James		

Peter Tinniswood   1936-   Humour

H E Bates   Annie Leith   Leslie Thomas
Guy Bellamy   Robert Llewellyn   Keith Waterhouse
George MacDonald Fraser   David Nobbs   P G Wodehouse
Tom Holt   Tom Sharpe

Alan Titchmarsh   Humour
www.alantitchmarsh.com

Katie Fforde   Tom Sharpe   Mark Wallington
David Nobbs   Leslie Thomas   Keith Waterhouse

Charles Todd   Crime: Police work - Br
www.charlestodd.com   ⚇ Insp Ian Rutledge - 1920s England

Pat Barker   Martha Grimes   Gillian Linscott
Robert Goddard   Laurie R King

Marilyn Todd   1958-   Crime: Historical
                                      ⚇ Claudia Seferius - Ancient Rome

Lindsey Davis   Rosemary Rowe   Peter Tremayne
Allan Massie   Steven Saylor   David Wishart

Colm Toibin   1955-   Ire   General

Peter Benson   Bernard MacLaverty   Encore   1993 ✹
Dermot Bolger   Brian Moore
Jennifer Johnston   David Park
Francis King   William Trevor
John McGahern   Niall Williams

J R R Tolkien   1892-1973   Fantasy: Epic

Terry Brooks   Katharine Kerr   R A Salvatore
David Eddings   C S Lewis   Roger Taylor
Robert Jordan   Philip Pullman   T H White
Guy Gavriel Kay   Michael Scott Rohan   Tad Williams

Peter Tonkin *1950-*

Sea: *Modern Mariner Series*

Gerry Carroll	Hammond Innes	Alistair MacLean
James Clavell	A E Langsford	Nicholas Monsarrat
Alan Evans	Mike Lunnon-Wood	Patrick Robinson
Duncan Harding	Philip McCutchan	

Peter Tonkin *1950-*

Crime: *Historical*
♀ *Tom Musgrave, Master of Defence - C16th England*

Fiona Buckley	Michael Clynes	Michael Jecks
P F Chisholm	Judith Cook	Edward Marston

Rebecca Tope *1948-*

Crime
www.rebeccatope.com ♀ *Drew Slocombe, Undertaker • PC Den Cooper - Devon*

Lizbie Brown	Liz Evans	Jill McGown
Mary Clayton	Ann Granger	Betty Rowlands
Tim Cockey	Joyce Holms	Scarlett Thomas
Judith Cutler	Hazel Holt	Stella Whitelaw

Eileen Townsend *Sco*

Saga
Scotland

Jessica Blair	Joan Eadith	Rosamunde Pilcher
Helen Cannam	Alison McLeay	Patricia Shaw
Teresa Crane		

Lindsay Townsend *1960-*

General

Evelyn Anthony	Mary Stewart
Charlotte Lamb	Phyllis A Whitney

Sue Townsend *1946-*

Humour

Clare Boylan	Kathy Lette	Mark Wallington
Laurie Graham	Sue Limb	Keith Waterhouse
Tom Holt	Helen Muir	Nigel Williams
India Knight		

T

Nigel Tranter
also wrote as Nye Tredgold — *1909-2000   Sco* — *Historical*

Nicholas Carter
Dorothy Dunnett
Howard Fast

Winston Graham
Edith Pargeter

Sharon Penman
Jean Plaidy

Barbara Trapido   *1941-* — *General*

Jane Austen
Amanda Craig
Alice Thomas Ellis
Catherine Fox

Joanne Harris
Barbara Neil
Susan Oudot

Tim Parks
Amanda Prantera
Polly Samson

Rose Tremain   *1943-* — *General*

William Bedford
Tracy Chevalier
Maggie Gee
Sheri Holman
Andrew Miller

Deborah Moggach
Robert Nye
Jane Stevenson
Graham Swift
Barry Unsworth

Black	*1992* ❀
Whitbread	*1999* ❀

Kate Tremayne
is Pauline Bentley — *Historical* — *Loveday Series - Cornwall*

Winston Graham
Susan Howatch

Linda Sole
Kay Stephens

E V Thompson

T Peter Tremayne   *1943-   Ire* — *Crime: Historical*
also writes as Peter Berresford Ellis
www.sisterfidelma.com

🏃 Sister Fidelma - C7th Ireland
Sir Keith Chace

Alys Clare
Lindsey Davis

Paul Harding
Michael Jecks

Ellis Peters
Marilyn Todd

John Trenhaile   *1949-* — *Adventure/Thriller*

Jeffrey Archer
Campbell Armstrong
Nelson DeMille

Daniel Easterman
Colin Forbes
Stephen Leather

Lawrence Sanders
Gerald Seymour
Murray Smith

William Trevor 1928- Ire *General*

John Banville	Brian Moore	*Whitbread 1976* ❀
Elizabeth Bowen	David Park	*Whitbread 1983* ❀
Ronald Frame	V S Pritchett	*Whitbread 1994* ❀
Susan Hill	Muriel Spark	
Jennifer Johnston	Colm Toibin	
John McGahern		

Antony Trew 1906-96 SA *Sea: Modern*

Brian Callison	Philip McCutchan	Douglas Reeman
Sam Llewellyn	Nicholas Monsarrat	Victor Suthren

Kathy Hogan Trocheck 1954- US *Crime*
http://kathytrocheck.com/ ☃ *Callahan Garrity, House cleaning business - Atlanta*

Lilian Jackson Braun	Martha Lawrence	Lindsay Maracotta
Jan Burke	Sharyn McCrumb	Margaret Maron
Janet Evanovich	Charlotte MacLeod	

Anthony Trollope 1815-82 *General*

Charles Dickens	William Golding
John Galsworthy	Susan Howatch

Joanna Trollope 1943- *Aga Saga*
also writes as Caroline Harvey

Diana Appleyard	Patricia Gaffney	*Parker 1980* ❀
Anne Doughty	Karen Hayes	
Catherine Dunne	Sian James	
Elizabeth Falconer	Karen Nelson	
Kate Fenton	Pam Rhodes	
Caro Fraser	Sophia Watson	

T

Don't forget lists of: *Genres * Characters * Literary prizes * Further reading* ☞

Janet MacLeod Trotter   1958-

Saga
NE England

Irene Carr	Elizabeth Gill	Brenda McBryde
Catherine Cookson	Una Horne	Denise Robertson
Valerie Georgeson	Sheila Jansen	Wendy Robertson

M J Trow   1949-   *Wales*

Crime: Historical
🕴 *Det Supt Sholto Lestrade - C19th England* ▪ *Peter Maxwell, Teacher*

W J Burley	Graham Hurley	Anne Perry
Arthur Conan Doyle	Gillian Linscott	Nicholas Rhea
Sarah Grazebrook	Peter Lovesey	Kate Ross
Ray Harrison	Amy Myers	Norman Russell

Lynne Truss

Humour

Susie Boyt	Lucy Ellman	Jane Green
Mavis Cheek	Helen Fielding	Arabella Weir
Isla Dewar		

Peter Turnbull   1950-

Crime: Police work - Br
🕴 *DCI Hennessy & DS Yellick - York* ▪ *P Division - Glasgow*

Jo Bannister	Quintin Jardine	William McIlvanney
Robert Barnard	Frank Lean	Frank Palmer
Pauline Bell	Frederic Lindsay	Stewart Pawson
Ken Bruen	Eugene McEldowney	Barbara Whitehead

T

Judy Turner   1936-
also writes as Kate Flynn & Judith Saxton

Saga
Norfolk

Margaret Dickinson	Judith Lennox
Jonathan Grant	Denise Robertson

Don't forget lists of: *Genres* ＊ *Characters* ＊ *Literary prizes* ＊ *Further reading* ☞

Scott Turow 1949- US   *Crime: Legal/financial*
www.scottturow.com

Alan M Dershowitz	John McLaren	CWA 1987 ❀
Dexter Dias	Phillip M Margolin	
William Diehl	Christopher Reich	
Colin Harrison	Nancy Taylor Rosenberg	
Craig Holden	Sheldon Siegel	
Paul Kilduff	Tony Strong	

Harry Turtledove 1949- US   *Fantasy: Epic*

Chris Bunch	Mike Jefferies	George R R Martin
Allan Cole	Paul Kearney	Roger Taylor

Anne Tyler 1941- US   *General*

Gail Anderson-Dargatz	Catherine Dunne	Pulitzer 1989 ❀
Suzanne Berne	Patricia Gaffney	
Candida Crewe	Elinor Lipman	
Agnes Desarthe	Mona Simpson	
Andre Dubus	Marly Swick	
Suzannah Dunn	Rebecca Wells	

Barry Unsworth 1930-   *Historical*

John Banville	Robert Nye	Booker 1992 ❀
William Bedford	Charles Palliser	
Bruce Chatwin	Amanda Prantera	
Jim Crace	Julian Rathbone	
Fred D'Aguiar	Rose Tremain	
Andrew Miller		

T
U

Caroline Upcher   *Glitz & Glamour*
also writes as Carly McIntyre

Sally Beauman	Judith Gould	Penny Vincenzi
Alexandra Campbell	June Flaum Singer	Fiona Walker
Jilly Cooper		

John Updike *1932- US* *General*

Saul Bellow	John Irving	
Ethan Canin	Norman Mailer	
Justin Cartwright	Rick Moody	
Don DeLillo	Vladimir Nabokov	
E L Doctorow	Paul Theroux	
Jonathan Franzen	Evelyn Waugh	

Pulitzer	*1982* ❀
Pulitzer	*1991* ❀

Leon Uris *1924- US* *General*

Howard Fast	Edward Rutherfurd	John Steinbeck
James A Michener	Isaac Bashevis Singer	Morris West

Jane Urquhart *1949- Can* *General*

Thomas Eidson	Peter Hoeg	Carol Shields
Barbara Esstman	Anne Michaels	Amy Tan
David Guterson	Ann Patchett	

Andrew Vachss *1942- US* *Crime: Modern*
www.vachss.com *⚐ Burke - New York*

James Crumley	Sam Reaves	Irvine Welsh
Dashiell Hammett	Jim Thompson	Charles Willeford
Joe R Lansdale		

Janwillem van de Wetering *1931- Neth* *Crime: Police work - foreign*
⚐ Adjutant Grijpstra & Sgt de Gier - Amsterdam, Netherlands

Nicolas Freeling	H R F Keating	Daniel Pennac
Juliet Hebden	Henning Mankell	Georges Simenon
Mark Hebden		

U
V

Jack Vance *1916- US* *Science Fiction: Space opera*

John Brunner	Frank Herbert	Vernor Vinge
L Sprague de Camp	Fritz Leiber	Gene Wolfe
Brian Herbert	Michael Moorcock	Roger Zelazny

Mario Vargas Llosa   1936-   Peru   General

Isabel Allende   Gabriel Garcia Márquez   Nicholas Shakespeare
Louis de Bernières   Kazuo Ishiguro

Jules Verne   1828-1905   Fr   Science Fiction

Robert A Heinlein   Kurt Vonnegut
C S Lewis   H G Wells

Salley Vickers   General
www.salleyvickers.com

Anita Brookner   Jane Gardam   Katharine McMahon
Stevie Davies   Joanne Harris   Barbara Pym
Catherine Feeny   Elizabeth Knox   Jill Paton Walsh
Penelope Fitzgerald

Gore Vidal   1925-   US   General
also writes as Edgar Box

Truman Capote   Norman Mailer   Mary Renault
Margaret George   James A Michener   Tom Wolfe
Robert Graves

Elizabeth Villars   1941-   US   Saga
is Ellen Feldman

Elizabeth Adler   Olivia Goldsmith   Janet Tanner
Janet Dailey   Lavyrle Spencer   Nicola Thorne

Penny Vincenzi   1939-   Glitz & Glamour V
www.penny-vincenzi.com

Elizabeth Adler   Shirley Conran   Frankie McGowan
Pat Booth   Olivia Goldsmith   Jill Mansell
Barbara Taylor Bradford   Roberta Latow   Caroline Upcher
Sandra Brown

Don't forget lists of: *Genres * Characters * Literary prizes * Further reading* ☞

Barbara Vine 1930-   Crime: Psychological
also writes as Ruth Rendell

Lisa Appignanesi	Frances Hegarty	CWA 1987 ✿
Martyn Bedford	Elizabeth McGregor	CWA 1991 ✿
Jeremy Dronfield	Susan Moody	
Kerstin Ekman	Margaret Murphy	
Penelope Evans	Julie Parsons	
Frances Galleymore	Tony Strong	

Vernor Vinge 1944- US   Science Fiction: Space and time

Brian W Aldiss	William Gibson	Larry Niven
Stephen Baxter	Ursula K Le Guin	Dan Simmons
C J Cherryh	Wil McCarthy	Jack Vance
Arthur C Clarke	Linda Nagata	Connie Willis

Anne Vivis Sco   Saga
Strathannan Series - Scotland

Doris Davidson	Alexandra Raife	Reay Tannahill
Christine Marion Fraser	Eileen Ramsay	Dee Williams
Nora Kay	Agnes Short	Mary Withall
Frances Paige	Linda Sole	

Kurt Vonnegut 1922- US   Science Fiction: Space and time

Brian W Aldiss	William Gibson	Jules Verne
J G Ballard	Jeff Noon	Jack Womack
Philip K Dick	John Sladek	Roger Zelazny
Thomas M Disch		

V
W Elizabeth Waite   Saga
London

Philip Boast	Pamela Evans	Elizabeth Lord
Harry Bowling	Patricia Grey	Elizabeth Warne
Helen Carey	Anna King	Audrey Willsher
Harry Cole	Peter Ling	

Don't forget lists of: *Genres * Characters * Literary prizes * Further reading* ☞

Martyn Waites

Crime: Modern
⚘ Stephen Larkin, journalist

John Baker	Paul Charles	Chris Paling
Adam Baron	Frank Lean	Ian Rankin
Ken Bruen	David Ralph Martin	Nicholas Royle

Alice Walker   1944-   US

General

Emma Donoghue	Toni Morrison	Pulitzer 1983 ⚘
Harper Lee	Gloria Naylor	
Terry McMillan	William Styron	

Elizabeth Walker

Saga
Yorkshire

Charlotte Vale Allen	Barbara Taylor Bradford	Sara Hylton
Aileen Armitage	Helen Cannam	Audrey Reimann
Jessica Blair	Joan Eadith	Kay Stephens

Fiona Walker   1969-

Chick Lit

Jessica Adams	Victoria Colby	Alexandra Potter
Catherine Alliott	Lucinda Edmonds	Victoria Routledge
Louise Bagshawe	Christina Jones	Patricia Scanlan
Susie Boyt	Freya North	Caroline Upcher

Robert W Walker   1948-   US

Crime

also writes as Geoffrey Caine,   ⚘ Dr Jessica Coran, Coroner - Texas, Houston
Glen Hale & Stephen Robertson

Patricia D Cornwell	Sarah Lovett	James Patterson
Lynn S Hightower	Margaret Maron	Claire Rayner

Robert James Waller   1939-   US

General

Nicholas Evans	Anita Shreve	Nicholas Sparks
Janice Graham	Jane Smiley	Larry Watson

W

Mark Wallington 1953- *Humour*

Stephen Fry	David Nobbs	Sue Townsend
John Lanchester	Alan Titchmarsh	Nigel Williams

Jill Paton Walsh 1937- *General*

Peter Ackroyd	Geraldine McCaughrean	Salley Vickers
Umberto Eco	Candia McWilliam	Marina Warner
Jane Gardam		

Minette Walters 1949- *Crime: Psychological*

Suzanne Berne	Margaret Murphy	CWA	1992 ❀
Kerstin Ekman	Julie Parsons	CWA	1994 ❀
Penelope Evans	Carol Smith		
Joanna Hines	Tony Strong		
Sarah Lovett	Alison Taylor		
J Wallis Martin	Aline Templeton		

Joseph Wambaugh 1937- US *Crime: Modern California*

William Diehl	Ed McBain	Mario Puzo
James Ellroy	Jefferson Parker	Stuart Woods
W E B Griffin		

Elizabeth Warne 1926- *Saga Bristol*

Brenda Clarke	Connie Monk	Janet Tanner
Lilian Harry	Eileen Stafford	Elizabeth Waite
Elizabeth Ann Hill		

Alan Warner 1964- Sco *General*

W

Iain Banks	Duncan McLean	S Maugham	1996 ❀
Guy Burt	Marc Pye	Encore	1998 ❀
Michel Faber	Paul Sayer		
Gordon Legge	Irvine Welsh		
Carl MacDougall			

Marina Warner 1946- General

Angela Carter
Lesley Glaister
Candia McWilliam

Amanda Prantera
Jane Rogers
Carol Shields

Graham Swift
Jill Paton Walsh

Tony Warren General

Dirk Bogarde
Michael Carson

Roy Hattersley
Stanley Middleton

Alan Sillitoe
Margaret Thornton

Freda Warrington 1956- Fantasy: Dark

Tom Arden
James Barclay
Alice Borchardt
Storm Constantine

Ellen Datlow
Kate Jacoby
J V Jones
Paul Kearney

Tanith Lee
Juliet E McKenna
K J Parker
Robert Silverberg

Keith Waterhouse 1929- Humour

Kingsley Amis
H E Bates
Malcolm Bradbury
Ben Elton

Sue Limb
David Lodge
Magnus Mills
John Mortimer

Leslie Thomas
Peter Tinniswood
Alan Titchmarsh
Sue Townsend

Sarah Waters 1966- Wales General

Jane Brindle
Tracy Chevalier
Stevie Davies
Philippa Gregory

Anne Haverty
Sheri Holman
Jane Stevenson
Jeanette Winterson

Sunday Times	2000 ❀
S Maugham	2000 ❀

Paul Watkins 1964- Wales General

Sebastian Faulks
Ernest Hemingway
Douglas Kennedy

Michael Ondaatje
Erich Maria Remarque
Derek Robinson

Encore	1990 ❀
Holtby	1995 ❀

W

Don't forget lists of: *Genres* * *Characters* * *Literary prizes* * *Further reading* ☞

Ian Watson 1943-   *Science Fiction*

J G Ballard
Iain M Banks
Stephen Baxter
Gregory Benford
John Brunner
Gwyneth Jones

Paul J McAuley
Larry Niven
Bob Shaw
Brian Stableford
Robert Charles Wilson

BSFA   *1977* ❀

Larry Watson 1947- US   *General*

Pete Dexter
Thomas Eidson
Louise Erdrich
Charles Frazier

Jim Harrison
Harper Lee
Cormac McCarthy

Peter Matthiessen
Stewart O'Nan
Robert James Waller

Sophia Watson 1962-   *Aga Saga*

Judy Astley
Amanda Brookfield

Elizabeth Pewsey
Rosie Thomas

Joanna Trollope

Daisy Waugh   *Chick Lit*

Victoria Corby
Helen Fielding
Wendy Holden

Lisa Jewell
India Knight
Claire Naylor

Freya North
Adele Parks

Evelyn Waugh 1903-66   *General*

E F Benson
Justin Cartwright
Joseph Connolly
Matthew Kneale

David Lodge
Olivia Manning
Pauline Melville
Paul Micou

Anthony Powell
William Sutcliffe
John Updike
Angus Wilson

Harriet Waugh   *General*

W

Lucy Ellman
Anne Fine

Esther Freud
Hilary Mantel

Pauline Melville

Don't forget lists of: *Genres* * *Characters* * *Literary prizes* * *Further reading* ☞

Hillary Waugh   1920-   US
also writes as H Baldwin Taylor & Harry Walker

Crime: Police work - US
⚐ Chief of Police Fred Fellows
Det Fred Sessions

K C Constantine
Paula Gosling

Donald Harstad
Reginald Hill

Walter Mosley

Teresa Waugh   1940-   General

Beryl Bainbridge
Jane Gardam

Linda Grant
Susan Hill

Alison Lurie

Arabella Weir   Chick Lit

Sherry Ashworth
Mavis Cheek
Helen Fielding

Laurie Graham
Sue Limb

Chris Manby
Lynne Truss

Margaret Weis   1948-   US   Fantasy: Epic

Terry Brooks
Steven Brust
David A Drake
Mercedes Lackey

Anne McCaffrey
L E Modesitt Jr
Elizabeth Moon
Melanie Rawn

Mickey Zucker Reichert
R A Salvatore
Jan Siegel

Jane Welch   1964-   Fantasy: Epic
www.janewelch.com

David Farland
David Gemmell
Terry Goodkind
Julia Gray

Simon R Green
Robin Hobb
Kate Jacoby
Guy Gavriel Kay

Stephen R Lawhead
Adam Nichols
K J Parker
Philip G Williamson

Fay Weldon   1933-   General

Beryl Bainbridge
Elizabeth Buchan
Angela Carter
Carol Clewlow

Janet Frame
Sara Maitland
Bel Mooney
Andrea Newman

Edna O'Brien
Wendy Perriam
Emma Tennant
Jeanette Winterson

W

Sue Welfare

Humour
East Anglia

Geraldine Bedell
Faith Bleasdale

Sarah Grazebrook
Wendy Holden

Carole Matthews
Isabel Wolff

H G Wells   1866-1946

Science Fiction: Space and time

Stephen Baxter
E M Forster

Greg Keyes
Tim Powers

Jules Verne
John Wyndham

Rebecca Wells   1963-   US
www.ya-ya.com

General
Louisiana

Kate Atkinson
Justin Cartwright
Louise Erdrich

Margaret Forster
Elinor Lipman
Anne Rivers Siddons

Marly Swick
Anne Tyler

Irvine Welsh   1958-   Sco
www.irvinewelsh.com

General

Des Dillon
Roddy Doyle
Sean Hughes

James Kelman
Marc Pye
Kevin Sampson

Will Self
Andrew Vachss
Alan Warner

Patricia Wendorf

Historical
The Patteran Trilogy

Kate Alexander
Diana Gabaldon

Cynthia Harrod-Eagles
Harriet Hudson

Caroline Stickland
T R Wilson

Patricia Wentworth   1878-1961
was Dora Amy Elles

Crime
🏃 Miss Maud Silver

Margery Allingham
Agatha Christie
Elizabeth Ferrars
Georgette Heyer

Michael Innes
Ngaio Marsh
Jennie Melville

Gladys Mitchell
Gwen Moffat
Dorothy L Sayers

W

Mary Wesley   1912-   *Aga Saga*

Clare Chambers	Fanny Frewen	Karen Nelson
Victoria Clayton	Janice Galloway	Kate Saunders
Elizabeth Falconer	Kate Hatfield	Diana Saville
Katie Fforde	Nora Naish	Peta Tayler

Valerie Wilson Wesley   1947-   US   *Crime: PI*
www.tamarahayle.com   ⚐ *Tamara Hayle - Newark, New Jersey*

Charlotte Carter	Sparkle Hayter	Terry McMillan
Janet Evanovich	Laura Lippman	Alexander McCall Smith

Christopher West   1954-   *Crime: Police work - foreign*
                                       ⚐ *Insp Wang Anzhuang - PR China*

Tony Hillerman	Donna Leon	Barbara Nadel
Roderic Jeffries	Peter May	Laura Joh Rowland
H R F Keating	Manuel Vázquez Montalbán	Peter Tasker

Morris West   1916-99   Aus   *General*

Colin Andrews	David Malouf	Brian Moore
Graham Greene	John Masters	Nevil Shute
Arthur Hailey	W Somerset Maugham	Leon Uris

Nigel West   1951-   *Adventure/Thriller*
is Rupert Allason

Len Deighton	Tim Sebastian
Philip Kerr	Gerald Seymour

Donald E Westlake   1933-   US   *Crime: Humour*
also writes as Tucker Coe & Richard Stark   ⚐ *John Dortmunder, Burglar*
www.donaldwestlake.com

Lawrence Block	Carl Hiaasen	Robert B Parker
Rita Mae Brown	Elmore Leonard	Charles Spencer
Tim Dorsey	John D MacDonald	

W

Edith Wharton   1862-1937   US   General

Jane Austen	Thomas Hardy	Alison Lurie
Penelope Fitzgerald	Henry James	Joyce Carol Oates
E M Forster		

Edmund White   1940-   US   General

Michael Carson	Alan Hollinghurst
Patrick Gale	Adam Mars-Jones

Gillian White   General
also writes as Georgina Fleming

Helen Dunmore	Richard Greensted	Kate Pullinger
Lesley Glaister	Deborah Moggach	Graham Swift

Gillian White   Adventure/Thriller: Psychological
also writes as Georgina Fleming

Harlan Coben	Bernard Taylor
Joanna Hines	Melanie Tem

Kirsty White   Saga
Scotland

Christine Marion Fraser	Elisabeth McNeill	Frances Paige
Gwen Kirkwood	Isobel Neill	Jessica Stirling

Patrick White   1912-90   Aus   General

Peter Carey	Rodney Hall	V S Naipaul
Robert Drewe	Henry James	Christina Stead
William Golding	Thomas Keneally	Tim Winton
Nadine Gordimer	David Malouf	

W

T H White   1906-64   Fantasy: Myth

Ursula K Le Guin	C S Lewis	J R R Tolkien

Barbara Whitehead   1930-   Crime: Police work - Br

⚐ DCI Bob Southwell - York

John Baker	D M Greenwood	Dorothy Simpson
Pauline Bell	Patricia Hall	Cath Staincliffe
Clare Curzon	Emma Page	June Thomson
Elizabeth Ferrars	Stewart Pawson	Peter Turnbull

Stella Whitelaw   Crime: PI

⚐ Jordan Lacey - Sussex

Simon Brett	Lauren Henderson	Cath Staincliffe
Judith Cutler	Joyce Holms	Scarlett Thomas
Liz Evans	David Roberts	Rebecca Tope

Charles Whiting   1926-   War: Modern
also writes as Duncan Harding & Leo Kessler

Brian Callison	Geoffrey Jenkins	Douglas Reeman
John Harris	Joseph Kanon	John Winton
Robert Jackson		

Jeanne Whitmee   Saga
London

Patricia Burns	Elizabeth Lord	Gilda O'Neill
Pamela Evans	Jenny Oldfield	Pamela Pope
Patricia Grey	Pamela Oldfield	

Barbara Whitnell   Saga
Cornwall

Rosemary Aitken	Cynthia S Roberts	E V Thompson
Iris Gower	Malcolm Ross	Nicola Thorne
Claire Lorrimer	Sarah Shears	Barbara Wood
Pamela Pope		

W

Phyllis A Whitney   1903-   US   Saga

Elizabeth Peters	Lindsay Townsend
Madge Swindells	Daoma Winston

Madeleine Wickham　　　　　　　　　　　　　　　　　*Aga Saga*

Judy Astley
Anne Atkins
Amanda Brookfield

Kate Fenton
Hazel Hucker
Jean Saunders

Peta Tayler
Willow Tickell
Marcia Willett

Marianne Wiggins　　*1947-　US*　　　　　　　　　*General*

William Golding
Michael Ondaatje

Salman Rushdie
Carol Shields

Charles Willeford　　*1919-88　US*　　**Crime:** *Police work - US*
♀ Sgt Hoke Moseley - Miami

Erle Stanley Gardner
George V Higgins
Jon A Jackson

Russell James
John D MacDonald
Walter Mosley

Reggie Nadelson
Jim Thompson
Andrew Vachss

Marcia Willett　　　　　　　　　　　　　　　　　　　　*Saga*
also writes as Willa Marsh　　　　　　　　　*♀ Chadwick Family*

Judy Astley
Marika Cobbold
Julia Lisle

Maggie Makepeace
Karen Nelson
Libby Purves

Mary Selby
Madeleine Wickham

Barnaby Williams　　　　　　　　　　　*Adventure/Thriller*

Len Deighton
Robert Harris

Robert Littell
Gerald Seymour

David Williams　　*1926-　Wales*　　**Crime:** *Police work - Br*
♀ Cl Merlin Parry & Sgt Gomer Lloyd - Police Br - Wales • Mark Treasure, Banking

Ann Cleeves
Jonathan Gash
Alan Hunter

Bill James
Janet Laurence
Roy Lewis

Charlotte MacLeod
Andrew Taylor

W

Dee Williams
Saga
East End, London

Jay Allerton
Patricia Burns
Helen Carey
Harry Cole

Pamela Evans
Peter Ling
Brenda McBryde
Connie Monk

Gilda O'Neill
Mary Jane Staples
Alison Stuart
Anne Vivis

Niall Williams   1958-   Ire
General

Dermot Bolger
Gabriel Garcia Márquez
Jennifer Johnston

Bernard MacLaverty
Edna O'Brien

Joseph O'Connor
Colm Toibin

Nigel Williams   1948-
Humour

David Baddiel
Terence Blacker
Jonathan Coe
Colin Douglas

Stephen Fry
John Lanchester
Helen Muir
Geoff Nicholson

David Nobbs
Sue Townsend
Mark Wallington

Tad Williams   1957-   US
Fantasy: Epic
www.tadwilliams.com/

Terry Brooks
Jonathan Carroll
David A Drake

David Eddings
Robin Hobb
Greg Keyes

Adam Nichols
Michael Scott Rohan
J R R Tolkien

Tad Williams   1957-   US
Science Fiction: Near future
www.tadwilliams.com

Steve Aylett
Alexander Besher

Eric Brown
Jon Courtenay Grimwood

Bruce Sterling

Henry Williamson   1895-1977
General

Richard Adams
William Horwood

Anthony Powell
Erich Maria Remarque

Joyce Stranger
Adam Thorpe

W

Philip G Williamson   1955-   Fantasy: Epic
also writes as Philip First & Joe Fish
www.ndirect.co.uk/~gormley/PGW

Terry Brooks	Robin Hobb	Jane Welch
David Farland	J V Jones	Janny Wurts

Connie Willis   1945-   US   Science Fiction: Space and time

Octavia E Butler	Diana Norman	Vernor Vinge
Orson Scott Card	Tim Powers	Robert Charles Wilson
William Gibson	Jan Siegel	

Tim Willocks   1957-   Adventure/Thriller

Philip Caveney	Andrew Klavan	David Lindsey
Thomas Harris	Dean R Koontz	

Audrey Willsher   Saga
London ▪ Leicestershire

Harriet Hudson	Lynda Page	Elizabeth Waite
Meg Hutchinson	Mary Jane Staples	Sally Worboyes
Gilda O'Neill	Alison Stuart	

A N Wilson   1950-   General

Kingsley Amis	Anthony Powell	*Mail* 1978 ❀
Julian Barnes	Barbara Pym	
Malcolm Bradbury	Bernice Rubens	
Iris Murdoch		

Angus Wilson   1913-91   General

Anthony Burgess	J B Priestley	Evelyn Waugh
A S Byatt	Piers Paul Read	

W

Derek Wilson   1935-   Crime
🏃 *Tim Lacy, Art world - modern ▪ George Keene - C18th France & America*

William Ardin	Roy Lewis	Hannah March
Kate Charles	John Malcolm	Iain Pears
Margaret Lawrence		

Laura Wilson
www.unusualsuspects.co.uk

Crime: Psychological

Frances Fyfield
Margaret Murphy
Gemma O'Connor

Ruth Rendell
Carol Smith

Veronica Stallwood
Andrew Taylor

Robert Wilson   1957-

Adventure/Thriller

🕺 Bruce Medway - Portugal

James Adams
Francis Bennett
Alan Furst
Philip Kerr

John Le Carré
J Wallis Martin
Henry Porter

CWA   1999 ❀

Robert Charles Wilson   1953-   Can

Science Fiction:
Space and time

David Brin
Wil McCarthy
Linda Nagata

Bob Shaw
Clifford D Simak

Ian Watson
Connie Willis

T R Wilson   1962-
also writes as Tim Wilson

Saga
East Anglia

Tessa Barclay
Margaret Dickinson
Jonathan Grant
Malcolm Macdonald

Mary Mackie
M R O'Donnell
Pamela Pope

Caroline Stickland
Graham Swift
Patricia Wendorf

Tim Wilson   1962-
also writes as T R Wilson

Horror

Mark Burnell
Peter James

Stephen Laws
Mark Morris

Phil Rickman

R D Wingfield

Crime: Police work - Br

🕺 DI Jack Frost - 'Denton'

W

Ken Bruen
Deborah Crombie
Jeff Gulvin
M R D Meek

Emma Page
Peter Robinson
Alan Scholefield

Stella Shepherd
Sally Spencer
Andrew Taylor

David Wingrove 1954- Science Fiction: Space and time

Greg Egan
William Gibson
Jon Courtenay Grimwood

Barry Hughart
Gwyneth Jones
Paul J McAuley

Wil McCarthy
Bruce Sterling

Mary Wings 1949- US Crime: PI
⚐ Emma Victor - San Francisco

Ace Atkins
Linda Barnes
Stephen Donaldson

Stella Duffy
Ellen Hart
Marcia Muller

Sandra Scoppettone
Manda Scott
Michelle Spring

Don Winslow 1953- US Crime
⚐ Neal Carey - Nevada

Robert Crais
Joseph Hansen

Carl Hiaasen
Elmore Leonard

Steve Womack

Daoma Winston 1922- US General

Virginia Andrews
Carol Clewlow
Janet Dailey

Victoria Holt
Barbara Michaels

Madge Swindells
Phyllis A Whitney

Jeanette Winterson 1959- General
www.jeanettewinterson.com

Angela Carter
Carol Clewlow
Emma Donoghue
Laura Esquivel
Michele Roberts

Bernice Rubens
Colin Thubron
Sarah Waters
Fay Weldon
Virginia Woolf

Whitbread   1985 ❀
Mail   1987 ❀

John Winton 1931-2001 Sea: Modern

W

Max Hennessy
Philip McCutchan

Douglas Reeman
Charles Whiting

Tim Winton   1960-   Aus   General

Peter Carey   Brian Moore
Rodney Hall   Patrick White

David Wishart   1952-   Sco   Crime: Historical
𝕏 Marcus Corvinus - Ancient Rome

Lindsey Davis   Rosemary Rowe   Marilyn Todd
Allan Massie   Steven Saylor

Mary Withall   Sco   Saga
Eisdalsa Island Trilogy - Scotland

Christine Marion Fraser   Gwen Kirkwood   Jessica Stirling
Evelyn Hood   Eileen Ramsay   Anne Vivis
Nora Kay

P G Wodehouse   1881-1975   Humour

E F Benson   Tom Holt   Peter Tinniswood
Stephen Fry   John Mortimer

Gene Wolfe   1931-   US   Fantasy: Literary

John Crowley   Tim Powers   BSFA   1981 ✳
Robert Holdstock   Adam Roberts
Barry Hughart   Jack Vance
Ursula K Le Guin   Roger Zelazny
Julian May

Tom Wolfe   1931-   US   General
www.tomwolfe.com

Stephen Amidon   Dominick Dunne   Norman Mailer
Truman Capote   Bret Easton Ellis   Paul Micou
Caleb Carr   Colin Harrison   Thomas Pynchon   **W**
Charles Dickens   Jay McInerney   Gore Vidal

Don't forget lists of: *Genres* * *Characters* * *Literary prizes* * *Further reading* ☞

Isabel Wolff
Humour

Raffaella Barker
Geraldine Bedell
Faith Bleasdale
Claire Calman

Wendy Holden
Amy Jenkins
India Knight

Josie Lloyd & Emlyn Rees
Sue Margolis
Sue Welfare

Jack Womack   *1956-   US*
Science Fiction: Near future

J G Ballard
John Brunner

Pat Cadigan
Paul J McAuley

Bruce Sterling
Kurt Vonnegut

Steve Womack   *1952-   US*
Crime: PI
www.womackbooks.com
↟ Harry James Denton - Nashville

Robert Crais
Loren D Estleman

Joe R Lansdale
Reggie Nadelson

Don Winslow

Barbara Wood
Historical
www.barbarawood.com

Janet Dailey
Iris Gower

Joanne Harris
E V Thompson

Nicola Thorne
Barbara Whitnell

Valerie Wood
Saga

Catherine Cookson
Inga Dunbar

Evelyn Hood
Audrey Howard

Wendy Robertson
Kay Stephens

Sarah Woodhouse   *1950-*
Historical

Kate Alexander
Elizabeth Buchan
Pamela Oldfield

Elizabeth Palmer
Cynthia S Roberts

Parker   1989 ❀

W Richard Woodman   *1944-*
Sea: Historical
↟ Nathaniel Drinkwater - C18th/19th England

Brian Callison
Tom Connery
David Donachie
Alexander Fullerton

Jonathan Lunn
Philip McCutchan
Jan Needle
Dudley Pope

Julian Stockwin
Showell Styles
Victor Suthren

Stuart Woods   1938-   US   Crime: Modern
www.stuartwoods.com/
🏃 Stone Barrington, PI - New York
Chief Holly Barker, Police - Florida

Ace Atkins	John Gilstrap	Andrew Klavan
Peter Blauner	Stuart Harrison	David Lindsey
Martina Cole	Patricia Highsmith	Jefferson Parker
Jeffery Deaver	Douglas Kennedy	Joseph Wambaugh

Virginia Woolf   1882-1941   General
www.utoronto.ca/IVWS

Joseph Conrad	Iris Murdoch	Patrick Süskind
E M Forster	Michele Roberts	Jeanette Winterson
James Joyce		

Sally Worboyes   Saga
London ▪ Kent

Patricia Burns	Lena Kennedy	Gilda O'Neill
Harry Cole	Anna King	Victor Pemberton
Elizabeth Daish	Jenny Oldfield	Audrey Willsher
Harriet Hudson		

Anne Worboys   1920-   Saga
also writes as Annette Eyre & Vicky Maxwell

Virginia Andrews	Elizabeth Peters
Mary E Pearce	Mary Stewart

Eric Wright   1929-   Can   Crime: Police work - foreign
🏃 Sgt Charlie Salter - Toronto, Canada ▪ Lucy Trimble Brenner

Jon Cleary	Frank Palmer	CWA 1983 ❀
Donald Harstad	Ridley Pearson	

W

Don't forget lists of: *Genres* ∗ *Characters* ∗ *Literary prizes* ∗ *Further reading* ☞

Glover Wright — *Adventure/Thriller*

James Follett   Duncan Kyle
Jack Higgins   Kenneth Royce

T M Wright — *US* — *Horror*

Ramsey Campbell   Richard Laymon   Robert McCammon
Stephen Gallagher   Brian Lumley   Peter Straub
Stephen King

Janny Wurts — *1953- US* — *Fantasy: Epic*
www.paravia.com/JannyWurts/

Steven Brust   Louise Cooper   L E Modesitt Jr
Chris Bunch   Sara Douglass   Elizabeth Moon
Jonathan Carroll   Raymond E Feist   Mickey Zucker Reichert
Allan Cole   Mike Jefferies   Philip G Williamson

Jonathan Wylie — *1953-* — *Fantasy: Epic*
is Mark & Julia Smith   *Island and Empire Trilogy*

Jonathan Carroll   Paul Kearney   Michael Scott Rohan
Ellen Datlow   L E Modesitt Jr

John Wyndham — *1903-69* — *Science Fiction*

Brian W Aldiss   Robert A Heinlein   H G Wells
John Brunner   Clifford D Simak   Roger Zelazny

Grace Wynne-Jones — *Ire* — *General*

Sarah Harrison   Susan Oudot
Marian Keyes   Judith Summers

W

Margaret Yorke 1924-

Crime: Psychological
↟ Patrick Grant

Jane Adams
Brian Battison
Louise Doughty
Elizabeth Ferrars
Gerald Hammond

Jessica Mann
Julie Parsons
Danuta Reah
Carol Smith
Alison Taylor

CWA   1999 ✿

Louisa Young

General
www.louisayoung.demon.co.uk   ↟ Evangeline Gower, ex Belly dancer

James Hawes
Hanif Kureishi

Zadie Smith
Meera Syal

Roger Zelazny 1937-95 US

Fantasy: Epic

Poul Anderson
A A Attanasio
Ray Bradbury
Steven Brust

Larry Niven
Robert Silverberg
Jack Vance

Kurt Vonnegut
Gene Wolfe
John Wyndham

David Zindell 1952-

Science Fiction: Space and time

Tom Arden
Iain M Banks

David Brin
Orson Scott Card

Mark Chadbourn
Brian Stableford

Y
Z

Authors listed by genre

It is almost impossible to identify accurately individual authors with one particular section of genre fiction; often there is no 'cut off' point between, for instance, *War* and *Adventure*; between *Fantasy, Science Fiction* and *Horror*; or between *Historical* and *Saga*. So, although in the main sequence this Guide indicates under the names of each author the genre in which they usually write, and these names are repeated again in the lists that follow, it is suggested that readers also refer to linking genres - and in particular to the main list - to discover new names that could become firm favourites.

Some categories - *Crime, Fantasy, Science Fiction, Sea Stories* and *War* - have been sub-divided to help readers find novelists they will enjoy. Do remember that some authors use a different name when they write in another genre, and others will produce an occasional book which is quite different in character to their usual style. Always look at the book jacket and the introduction before you borrow or purchase.

Stories with fast moving plots, exotic settings and usually larger-than-life main characters and with the action full of thrilling and daring feats. Many of these authors specialised in stories set in the period of the cold war but increasingly now they have a political, financial, industrial espionage or terrorist background.

Paul Adam	Kit Craig	Stuart Harrison
James Adams	Conor Cregan	Jack Harvey
Ted Allbeury	Clive Cussler	Humphrey Hawksley
Eric Ambler	Lionel Davidson	Richard Herman
Colin Andrews	Linda Davies	Jack Higgins
Evelyn Anthony	Murray Davies	Joanna Hines
Lisa Appignanesi	John Gordon Davis	Philip Hook
Geoffrey Archer	Victor Davis	Gwen Hunter
Campbell Armstrong	Nelson DeMille	Stephen Hunter
Desmond Bagley	Len Deighton	Graham Hurley
Keith Baker	Peter Driscoll	David Ignatius
David Baldacci	Jeremy Dronfield	Greg Iles
Francis Bennett	June Drummond	Hammond Innes
Suzanne Berne	Brendan Dubois	Donald James
Tim Binding	Daniel Easterman	Geoffrey Jenkins
Harry Bingham	Clive Egleton	Alan Judd
Alice Blanchard	Gavin Esler	Joseph Kanon
Peter Blauner	Colin Falconer	Judith Kelman
Larry Bond	Joseph Finder	Douglas Kennedy
Martin Booth	Ian Fleming	Philip Kerr
Tom Bradby	James Follett	Michael Kimball
David Brierley	Ken Follett	Andrew Klavan
Dale Brown	Bryan Forbes	Duncan Kyle
James Buchan	Colin Forbes	Derek Lambert
John Buchan	Frederick Forsyth	John Lawton
John Burdett	Clare Francis	John Le Carré
Guy Burt	Brian Freemantle	Stephen Leather
Bethany Campbell	Nicci French	David Lindsey
Stephen J Cannell	Alexander Fullerton	Robert Littell
Lorenzo Carcaterra	Alan Furst	Sam Llewellyn
Lee Child	Frances Galleymore	Robert Ludlum
Windsor Chorlton	John Gardner	Eric Lustbader
Tom Clancy	Lisa Gardner	Gavin Lyall
Mary Higgins Clark	John Gilstrap	Patrick Lynch
James Clavell	Robert Goddard	Amin Maalouf
Jon Cleary	Richard Greensted	Alistair MacLean
Nicholas Coleridge	Arthur Hailey	J Wallis Martin
Richard Condon	Palma Harcourt	David Mason
Robin Cook	John Harris	John R Maxim
Stephen Coonts	Robert Harris	Jenny Maxwell
Bryce Courtenay	Thomas Harris	J K Mayo
Harold Coyle	Colin Harrison	Glenn Meade

Adventure/Thriller

Brad Meltzer
David Morrell
John Nichol
Christopher Nicole
Hilary Norman
Marc Olden
Chris Paling
Michael Palmer
Julie Parsons
Henry Porter
Anthony Price
A J Quinnell
Julian Rathbone
Matthew Reilly
Michael Ridpath

Kenneth Royce
Chris Ryan
Lawrence Sanders
Julian Jay Savarin
Tim Sebastian
Gerald Seymour
Sidney Sheldon
Nevil Shute
Daniel Silva
Dov Silverman
Paullina Simons
William Smethurst
Murray Smith
Scott Smith
Wilbur Smith

Gordon Stevens
Grant Stewart
Melanie Tem
Douglas Terman
James Thayer
Craig Thomas
Gordon Thomas
John Trenhaile
Nigel West
Gillian White
Barnaby Williams
Tim Willocks
Robert Wilson
Glover Wright

Aga Saga

A phrase that came into being in the early 1990s, the Aga Sagas are novels based upon the middle-class surroundings of the type of person that typically owns Aga cookers but who is not immune to the emotional dilemmas that can confront all classes of society.

Diana Appleyard
Judy Astley
Anne Atkins
Anna Barrie
Caroline Bridgwood
Amanda Brookfield
Elizabeth Buchan
Lucy Clare
Victoria Clayton
Marika Cobbold
Nina Dufort

Elizabeth Falconer
Patricia Fawcett
Kate Fenton
Katie Fforde
Kate Fielding
Fanny Frewen
Julia Hamilton
Hazel Hucker
Charlotte Moore
Nora Naish
Elizabeth Palmer

Rosamunde Pilcher
Jean Saunders
Kate Saunders
Diana Saville
Henrietta Soames
Ann Swinfen
Joanna Trollope
Sophia Watson
Mary Wesley
Madeleine Wickham

Stories written by young women for other young women, usually with a central plot of boyfriend mishaps and the problems of staying in shape.

Jessica Adams	Jane Green	Sue Margolis
Catherine Alliott	Sarah Harris	Carole Matthews
Louise Bagshawe	Sarah Harvey	Anna Maxted
Zoë Barnes	Wendy Holden	Melissa Nathan
Geraldine Bedell	Amy Jenkins	Claire Naylor
Susie Boyt	Lisa Jewell	Freya North
Colette Caddle	Christina Jones	Tyne O'Connell
Claire Calman	Cathy Kelly	Sheila O'Flanagan
Rebecca Campbell	Marian Keyes	Adele Parks
Francesca Clementis	Sophie Kinsella	Alexandra Potter
Victoria Colby	Kathy Lette	Victoria Routledge
Jenny Colgan	Josie Lloyd & Emlyn Rees	Patricia Scanlan
Victoria Corby	L McCrossan	Stephanie Theobald
Claudine Cullimore	Serena Mackesy	Fiona Walker
Martina Devlin	Chris Manby	Daisy Waugh
Helen Fielding	Jill Mansell	Arabella Weir

Crime

Genres

This type of novel is usually characterised by the clues which gradually lead the reader to the final solution, often within an atmosphere of rising tension or danger. Although there are basically two types of detective, the private investigator *(PI)* and the official policeman, there are an increasing number of subgenres within these two broad headings. The style of crime writing has been divided, in the majority of cases, into separate headings, and under each is shown the list of authors who usually but not always write in that vein.

William Ardin
Jake Arnott
Ace Atkins
Nevada Barr
Martyn Bedford
Nicholas Blincoe
Lawrence Block
Matthew Branton
Christopher Brookmyre
Lizbie Brown
Edna Buchanan
Jan Burke
John Dickson Carr
Charlotte Carter
Kate Charles
James Hadley Chase
Tim Cockey
Liza Cody
Anthea Cohen
Natasha Cooper
Patricia D Cornwell
John Creasey
Edmund Crispin
Amanda Cross
Judith Cutler
Denise Danks
Jeffery Deaver
Eileen Dewhurst
Anabel Donald
Arthur Conan Doyle
Martin Edwards
Ron Ellis
Janet Evanovich
Elizabeth Ferrars
Robert Ferrigno
Dick Francis
John Francome
Kinky Friedman
Frances Fyfield

Jonathan Gash
Joseph Glass
Lesley Grant-Adamson
D M Greenwood
Gerald Hammond
Ellen Hart
Veronica Heley
Vicki Hendricks
Georgette Heyer
George V Higgins
Elizabeth Ironside
Jonnie Jacobs
Russell James
Iris Johansen
Morag Joss
Nora Kelly
Valerie Kershaw
Sarah Lacey
Joe R Lansdale
Emma Lathen
Janet Laurence
Martha Lawrence
Roy Lewis
Martin Limon
Sarah Lovett
Rory McCormac
Val McDermid
Marianne MacDonald
John Malcolm
Jessica Mann
Lindsay Maracotta
M R D Meek
Denise Mina
Gladys Mitchell
Gwen Moffat
Walter Mosley
Chris Niles
Kem Nunn
Roger Ormerod
Robert B Parker

Iain Pears
Mike Phillips
Richard Pitman
Richard Preston
Robert T Price
Donald Rawley
Claire Rayner
Kathy Reichs
Mike Ripley
David Roberts
Annette Roome
Betty Rowlands
Nicholas Royle
James Sallis
Dorothy L Sayers
Manda Scott
Stella Shepherd
John Sherwood
Joan Smith
John B Spencer
Veronica Stallwood
Les Standiford
Susan Sussman with
    Sarajane Avidon
Scarlett Thomas
Jim Thompson
Rebecca Tope
Kathy Hogan Trocheck
Robert W Walker
Patricia Wentworth
Derek Wilson
Don Winslow

Historical

Bruce Alexander
Stephanie Barron
Fiona Buckley
Caleb Carr
P F Chisholm
Alys Clare

Michael Clynes
Judith Cook
Lindsey Davis
Paul Doherty
Richard Grayson
Susanna Gregory
Paul Harding
Ray Harrison
Keith Heller
Michael Jecks
Alanna Knight
Bernard Knight
Deryn Lake
Margaret Lawrence
Gillian Linscott
Peter Lovesey
Hannah March
Edward Marston
Viviane Moore
Fidelis Morgan
Ian Morson
Amy Myers
Michael Pearce
Anne Perry
Elizabeth Peters
Ellis Peters
Candace Robb
Roberta Rogow
Kate Ross
Rosemary Rowe
Laura Joh Rowland
Norman Russell
Steven Saylor
Kate Sedley
Marilyn Todd
Peter Tonkin
Peter Tremayne
M J Trow
David Wishart

Humour

Marian Babson
Marc Blake
Anthony Bourdain
Lilian Jackson Braun
Simon Brett
Rita Mae Brown

John Burns
Tim Dorsey
Ruth Dudley Edwards
Bill Fitzhugh
Alma Fritchley
Peter Guttridge
Sparkle Hayter
Tim Heald
Carl Hiaasen
Douglas Lindsay
Nancy Livingston
Charlotte MacLeod
Pauline McLynn
Daniel Pennac
Laurence Shames
Simon Shaw
Charles Spencer
Donald E Westlake

Legal/financial

Catherine Arnold
Po Bronson
Jonathan Davies
Rankin Davis
Alan M Dershowitz
Dexter Dias
William Diehl
Paul Erdman
Linda Fairstein
Stephen Frey
Philip Friedman
Erle Stanley Gardner
John Grisham
Craig Holden
Paul Kilduff
John T Lescroart
John McLaren
Phillip M Margolin
Steve Martini
Richard North Patterson
Christopher Reich
Nancy Taylor Rosenberg
Lisa Scottoline
Sheldon Siegel
Robert K Tanenbaum
Scott Turow

Medical

Paul Carson
Tess Gerritsen
Ken McClure
Andrew Puckett
Leah Ruth Robinson

Modern

Mark Burnell
Jeremy Cameron
Philip Caveney
Martina Cole
Thomas H Cook
James Ellroy
Elmore Leonard
Jefferson Parker
Marc Pye
Jerry Raine
Boston Teran
Andrew Vachss
Martyn Waites
Joseph Wambaugh
Stuart Woods

Police work

Jane Adams *Br*
Catherine Aird *Br*
David Armstrong *Br*
Vivien Armstrong *Br*
Jeffrey Ashford *Br*
Jo Bannister *Br*
Robert Barnard *Br*
Brian Battison *Br*
M C Beaton *Br*
Pauline Bell *Br*
Janie Bolitho *Br*
Hilary Bonner *Br*
Stephen Booth *Br*
John Brady *foreign*
Ken Bruen *Br*
James Lee Burke *US*
W J Burley *Br*
Gwendoline Butler *Br*
Joanna Cannan *Br*
Paul Charles *Br*
Jon Cleary *foreign*
Ann Cleeves *Br*

Police work (cont)

Michael Connelly *US*
K C Constantine *US*
Brian Cooper *Br*
Deborah Crombie *Br*
Clare Curzon *Br*
Colin Dexter *Br*
Michael Dibdin *foreign*
Margaret Duffy *Br*
Marjorie Eccles *Br*
Kate Ellis *Br*
John Farrow *foreign*
Raymond Flynn *Br*
Malcolm Forsythe *Br*
Anthea Fraser *Br*
Nicolas Freeling *foreign*
Elizabeth George *Br*
B M Gill *Br*
Bartholomew Gill *foreign*
Paula Gosling *US*
Caroline Graham *Br*
Ann Granger *Br*
Christine Green *Br*
J M Gregson *Br*
W E B Griffin *US*
Martha Grimes *Br*
Jeff Gulvin *Br*
Patricia Hall *Br*
Hugo Hamilton *foreign*
Cynthia Harrod-Eagles *Br*
Donald Harstad *US*
John Harvey *Br*
Janet Harward *Br*
Juliet Hebden *foreign*
Mark Hebden *foreign*
Lynn S Hightower *US*
Reginald Hill *Br*
Tony Hillerman *US*
Alan Hunter *Br*
Graham Hurley *Br*
Michael Innes *Br*
Jon A Jackson *US*
Bill James *Br*
P D James *Br*
J A Jance *US*
J Robert Janes *foreign*

Quintin Jardine *Br*
Roderic Jeffries *foreign*
H R F Keating *foreign*
Faye Kellerman *US*
Jonathan Kellerman *US*
Susan Kelly *Br*
Laurie R King *US*
Bill Knox *Br*
Rochelle Krich *US*
Lynda La Plante *Br/US*
Donna Leon *foreign*
Frederic Lindsay *Br*
Jim Lusby *foreign*
Ed McBain *US*
Eugene McEldowney *Br*
Jill McGown *Br*
William Mcilvanney *Br*
Claire McNab *foreign*
Barry Maitland *Br*
Henning Mankell *foreign*
Margaret Maron *US*
Ngaio Marsh *Br*
David Ralph Martin *Br*
Priscilla Masters *Br*
Peter May *foreign*
Jennie Melville *Br*
Kay Mitchell *Br*
Magdalen Nabb *foreign*
Barbara Nadel *foreign*
Janet Neel *Br*
Maureen O'Brien *Br*
Carol O'Connell *US*
Nick Oldham *Br*
Emma Page *Br*
Frank Palmer *Br*
Stewart Pawson *Br*
David Peace *Br*
Ridley Pearson *US*
John Penn *Br*
Ann Quinton *Br*
Ian Rankin *Br*
Ruth Rendell *Br*
Nicholas Rhea *Br*
Peter Robinson *Br*
John Sandford *US*
Alan Scholefield *Br*

Georges Simenon *foreign*
Dorothy Simpson *Br*
Martin Cruz Smith *foreign*
Sally Spencer *Br*
Staynes & Storey *Br*
Julian Symons *Br*
Alison Taylor *Br*
Andrew Taylor *Br*
Josephine Tey *Br*
June Thomson *Br*
Charles Todd *Br*
Peter Turnbull *Br*
Janwillem van de
    Wetering *foreign*
Hillary Waugh *US*
Christopher West *foreign*
Barbara Whitehead *Br*
Charles Willeford *US*
David Williams *Br*
R D Wingfield *Br*
Eric Wright *foreign*

Private investigator (PI)

Margery Allingham
Phil Andrews
John Baker
Linda Barnes
Adam Baron
Raymond Chandler
Agatha Christie
Carol Higgins Clark
Mary Clayton
Harlan Coben
Robert Crais
James Crumley
Stephen Dobyns
Stephen Donaldson
Stella Duffy
Sarah Dunant
Loren D Estleman
Liz Evans
Sue Grafton
James Hall
Steve Hamilton
Dashiell Hammett
Joseph Hansen

Lauren Henderson
Joyce Holms
Hazel Holt
Paul Johnston
Alison Joseph
Stuart M Kaminsky
Sarah Lacey
Frank Lean
Dennis Lehane
Irene Lin-Chandler
Laura Lippman
John D MacDonald
Ross Macdonald
Michael McGarrity
Manuel Vázquez Montalbán
Susan Moody
Marcia Muller
Reggie Nadelson
Geoffrey Norman
Sara Paretsky
George P Pelecanos
Sam Reaves
Sandra Scoppettone
Gillian Slovo
Alexander McCall Smith
Michelle Spring
Cath Staincliffe
Rex Stout
John Straley
Doug J Swanson
Peter Tasker
Leslie Thomas
Mark Timlin
Valerie Wilson Wesley
Stella Whitelaw
Mary Wings
Steve Womack

Psychological

John Connolly
Kerstin Ekman
Penelope Evans
Joy Fielding
Gregory Hall
Mo Hayder
Frances Hegarty
Patricia Highsmith
Tami Hoag
Sharyn McCrumb
Elizabeth McGregor
Margaret Murphy
Gemma O'Connor
James Patterson
Chris Petit
Danuta Reah
Carol Smith
Tony Strong
Aline Templeton
Barbara Vine
Minette Walters
Laura Wilson
Margaret Yorke

Fantasy

Fantasy novels - as distinct from Science Fiction - deal with the impossible, being based on magic or the supernatural. They follow no scientific 'rules' - only the whim of the author. While there are many sub-divisions in the world of Fantasy, we have used six sub-genres to help readers find the kind of book they most enjoy. *Contemporary* The intrusion of the fantastic into modern life. *Dark* Fantasy which incorporates a sense of horror. *Epic* Books in which heroes and heroines wage epic combat with forces of evil. *Myth* Authors who place their stories in worlds of myth, saga and legend particularly Celtic. *Humour* Not all fantasy is dark, and these authors write light and humorous stories, often including elements of familiar folk tales. *Literary* The characters of fiction and literature in general take on reality in a fantasy world rich in literary allusion.

Storm Constantine
Barbara Hambly
Philip Pullman
Michael Scott Rohan

Contemporary

Gene Brewer
Mark Chadbourn
John Crowley
Charles de Lint
Neil Gaiman
Tim Powers

Dark

Jonathan Carroll
Tanith Lee
Freda Warrington

Epic

Mark Anthony
Tom Arden
Robert Asprin
James Barclay
Marion Zimmer Bradley
Terry Brooks
Steven Brust
Chris Bunch
Allan Cole
Louise Cooper
Stephen Donaldson
Sara Douglass
David A Drake
David Eddings

Kate Elliott
Steven Erikson
David Farland
Raymond E Feist
Maggie Furey
David Gemmell
Mary Gentle
Terry Goodkind
Julia Gray
Simon R Green
Elizabeth Haydon
Robin Hobb
William Horwood
Kate Jacoby
Mike Jefferies
J V Jones
Robert Jordan
Guy Gavriel Kay
Paul Kearney
Greg Keyes
Katherine Kurtz
Mercedes Lackey
Ursula K Le Guin
Fritz Leiber
Valery Leith
Megan Lindholm
Holly Lisle
Juliet E McKenna
John Marco
George R R Martin
Julian May
L E Modesitt Jr
Elizabeth Moon
Michael Moorcock

Adam Nichols
K J Parker
Melanie Rawn
Mickey Zucker Reichert
Jennifer Roberson
R A Salvatore
Jan Siegel
Judith Tarr
Roger Taylor
Sheri S Tepper
J R R Tolkien
Harry Turtledove
Margaret Weis
Jane Welch
Tad Williams
Philip G Williamson
Janny Wurts
Jonathan Wylie
Roger Zelazny

Humour

Piers Anthony
L Sprague de Camp
Craig Shaw Gardner
Andrew Harman
Tom Holt
Nick Nielsen
Terry Pratchett
Martin Scott

Literary

Robert Holdstock
C S Lewis
Gene Wolfe

Myth

Peter S Beagle	Barry Hughart	Juliet Marillier
Alice Borchardt	Katharine Kerr	Caiseal Mor
C J Cherryh	Stephen R Lawhead	T H White
Ellen Datlow		

Glitz & Glamour

This genre features the modern world of big business and entertainment, with generous proportions of sex, violence and avarice.

Maria Barrett	Jude Deveraux	Susan Lewis
Sally Beauman	Laramie Dunaway	Johanna Lindsey
Pat Booth	Lucinda Edmonds	Frankie McGowan
Celia Brayfield	Julie Ellis	Judith Michael
Sandra Brown	Elizabeth Gage	Fern Michaels
Alexandra Campbell	Olivia Goldsmith	Una-Mary Parker
Jackie Collins	Judith Gould	Harold Robbins
Joan Collins	Judi James	June Flaum Singer
Shirley Conran	Judith Krantz	Madge Swindells
Jilly Cooper	Jayne Ann Krentz	Caroline Upcher
Jenn Crowell	Roberta Latow	Penny Vincenzi
Barbara Delinsky		

Historical

Another very popular category, where fictional characters are set against an actual historical perspective, with close and realistic links between fiction and fact. Some are based on real people and events, while others are purely imaginary.

Vanessa Alexander	Sandra Gulland	Andrew Miller
Evelyn Anthony	Cynthia Harrod-Eagles	Diana Norman
Jean M Auel	Caroline Harvey	Charles Palliser
William Bedford	Anne Haverty	Edith Pargeter
Elizabeth Boyle	Elizabeth Hawksley	Margaret Pemberton
Philippa Carr	Georgette Heyer	Sharon Penman
Nicholas Carter	Domini Highsmith	Maureen Peters
Elizabeth Chadwick	Pamela Hill	Jean Plaidy
Joy Chambers	Joanna Hines	Steven Pressfield
Marion Chesney	Jane Aiken Hodge	Amanda Quick
Tracy Chevalier	Helen Hollick	Julian Rathbone
Gloria Cook	Sheri Holman	Mary Renault
Catherine Coulter	Victoria Holt	Cynthia S Roberts
Teresa Crane	Christian Jacq	Edward Rutherfurd
Stevie Davies	Tim Jeal	Simon Scarrow
Emma Drummond	Elizabeth Jeffrey	Anya Seton
June Drummond	Ross King	Patricia Shaw
Dorothy Dunnett	Matthew Kneale	Agnes Short
Robert Edric	Rosalind Laker	Linda Lay Shuler
Barbara Erskine	Dinah Lampitt	Wilbur Smith
Diana Gabaldon	Ross Leckie	Jane Stevenson
Pauline Gedge	Morgan Llywelyn	E V Thompson
Margaret George	Genevieve Lyons	Nigel Tranter
Valerie Georgeson	Colleen McCullough	Kate Tremayne
Anne Goring	Valerio Massimo Manfredi	Barry Unsworth
Winston Graham	Allan Massie	Patricia Wendorf
Jonathan Grant	Robin Maxwell	Barbara Wood
Philippa Gregory	Rosalind Miles	Sarah Woodhouse

This section includes authors who frequently write suspense and horror, where the storyline involves pursuit and eventual escape - often from the supernatural, demonic or the occult.

Jonathan Aycliffe
Richard Bachman
Clive Barker
Anne Billson
Campbell Black
David Bowker
Chaz Brenchley
Poppy Z Brite
Ramsey Campbell
Jonathan Carroll
Simon Clark
Douglas Clegg
Nancy Collins
Joe Donnelly
John Douglas
Dennis Etchison
John Farris
Christopher Fowler
Stephen Gallagher
Robert Girardi

Muriel Gray
Diane Guest
Laurell K Hamilton
Steve Harris
James Herbert
Tom Holland
Shaun Hutson
Peter James
Jenny Jones
Graham Joyce
Jeanne Kalogridis
Stephen King
Dean R Koontz
Stephen Laws
Richard Laymon
Bentley Little
H P Lovecraft
Brian Lumley
Robert McCammon
David Martin

Graham Masterton
Richard Matheson
Mark Morris
Gloria Murphy
Kim Newman
Christopher Pike
Anne Rice
Phil Rickman
John Saul
Dan Simmons
Michael Slade
Guy N Smith
S P Somtow
Steven Spruill
Michael Stewart
Peter Straub
Whitley Strieber
Bernard Taylor
Tim Wilson
T M Wright

Humour

A select group of authors whose novels are mainly written to amuse.

Sherry Ashworth
Colin Bateman
H E Bates
Guy Bellamy
E F Benson
Terence Blacker
Faith Bleasdale
Mavis Cheek
Jonathan Coe
Joseph Connolly
Colin Douglas
Roddy Doyle
George MacDonald Fraser
Michael Frayn
Stephen Fry

Maggie Gibson
James Hawes
Charles Higson
Tom Holt
Sean Hughes
Garrison Keillor
Sue Limb
Robert Llewellyn
John McCabe
Magnus Mills
John Mortimer
Helen Muir
Geoff Nicholson
David Nobbs
Joseph O'Connor

Ardal O'Hanlon
Kate O'Riordan
Tom Sharpe
William Sutcliffe
Linda Taylor
Peter Tinniswood
Alan Titchmarsh
Sue Townsend
Lynne Truss
Mark Wallington
Keith Waterhouse
Sue Welfare
Nigel Williams
P G Wodehouse
Isabel Wolff

Lad Lit

The male equivalent to Chick Lit therefore written about men in the same age range who have trouble expressing their emotions.

David Baddiel
Mark Barrowcliffe
Matthew Beaumont
Nick Earls
Ben Elton

Mike Gayle
Alex George
Nick Hornby
Tim Lott

Tony Parsons
Kevin Sampson
Sean Thomas
Matt Thorne

Romance

Most libraries and bookshops will have a separate section of shelves devoted entirely to Romance - novels usually written by women for women, with love and romance as the principal theme. In recent years two significant and popular subgenre have appeared – romance with a *Medical* theme and *Historical* romance. This list of contemporary authors starts with writers of general romances, followed by sections on the two subgenres. Authors in this section do not appear in the main sequence of this Guide.

Nancy Campbell Allen
Lindsay Armstrong
Stella Bagwell
Jacqueline Baird
Patricia Ballard
Lois Battle
Helen Bianchin
Beverly Bird
Helen Brooks
Amanda Browning
Elizabeth Cadell
Barbara Cartland
Grace Chaplin
Daphne Clair
Donna Clayton
Lynne Collins
Vera Cowie
Caroline Cross
Emma Darcy
Trisha David
Janelle Denison
Robyn Donald

Jennifer Drew
Sandra Field
Liz Fielding
Rae Foley
Natalie Fox
Susan Fox
Hayley Gardner
Lynne Graham
Andrew M Greeley
Karen Hawkins
Grace Livingston
Kay Hooper
Jenny Hughes
Sharon Kendrick
Patricia Knoll
Day Leclaire
Miranda Lee
Julia London
Roberta H Mandell
Victoria Marquez
Sandra Marton
Anne Mather

Anne McAllister
Kay L McDonald
K C McKinnon
Barbara McMahon
Julianna Morris
Carole Mortimer
Betty Neels
Kathleen O'Brien
Margaret O'Neill
Valerie Parv
Pat Phillips
Susan Plunkett
Michelle Reid
Glenda Sanders
Beatrice Small
Jessica Steele
Rowena Summers
Kay Thorpe
Kate Walker
Anne Weale
Sara Wood
Hill Karen Young

Medical

Christine Adams
Caroline Anderson
Margaret Barker
Sheila Danton
Lilian Darcy
Barbara Hart
Rebecca Lang
Marion Lennox
Laura MacDonald
Leah Martyn
Jessica Matthews
Margaret O'Neill
Colleen L Reece
Elisabeth Scott
Claire Vernon
Meredith Webber

Historical

Nita Abrams
Kathryn Alexander
Susan Andersen
Jane Ashford
Cassandra Austin
Lynn Bailey
Faith Baldwin
Mary Balogh
Julie Beard
Lillian Beckwith
Patti Berg
Rosanne Bittner
Jennifer Blake
Mary Brendan
Connie Brockway
Marsha Canham
Lynda Carpenter
Linda Lea Castle
Elaine Coffman
Emma Craig
Ann Cree
Claire Delacroix
Natalie Dunbar
Kathleen Eagle

Patricia Favier
Heather Graham
Nora Hague
Renee Halverson
Kristin Hannah
Miranda Jarrett
Karen Kay
Judith A Lansdowne
Emilie Baker Loring
Debbie Macomber
Thomas Mallon
Paula Marshall
Julie Moffett
Jacqueline Navin
Laura Paquet
Elizabeth Powell
Kimberly Raye
Karen Robards
Donna Simpson
Anne Stuart
Elizabeth Thornton
Karen White
Susan Wiggs
Christine Young

Saga

A popular genre, frequently set against an historical background, telling the story of two or more generations of a family, with the plot often revolving around the purchase of property or the development of a family business.

Elizabeth Adler	R F Delderfield	Judith Lennox
Rosemary Aitken	Margaret Dickinson	Freda Lightfoot
Kate Alexander	Inga Dunbar	Peter Ling
Charlotte Vale Allen	Joan Eadith	Elizabeth Lord
Jay Allerton	Doreen Edwards	Claire Lorrimer
Lyn Andrews	Elizabeth Elgin	Brenda McBryde
Aileen Armitage	Rosemary Enright	Malcolm Macdonald
Anne Baker	Pamela Evans	Hilda McKenzie
Donna Baker	Katie Flynn	Mary Mackie
Tessa Barclay	Helen Forrester	Alison McLeay
Anne Bennett	June Francis	Elisabeth McNeill
Maeve Binchy	Christine Marion Fraser	Maggie Makepeace
Emma Blair	Sara Fraser	Margaret Mayhew
Jessica Blair	Elizabeth Gill	Anne Melville
Philip Boast	Judith Glover	Mary Minton
Rose Boucheron	Suzanne Goodwin	Connie Monk
Harry Bowling	Iris Gower	Catrin Morgan
Clare Boylan	Margaret Graham	Elizabeth Murphy
Barbara Taylor Bradford	Patricia Grey	Annie Murray
Rita Bradshaw	Ruth Hamilton	Isobel Neill
Louise Brindley	Lilian Harry	M R O'Donnell
Julia Bryant	Meg Henderson	Gilda O'Neill
Patricia Burns	Elizabeth Ann Hill	Joan O'Neill
Betty Burton	Evelyn Hood	Jenny Oldfield
Helen Cannam	Una Horne	Pamela Oldfield
Helen Carey	Audrey Howard	Lynda Page
Irene Carr	Susan Howatch	Frances Paige
Jean Chapman	Harriet Hudson	Mary E Pearce
Brenda Clarke	Meg Hutchinson	Victor Pemberton
Harry Cole	Sara Hylton	Belva Plain
Catrin Collier	Anna Jacobs	Pamela Pope
Kathleen Conlon	Sheila Jansen	D M Purcell
Alexandra Connor	Joan Jonker	Alexandra Raife
Catherine Cookson	Penny Jordan	Eileen Ramsay
Josephine Cox	Marie Joseph	Kitty Ray
Elaine Crowley	Nora Kay	Claire Rayner
Janet Dailey	Sheelagh Kelly	Miss Read
Elizabeth Daish	Lena Kennedy	Audrey Reimann
Emma Dally	Anna King	Elvi Rhodes
Elizabeth Darrell	Beryl Kingston	Pam Rhodes
Doris Davidson	Gwen Kirkwood	Ann Victoria Roberts
Margaret Thomson Davis	Mary A Larkin	Denise Robertson
Frank Delaney	Maureen Lee	Wendy Robertson

Malcolm Ross
Liz Ryan
Susan Sallis
Judith Saxton
Arabella Seymour
Sarah Shears
Anne Rivers Siddons
Alison Skelton
Harriet Smart
Linda Sole
Lavyrle Spencer
Sally Spencer
Eileen Stafford
Diana Stainforth
Mary Jane Staples
Danielle Steel
Kay Stephens

Sally Stewart
Caroline Stickland
Jessica Stirling
Alison Stuart
Jean Stubbs
Sue Sully
Margaret Sunley
Reay Tannahill
Janet Tanner
Alice Taylor
Rosie Thomas
Grace Thompson
Nicola Thorne
Margaret Thornton
Eileen Townsend
Janet Macleod Trotter
Judy Turner

Elizabeth Villars
Anne Vivis
Elizabeth Waite
Elizabeth Walker
Elizabeth Warne
Kirsty White
Jeanne Whitmee
Barbara Whitnell
Phyllis A Whitney
Marcia Willett
Dee Williams
Audrey Willsher
T R Wilson
Mary Withall
Valerie Wood
Sally Worboyes
Anne Worboys

Science fiction

Although Science Fiction (SF) and Fantasy are often mixed, SF deals with the possible, and is based (often tenuously) on scientific knowledge obeying the laws of nature in the universe - however fantastic some of the stories may seem. The literature of SF is substantial and we have used five subgenres to help you find the type of author you want to read. **Near future** Stories concerning all pervasive technologies, their use and misuse, normally set within the next hundred years. **Space opera** Space adventure stories of extravagant dimensions, often involving galactic empires and space battles. **Space and time** Travel into either the past or the future, exploring history as it might have been, or the future as the author sees it. **Technical** SF novels with an overriding emphasis on the technical and scientific achievement, usually involving flight into outer space. **Humour** Authors whose books highlight the humorous aspects of SF.

Brian W Aldiss
Kristine Kathryn Rusch
Mary Doria Russell
Jules Verne
Ian Watson
John Wyndham

Humour

Douglas Adams
Rob Grant
Harry Harrison
Robert Rankin
Bob Shaw

Near future

Steve Aylett
John Barnes
Alexander Besher
Eric Brown
John Brunner
Pat Cadigan
Greg Egan
William Gibson
Jon Courtenay Grimwood
Gwyneth Jones
James Lovegrove
Jeff Noon
Rachel Pollack
Richard Powers
Kim Stanley Robinson
Lucius Shepard
Michael Marshall Smith
Neal Stephenson

Bruce Sterling
Tad Williams
Jack Womack

Space and time

Isaac Asimov
Ben Bova
Ray Bradbury
Octavia E Butler
Philip K Dick
Christopher Evans
Robert A Heinlein
Anne McCaffrey
Jack McDevitt
Ian McDonald
Ken MacLeod
China Miéville
Larry Niven
Robert Silverberg
Clifford D Simak
Vernor Vinge
Kurt Vonnegut
H G Wells
Connie Willis
Robert Charles Wilson
David Wingrove
David Zindell

Space opera

Poul Anderson
A A Attanasio
Iain M Banks
David Brin

Lois McMaster Bujold
Orson Scott Card
C J Cherryh
Alan Dean Foster
Colin Greenland
Joe Haldeman
Peter F Hamilton
Brian Herbert
Frank Herbert
Alastair Reynolds
Adam Roberts
Dan Simmons
Jack Vance

Technical

J G Ballard
Stephen Baxter
Greg Bear
Gregory Benford
Arthur C Clarke
Thomas M Disch
K W Jeter
Paul J McAuley
Wil McCarthy
John Meaney
Linda Nagata
John Sladek
Brian Stableford

A popular category where many authors have made a well-deserved reputation for writing about the sea either in an historical or a modern setting. Many novelists in this genre will also be found under *Adventure/Thriller* and also under *War stories*.

Historical	Historical & Modern	Modern
Tom Connery	Philip McCutchan	Brian Callison
David Donachie	Dudley Pope	Gerry Carroll
C S Forester		James Cobb
Alexander Kent		P T Deutermann
A E Langsford		Alan Evans
Jonathan Lunn		Duncan Harding
Jan Needle		Nicholas Monsarrat
James L Nelson		Douglas Reeman
Patrick O'Brian		Patrick Robinson
Marcus Palliser		Justin Scott
Dan Parkinson		Peter Tonkin
Julian Stockwin		Antony Trew
Showell Styles		John Winton
Victor Suthren		
Richard Woodman		

War

Authors who have written widely but not exclusively about war, generally within the 19th and 20th centuries. Many books about war will also be found under *Adventure/Thriller* and *Sea stories*. Some *General* novelists have also written individual books about war.

Historical	Modern	
Bernard Cornwell	Peter Cave	Robert Jackson
Garry Douglas	Shaun Clarke	Leo Kessler
Richard Howard	W E B Griffin	Mike Lunnon-Wood
Allan Mallinson	John Harris	Andy McNab
	Eric L Harry	Derek Robinson
	Max Hennessy	Alan Savage
	Johnny 'Two Combs' Howard	Terence Strong
		Charles Whiting

Western

As with Romance, most libraries have a separate section for stories set in the old American West during the middle and end of the 19th century. The authors listed below are a small selection of the many writers still in print in this genre. They do not appear in the main sequence of this Guide.

Luke Adams	Bill Gulick	George J Prescott
Tom Anson	Malcolm Hartley	Jack Reason
Todhunter Ballard	Ken Hodgson	Henry Remington
Frederic Bean	John Hunt	Rick Riordan
Tom Benson	Alan Irwin	Les Savage
Matt Braun	Terry C Johnston	Frank Scarman
Wes Calhoun	Hank J Kirby	Billy L Stephens
Tim Champlin	Jake Logan	Louis Trimble
Ralph Cotton	John S McCord	Robert Vaughan
Dan Cushman	Earl Murray	Richard S Wheeler
John Dyson	Ray Nolan	Jim R Woolard
Loren D Estleman	Dennis O'Keefe	Adam Wright
Steve Frazee	Wayne D Overholser	Don Wright
Zane Grey		

Characters

This section lists in principal name order all the **Characters**, **Series** and **Family** names which appear in the main A-Z sequence of the guide. Where there are two linked characters, eg *Sgt Abbot & Insp Thorne*, there is a reverse entry under the second name, ie *Insp Thorne & Sgt Abbot*.

Character	Author
Sgt Abbot & Insp Thorne	John Penn
Ben Abbott	Justin Scott
Simon Abelard	Bill James
Mick 'Brew' Axbrewder & Ginny Fistoulari	Stephen Donaldson
Johnny Ace	Ron Ellis
Laura Ackroyd & DCI Michael Thackeray	Patricia Hall
Gillian Adams	Nora Kelly
Adams Family	Mary Jane Staples
Age of Misrule Series	Mark Chadbourn
Sister Agnes Bourdillon	Alison Joseph
Alexander The Great	Valerio Massimo Manfredi
DI Roderick Alleyn	Ngaio Marsh
DI Alvarez	Roderic Jeffries
Amerotke	Paul Doherty
Robert Amiss & Baroness Troutbeck	Ruth Dudley Edwards
Peter Amsterdam	Laurence Shames
Fitzroy MacLean Angel	Mike Ripley
Anno Dracula Series	Kim Newman
Anvil of The World Series	Michael Scott Rohan
Insp Wang Anzhuang	Christopher West
DI John Appleby	Michael Innes
Appletree Saga	Mary E Pearce
Lew Archer	Ross Macdonald
Owen Archer	Candace Robb
Comm Jan Argand	Julian Rathbone
Jonathan Argyll	Iain Pears
Arms Trade Series	Christopher Nicole
Sheriff Spenser Arrowood	Sharyn McCrumb
Arthurian Trilogy	Helen Hollick
Countess of Ashby-de-la-Zouche	Fidelis Morgan
DI Carol Ashton	Claire McNab
Peter Ashton	Clive Egleton
DCI Jim Ashworth & DS Holly Bedford	Brian Battison
Askham Family	Nicola Thorne
Brother Athelstan & Sir Hugh Corbett	Paul Doherty
Brother Athelstan & Sir John Cranston	Paul Harding

Characters

Jack Aubrey & Stephen Maturin	Patrick O'Brian
Dr David Audley	Anthony Price
Jane Austen	Stephanie Barron
Kate Austen	Jonnie Jacobs
Avalon Series	Marion Zimmer Bradley
Badge of Honour Series	W E B Griffin
Kate Baeier	Gillian Slovo
Bill Bailey	Catherine Cookson
Geoffrey Bailey & Helen West	Frances Fyfield
Jonathan Bale & Christopher Redmayne	Edward Marston
Chief Mario Balzac	K C Constantine
CI Alan Banks	Peter Robinson
Paul Bannerman	John R Maxim
Chief Holly Barker	Stuart Woods
Barleybridge Series	Rebecca Shaw
Dr George Barnabas	Claire Rayner
DCI Tom Barnaby & Sgt Troy	Caroline Graham
The Baron	John Creasey
Stone Barrington	Stuart Woods
Matthew Bartholomew	Susanna Gregory
Miriam Bartimeus	Paul Doherty
Ernie Bascom & George Suenno	Martin Limon
Andrew Basnett	Elizabeth Ferrars
Det J P Beaumont	J A Jance
Holly Beckman	Jessica Stirling
DS Holly Bedford & DCI Jim Ashworth	Brian Battison
The Belgaried	David Eddings
Beloved People Trilogy	Denise Robertson
Will Benson	Charles Spencer
William Bentley	Jan Needle
Dr Fidelis Berlin	Jessica Mann
Sgt William Bird & DI Richard Montgomery	Stella Shepherd
Max Bittersohn & Sarah Kelling	Charlotte MacLeod
Oz Blackstone & Primavera Phillips	Quintin Jardine
Mike Blackwood	Douglas Reeman
Elizabeth Blair	Lizbie Brown
Det Sonora Blair	Lynn S Hightower
Anita Blake	Laurell K Hamilton
DI Josephine Blake	Janet Harward
Ursula Blanchard	Fiona Buckley
Insp Bland	Julian Symons
Simon Bognor	Tim Heald
Sgt Lou Boldt	Ridley Pearson
Myron Bolitar	Harlan Coben
Richard Bolitho	Alexander Kent
Bonaparte Series	Richard Howard
Supt Bone	Staynes & Storey
Bonn & Dr Clare Burtonall	Jonathan Gash
Harry Bosch	Michael Connelly

Sgt Bottomley & DI Saul Jackson	Norman Russell
Eva Bower	Aileen Armitage
Nicholas Bracewell	Edward Marston
John Bradedge & Dr Simon Forman	Judith Cook
Dame Beatrice Bradley	Gladys Mitchell
Charlie Bradshaw	Stephen Dobyns
Sheriff Joanna Brady	J A Jance
Sgt Bragg & PC Morton	Ray Harrison
Deacon Theodora Braithwaite	D M Greenwood
Dave Brandstetter	Joseph Hansen
Kate Brannigan	Val McDermid
DS Brant & DCI Roberts	Ken Bruen
Nell Bray	Gillian Linscott
Breadmakers Series	Margaret Thomson Davis
Dr Temperance Brennan	Kathy Reichs
Lucy Trimble Brenner	Eric Wright
Gervase Bret & Ralph Delchard	Edward Marston
Brethren of the Coast Trilogy	James L Nelson
Insp John Bright	Maureen O'Brien
DCI David Brock & DS Kathy Kolla	Barry Maitland
Brotherhood of War Series	W E B Griffin
CI Browne & DC Jennie Taylor	Pauline Bell
Verity Browne & Lord Edward Corinth	David Roberts
Commissario Guido Brunetti	Donna Leon
Tam Buchanan & Fizz Fitzgerald	Joyce Holms
Burke	Andrew Vachss
Nicky Burkett	Jeremy Cameron
DI Kate Burrows	Martina Cole
Dr Clare Burtonall & Bonn	Jonathan Gash
Brother Cadfael	Ellis Peters
DI Jack Caffery	Mo Hayder
Sgt Denise Caldecote & DI Thomas Rydell	Christine Green
Calder Family	Janet Dailey
Keith Calder	Gerald Hammond
Donald Cameron	Philip McCutchan
Fiona Cameron	Val McDermid
Letty Campbell	Alma Fritchley
Margaret Campbell & Det Li Yan	Peter May
Albert Campion	Margery Allingham
Canaletto	Janet Laurence
Det Steve Carella	Ed McBain
Neal Carey	Don Winslow
Sir Robert Carey	P F Chisholm
Carlotta Carlyle	Linda Barnes
Agnes Carmichael	Anthea Cohen
Insp James Carrick	Margaret Duffy
Pepe Carvalho	Manuel Vázquez Montalbán
Henri Castang	Nicolas Freeling
Quintus Licinius Cato	Simon Scarrow

Sir Keith Chace	Peter Tremayne
Chadwick Family	Marcia Willett
Champagne Series	Nicola Thorne
Roger the Chapman	Kate Sedley
Max Chard	John Burns
Elizabeth Chase	Martha Lawrence
Jim Chee & Joe Leaphorn	Tony Hillerman
Cheysuli Series	Jennifer Roberson
DI Henry Christie	Nick Oldham
Chronicles of Magravadias	Storm Constantine
Chronicles of the Raven Series	James Barclay
Church of England Series	Susan Howatch
DS Emile Cinq-Mars	John Farrow
DC Siobhan Clarke & DI John Rebus	Ian Rankin
Denise Cleever	Claire McNab
Com John Coffin	Gwendoline Butler
Artie Cohen	Reggie Nadelson
Elvis Cole	Robert Crais
Lewis Cole	Brendan Dubois
Hap Collins & Leonard Pine	Joe R Lansdale
The Continental Op	Dashiell Hammett
Conway Family	Jessica Stirling
Alexandra Cooper	Linda Fairstein
DC Ben Cooper & DS Diane Fry	Stephen Booth
PC Den Cooper	Rebecca Tope
Coppins Bridge Series	Elizabeth Daish
Dr Jessica Coran	Robert W Walker
Sir Hugh Corbett & Brother Athelstan	Paul Doherty
Cordwainer Series	Iris Gower
Det John Corey & Kate Mayfield	Nelson DeMille
Lord Edward Corinth & Verity Browne	David Roberts
Grace Cornish	Simon Shaw
Corps Series	W E B Griffin
Corvill Family	Tessa Barclay
Marcus Corvinus	David Wishart
Pat Coyne	Hugo Hamilton
Craddock Family	R F Delderfield
Melissa Craig	Betty Rowlands
Craigallan Family	Tessa Barclay
Sir John Cranston & Brother Athelstan	Paul Harding
Francis Crawford of Lymond	Dorothy Dunnett
Thea Crawford	Jessica Mann
Tildy Crawford	Sara Fraser
Creasy	A J Quinnell
Sgt Cribb & PC Thackeray	Peter Lovesey
DI Mike Croft	Jane Adams
DC John Cromer & DS Vic Hallam	David Ralph Martin
DS Crosby & DI Sloan	Catherine Aird
Det Alex Cross	James Patterson

Sgt Jack Crossman	Garry Douglas
DI Crow	Roy Lewis
Dave Cunane	Frank Lean
John Cunningham	Gerald Hammond
Richard Cypher	Terry Goodkind
Supt Adam Dalgleish	P D James
Quintilian Dalrymple	Paul Johnston
Patrick Dalton	Dan Parkinson
DI Dalziel & DS Pascoe	Reginald Hill
DI Charmian Daniels	Jennie Melville
Josse D'Acquin & Abbess Helewise	Alys Clare
Dark Materials Trilogy	Philip Pullman
Darkover Series	Marion Zimmer Bradley
Lucas Davenport	John Sandford
'Dangerous' Davies	Leslie Thomas
Sgt de Gier & Adjutant Grijpstra	Janwillem van de Wetering
John Deal	Les Standiford
Sam Dean	Mike Phillips
Lt Pete Decker	Faye Kellerman
Alex Delaware & Det Milo Sturgis	Jonathan Kellerman
Ralph Delchard & Gervase Bret	Edward Marston
John Delmas	Raymond Chandler
Sgt Denny & Major Mearns	Gwendoline Butler
Harry James Denton	Steve Womack
Deryni Series	Katherine Kurtz
Deverry Series	Katharine Kerr
Harry Devlin	Martin Edwards
Peter Diamond	Peter Lovesey
Auguste Didier	Amy Myers
Sean Dillon	Jack Higgins
Discworld Series	Terry Pratchett
Trixie Dolan & Evangeline Sinclair	Marian Babson
Sgt Cal Donovan & DI Liz Graham	Jo Bannister
John Dortmunder	Donald E Westlake
Arthur Conan Doyle	Roberta Rogow
Family Dracul	Jeanne Kalogridis
Det Jessie Drake	Rochelle Krich
Drenai Series	David Gemmell
Nathaniel Drinkwater	Richard Woodman
Drummond Family	Emma Blair
Eve Duncan	Iris Johansen
Easter Empire	Beryl Kingston
Eisdalsa Island Trilogy	Mary Withall
Elita Series	Kate Jacoby
The Ellenium	David Eddings
Emma	Elizabeth Daish
Fairacre	Miss Read
Robert Fairfax	Hannah March
Marcus Didius Falco	Lindsey Davis

Characters

Gordianus the Finder	Steven Saylor
Lindsay Gordon	Val McDermid
Evangeline Gower	Louisa Young
Davina Graham	Evelyn Anthony
DI Liz Graham & DS Cal Donovan	Jo Bannister
DCI Robert Graham	Raymond Flynn
DI Alan Grant	Josephine Tey
Celia Grant	John Sherwood
Patrick Grant	Margaret Yorke
Cordelia Gray	P D James
Greg Mandell Series	Peter F Hamilton
Lew Griffin	James Sallis
Adjutant Grijpstra & Sgt de Gier	Janwillem van de Wetering
Marshal Guarnaccia	Magdalen Nabb
St Vincent Halfhyde	Philip McCutchan
DS Vic Hallam & DC John Cromer	David Ralph Martin
Judy Hammer	Patricia D Cornwell
Supt Hannasyde & DI Hemingway	Georgette Heyer
Hannibal	Ross Leckie
Sigrid Harald	Margaret Maron
Hardie Family	Anne Melville
Dismas Hardy	John T Lescroart
Mary Haristean & Mrs Murphy (a cat)	Rita Mae Brown
Ch Supt Colin Harpur & ACC Desmond Iles	Bill James
Emma Harte	Barbara Taylor Bradford
DS Barbara Havers & DCI Thomas Lynley	Elizabeth George
Det Al Hawkin & Det Kate Martinelli	Laurie R King
Hawksmoor Series	Aileen Armitage
Det Stuart Haydon	David Lindsey
Nanette Hayes	Charlotte Carter
Tamara Hayle	Valerie Wilson Wesley
Heart of Gold Series	Catrin Collier
Abbess Helewise & Josse D'Aquin	Alys Clare
DI Hemingway & Supt Hannasyde	Georgette Heyer
DCI Hennessy & DS Yellick	Peter Turnbull
Heron Saga	Pamela Oldfield
Matthew Hervey	Allan Mallinson
DI Judy Hill & DCI Lloyd	Jill McGown
Dr Tony Hill & DCI Carol Jordan	Val McDermid
Hillsbridge Family	Janet Tanner
Kate Hilton	Margaret Dickinson
Holly-Jean Ho	Irene Lin-Chandler
Dido Hoare	Marianne MacDonald
Billy-Bob Holland	James Lee Burke
Sherlock Holmes & Mary Russell	Laurie R King
Sherlock Holmes & Dr John Watson	Arthur Conan Doyle
DI Nick Holroyd	Ann Quinton
Det Hook & Det Lambert	J M Gregson
DS Angela Hope & DCI Nick Trevelyan	Susan Kelly

Characters

Supt Duncan Kincaid & Sgt Gemma James	Deborah Crombie
Willow King	Natasha Cooper
Kings Series	Christine Marion Fraser
Lucy Kingsley & David Middleton-Brown	Kate Charles
Kate Kinsella	Christine Green
Deborah Knott	Margaret Maron
Hermann Kohler & Jean-Louis St-Cyr	J Robert Janes
DS Kathy Kolla & DCI David Brock	Barry Maitland
DS Mike Korpanski & DI Joanna Piercy	Priscilla Masters
Koto & Yum Yum	Lilian Jackson Braun
Big Herbie Kruger	John Gardner
Thomas Paine Kydd	Julian Stockwin
Jordan Lacey	Stella Whitelaw
Tim Lacy	Derek Wilson
DI Jack Laidlaw	William McIlvanney
Det Lambert & Det Hook	J M Gregson
DS Lambert & DCI Kelsey	Emma Page
Arnold Landon	Roy Lewis
Lilac Larkin	Katie Flynn
Stephen Larkin	Martyn Waites
Dr Samantha Laschen	Nicci French
Last of the Renshai Series	Mickey Zucker Reichert
Lauren Laurano	Sandra Scoppettone
Sgt Alain Lausard	Richard Howard
C S Vernon Lavelle	David Bowker
Lavender Road Series	Helen Carey
Jane Lawless	Ellen Hart
Loretta Lawson	Joan Smith
Joe Leaphorn & Jim Chee	Tony Hillerman
Dr Hannibal Lecter	Thomas Harris
Anna Lee	Liza Cody
John Lempriere	Lawrence Norfolk
Chevalier Galeran de Lesnevan	Viviane Moore
Det Supt Sholto Lestrade	M J Trow
Libertus	Rosemary Rowe
Saga of the Light Isles	Juliet Marillier
DS Lineham & DI Luke Thanet	Dorothy Simpson
Nicholas Linnear	Eric Lustbader
Darina Lisle	Janet Laurence
DCI Lloyd & DI Judy Hill	Jill McGown
Sgt Gomer Lloyd & CI Merlin Parry	David Williams
Matthew Loftus	Marcus Palliser
Ben London	Philip Boast
London Sequence	Margaret Pemberton
Lorimer Family	Anne Melville
Loveday Series	Kate Tremayne
Lovejoy	Jonathan Gash
John Lubbock & CI Mark Tench	Brian Cooper
Harry Ludlow	David Donachie

Major Mearns & Sgt Denny	Gwendoline Butler
Bruce Medway	Robert Wilson
Supt Cecil Megarry	Eugene McEldowney
DI Jim Meldrum	Frederic Lindsay
David Middleton-Brown & Lucy Kingsley	Kate Charles
Kinsey Millhone	Sue Grafton
DCI Millson & DS Scobie	Malcolm Forsythe
Milo Milodragovitch	James Crumley
Insp Matt Minogue	John Brady
Minster Family	Peter Ling
DI Benny Mitchell	Pauline Bell
Meredith Mitchell & Div Supt Alan Markby	Ann Granger
Mitch Mitchell	Valerie Kershaw
Mitford Series	Jan Karon
Tess Monaghan	Laura Lippman
Insp William & Hester Monk	Anne Perry
Monkton Family	Margaret Thomson Davis
Britt Montero	Edna Buchanan
DI Richard Montgomery & Sgt William Bird	Stella Shepherd
Monty & Sarah Patrick	Iris Johansen
DI Abigail Moon & Supt Gil Mayo	Marjorie Eccles
Phyllida Moon	Eileen Dewhurst
Kazuo Mori	Peter Tasker
Morland Dynasty	Cynthia Harrod-Eagles
CI John Morrissey	Kay Mitchell
DI Morse	Colin Dexter
PC Morton & Sgt Bragg	Ray Harrison
Sgt Hoke Moseley	Charles Willeford
DI Moss & DCI Colin Thane	Bill Knox
Sgt Angus Mott & Supt Mike Yeadings	Clare Curzon
Charlie Muffin	Brian Freemantle
Sgt 'Fang' Mulheisen	Jon A Jackson
Mrs Murphy (a cat) & Mary Haristean	Rita Mae Brown
Tom Musgrave	Peter Tonkin
Myth Adventures Series	Robert Asprin
Net Force Explorers	Tom Clancy
Neyler Family	Judith Saxton
Nicholson Family	Jessica Stirling
Night Dawn Trilogy	Peter F Hamilton
Noble Series	Christine Marion Fraser
Insp Guy Northeast	Joanna Cannan
Nugent Family	Betty Burton
Oak Family	Margaret Sunley
Kali O'Brien	Jonnie Jacobs
Det Supt Oddie & DC Charlie Peace	Robert Barnard
Maureen O'Donnell	Denise Mina
O'Hara Family	Elaine Crowley
DCI Connor O'Neill & DS Fran Wilson	Christine Green
Orokon Series	Tom Arden

Michael Osbourne	Daniel Silva
P Division	Peter Turnbull
Sam Packer	Geoffrey Archer
Lorraine Page	Lynda La Plante
Christopher Paget	Richard North Patterson
George & Molly Palmer-Jones	Ann Cleeves
Mrs Pargeter	Simon Brett
PC Nick Parish	Nicholas Rhea
Charlie "Bird" Parker	John Connolly
Jack Parlabane	Christopher Brookmyre
Charles Parris	Simon Brett
CI Merlin Parry & Sgt Gomer Lloyd	David Williams
Annie Parsons	Sarah Shears
Parsons Family	Jenny Oldfield
Lily Pascale	Scarlett Thomas
DS Pascoe & DI Dalziel	Reginald Hill
Sarah Patrick & Monty	Iris Johansen
Stephanie Patrick	Mark Burnell
The Patteran Trilogy	Patricia Wendorf
Patterson Family	Jessica Stirling
Richard & Amelia Patton	Roger Ormerod
Amelia Peabody	Elizabeth Peters
DC Charlie Peace & Det Supt Oddie	Robert Barnard
DI Percy Peach	J M Gregson
Insp Evariste Pel	Juliet Hebden / Mark Hebden
John Pellam	Jeffery Deaver
DS Mark Pemberton	Nicholas Rhea
Pendragon Island Series	Grace Thompson
Performers Series	Claire Rayner
Douglas Perkins & Gerry Tate	Marian Babson
Karen Perry-Mondori	Catherine Arnold
Toby Peters	Stuart M Kaminsky
DS Wesley Peterson	Kate Ellis
Primavera Phillips & Oz Blackstone	Quintin Jardine
Phule's Saga	Robert Asprin
DI Joanna Piercy & DS Mike Korpanski	Priscilla Masters
Anna Pigeon	Nevada Barr
Leonard Pine & Hap Collins	Joe R Lansdale
Melinda Pink	Gwen Moffat
DCI Rose Piper	Hilary Bonner
Dirk Pitt	Clive Cussler
Insp Thomas & Charlotte Pitt	Anne Perry
Pliocene Saga	Julian May
DI Montague Pluke	Nicholas Rhea
Stephanie Plum	Janet Evanovich
DS Romulus Poe	Faye Kellerman
Hercule Poirot	Agatha Christie
Poppy Chronicles	Claire Rayner
DS Kate Power	Judith Cutler

Georgina Powers	Denise Danks
DI Ian Preston	Vivien Armstrong
DI Charlie Priest	Stewart Pawson
Prince Family	Sheelagh Kelly
Laura Principal	Michelle Spring
Mr G D H Pringle	Nancy Livingston
Simon Puttock & Sir Baldwin Furnshill	Michael Jecks
Tilly Quentin	Claire Rayner
Ellie Quick	Veronica Heley
Terry Quinn & Derek Strange	George P Pelecanos
Jim Qwilleran	Lilian Jackson Braun
Agatha Raisin	M C Beaton
Rambo	David Morrell
Precious Ramotswe	Alexander McCall Smith
Charles Ramsay	William Ardin
DI Stephen Ramsay	Ann Cleeves
PI Sunny Randall	Robert B Parker
Captain Matthew Ranklin	Gavin Lyall
Ravensdale Series	Kate Fielding
John Rawlings	Deryn Lake
Dolly Rawlins	Lynda La Plante
Easy Rawlins	Walter Mosley
Jack Reacher	Lee Child
DI John Rebus & DC Siobhan Clarke	Ian Rankin
Red Riding Quartet	David Peace
Christopher Redmayne & Jonathan Bale	Edward Marston
Clio Rees	Jo Bannister
Regan Reilly	Carol Higgins Clark
The Reindeer People	Megan Lindholm
Insp Arkady Renko	Martin Cruz Smith
DI Charlie Resnick	John Harvey
Retallick Family	E V Thompson
Ex-Insp John Reynolds	Mary Clayton
Sukey Reynolds	Betty Rowlands
Rhanna Series	Christine Marion Fraser
Rhapsody Trilogy	Elizabeth Haydon
Bernie Rhodenbarr	Lawrence Block
Lincoln Rhyme	Jeffery Deaver
Madoc Rhys	Charlotte MacLeod
DI Tom Richmond	Marjorie Eccles
Sam Ridley	Chris Niles
Riftwar Saga	Raymond E Feist
Rim Series	Alexander Besher
Tom Ripley	Patricia Highsmith
Rising Family	Susan Sallis
Sophie Rivers	Judith Cutler
DCI Roberts & DS Brant	Ken Bruen
Dave Robicheaux	James Lee Burke
Rochford Family	Claire Lorrimer

DCI Bob Southwell	Barbara Whitehead
Sam Spade	Dashiell Hammett
Spellsinger Series	Alan Dean Foster
Spenser	Robert B Parker
DI Vera Stanhope	Ann Cleeves
Staples Family	Mary Jane Staples
Nathaniel Starbuck	Bernard Cornwell
Dan Starkey	Colin Bateman
Nick Stefanos	George P Pelecanos
Sten Series	Chris Bunch
Stevenson Family Series	Malcolm Macdonald
Dr Kellen Stewart	Manda Scott
Jesse Stone	Robert B Parker
Stonemoor Series	Kay Stephens
Serge Storms	Tim Dorsey
Derek Strange & Terry Quinn	George P Pelecanos
Sylvia Strange	Sarah Lovett
Strathannan Series	Anne Vivis
Leo Street	Pauline McLynn
Pearl Street	Maureen Lee
Steve Strong	Phil Andrews
Lt Jack Stryker	Paula Gosling
Det Milo Sturgis & Alex Delaware	Jonathan Kellerman
George Sueno & Ernie Bascom	Martin Limon
C W Sughrue	James Crumley
Sheriff John Victor Sully	Boston Teran
Supt Gregory Summers	Susan Kelly
Dr Evelyn Sutcliffe	Leah Ruth Robinson
Sutton Family	Elizabeth Elgin
Cassie Swann	Susan Moody
Swann Family	R F Delderfield
Sweet Rosie Series	Iris Gower
Sword of Truth Series	Terry Goodkind
The Tamuli	David Eddings
Alex Tanner	Anabel Donald
Tanner Trilogy	Harry Bowling
Tanquillan Series	Louise Brindley
DCI Tansey	John Penn
Gerry Tate & Douglas Perkins	Marian Babson
Taylor Family	Sally Spencer
DC Jennie Taylor & CI Browne	Pauline Bell
Morgan Taylor	Susan Sussman with Sarajane Avidon
CI Mark Tench & DCI John Lubbock	Brian Cooper
DCI Jane Tennison	Lynda La Plante
PC Thackeray & Sgt Cribb	Peter Lovesey
DCI Michael Thackeray & Laura Ackroyd	Patricia Hall
DCI Colin Thane & DI Phil Moss	Bill Knox
DI Luke Thanet & DS Lineham	Dan Simmons

John Putnam Thatcher	Emma Lathen
Thomas Covenant Chronicles	Stephen Donaldson
Barney Thomson	Douglas Lindsay
Thorn	James Hall
Insp Thorne & Sgt Abbot	John Penn
DI Richard Thornhill & Jill Francis	Andrew Taylor
Charles Thoroughgood	Alan Judd
Thrush Green	Miss Read
Leslie Titmus	John Mortimer
Asst CC Phil 'Sweeney' Todd	Frank Palmer
The Toff	John Creasey
Tramont Family	Tessa Barclay
Nick Travers	Ace Atkins
Mark Treasure	David Williams
Supt Perry Trehowan	Robert Barnard
DCI Nick Trevelyan & DS Angela Hope	Susan Kelly
Rose Trevelyan	Janie Bolitho
Hannah Trevor	Margaret Lawrence
Prof Kate Trevorne	Paula Gosling
Tilly Trotter	Catherine Cookson
Baroness Troutbeck & Robert Amiss	Ruth Dudley Edwards
Sgt Troy & DCI Tom Barnaby	Caroline Graham
Frederick Troy	John Lawton
Sam Turner	John Baker
Turnham Malpas Series	Rebecca Shaw
Francis Urquhart Trilogy	Michael Dobbs
Inspector Vadim	Donald James
Martin Vail	William Diehl
Valley Series	Grace Thompson
Insp Van Der Valk	Nicolas Freeling
DCI Aden Vanner	Jeff Gulvin
Fran Varady	Ann Granger
Emma Victor	Mary Wings
Vlad Taltos Series	Steven Brust
Miles Vorkosigan	Lois McMaster Bujold
Amos Walker	Loren D Estleman
Supt Mike Walker	Lynda La Plante
Insp Kurt Wallander	Henning Mankell
Lily Walters	Catrin Morgan
Penny Wanawake	Susan Moody
Eric Ward	Roy Lewis
Ward Family	Elizabeth Murphy
DS Tom Ward	Aline Templeton
V I Warshawski	Sara Paretsky
Dr John Watson & Sherlock Holmes	Arthur Conan Doyle
Wayman Family	Mary E Pearce
Weavers Series	Donna Baker
DCI David Webb & DS Ken Jackson	Anthea Fraser
Werner Family	Belva Plain

DI West	John Creasey
Helen West & DS Geoffrey Bailey	Frances Fyfield
DCI George Wexford	Ruth Rendell
Wheel of Time Series	Robert Jordan
Elinor Whiteblade	Adam Nichols
Lu Wilmott	Betty Burton
DS Fran Wilson & DCI Conor O'Neill	Christine Green
Francesca Wilson & DCI John McLeish	Janet Neel
Lord Peter Wimsey	Dorothy L Sayers
Hannah Wolfe	Sarah Dunant
Sir John de Wolfe	Bernard Knight
Nero Wolfe & Archie Goodwin	Rex Stout
Women's Murder Club'	James Patterson
CI Charlie Woodend	Sally Spencer
Becky Worrell	Sally Spencer
Supt Wycliffe	W J Burley
Eva Wylie	Liza Cody
Xanth Series	Piers Anthony
Det Li Yan & Margaret Campbell	Peter May
Supt Mike Yeadings & Sgt Angus Mott	Clare Curzon
DS Yellick & DCI Hennessy	Peter Turnbull
Cecil Younger	John Straley
Yum Yum & Koto	Lilian Jackson Braun
The Mamur Zapt (Gareth Owen)	Michael Pearce
Aurelio Zen	Michael Dibdin

Literary prizes and awards

There are currently over 150 literary prizes and awards available in the United Kingdom, of which some 32 relate to fiction. These are listed in this section with a brief description of each award followed by the names of the winning authors and titles. Further details of all awards can be found by contacting the Book Trust at Book House, 45 East Hill, London SW18 2QZ or at www.booktrust.org.uk/prizes.

Authors' Club First Novel Award

Prizes

This is given to the most promising First Novel published by a writer in Great Britain. Introduced by Laurence Meynell in 1954.

1970	Rachel Ingalls	*Theft*
1971	Rosemary Hawley Jarman	*We speak no treason*
1973	Jennifer Johnston	*The captains and the kings*
1975	Sasha Moorsom	*A lavender trip*
1977	Barbara Benson	*The underlings*
1978	Katherine Gordon	*The emerald peacock*
1979	Martin Page	*The pilate plot*
1980	Dawn Lowe-Watson	*The good morrow*
1981	Dr Anne Smith	*The magic glass*
1982	Frances Vernon	*The privileged children*
1983	Katharine Moore	*Summer at the haven*
1984	Frederick Hyde-Chambers	*Lama, a novel of Tibet*
1985	Magda Sweetland	*Eightsome reel*
1986	Helen Harris	*Playing fields in winter*
1987	Peter Benson	*The levels*
1988	Gilbert Adair	*The holy innocents*
1989	Lindsey Davis	*The silver pigs*
1990	Alan Brownjohn	*The way you tell them*
1991	Zina Rohan	*The book of wishes and complaints*
1992	David Park	*The healing*
1993	Nadeem Aslam	*Season of the rainbirds*
1994	Andrew Cowan	*Pig*
1995	T J Armstrong	*Walter and the resurrection of G*
joint winners 1996	Yinka Adebayo	*A kind of black*
1996	Rhidian Brook	*The testimony of Taliesin Jones*
1997	Mick Jackson	*The underground man*
1998	Jackie Kay	*Trumpet*
1999	Ann Harries	*Manly pursuits*
2000	Brian Clarke	*The stream*
2001	Carl Tighe	*Burning worm*

James Tait Black Memorial Prizes

The James Tait Black Memorial Prizes, founded in memory of a partner in the publishing house A & C Black Ltd, were instituted in 1918. Two prizes are awarded annually: one for the best biography or work of that type and the other for the best work of fiction published during the calendar year.

joint winners {	1981	Salman Rushdie	*Midnight's children*
	1981	Paul Theroux	*The mosquito coast*
	1982	Bruce Chatwin	*On the black hill*
	1983	Jonathan Keates	*Allegro postillions*
joint winners {	1984	Angela Carter	*Nights at the circus*
	1984	J G Ballard	*Empire of the sun*
	1985	Robert Edric	*Winter garden*
	1986	Jenny Joseph	*Persephone*
	1987	George Mackay Brown	*The golden bird: two Orkney stories*
	1988	Piers Paul Read	*A season in the West*
	1989	James Kelman	*A disaffection*
	1990	William Boyd	*Brazzaville Beach*
	1991	Iain Sinclair	*Downriver*
	1992	Rose Tremain	*Sacred country*
	1993	Caryl Phillips	*Crossing the river*
	1994	Alan Hollinghurst	*The folding star*
	1995	Christopher Priest	*The prestige*
joint winners {	1996	Graham Swift	*Last orders*
	1996	Alice Thompson	*Justine*
	1997	Andrew Miller	*Ingenious pain*
	1998	Beryl Bainbridge	*Master Georgie*
	1999	Timothy Mo	*Renegade or Halo 2*
	2000	Zadie Smith	*White teeth*

Booker Prize for Fiction

Established in 1968 by Booker McConnell Ltd. Eligible novels must be written in English by a citizen of Britain, the Commonwealth or the Republic of Ireland. From 2002 sponsorship is by the Man Group and the prize will in future be known as the Man Booker Prize.

	1969	P H Newby	*Something to answer for*
	1970	Bernice Rubens	*The elected member*
	1971	V S Naipaul	*In a free state*
	1972	John Berger	*G*
	1973	J G Farrell	*The siege of Krishnapur*
joint winners	1974	Nadine Gordimer	*The conservationist*
	1974	Stanley Middleton	*Holiday*
	1975	Ruth Prawer Jhabvala	*Heat and dust*
	1976	David Storey	*Saville*
	1977	Paul Scott	*Staying on*
	1978	Iris Murdoch	*The sea, the sea*
	1979	Penelope Fitzgerald	*Offshore*
	1980	William Golding	*Rites of passage*
	1981	Salman Rushdie	*Midnight's children*
	1982	Thomas Keneally	*Schindler's ark*
	1983	J M Coetzee	*Life & times of Michael K*
	1984	Anita Brookner	*Hotel du Lac*
	1985	Keri Hulme	*The bone people*
	1986	Kingsley Amis	*The old devils*
	1987	Penelope Lively	*Moon tiger*
	1988	Peter Carey	*Oscar and Lucinda*
	1989	Kazuo Ishiguro	*The remains of the day*
	1990	A S Byatt	*Possession*
	1991	Ben Okri	*The famished road*
joint winners	1992	Michael Ondaatje	*The English patient*
	1992	Barry Unsworth	*Sacred hunger*
	1993	Roddy Doyle	*Paddy Clarke ha ha ha*
	1994	James Kelman	*How late it was, how late*
	1995	Pat Barker	*The ghost road*
	1996	Graham Swift	*Last orders*
	1997	Arundhati Roy	*The god of small things*
	1998	Ian McEwan	*Amsterdam*
	1999	J M Coetzee	*Disgrace*
	2000	Margaret Atwood	*The blind assassin*
	2001	Peter Carey	*True history of the Kelly Gang*

Harry Bowling Prize

Awarded in alternate years from 2000 and sponsored by Headline Book Publishing in honour of Harry Bowling "the King of Cockney Sagas" who died in 1999. Entry is open to anyone who has not previously had an adult novel published.

2000   Pip Granger   *Not all tarts are apple*

British Science Fiction Association Awards

Awarded annually after a ballot of members, by the British Science Fiction Association (BSFA). Winners of the Best Novel prize are listed below.

1969	John Brunner	*Stand on Zanzibar*
1970	John Brunner	*The jagged orbit*
1971/72	*No award*	
1973	Arthur C Clarke	*Rendezvous with Rama*
1974	Christopher Priest	*Inverted world*
1975	Bob Shaw	*Orbitsville*
1976	Michael G Coney	*Brontomek!*
1977	Ian Watson	*The Jonah kit*
1978	Philip K Dick	*A scanner darkly*
1979	J G Ballard	*The Unlimited Dream Company*
1980	Gregory Benford	*Timescape*
1981	Gene Wolfe	*The shadow of the torturer*
1982	Brian Aldiss	*Helliconia spring*
1983	John Sladek	*Tik-tok*
1984	Robert Holdstock	*Mythago Wood*
1985	Brian Aldiss	*Helliconia winter*
1986	Bob Shaw	*The ragged astronauts*
1987	Keith Roberts	*Grainne*
1988	Robert Holdstock	*Lavondyss*
1989	Terry Pratchett	*Pyramids*
1990	Colin Greenland	*Take back plenty*
1991	Dan Simmons	*The fall of Hyperion*
1992	Kim Stanley Robinson	*Red Mars*
1993	Christopher Evans	*Aztec century*
1994	Iain M Banks	*Feersum endjinn*
1995	Stephen Baxter	*The time ships*
1996	Iain M Banks	*Excession*
1997	Mary Doria Russell	*The sparrow*
1998	Christopher Priest	*The extremes*
1999	Ken MacLeod	*The sky road*
2000	Mary Gentle	*Ash: a secret history*
2001	Alastair Reynolds	*Chasm city*

Arthur C Clarke Award

Established in 1986 the Arthur C Clarke award is supported and judged jointly by the British Science Fiction Association, the Science Fiction Foundation and the Science Museum. It is for a Science Fiction novel and there are no limits on the country of origin. Horror and Fantasy are excluded unless there is a strong Science Fiction element in the book.

1987	Margaret Atwood	*The handmaid's tale*
1988	George Turner	*The sea and summer*
1989	Rachel Pollack	*Unquenchable fire*
1990	Geoff Ryman	*The child garden*
1991	Colin Greenland	*Take back plenty*
1992	Pat Cadigan	*Synners*
1993	Marge Piercy	*Body of glass*
1994	Jeff Noon	*Vurt*
1995	Pat Cadigan	*Fools*
1996	Paul J McAuley	*Fairyland*
1997	Amitav Ghosh	*The Calcutta chromosome*
1998	Mary Doria Russell	*The sparrow*
1999	Tricia Sullivan	*Dreaming in smoke*
2000	Bruce Sterling	*Distraction*
2001	China Miéville	*Perdido Street station*
2002	Gwyneth Jones	*Bold as love*

Commonwealth Writers Prize

Established in 1987 by the Commonwealth Foundation in association with the Book Trust and the Royal Overseas League, the award is administered annually within one of four regions of the Commonwealth. Entries submitted by publishers must be novels or short stories.

1987	Olive Senior	*Summer lightning*
1988	Festus Iyayi	*Heroes*
1989	Janet Frame	*The Carpathians*
1990	Mordecai Richler	*Solomon Gursky*
1991	David Malouf	*The great world*
1992	Rohinton Mistry	*Such a long journey*
1993	Alex Miller	*The ancestor game*
1994	Vikram Seth	*A suitable boy*
1995	Louis de Bernières	*Captain Corelli's mandolin*
1996	Rohinton Mistry	*A fine balance*
1997	Earl Lovelace	*Salt*
1998	Peter Carey	*Jack Maggs*
1999	Murray Bail	*Eucalyptus*
2000	J M Coetzee	*Disgrace*
2001	Peter Carey	*True history of the Kelly Gang*
2002	Richard Flanagan	*Gould's book of fish*

Crime Writers' Association

The first meeting of the Association was convened by John Creasey in November 1953 and awards have been presented since 1955 for the best crime novel of the year. Originally called the Crossed Red Herrings Award it is now the **Macallan Gold Dagger,** awarded for the best thriller, suspense novel or spy fiction published in the UK in the English language. The **Macallan Silver Dagger** goes to the runner up. The **John Creasey Memorial Award (JCMA)**, instituted to commemorate his death in 1973, is for the best crime novel by an author who has not previously published a full length work of fiction. From 1985 to 1987, the *Police Review* sponsored an award for the crime novel which best portrayed police work and procedure. In 1988 for one year only, *Punch* magazine sponsored a prize for the funniest crime book of the year. This was superseded by **The Last Laugh Award** (currently suspended). In 1990, Hazel Wynn Jones instituted the **CWA '92 Award** to run for three years for a crime novel partly or wholly set in Europe. Also in 1990 the *New Law Journal* sponsored the biennial **Rumpole Award** for a crime novel with a British legal setting. From 1999 a new award for an historical crime story commemorates the novelist Ellis Peters. All these awards are set out below under each year.

Year	Author	Award	Title
1970	Joan Fleming	Gold Dagger	*Young man I think you're dying*
	Anthony Price	Silver Dagger	*The labyrinth makers*
1971	James McClure	Gold Dagger	*The steam pig*
	P D James	Silver Dagger	*Shroud for a nightingale*
1972	Eric Ambler	Gold Dagger	*The levanter*
	Victor Canning	Silver Dagger	*The rainbird pattern*
1973	Robert Littell	Gold Dagger	*The defection of A J Lewinter*
	Gwendoline Butler	Silver Dagger	*A coffin for Pandora*
	Kyril Bonfiglioli	JCMA	*Don't point that thing at me*
1974	Anthony Price	Gold Dagger	*Other paths to glory*
	Francis Clifford	Silver Dagger	*The Grosvenor Square goodbye*
	Roger L Simon	JCMA	*The big fix*
1975	Nicholas Meyer	Gold Dagger	*The seven per cent solution*
	P D James	Silver Dagger	*The black tower*
	Sara George	JCMA	*Acid drop*
1976	Ruth Rendell	Gold Dagger	*A demon in my view*
	James McClure	Silver Dagger	*Rogue eagle*
	Patrick Alexander	JCMA	*Death of a thin skinned animal*
1977	John le Carré	Gold Dagger	*The honourable schoolboy*
	William McIlvanney	Silver Dagger	*Laidlaw*
	Jonathan Gash	JCMA	*The Judas pair*
1978	Lionel Davidson	Gold Dagger	*The Chelsea murders*
	Peter Lovesey	Silver Dagger	*Waxwork*
	Paula Gosling	JCMA	*A running duck*
1979	Dick Francis	Gold Dagger	*Whip hand*
	Colin Dexter	Silver Dagger	*Service of all the dead*
	David Serafin	JCMA	*Saturday of glory*

1980	H R F Keating	Gold Dagger	*The murder of the Maharajah*
	Ellis Peters	Silver Dagger	*Monk's hood*
	Liza Cody	JCMA	*Dupe*
1981	Martin Cruz Smith	Gold Dagger	*Gorky Park*
	Colin Dexter	Silver Dagger	*The dead of Jericho*
	James Leigh	JCMA	*The Ludi victor*
1982	Peter Lovesey	Gold Dagger	*The false Inspector Dew*
	S T Haymon	Silver Dagger	*Ritual murder*
	Andrew Taylor	JCMA	*Caroline Minuscule*
1983	John Hutton	Gold Dagger	*Accidental crimes*
	William McIlvanney	Silver Dagger	*The papers of Tony Veitch*
Tied	Carol Clemeau	JCMA	*The Ariadne clue*
	Eric Wright		*The night the gods smiled*
1984	B M Gill	Gold Dagger	*The twelfth juror*
	Ruth Rendell	Silver Dagger	*The tree of hands*
	Elizabeth Ironside	JCMA	*A very private enterprise*
1985	Paula Gosling	Gold Dagger	*Monkey puzzle*
	Dorothy Simpson	Silver Dagger	*Last seen alive*
	Robert Richardson	JCMA	*The Latimer mercy*
	Andrew Arncliffe	*Police Review* Award	*After the holiday*
1986	Ruth Rendell	Gold Dagger	*Live flesh*
	P D James	Silver Dagger	*A taste for death*
	Neville Steed	JCMA	*Tinplate*
	Bill Knox	*Police Review* Award	*The crossfire killings*
1987	Barbara Vine	Gold Dagger	*A fatal inversion*
	Scott Turow	Silver Dagger	*Presumed innocent*
	Denis Kilcommons	JCMA	*Dark apostle*
	Roger Busby	*Police Review* Award	*Snowman*
1988	Michael Dibdin	Gold Dagger	*Ratking*
	Sara Paretsky	Silver Dagger	*Toxic shock*
	Janet Neel	JCMA	*Death's bright angel*
	Nancy Livingston	*Punch* Prize	*Death in a distant land*
1989	Colin Dexter	Gold Dagger	*The wench is dead*
	Desmond Lowden	Silver Dagger	*The shadow run*
	Annette Roome	JCMA	*A real shot in the arm*
	Mike Ripley	Last Laugh Award	*Angel touch*
1990	Reginald Hill	Gold Dagger	*Bones and silence*
	Mike Phillips	Silver Dagger	*The late candidate*
	Patricia D Cornwell	JCMA	*Postmortem*
	Simon Shaw	Last Laugh Award	*Killer Cinderella*
	Michael Dibdin	CWA '92 Award	*Vendetta*
	Frances Fyfield	Rumpole Award	*Trial by fire*
1991	Barbara Vine	Gold Dagger	*King Solomon's carpet*
	Frances Fyfield	Silver Dagger	*Deep sleep*
	Walter Mosley	JCMA	*Devil in a blue dress*
	Mike Ripley	Last Laugh Award	*Angels in arms*
	Barbara Wilson	CWA '92 Award	*Gaudi afternoon*

1992	Colin Dexter	Gold Dagger	*The way through the woods*
	Liza Cody	Silver Dagger	*Bucket nut*
	Minette Walters	JCMA	*The ice house*
	Carl Hiaasen	Last Laugh Award	*Native tongue*
	Timothy Williams	CWA '92 Award	*Black August*
	Peter Rawlinson	Rumpole Award	*Hatred and contempt*
1993	Patricia D Cornwell	Gold Dagger	*Cruel and unusual*
	Sarah Dunant	Silver Dagger	*Fatlands*
	No award	JCMA	
	Michael Pearce	Last Laugh Award	*The Mamur Zapt and the spoils of Egypt*
1994	Minette Walters	Gold Dagger	*The scold's bridle*
	Peter Hoeg	Silver Dagger	*Miss Smilla's feeling for snow*
	Doug J Swanson	JCMA	*Big town*
	Simon Shaw	Last Laugh Award	*The villain of the earth*
1995	Val McDermid	Gold Dagger	*The mermaid's singing*
	Peter Lovesey	Silver Dagger	*The summons*
	Janet Evanovich	JCMA	*One for the money*
	Laurence Shames	Last Laugh Award	*Sunburn*
1996	Ben Elton	Gold Dagger	*Popcorn*
	Peter Lovesey	Silver Dagger	*Bloodhounds*
	No award	JCMA	
	No award	Last Laugh Award	
1997	Ian Rankin	Gold Dagger	*Black & blue*
	Janet Evanovich	Silver Dagger	*Three to get deadly*
	Paul Johnston	JCMA	*Body politic*
1998	James Lee Burke	Gold Dagger	*Sunset limited*
	Nicholas Blincoe	Silver Dagger	*Manchester slingback*
	Denise Mina	JCMA	*Garnethill*
1999	Robert Wilson	Gold Dagger	*A small death in Lisbon*
	Adrian Matthews	Silver Dagger	*Vienna blood*
	Dan Fesperman	JCMA	*Lie in the dark*
	Lindsey Davis	Historical Dagger	*Two for the lions*
2000	Jonathan Lethem	Gold Dagger	*Motherless Brooklyn*
	Donna Leon	Silver Dagger	*Friends in high places*
	Boston Teran	JCMA	*God is a bullet*
	Gillian Linscott	Historical Dagger	*Absent friends*
2001	Henning Mankell	Gold Dagger	*Sidetracked*
	Giles Blunt	Silver Dagger	*Forty words for sorrow*
	Susanna Jones	JCMA	*The earthquake bird*
	Andrew Taylor	Historical Dagger	*The office of the dead*

Prizes

Encore Award

Awarded to the best second novel of the year published in that calendar year. The winner is chosen by a panel of judges from entries submitted by publishers. The award is administered by the Society of Authors.

joint winners {	1990	Peter Benson	*A lesser dependency*
	1990	Paul Watkins	*Calm at sunset, calm at dawn*
	1991	Carey Harrison	*Richard's feet*
	1992	Iain Sinclair	*Downriver*
	1993	Colm Toibin	*The heather blazing*
	1994	Amit Chaudhuri	*Afternoon raag*
	1995	Dermot Healy	*A goat's song*
	1996	A L Kennedy	*So I am glad*
	1997	David Flusfeder	*Like plastic*
joint winners {	1998	Timothy O'Grady	*I could read the sky*
	1998	Alan Warner	*These demented lands*
	1999	Christina Koning	*Undiscovered country*
joint winners {	2000	John Burnside	*The mercy boys*
	2000	Claire Messud	*The last life*
	2000	Matt Thorne	*Eight minutes idle*
	2000	Phil Whitaker	*Triangulation*
	2001	Ali Smith	*Hotel world*

Geoffrey Faber Memorial Prize

As a memorial to the founder and first Chairman of the firm, Faber and Faber Limited established the prize in 1963. Awarded annually it is given in alternate years for a volume of verse and for a volume of prose fiction published originally in this country by writers who are under 40 years of age. The following is the list of fiction prize winners:-

1971	J G Farrell	*Troubles*
1973	David Storey	*Pasmore*
1975	Richard Wright	*The middle of a life*
1977	Carolyn Slaughter	*The story of the weasel*
1979	Timothy Mo	*The monkey king*
1981	J M Coetzee	*Waiting for the Barbarians*
1983	Graham Swift	*Shuttlecock*
1985	Julian Barnes	*Flaubert's parrot*
1987	Guy Vanderhaeghe	*Man descending*
1989	David Profumo	*Sea music*
1991	Carol Birch	*The fog line*
1993	Will Self	*The quantity theory of insanity*
1995	Livi Michael	*Their angel reach*
1997	Emily Perkins	*Not her real name*
1999	Gavin Kramer	*Shopping*
2001	Trezza Azzopardi	*The hiding place*

Guardian Fiction Prize

Awarded annually from 1965 to 1999 for a work of fiction by a British or Commonwealth writer and published in the United Kingdom. Succeeded by the Guardian First Book Award which is open to fiction and non-fiction titles.

1965	Clive Barry	*Crumb borne*
1966	Archie Hind	*The dear green place*
1967	Eva Figes	*Winter journey*
1968	P J Kavanagh	*A song and dance*
1969	Maurice Leitch	*Poor Lazarus*
1970	Margaret Blount	*When did you last see your father?*
1971	Thomas Kilroy	*The big chapel*
1972	John Berger	*G*
1973	Peter Redgrove	*In the country of the skin*
1974	Beryl Bainbridge	*The bottle factory outing*
1975	Sylvia Clayton	*Friends and Romans*
1976	Robert Nye	*Falstaff*
1977	Michael Moorcock	*The condition of Muzak*
1978	Roy A K Heath	*The murderer*
1979	Neil Jordan	*Night in Tunisia*
1980	J L Carr	*A month in the country*
1981	John Banville	*Kepler*
1982	Glyn Hughes	*Where I used to play on the green*
1983	Graham Swift	*Waterland*
1984	J G Ballard	*Empire of the sun*
1985	Peter Ackroyd	*Hawksmoor*
1986	Jim Crace	*Continent*
1987	Peter Benson	*The levels*
1988	Lucy Ellman	*Sweet desserts*
1989	Carol Lake	*Rosehill: portraits from a midlands city*
1990	Pauline Melville	*Shape-shifter*
1991	Alan Judd	*The devil's own work*
1992	Alasdair Gray	*Poor things*
1993	Pat Barker	*The eye in the door*
1994	Candia McWilliam	*Debatable land*
1995	James Buchan	*Heart's journey into winter*
1996	Seamus Deane	*Reading in the dark*
1997	Anne Michaels	*Fugitive pieces*
1998	Jackie Kay	*Trumpet*

Guardian First Book Award

This award replaces the Guardian Fiction Prize from 1999. It will recognise and reward new writing by honouring an author's first book which may be fiction or non-fiction.

1999	No award to fiction	
2000	Zadie Smith	White teeth
2001	Chris Ware	Jimmy Corrigan: the smartest kid on earth

Hawthornden Prize

Founded in 1919 by Miss Alice Warrender, it is the oldest of the famous British literary prizes. Awarded annually to an English writer for the best work of imaginative literature, it is especially designed to encourage young authors, and the word 'imaginative' is given a broad interpretation.

The following dates are the years for which the award was given to a work of fiction:

1970	Piers Paul Read	Monk Dawson
1975	David Lodge	Changing places
1976	Robert Nye	Falstaff
1978	David Cook	Walter
1979	P S Rushforth	Kindergarten
1982	Timothy Mo	Sour sweet
1983	Jonathan Keates	Allegro postillions
1992	Ferdinand Mount	Of love and asthma
1993	Andrew Barrow	The tap dancer
1994	Tim Pears	In the place of fallen leaves
1996	Hilary Mantel	An experiment in love
1997	John Lanchester	The debt to pleasure
1998	No award to fiction	
1999	No award to fiction	
2000	No award to fiction	
2001	Helen Simpson	Hey yeah right get a life

David Higham Prize for Fiction

An annual award for a first novel or book of short stories published in the UK in the year of the award, by an author who is a citizen of Britain, the Commonwealth or the Republic of Ireland. Sponsored by David Higham Associates. The award in its present form has now been discontinued.

joint winners	1975	Jane Gardam	*Black faces/white faces*
	1975	Matthew Vaughan	*Chalky*
	1976	Caroline Blackwood	*The stepdaughter*
	1977	Patricia Finney	*A shadow of gulls*
	1978	Leslie Norris	*Sliding*
	1979	John Harvey	*The plate shop*
	1980	Ted Harriot	*Keep on running*
	1981	Christopher Hope	*A separate development*
	1982	Glyn Hughes	*Where I used to play on the green*
	1983	R M Lamming	*The notebook of Gismondo Cavalletti*
	1984	James Buchan	*A parish of rich women*
	1985	Patricia Ferguson	*Family myths and legends*
	1986	Jim Crace	*Continent*
	1987	Adam Zameenzad	*The 13th house*
	1988	Carol Birch	*Life in the palace*
	1989	Timothy O'Grady	*Motherland*
	1990	Russell Celyn Jones	*Soldiers and innocents*
	1991	Elspeth Barker	*O Caledonia*
	1992	John Loveday	*Halo*
	1993	Nicola Barker	*Love your enemies*
	1994	Fred D'Aguiar	*The longest memory*
	1995	Vikram Chandra	*Red earth and pouring rain*
	1996	Linda Grant	*The cast iron shore*
	1997	Ronald Wright	*A scientific romance*
	1998	Gavin Kramer	*Shopping*

Winifred Holtby Memorial Prize

In 1966 Vera Brittain gave to the Royal Society of Literature a sum of money to provide an annual prize in honour of Winifred Holtby. It is for the best regional novel of the year written in the English language. Winners since 1980 are:-

1980	Elsa Joubert	*Poppie*
1981	Alan Judd	*A breed of heroes*
1982	Kazuo Ishiguro	*A pale view of hills*
1983	Graham Swift	*Waterland*
1984	Balraj Khanna	*Nation of fools*
1985	*No award*	
1986	Maggie Hemingway	*The bridge*
1987	*No award*	
1989	Shusha Guppy	*The blindfold horse*
1990	Hilary Mantel	*Fludd*
1991	Nino Ricci	*The lives of the saints*
1992	Elspeth Barker	*O Caledonia*
1993	Adam Thorpe	*Ulverton*
1994	Jim Crace	*Signals of distress*
1995	Paul Watkins	*Archangel*
1996	Rohinton Mistry	*A fine balance*
1997	Eden Robinson	*Traplines*
1998	Giles Foden	*The last king of Scotland*
1999	Andrew O'Hagan	*Our fathers*
2000	Donna Morrissey	*Kit's law*
2001	Anna Burns	*No bones*

'Independent' Foreign Fiction Award

Funded by the Arts Council and promoted by *The Independent* newspaper, an annual prize for the best contemporary work of prose fiction translated into English from any other tongue and published between 1 January and 31 December each year.

2001   Marta Morazzoni   *The Alphonse Courriér Affair*
translated from the Italian by Emma Rose

2002   W G Sebald   *Austerlitz*
translated from the German by Anthea Bell

International IMPAC Dublin Literary Award

Established in 1996 and awarded to a work of fiction written and published in the English language or written in a language other than English and published in English translation. The winner is chosen by nominations made by selected public libraries.

1996	David Malouf	*Remembering Babylon*
1997	Javier Marias	*A heart so white*
1998	Herta Müller	*The land of green plums*
1999	Andrew Miller	*Ingenious pain*
2000	Nicola Barker	*Wide open*
2001	Alistair MacLeod	*No great mischief*
2002	Michel Housellebecq	*Atomised*

Irish Times International Fiction Prize

Awarded biennially to the author of a work of fiction written in the English language and published in Ireland, the United Kingdom or the United States. The winner is selected by an international panel of judges.

1989	Don DeLillo	*Libra*
1990	A S Byatt	*Possession*
1991	Louis Begley	*Wartime lies*
1992	Norman Rush	*Mating*
1993	E Annie Proulx	*The shipping news*
1995	J M Coetzee	*The master of Petersberg*
1997	Seamus Deane	*Reading in the dark*
1999	Lorrie Moore	*Birds of America*

Jewish Quarterly / Wingate Literary Prize for Fiction

Sponsored by the Harold Hyman Wingate Foundation and awarded to a work of fiction and non-fiction which stimulates an interest in themes of Jewish concern.

1997	Anne Michaels	*Fugitive*
1998	Dorit Rabinyan	*Persian brides*
1999	Howard Jacobson	*The mighty walzer*
2000	Mona Yahia	*When the grey beetles took over Baghdad*
2001	W G Sebald	*Austerlitz*

Mail on Sunday / John Llewellyn Rhys Prize

Founded in 1942 by Jane Oliver, the widow of John Llewellyn Rhys, a young writer killed in action in World War II. Open to writers aged under 35, the work may be any form of literature: fiction, short stories, poetry, drama, biography or literary non-fiction written by a British or Commonwealth writer. The following dates are the years for which an award was given to a work of fiction.

1971	Shiva Naipaul	*Fireflies*
1972	Susan Hill	*The albatross*
1973	Peter Smalley	*A warm gun*
1974	Hugh Fleetwood	*The girl who passed for normal*
1975	Tim Jeal	*Cushing's crusade*
1978	A N Wilson	*The sweets of Pimlico*
1980	Desmond Hogan	*The diamonds at the bottom of the sea*
1982	William Boyd	*An ice-cream war*
1983	Lisa St Aubin de Teran	*The slow train to Milan*
1985	John Milne	*Out of the blue*
1986	Tim Parks	*Loving Roger*
1987	Jeanette Winterson	*The passion*
1988	Matthew Yorke	*The March fence*
1992	Matthew Kneale	*Sweet Thames*
1994	Jonathan Coe	*What a carve up!*
1995	Melanie McGrath	*Motel Nirvana*
1996	Nicola Barker	*Heading inland*
1997	Phil Whitaker	*Eclipse of the sun*
1998	Peter H Davis	*The ugliest house in the world*
1999	David Mitchell	*Ghostwritten*
2000	Edward Platt	*Leadville*

Somerset Maugham Awards

The purpose of these annual awards is to encourage young writers to travel, and the emphasis of the founder is on originality and promise. Authors must be under 35 years of age, a British subject by birth, and ordinarily resident in the United Kingdom. Poetry, fiction and non-fiction are all eligible. The fiction winners from 1981 are listed below.

	1981	Julian Barnes	*Metroland*
joint winners	1982	William Boyd	*A good man in Africa*
	1982	Adam Mars-Jones	*Lantern lecture*
	1983	Lisa St Aubin de Teran	*Keepers of the house*
	1984	Peter Ackroyd	*The last testament of Oscar Wilde*
	1985	Jane Rogers	*Her living image*
joint winners	1986	Patricia Ferguson	*Family myths and legends*
	1986	Tim Parks	*Tongues of flame*
	1987	Stephen Gregory	*The cormorant*
	1988	Matthew Kneale	*Whore banquets*
joint winners	1989	Alan Hollinghurst	*The swimming pool library*
	1989	Deidre Madden	*The birds of the innocent wood*
	1990	Nicholas Shakespeare	*The vision of Elena Silves*
joint winners	1991	Peter Benson	*The other occupant*
	1991	Lesley Glaister	*Honour thy father*
	1991	Helen Simpson	*Four bare legs*
	1992	Geoff Dyer	*But beautiful*
	1993	Duncan McLean	*Bucket of tongues*
	1994	A L Kennedy	*Looking for the possible dance*
	1995	*No award to fiction*	
	1996	Alan Warner	*Morvern Callar*
joint winners	1997	Rhidian Brook	*The testimony of Tailiesin Jones*
	1997	Philip Hensher	*Kitchen venom*
	1998	Rachel Cusk	*The country life*
joint winners	1999	Andrea Ashworth	*Once in a house on fire*
	1999	Paul Farley	*The boy from the chemist is here to see you*
	1999	Giles Foden	*The last King of Scotland*
	1999	Jonathan Freedland	*Bring home the revolution*
	2000	Sarah Waters	*Affinity*
	2001	Ben Rice	*Pobby and Dingan*
joint winners	2002	Charlotte Hobson	*Black earth city*
	2002	Marcel Theroux	*The paper chase*

McKitterick Prize

Endowed by the late Tom McKitterick the award is made to a first novel (published or unpublished) by an author over the age of 40.

1990	Simon Mawer	*Chimera*
1991	John Loveday	*A summer to halo*
1992	Alberto Manguel	*News from a foreign country came*
1993	Andrew Barrow	*The tap dancer*
1994	Helen Dunmore	*Zennor in darkness*
1995	Christopher Bigsby	*Hester*
1996	Stephen Blanchard	*Gagarin and I*
1997	Patricia Duncker	*Hallucinating Foucault*
1998	Eli Gottlieb	*The boy who went away*
1999	Magnus Mills	*The restraint of beasts*
2000	Chris Dolan	*Ascension day*
2001	Giles Waterfield	*The long afternoon*
2002	Manil Suri	*The death of Vishnu*

The Orange Prize

Founded in 1996, this award is open to women authors of any nationality, provided that entries have been published in the United Kingdom. Administered by the Book Trust.

1996	Helen Dunmore	*A spell of winter*
1997	Anne Michaels	*Fugitive pieces*
1998	Carol Shields	*Larry's party*
1999	Suzanne Berne	*A crime in the neighbourhood*
2000	Linda Grant	*When I lived in modern times*
2001	Kate Grenville	*The idea of perfection*
2002	Ann Patchett	*Bel Canto*

Parker Romantic Novel of the Year

Established in 1960 the award, now sponsored by the Parker Pen Company, is for the best romantic novel of the year by a United Kingdom citizen.

joint winners {	1970	Margaret Maddocks	*Thea*
	1970	Joanne Marshall	*Cat on a broomstick*
	1970	Rona Randall	*Broken tapestry*
	1971	Joanne Marshall	*Flower of silence*
	1972	Maynah Lewis	*The pride of innocence*
	1973	Constance Heaven	*The House of Kuragin*
	1974	Frances Murray	*The burning lamp*
	1975	Jay Allerton	*Vote for a silk gown*
	1976	Anna Gilbert	*The look of innocence*
	1977	Anne Worboys	*Every man a king*
	1978	Madeleine Brent	*Merlin's Keep*
	1979	Josephine Edgar	*Countess*
	1980	Joanna Trollope	*Parson Harding's daughter*
	1981	Gwendoline Butler	*The red staircase*
	1982	Valerie Fitzgerald	*Zemindar*
	1983	Eva Ibbotson	*Magic flutes*
	1984	Sheila Walsh	*A highly respectable marriage*
	1985	Rosie Thomas	*Sunrise*
	1986	Brenda Jagger	*A song twice over*
	1987	Marie Joseph	*A better world than this*
	1988	Audrey Howard	*The juniper bush*
	1989	Sarah Woodhouse	*The peacock's feather*
	1990	Reay Tannahill	*Passing glory*
	1991	Susan Kay	*Phantom*
	1992	June Knox-Mawer	*Sandstorm*
	1993	Cynthia Harrod-Eagles	*Emily*
	1994	Elizabeth Buchan	*Consider the lily*
	1995	Charlotte Bingham	*Change of heart*
	1996	Rosamunde Pilcher	*Coming home*
	1997	Sue Gee	*The hours of the night*
	1998	Angela Lambert	*Kiss and kin*
	1999	Clare Chambers	*Learning to swim*
	2000	Maureen Lee	*Dancing in the dark*
	2001	Cathy Kelly	*Someone like you*
	2002	Philippa Gregory	*The other Boleyn girl*

Pulitzer Prize for Fiction

Joseph Pulitzer, reporter, editor, publisher and a founder of the Graduate School of Journalism at Columbia University, established in 1903 a system of prizes to encourage 'public service, public morals, American literature and the advancement of education'. The Fiction Prize was first awarded in 1948.

1970	Jean Stafford	*Collected stories*
1971	*No award*	
1972	Wallace Stegner	*Angle of repose*
1973	Eudora Welty	*The optimist's daughter*
1974	*No award*	
1975	Michael Shaara	*The killer angels*
1976	Saul Bellow	*Humboldt's gift*
1977	*No award*	
1978	James Alan McPherson	*Elbow room*
1979	John Cheever	*The stories of John Cheever*
1980	Norman Mailer	*The executioner's song*
1981	John Kennedy Toole	*A confederacy of dunces*
1982	John Updike	*Rabbit is rich*
1983	Alice Walker	*The color purple*
1984	William Kennedy	*Ironweed*
1985	Alison Lurie	*Foreign affairs*
1986	Larry McMurtry	*Lonesome dove*
1987	Peter Taylor	*A summons to Memphis*
1988	Toni Morrison	*Beloved*
1989	Anne Tyler	*Breathing lessons*
1990	Oscar Hijuelos	*The mambo kings play songs of love*
1991	John Updike	*Rabbit at rest*
1992	Jane Smiley	*A thousand acres*
1993	Robert Olen Butler	*A good scent from a strange mountain*
1994	E Annie Proulx	*The shipping news*
1995	Carol Shields	*The stone diaries*
1996	Richard Ford	*Independence day*
1997	Steven Millhauser	*Martin Dressler: The tale of an American dreamer*
1998	Philip Roth	*American pastoral*
1999	Michael Cunningham	*The hours*
2000	Jhumpa Lahiri	*Interpreter of maladies*
2001	Michael Chabon	*The amazing adventures of Kavalier and Clay*
2002	Richard Russo	*Empire Falls*

Sagittarius Prize

Awarded to a first novel by a writer over 60 years of age, first published in the United Kingdom during the year preceding the year in which the award is presented. Administered by the Society of Authors.

1991	Judith Hubback	*The sea has many voices*
1992	Hugh Leonard	*Parnell and the English woman*
1993	Brian O'Doherty	*The strange case of Mademoiselle P*
1994	George Hummer	*Red branch*
1995	Fred Plisner	*Gravity is getting me down*
1996	Samuel Lock	*As luck would have it*
1997	Barbara Hardy	*London lovers*
1998	A Sivanandan	*When memory dies*
1999	Ingrid Mann	*The Danube testament*
2000	David Crackanthorpe	*Stolen marches*
2001	Michael Richardson	*The pig bin*
2002	Zvi Jagendorf	*Wolfy and the strudelbakers*

W H Smith - Book Awards

From the year 2000 prizes are awarded annually as a result of votes cast by members of the public. Two awards may relate to fiction and one is specific to the genre.

❋ Fiction Award

2000	Maeve Binchy	*Scarlet feather*
2001	Nick Hornby	*How to be good*

❋ Literary Award

2000	Philip Roth	*The human stain*
2001	Ian McEwan	*Atonement*

❋ New Talent Award

2000	Zadie Smith	*White teeth*
2001	Emily Barr	*Backpack*

Sunday Times Young Writer of the Year Award

Awarded to a writer who is under the age of 35 on the strength of the promise shown by a full-length published work of fiction, non-fiction or poetry.

1991	Helen Simpson	*Four bare legs in a bed*
1992	Caryl Phillips	*Cambridge*
1993	*No award to fiction*	
1994	*No award to fiction*	
1995	Andrew Cowen	*Pig*
1996	Katherine Pierpoint	*Truffle beds*
1997	Francis Spufford	*I may be some time*
1998	Patrick French	*Liberty or death*
1999	*No award to fiction*	
2000	Sarah Waters	*Affinity*
2001	Zadie Smith	*White teeth*

Thumping Good Read Book Award

Awarded to a novel that is judged by a panel of W H Smith's customers to be an "accessible and page-turning good read".

1992	Robert Goddard	*Into the blue*
1993	Robert Harris	*Fatherland*
1994	Dominick Dunne	*A season in purgatory*
1995	Thomas Eidson	*St Agnes' stand*
1996	Andrew Klavan	*True crime*
1997	David Baldacci	*Absolute power*
1998	Douglas Kennedy	*The big picture*
1999	Lee Child	*Die trying*
2000	Boris Starling	*Storm*
2001	Jeffery Deaver	*The empty chair*

Tom-Gallon Trust

Founded by the late Miss Nellie Tom-Gallon, the award is made biennially to fiction writers of limited means who have had at least one short story accepted for publication. The award is made for a short story.

	1943	Elizabeth Myers	*A well full of leaves*
	1945	Jack Aistrop	*Death in the midst of what*
	1947	Dorothy K Haynes	*The head*
	1949	Olivia Manning	*The children*
	1951	Fred Urquhart	*The ploughing match*
	1953	Maurice Cranston	*A visit to the author*
	1955	Robert Roberts	*Conducted tour*
	1957	E W Hildick	*A casual visit*
	1959	Harold Elvin	*God's right hand upon my shoulder*
1961 and 1963		*No award*	
joint winners	1964	Peter Greave	*The wonderful day*
	1964	Jean Stubbs	*A child's four seasons*
	1966	Gillian Edwards	*An evening in September*
	1968	*No award*	
joint winners	1970	A Craig Bell	*The nest*
	1970	Aileen Pennington	*The princess and the pussycat*
	1972	Kathleen Julian	*Catch two*
	1974	Neilson Graham	*Anscombe*
	1976	Jackson Webb	*Vassili*
	1978	Michael Morrissey	*An evening with Ionesco*
	1980	A McConnell-Duff	*The comrades marathon*
	1982	Dermot Healy	*The tenant*
	1984	Janni Howker	*The egg man*
	1986	Lawrence Scott	*The house of funerals*
	1988	Alan Beard	*Taking Doreen out of the sky*
	1990	Richard Austin	*Sister Monica's last journey*
	1992	David Callard	*Reading the signals*
	1994	Janice Fox	*A good place to die*
	1996	Leo Madigan	*Packing for Wednesday*
	1998	Grace Ingoldby	*The notion of deuce*
	2000	Paul Blaney	*Apple tennis*

Betty Trask Awards

Started in 1984 and administered by the Society of Authors, the awards are for the benefit of young authors (under 35), and are given on the strength of the manuscript of a first novel of a romantic or traditional - rather than experimental - nature. The winners are required to use the money for foreign travel. The principal winners are:

joint winners {	1984	Ronald Frame	*Winter journey*
	1984	Clare Nonhebel	*Cold showers*
	1985	Susan Kay	*Legacy*
	1986	Tim Parks	*Tongues of flame*
	1987	James Maw	*Hard luck*
	1988	Alex Martin	*The general interruptor*
	1989	Nigel Watts	*The life game*
	1990	Robert McLiam Wilson	*Ripley bogle*
	1991	Amit Chaudhuri	*A strange and sublime address*
	1992	Liane Jones	*The dream stone*
	1993	Mark Blackaby	*You'll never be here again* (unpublished)
	1994	Colin Bateman	*Divorcing Jack*
	1995	Robert Newman	*Dependence day*
	1996	John Lanchester	*The debt to pleasure*
	1997	Alex Garland	*The beach*
	1998	Kiran Desai	*Hullabaloo in the guava orchard*
	1999	Elliot Perlman	*Three dollars*
	2000	Jonathan Tulloch	*The season ticket*
	2001	Zadie Smith	*White teeth*
	2002	Hari Kunzru	*The Impressionist*

Prizes

Whitbread Book of the Year and Literary Awards

Established in 1971, the Whitbread Co. prizes now reward five categories of book. These are: Novel; First Novel; Children's Novel; Poetry and Biography. Writers must have been resident in Great Britain or the Republic of Ireland for three years or more. Nominations are selected by the panel of judges from each category and one of the category winners is then voted Whitbread Book of the Year. The awards are administered by the Booksellers Association.

	Year	Author	Title
	1971	Gerda Charles	*The destiny waltz*
	1972	Susan Hill	*The bird of night*
	1973	Shiva Naipaul	*The chip chip gatherers*
	1974	Iris Murdoch	*The sacred and profane love machine*
	1975	William McIlvanney	*Docherty*
	1976	William Trevor	*The children of Dynmouth*
	1977	Beryl Bainbridge	*Injury time*
	1978	Paul Theroux	*Picture palace*
	1979	Jennifer Johnston	*The old jest*
'Book of the Year'	1980	David Lodge	*How far can you go?*
Novel	1981	Maurice Leitch	*Silver's city*
First Novel	1981	William Boyd	*A good man in Africa*
Novel	1982	John Wain	*Young shoulders*
First Novel	1982	Bruce Chatwin	*On the black hill*
Novel	1983	William Trevor	*Fools of fortune*
First Novel	1983	John Fuller	*Flying to nowhere*
Novel	1984	Christopher Hope	*Kruger's Alp*
First Novel	1984	James Buchan	*A parish of rich women*
Novel	1985	Peter Ackroyd	*Hawksmoor*
First Novel	1985	Jeanette Winterson	*Oranges are not the only fruit*
Novel & 'Book of the Year'	1986	Kazuo Ishiguro	*An artist of the floating world*
First Novel	1986	Jim Crace	*Continent*
Novel	1987	Ian McEwan	*The child in time*
First Novel	1987	Francis Wyndham	*The other garden*
Novel	1988	Salman Rushdie	*The satanic verses*
First Novel & 'Book of the Year'	1988	Paul Sayer	*The comforts of madness*
Novel	1989	Lindsay Clarke	*The chymical wedding*
First Novel	1989	James Hamilton-Paterson	*Gerontius*
Novel & 'Book of the Year'	1990	Nicholas Mosley	*Hopeful monsters*
First Novel	1990	Hanif Kureishi	*The Buddha of suburbia*

Prizes

Novel	1991	Jane Gardam	*The queen of the tambourine*
First Novel	1991	Gordon Burn	*Alma Cogan*
Novel	1992	Alasdair Gray	*Poor things*
First Novel & 'Book of The Year'	1992	Jeff Torrington	*Swing hammer swing!*
Novel & 'Book of The Year'	1993	Joan Brady	*Theory of war*
First Novel	1993	Rachel Cusk	*Saving Agnes*
Novel & 'Book of The Year'	1994	William Trevor	*Felicia's journey*
First Novel	1994	Fred D'Aguiar	*The longest memory*
First Novel	1995	Kate Atkinson	*Behind the scenes at the museum*
Novel	1995	Salman Rushdie	*The moor's last sigh*
First Novel	1996	John Lanchester	*The debt to pleasure*
Novel	1996	Beryl Bainbridge	*Every man for himself*
First Novel	1997	Pauline Melville	*The ventriloquist's tale*
Novel	1997	Jim Crace	*Quarantine*
First Novel	1998	Giles Foden	*The last king of Scotland*
Novel	1998	Justin Cartwright	*Leading the cheers*
First Novel	1999	Tim Lott	*White city blue*
Novel	1999	Rose Tremain	*Music and silence*
First Novel	2000	Zadie Smith	*White teeth*
Novel & 'Book of The Year'	2000	Matthew Kneale	*English passengers*
First Novel	2001	Sid Smith	*Something like a house*
Novel	2001	Patrick Neate	*Twelve bar blues*

Prizes

Further reading

This short list of twelve items contains books which should be readily available in most public library systems. They form an invaluable complement to *Who else writes like...?* and will help the reader explore a particular genre, pursue the reading of a series, or follow up a more detailed path from one specific author and title to another.

With the growth of the Internet there is an increasing range of websites which can assist the reader to expand their interest in particular authors and their works. Here are some sites which should prove useful but please note that although they were accurate at the time of going to press, they may very well change during the life of this edition.

www.Amazon.co.uk
www.bbc.co.uk/arts/books
www.bookbrowser.com/pseudonyms
www.branching-out.net/forager/forager.htm
www.mysteryguide.com
www.overbooked.org
www.sfsite.com
www.stopyourekillingme.com
www.twbooks.co.uk
www.Waterstones.co.uk
www.word-of-mouth.org.uk
www.readinggroupguides.com

Bloomsbury good reading guide

by Kenneth McLeish, *Bloomsbury Publishing Ltd,*
5th rev edition edited by Nick Rennison 2001

A natural 'follow up' to *Who else writes like...?* It contains articles on some 375 authors describing the type of books they write – listing over 3,500 individual books, suggesting alternative and 'follow up' authors and titles.

Cumulated fiction index

Career Development Group of CILIP

1945-1960	by G B Cotton and Alan Glencross
1960-1969	by Raymond Smith
1970-1974	by Raymond Smith and Anthony J Gordon
1975-1979	by Marilyn E Hicken
1980-1989	by Marilyn E Hicken
1990-1994	by Marilyn E Hicken
1995-1999	by Marilyn E Hicken

This series indexes the majority of novels published in the United Kingdom since the end of the Second World War. The subject headings indicate places, persons, and periods of history as well as showing genres and techniques. It is particularly helpful to readers of crime fiction as the index divides this genre into thirteen groups.

Dictionary of literary pseudonyms in the English language

compiled by Terence Carty, *Mansell*, 1995

Lists 12,000 English language literary pseudonyms to give the real names of around 7,500 authors, from the early seventeenth century to the present day.

Encyclopaedia of fantasy

edited by John Clute and John Grant, *Orbit*, 1999

A companion volume to the *Encyclopaedia of science fiction*, it contains over 4,000 entries covering every aspect of fantasy in literature, films, television, opera, art and comics.

Encyclopaedia of science fiction

edited by John Clute and Peter Nichols, *Orbit, 2nd ed, 1993 (rev paperback ed, 1999)*

The essential reference work on science fiction due to its coverage and scholarship.

Good fiction guide

edited by Jane Rogers, *OUP*, 2001

Features over 1,000 writers from Maeve Binchy to Emile Zola, each entry recommends alternative authors and also suggests new areas of literature to explore.

Further reading

Mammoth encyclopaedia of modern crime fiction

compiled by Mike Ashley, *Constable and Robinson*, 2002

A welcome addition to the reference shelves, and the first title to include all the major new discoveries of the last couple of decades.

The modern library: the two hundred best novels in English since 1950

by Carmen Callil and Colm Toibin, *Picador*, 1999

A personal choice of contemporary novels with a full annotation for each, together with lists of related biographies and memoirs and a short list of international literary prizewinners.

Oxford dictionary of writers and their works

edited by Michael Cox, *OUP*, 2001

A selective listing of over 25,000 titles from nearly 3,000 well known British, American & Commonwealth authors including major European and Classical figures.

Science fiction: the illustrated encyclopaedia

edited by John Clute, *Dorling Kindersley*, 1995

Covers the history of the genre in all its forms. Lavishly illustrated. Over 100 short biographies of SF writers.

Sequels Vol 1: Adult Books

compiled by Mandy Hicken, Career Development Group, CILIP,
13th ed to be published 2003

Lists novels in which the same characters appear; sequences of novels connected by theme; sequences of novels with a geographical or historical connection; and non-fiction, mainly autobiographical, which is intended to be read in sequence. The arrangement is primarily under the author, with an index of series and characters. Invaluable if you want to read a series in order.

Who's who of twentieth century novelists

edited by Tim Woods, *Routledge*, 2001

Contains 1,000 biographical entries of novelists who have influenced 20th century fiction. Drawn from a broad range of countries, genres and styles including writers of popular genre fiction. The emphasis is on post 1945 writers.